From Corpus to Classroom:
language use and
language teaching

From Corpus to Classroom:
language use and
language teaching

Anne O'Keeffe

Michael McCarthy

& Ronald Carter

CAMBRIDGE
UNIVERSITY PRESS

CAMBRIDGE UNIVERSITY PRESS
Cambridge, New York, Melbourne, Madrid, Cape Town, Singapore, São Paulo

Cambridge University Press
The Edinburgh Building, Cambridge CB2 2RU, UK

www.cambridge.org
Information on this title: www.cambridge.org/9780521616867

First published 2007

Printed in the United Kingdom at the University Press, Cambridge

A catalogue record for this publication is available from the British Library

ISBN-13 978-0-521-85146-6 hardback
ISBN-13 978-0-521-61686-7 paperback

Acknowledgements

In writing this book, we have received help, support and inspiration from many sources. First and foremost, we thank Alison Sharpe, Associate Publishing Director, ELT, at Cambridge University Press, who decided to run with this particular idea and who has been a constant source of support to our work over many years. We are also extremely grateful to Jane Walsh, Senior Development Editor, for managing this endeavour. We appreciated greatly her support from start to finish. Thanks also to Geraldine Mark who edited the book and took it through its final stages.

This book stands on the shoulders of a huge amount of work over the last thirty years in the areas of corpus linguistics and applied linguistics. Developments in corpus linguistics have inspired each of us in how we look at language, how we design materials and how we teach, and research in applied linguistics has offered us broad frameworks in which to make sense of it all. We therefore acknowledge the work that has been done to bring us to where we are. Above all, we acknowledge the work of John Sinclair. Every chapter of this book is influenced by his ideas. For each of us, he has generously inspired and nurtured our work over the years. The work of Luke Prodromou is also very influential for us in this book. His work on 'Successful Users of English' provides a paradigm shift in how we view English language use in a global context, and one which is particularly salient in current debates.

This book is the first to come out of the Inter-Varietal Applied Corpus Studies (IVACS) inter-institutional collaboration between the University of Limerick, Ireland, the University of Nottingham and the Queen's University Belfast, UK. What brings us together is reflected in this book: an interest in the applications of corpus linguistics for the analysis of language in use and what this can tell us about how and what we teach. We acknowledge our colleagues in IVACS for their part in making this book happen: Svenja Adolphs, Carolina Amador Moreno, James Binchy, Brian Clancy, Jane Evison, Fiona Farr, Loretta Fung, Michael Handford, Dawn Knight, Barbara Malveira Orfanó, Bróna Murphy, Róisín Ní Mhocháin, Aisling O'Boyle, María Palma Fahey, Nikoleta Rapti, Paul Roberts, Norbert Schmitt, Ivor Timmis, Elaine Vaughan, Steve Walsh and Wang Shih-Ping. Other colleagues and friends who have inspired us during the course of writing this book include Angela Chambers, Winnie Cheng, Paul Heacock, Michael Hoey, Almut Koester, James Lantolf, Nigel McQuitty, Rosamund Moon, Jeanne McCarten, Felicity O'Dell, Barry O'Sullivan, Randi Reppen, Helen Sandiford, Howard Siegelman, Peter Stockwell, Steve Thorne, Koen Van Landeghem, Mary Vaughn and Martin Warren.

We owe a huge debt of gratitude to Susan Hunston, who provided detailed comments and constructive criticism for us on the first draft of the manuscript. The final version of this book has benefited enormously from her clear and generous feedback. We are also grateful to Dave Evans for his extensive work with us on the index. As the cliché goes, responsibility for any inadequacies which remain in the book rests firmly at the door of the authors.

Most of all we thank our respective partners, Ger Downes, Jeanne McCarten and Jane Carter, without whose support this book would have no meaning.

ANNE O'KEEFFE
MICHAEL MCCARTHY
RONALD CARTER

Contents

Acknowledgements v
Preface xi

1 **Introduction** *1*
1.1 Introduction: the basics *1*
1.2 What is a corpus and how can we use it? *1*
1.3 Which corpus, what for and what size? *3*
1.4 How to make a basic corpus *5*
1.5 Basic corpus linguistic techniques *8*
1.6 Lexico-grammatical profiles *14*
1.7 How have corpora been used? *17*
1.8 How have corpora influenced language teaching? *21*
1.9 Issues and debates in the use of corpora in language teaching *25*

2 **Establishing basic and advanced levels in vocabulary learning** *31*
2.1 Introduction *31*
2.2 Frequency and native-speaker vocabulary size *31*
2.3 The most frequent words and the core vocabulary *33*
2.4 The broad categories of a basic vocabulary *37*
2.5 Chunks at the basic level *46*
2.6 The basic level: conclusion *46*
2.7 The advanced level *47*
2.8 Targets *48*
2.9 The vocabulary curve *49*
2.10 The 6,000 to 10,000 word band *50*
2.11 Meanings and connotations *53*
2.12 Breadth and depth *54*

3 **Lessons from the analysis of chunks** *58*
3.1 Introduction *58*
3.2 The single word *58*
3.3 Collocation *59*
3.4 Strings of words in corpora *60*
3.5 Phraseology and idiomaticity *62*
3.6 Looking at corpus data *64*
3.7 Interpreting the data: chunks and single words *69*
3.8 Chunks and units of interaction *70*
3.9 Conclusions and implications *75*

4   **Idioms in everyday use and in language teaching** *80*

4.1   Introduction *80*

4.2   Finding and classifying idioms *82*

4.3   Frequency *84*

4.4   Meaning *86*

4.5   Functions of idioms *87*

4.6   Idioms in specialised contexts *90*

4.7   Idioms in teaching and learning *94*

5   **Grammar and lexis and patterns** *100*

5.1   Introduction *100*

5.2   The example of *border* *102*

5.3   Grammar rules and patterns: deterministic and probabilistic *104*

5.4   The *get*-passive: an extended case study *106*

5.5   Previous studies of the *get*-passive *106*

5.6   *Get*-passives and related forms *108*

5.7   Core *get*-passive constructions in the CANCODE sub-corpus *109*

5.8   Discussion *113*

5.9   Grammar as structure and grammar as probabilities: the example of ellipsis *114*

5.10 Conclusions and implications *115*

6   **Grammar, discourse and pragmatics** *120*

6.1   Introduction *120*

6.2   Non-restrictive *which*-clauses *120*

6.3   Previous studies of *which*-clauses *122*

6.4   Concordance analysis of *which*-clauses *122*

6.5   *If*-clauses *127*

6.6   *Wh*-cleft clauses *130*

6.7   Bringing the insights together *136*

6.8   Corpus grammar and pedagogy *137*

7   **Listenership and response** *140*

7.1   Introduction *140*

7.2   Forms of listenership *142*

7.3   Response tokens across varieties of English *145*

7.4   Functions of response tokens *148*

7.5   Conclusions and implications *155*

8   **Relational language** *159*

8.1   Introduction *159*

8.2   Conversational routines *163*

8.3   Small talk *168*

8.4   Discourse markers *171*

8.5   Hedging *174*

8.6   Vagueness and approximation *176*
8.7   Conclusions and implications *181*

  9   **Language and creativity: creating relationships** *184*
9.1   Introduction *184*
9.2   Spoken language and creativity *184*
9.3   Corpora and creativity *188*
9.4   Creative speakers *190*
9.5   Applications to pedagogy *191*
9.6   Corpus to pedagogy: creating relationships *192*
9.7   SUEs and creativity *192*
9.8   Quantitative and qualitative *196*
9.9   Conclusions *197*

 10   **Specialising: academic and business corpora** *198*
10.1   Introduction *198*
10.2   Written academic English *198*
10.3   Written academic English: examples of frequency *200*
10.4   Spoken academic corpora *203*
10.5   Spoken academic English, conversation and spoken business English *204*
10.6   The CANBEC business corpus *206*
10.7   Chunks *210*
10.8   *Problem* and its institutional construction in CANBEC *214*
10.9   Summary *216*
10.10   Pedagogical implications *216*

 11   **Exploring teacher corpora** *220*
11.1   Introduction *220*
11.2   Classroom discourse *222*
11.3   Frameworks for the analysis of classroom language *222*
11.4   Applying the frameworks to a corpus of classroom data *229*
11.5   Looking at questioning in the classroom *233*
11.6   Teacher corpora in professional development *240*
11.7   Conclusions and considerations *243*

      Coda *246*
      References *249*
      Appendix 1 *284*
      Appendix 2 *297*
      Appendix 3 *301*
      Author index *305*
      Subject index *310*
      Publisher's acknowledgements *314*

Preface

In recent years, conferences on applied linguistics and teacher development, as well as published material such as books, articles and newsletters, frequently refer to developments and findings in the field of corpus linguistics. An increasing number of materials and resources for use in language teaching and learning now boast that they are 'corpus-based' or 'corpus-informed'. Indeed, in the pioneering area of learners' dictionaries, one could hardly imagine any major publisher nowadays putting out a dictionary that was not based on a corpus, such was the revolution sparked off by Sinclair's COBUILD dictionary project in the 1980s. Similarly, corpus information, in recent years, seems to be becoming *de rigueur* as the basis of the compilation of major reference grammars, and, more and more, as a major feature of coursebooks, though here the picture is more patchy at the time of writing.

However, widespread use of 'corpus linguistics' does not mean that the term or its findings are necessarily fully or widely understood in the context of language pedagogy. In addition, many important developments in the field of corpus linguistics are not always communicated or usefully mediated in terms of their implications for language teaching. This is possibly because corpus linguists are very often not language teachers and spend a lot of time talking with one another rather than with teachers. This book aims to address the frequent mismatch between corpus linguistics research and what goes into materials and resources, and what goes on in the language classroom. It aims to highlight the outcomes which we consider to be relevant and transferable in terms of how they can inform pedagogy, or challenge how and what we teach. But the book stops at the classroom door. We do not intend to tell you how to teach and what to do in your own classes; only you can know best what is effective and appropriate in your specific local context, and you are by far the best person to take the final, practical steps in applying our 'applied' linguistics, if you judge the book to have value.

Not all descriptive findings about language are of relevance to how and what we teach, but very many of them are. Here we aim to start with the basics. We do not assume any prior knowledge or experience of corpus linguistics. The book begins by explaining what is meant by a corpus, how one is made, and the most common techniques that can be used to analyse language in a corpus. We also aim to identify what we see as key findings that may lead to new pedagogical insights for language teachers. In so doing, the book aims to provide the critical knowledge and stimulus for language teachers to get involved in the exciting area of corpus linguistics and to make informed decisions about corpus findings in terms of how, or whether, these can inform their teaching, translate into classroom practice, or inform their choices of materials and other resources. Nowadays, given the bewildering range of available materials and the inevitable claims of publishers that theirs are the best, it helps more than ever to be able, calmly and confidently, to question and evaluate claims made about materials, especially in the relatively new area of corpus-informed ones.

We are aware that a book entitled *From Corpus to Classroom* promises many things. It is helpful, at this stage, to make clear what it is not. This book is not about data-driven learning (often referred to as DDL), that is, where data from language corpora (most typically concordances) are used in a hands-on manner in the classroom by the learners. There are many existing publications which address and facilitate this approach. This book is not about telling language teachers how to teach. We are not saying 'this is what it says in a corpus and so you have to teach it'. This book does not provide 'off-the-shelf' solutions or materials that can be rolled out in any and every classroom. It is about informing the reader of the relevant research that is on-going in the field of corpus linguistics and summarising the findings in terms of what we, its authors, consider to have relevance to language teaching. It is about making such research accessible by explaining key concepts, beginning with the assumption of zero background knowledge in the area. Our aim is to facilitate a discerning understanding of what it actually means when claims are made that such things as syllabuses, reference resources and teaching materials are 'corpus-based'.

Most of the chapters in this book draw primarily on spoken language corpora, so much so that at one point, we debated whether the word 'spoken' should be included in the title. However, given that most books on corpora draw primarily on written data and do not feel any need to make this explicit in their titles, we have decided not to apologise for our attempt to redress the balance. Most of our research, over the years, has endeavoured to challenge the dominance of the written word. We hope that this is also the case here. We are also very conscious in this book that there is a proliferation of corpora dedicated to the English language. Where possible we try to use as many types of Englishes as we have been able to access, and we sometimes refer to research that relates to languages other than English. We accept that we come nowhere near finding a balance, and could hardly do so in a book aimed at a wide international readership for whom English is typically the professional lingua franca, but we think that it is important to highlight this point at the outset. At the time of writing, there is far more corpus-based research into English than into any other language (see Wilson, Rayson and McEnery 2003 for more on corpora of languages other than English). Perhaps some of the readers of this book can contribute to redressing the imbalance by building on the existing work using non-English data.

The book opens with a foundational chapter which aims to provide the critical knowledge for building and using a corpus. It also focuses on key issues and debates that have emerged around corpus research. We feel these need to be addressed as a backdrop to the chapters which follow. These issues centre mostly around debates about authenticity and native speakers versus non-native speakers. We are conscious throughout the book to avoid absolutism in relation to native versus non-native speakers of a language. We take the position that the concept of the ideal native speaker is an ephemeral one, and we search in vain for that elusive phantom in our corpora. Real speakers whose utterances we analyse in corpus examples are very often struggling with the demands of real-time communication. Indeed, if we compare the everyday human activities of talking and walking, talking has been compared to a series of uncertain lurches rather than to smooth walking (Krauss et al. 1995). We therefore find the term 'Successful User of English' (SUE), after the work of Luke Prodromou (2003a), to be a much more appropriate term than 'native speaker'. This is discussed and exemplified in chapter one.

All three authors of this book have been inspired by the seminal work of John Sinclair in the field of corpus linguistics, and the structure of the book is motivated by the importance that his work places on the word as the starting point for the description of meaning. As he puts it, 'the word is the unit that aligns grammar and vocabulary' (Sinclair 1996a: 75). Hence the body of the book is structured so that it moves from the word to everyday strings of words (or *chunks*) and idioms, then onto grammar, which subsequently leads us into pragmatics, discourse and creativity. Finally, the closing chapters of the book look at specialised corpora in the areas of teacher development and the institutional contexts of academic and business communication.

Chapter 2 looks at the most frequently occurring words in written and spoken English. It focuses on the pedagogical relevance of corpus findings in terms of our understanding of the vocabulary needs of second language learners. We explore how this information can be beneficial for establishing benchmarks by which learners' vocabulary levels can be assessed and by which we may come to some general agreement as to what constitutes the various levels of proficiency in vocabulary knowledge.

Chapter 3 brings us from the single word to clusters of words, or chunks. Corpus software can tell us what the most frequent chunks in a language are, but this information in its raw form is not terribly illuminating. This chapter proposes a functional categorisation for the most frequent items and explores some of the issues connected with working with chunks in the classroom.

Chapter 4 addresses idioms. This chapter gives consideration to how we define idioms and how they can be extracted from a corpus. This is a qualitative and interpretive process (a computer does not know what an idiom is), and one which we hope can be replicated by those interested in exploring this area further. We take a broad view of idioms and we believe the classification has transfer for the classroom and, particularly, for the design of materials for the teaching of idioms.

In the progression from the single word and lexical chunks, chapter 5 brings us to the next level 'up', that is the interface between lexis and grammar, or 'lexico-grammar'. The phraseological or lexico-grammatical patterns that we explore here, such as choices between *he's not* and *he isn't*, are found to be systematic and go beyond a straightforward grammatical description.

Chapter 6 brings us from phrasal- and clausal-level considerations to discourse and pragmatics. This is contextualised using two structures which are very familiar to language teachers: non-restrictive (sometimes called non-defining) *which*-clauses, and *if*-clauses. We aim to show how a corpus can reveal a lot about the pragmatic force of grammatical choices.

In chapter 7 we focus on one aspect of discourse which we see as having great relevance to language pedagogy and the promotion of fluency. Here we concentrate on the notion of *listenership*, whereby interaction is seen as a two way speaker-hearer process. For spoken discourse to be successful, it demands that the listener responds appropriately to the ongoing speaker turns. The markers of successful listenership are explored, using corpus data, both in terms of the typical structures that are used by listeners and in terms of how they can perform different functions.

Chapter 8 brings together all the chapters that precede it by focusing on how words, chunks and lexico-grammatical patterns can have relational functions. It focuses on areas of spoken language which, in the past, have mostly been the domain of pragmatics and conversation analysis, but which can be explored very effectively in both a quantitative and qualitative way using corpora (for example, small talk, conversational routines, hedging, vague language).

Chapter 9 explores corpus examples in terms of the everyday creativity of users and addresses how this can be appreciated and enjoyed in the classroom. This chapter is a good example of our attempts to redress the balance between spoken and written English. We are very used to talking about creativity in written prose and poetry, but rarely consider it in spoken language. Now that the ephemerality of the spoken word can be overcome by looking at spoken corpus data, we see this as an important contribution to the building of frameworks for looking at spoken language in this way. We also hope that this chapter will go some way to redress the bias towards the rather utilitarian views of language immanent in many versions of communicative language teaching.

Chapter 10 deals with academic and business corpora and what lessons these have for the courses that we teach and the materials that we use. Here both written and spoken data are used and high frequency vocabulary items are discussed. The chapter aims to show the value of smaller and specialised corpora in contrast to the ever-bigger, billion-word-plus corpora built by major publishers primarily to serve the needs of lexicographers.

The final chapter in the body of the book is intended to facilitate the use of corpora in teacher education and development. It is a very broad chapter in a number of ways, and indeed it differs from all the previous chapters. It is broad in the sense that it offers the possibility of a corpus as a collection of transcribed classroom interactions, even if it is just following one class or group of students. This is sufficient, we believe, as a starting point to using a corpus for teacher reflection. As little as one class can provide enough material to facilitate scrutiny of the commonest processes of classroom interaction. It is also broad in the sense that it provides three frameworks which can be used by teachers as the basis for reflecting on practice. None of these frameworks comes from corpus linguistics (and many of our readers may already be aware of them), but they all have much to offer to the interpretation of classroom discourse in a corpus. We end the book with a coda, which looks forward to the future.

We have enjoyed writing this book very much. It has challenged us to look at what we do and articulate its relevance and implications for pedagogy. We hope that by the end of the book you are as excited about what corpus linguistics has to offer language pedagogy as we are, and that the book will have bridged a conceptual gap, and facilitated access to an area of immense potential for language teachers, syllabus designers and materials writers and researchers in the area of applied linguistics.

ANNE O'KEEFFE
MICHAEL MCCARTHY
RONALD CARTER

1　Introduction

1.1　Introduction: the basics

Here we look at the basics of corpus linguistics, from what a corpus is to how to build one. We outline the basic functions of corpus software, such as generating word frequency lists and concordance lines of words and clusters (or chunks). We also try to give an idea of the wide range of applications of a corpus to fields as diverse as forensic linguistics and language teaching. Creating a corpus also brings up a number of issues, for example, whose language it is representing. This is particularly the case in relation to corpora of English in the context of native versus non-native speaker users of the language.

1.2　What is a corpus and how can we use it?

A corpus is a collection of texts, written or spoken, which is stored on a computer. In the past the term was more associated with a body of work, for example all of the writings of one author. However, since the advent of computers large amounts of texts can be stored and analysed using analytical software. Another feature of a corpus, as Biber, Conrad and Reppen (1998) point out, is that it is a *principled* collection of texts available for *qualitative* and *quantitative* analysis. This definition is useful because it captures a number of important issues:

A corpus is a principled collection of texts

Any old collection of texts does not make a corpus. It must represent something and its merits will often be judged on how representative it is. For example, if we decided to build a corpus representing classroom discourse in the context of English Language Teaching (ELT), how do we design it so as to best represent this? Would four hours of recordings from an intermediate level class in a London language school suffice? Great care is usually taken at the design stage of a corpus so as to ensure that it is representative. If we wished to build a corpus to represent classroom discourse in ELT, we would have to create a design matrix that would ideally capture all the essential variables of age, gender, location, type of school (e.g. state or private sector), level, teacher (e.g. gender, qualifications, years of experience, whether native or non-native speaker), class size (large groups, small groups or one-to-one), location, nationalities and so on. It is important to scrutinise how a corpus is designed when considering buying or accessing one, or when evaluating any findings based on it. The design criteria of a corpus allow us to assess its representativeness. Crowdy (1993), Biber (1993), McEnery and

Wilson (1996), McCarthy (1998), Biber, Conrad and Reppen (1998), Kennedy (1998), Meyer (2002), Thompson (2005a), Wynne (2005a), Adolphs (2006) and McEnery, Xiao and Tono (2006), among others, are essential reading if you are considering designing your own corpus.

A corpus is a collection of electronic texts usually stored on a computer

Because corpora are stored on a computer, this allows for very large amounts of text to be amassed and analysed using specially designed software. Language corpora can be composed of written or spoken texts, or a mix of both, and nowadays the capability exists to add multimedia elements, such as video clips, to corpora of spoken language. If it is a corpus of written language, texts may be entered into a computer by scanning, typing, downloading from the internet or by using files that already exist in electronic form.[1] For example, you may wish to build a corpus of your students' written work over a one-year period so as to track their vocabulary acquisition and to compare this with other data. This could be done easily by asking your students to email you their work (see section 1.4 for further details on creating your own corpus).[2] Corpora of spoken language, on the other hand, are much more time-consuming to assemble. For instance, if you wished to build a corpus of your own classroom interactions, you would first need to record the classes and then transcribe them. One hour of recorded speech usually yields approximately between 12,000 and 15,000 words of data and it takes around two days to transcribe, depending on the level of coding you decide to use in transcription (O'Keeffe and Farr 2003 discuss the pros and cons of building versus buying a corpus). For example, a spoken corpus may be coded for different speaker turns, interruptions, speaker overlaps, truncated utterances, extra-linguistic information such as 'giggling', 'door closes in background', 'dog barking' (see section 1.4). More detailed transcriptions include prosodic information as found in the London-Lund Corpus (Svartvik and Quirk 1980), the Lancaster/IBM Spoken English Corpus (Knowles 1990; Leech 2000) and the Hong Kong Corpus of Spoken English (Cheng and Warren 1999, 2000, 2002). Not surprisingly, written corpora are much more plentiful and usually much larger than spoken ones.

A corpus is available for qualitative and quantitative analysis

We can look at a language feature in a corpus in different ways. For example, using a corpus of newspapers, we could examine how many times the words *fire* and *blaze* occur. This will give us quantitative results, that is, numbers of occurrences, which we can then compare with frequencies in other corpora, such as casual conversation or general written English. This might lead us to conclude that the word *blaze* is more frequently used in newspaper articles than in general English conversation or writing, when talking about destructive outbreaks of fire. This conclusion is arrived at through quantitative means. However, another approach is to look more qualitatively at how a word or phrase is used across a corpus. To do this, we need to look beyond the frequency of the word's occurrence.

---

[1] It is essential to remember that most texts are covered by copyright, and that permission to use a text may need to be obtained before it can be stored or exploited in any way.

[2] Teachers may find that their institutions have strict ethical guidelines for using students' work in research, and these should always be observed.

As we will exemplify below, looking at concordance lines can help us do this and to see qualitative patterns of use beyond frequency.

1.3 Which corpus, what for and what size?

There is no one corpus to suit all purposes. The one we choose to work with is the one that best suits our needs at any given time. Begin with the question: *why do I need to use a corpus?* The answer to this question will vary widely. For example, some may wish to use a corpus for research purposes to study how a lexical item or pattern is used. Others may wish to compare the use of an item in different language varieties, for example *will* and *shall* in American versus British English (see Carter and McCarthy 2006: 880–881). In such cases, the corpus which is chosen must best represent the language or language variety, and, if comparing varieties, the corpora themselves must be comparable. For example, comparing *will* and *shall* in American and British English using a corpus of American academic textbooks from the 1960s and a corpus of contemporary spoken British English will obviously yield flawed results (unless one is conducting a study of language change and the possible backwash effects of spoken language on written language). In a pedagogic context, a corpus may also be utilised for reference purposes, for example, a teacher may advise students to search a corpus to find out what preposition most commonly follows *bargain* as a verb. Many of these types of questions can also be answered by looking things up in a dictionary. The advantage of looking up a lexico-grammatical query in a corpus is that it provides us with many examples of the search item in its context of use. However, a corpus will not tell us the meaning of the word or phrase. This is something that we have to deduce from the many examples that are generated. Combining a dictionary and a corpus can be a valuable route in a pedagogical context. Let us look the word *bargain* using a dictionary and some corpus examples:

Figure 1: Main entries for *bargain* from the *Cambridge Advanced Learner's Dictionary* (CD-ROM 2003)

bargain (AGREEMENT) ◀)) ◀)) 🖉 /ˈbɑː.ɡɪn/ ⑯ /ˈbɑːr-/ *noun* [C]
   an agreement between two people or groups in which each promises to
      do something in exchange for something else:
      "I'll tidy the kitchen if you clean the car." "OK, it's a bargain."
      The management and employees eventually **struck/made** *a bargain*
         (= reached an agreement).

bargain ◀)) ◀)) 🖉 /ˈbɑː.ɡɪn/ ⑯ /ˈbɑːr-/ *verb* [I or T] (Verb Endings)
   Unions bargain **with** *employers for better rates of pay each year.*
   I realized that by trying to gain security I had bargained **away** *my*
      freedom (= exchanged it for something of less value).

bargain for/on *sth* *phrasal verb*
   to expect or be prepared for something:
      We hadn't bargained on such a long wait.
      The strength of the opposition was rather **more than** *she'd*
         bargained **for**.

Figure 2: Sample of concordance lines for *bargain* from the Cambridge International Corpus (see Appendix 1 for details)

```
1    blic-sector unions have been allowed to bargain away jobs for pay.     In a deal
2    over ... The chancellor also asks us to bargain away whatever obligations or int
3    : your loss is Southampton's gain.     A bargain buy at pounds 1 million this sea
4    weapons; and that the Russians will not  bargain for cuts in something that Labou
5    in his shirt front. Scurra has struck a  bargain,' he called out as he bustled fu
6    e, and even the possibility of making a  bargain,he turned his back on them for
7    tologists had kept to their side of the  bargain;he'd make their deaths quick...
8    he airport.'    I see now why this is a  bargain holiday. Once the clients have p
9    erm        these really s5 sort of quite bargain holidays where you take+
10           Chuffed.         You little     bargain hunter you.              laughs
11    Events' are manna from heaven for the   bargain hunter.    When shares get marke
12    ost of the phone calls I took were from bargain hunters,' Steve says.    While L
13    junkies, pop history freaks and casual  bargain hunters. Record Collector magazi
14   as keen on trail running as they are on  bargain hunting. A spokeswoman for PR co
15    and you'll lose a lot of wine into the  bargain.     Reading a champagne label
16   point and got a little success into the  bargain, she'll go back to what she was
17    And it's invariably dishonest into the  bargain."    So how has he managed to we
18   tanding but seem pretty boring into the  bargain.     THERE was a moment about a t
19   t free tickets. He's a widower into the  bargain, they say. Quite a catch for som
20   ess accepted separate electorates and a  bargain was struck over the distribution
21   chaser and it really is if you like the  bargain we will strike and I like to thi
22   ents that they can actually strike up a  bargain with a patient. Em and things ca
23    occurred to me that I might be able to  bargain with him. If you really are a Ke
24   es."    But you're not. All you have to  bargain with now is a copy of the decode
25   added.    The Americans are prepared to  bargain with the Russians on almost anyt
26   ers from their beds each day at five to  bargain with the     wholesalers, which g
```

As well as illustrating a range of prepositions that follow *bargain*, the concordance lines also give a rich insight into how the word collocates with other words (see below and chapter 2), for example, *to strike a bargain*, or *bargain hunters*. We also find idiomatic usage, such as *into the bargain* meaning 'as well'.

On the question of corpus size, in the case of *bargain*, we had to search over 10 million words of data to find a range of instances. This is because it is not a core vocabulary item in English. If, on the other hand, we were looking at a word or structure that was quite common, a smaller corpus would suffice. Aston (1997), Maia (1997) and Tribble (1997) suggest using a small corpus if we are dealing with a very specialised language register, for words of caution, see Gavioli (2002) (see also chapter 8 which makes a case for using small corpora to look at relational language). In terms of what constitutes a large or a small corpus, it depends on whether it is a spoken or written corpus and what it is seeking to represent. For corpora of spoken language, anything over a million words is considered to be large; for written corpora, anything below five million is quite small. In terms of suitability, however, it is often the design of a corpus as opposed to its size which is the determining factor. For example, a corpus containing only highly technical engineering language will be largely inappropriate for language teacher trainees wanting to investigate general vocabulary. Therefore, while size is an issue, it should be considered hand-in-hand with the appropriateness of corpus design (for further discussion of these and other issues relating to size and corpus design see: Sinclair 1991a; Thomas and Short 1996; Aston 1997; Maia 1997; Tribble 1997; Biber et al. 1998; McCarthy 1998; Biber et al. 1999; Coxhead 2000; Carter and McCarthy 2001; Hunston 2002; O'Keeffe and Farr 2003; Thompson 2005a; Wynne 2005a; Adolphs 2006 and McEnery et al. 2006).

Overview of existing corpora

There are many corpora available and some can be bought, some are free and some are not publicly available (e.g. corpora compiled by publishers for the specific commercial purposes of producing language teaching resources and materials, or corpora where the consent agreement of writers or speakers may only allow for restricted use). Appendix 1 provides an overview of a wide range of language corpora and how to find out more about them. Throughout this book we will be referring to a number of these corpora in our illustrations and analyses.

1.4   How to make a basic corpus

A basic language corpus can be assembled from spoken or written texts and can be used with commercially available corpus software such as *Wordsmith Tools* (Scott 1999) and *Monoconc Pro* (2000), which any average home computer user can manipulate with relative ease. A spoken corpus takes considerably longer to build, as discussed above, because speech has to be transcribed and possibly coded for some of its non-verbal features. Written corpora, on the other hand, can be made very quickly using the internet as a source (though international copyright must always be respected in the usual ways).

Stages of building a spoken corpus

1 Create a design rationale

Your corpus will need some design principle (see above on representativeness). When considering the design of a spoken (or written corpus), considerations of feasibility (what is available, what is ethical, what is legal?) will need to be a guiding factor also. Decide what it is you wish to represent and consider how best you can represent this for your purposes. This will guide your decision as to how much data you want to collect. For example, you might wish to create a corpus of news reports to use in class. You could decide to collect ten news reports or a hundred. You may wish to only record business reports or political reports and so on.

2 Record data

It is useful to keep in mind that one hour of continuous everyday, informal conversation yields approximately 12,000 to 15,000 words. The mode of recording is also worth consideration. There are a number of options including analogue cassettes, digital media and audiovisual digital recorders. Traditional analogue, though they are inexpensive, have a number of drawbacks. They are cumbersome to store and unlike digital recordings, they cannot easily be computerised and aligned with the transcription later. Using digital devices leaves open the option of aligning sound (and image if you use an audiovisual recorder) with your transcription. Permission to record should be cleared in advance with the speakers and consent forms should be signed off authorising the use of the recordings for research or commercial pedagogical materials, etc. It may be necessary to specify how the recordings will be used when obtaining permission; for example, is the speaker signing permission just for the transcript to be used, or for his/her actual voice to be used in research or any publication?

3 Transcribe recordings and save as text files

Spoken data needs to be manually transcribed and this is what makes corpora of spoken language such a challenge. They are best stored as 'plain text' files, as this offers the maximum flexibility of use with different software suites. As mentioned above, every one hour of recorded speech can take approximately two working days to transcribe. In most cases, every word, vocalisation, truncation, hesitation, overlap, and so on, is transcribed, as opposed to a cleaned-up version of what the speakers said. The level of detail of the transcription is relative to the purpose of your corpus. If you have no requirement to know where overlapping utterances and interruptions occur, then there is no point in spending time transcribing to that level of detail. Figure 3 shows an example of an extract from a transcript from the Limerick Corpus of Irish English (LCIE) (see appendix 1). Our data extracts in this book will use these conventions to a greater or lesser extent:

TRANSCRIPTION CODING KEY

<$1>, <$2>, etc.	these mark the different speakers in the order in which they appear on the recording
+	interruptions can be marked from where they occur and from where the utterance is resumed (often called 'latched turns')
=	unfinished or truncated words can be marked, for example, yester=
<?>	unintelligible utterance
<$E> laugh <\$E>	extralinguistic information such as 'laughing', 'sound of someone leaving the room', 'coughing', 'dog barking' can be useful background information

Figure 3: Extract of a transcript of a recording of family members changing a printer cartridge while looking at the instruction manual (from LCIE)

```
<$1> Oki Jet. Isn't that what we have?

<$2> Yeah but that's not the <$E> pause one second <\$E> there's a <?>. Here it is.
     Here Brendan. Here. Look. <$E> intercom goes off in the kitchen <\$E>

<$1> Knock that off now. <$E> sound of intercom being switched off <\$E>

<$2> There's about six different languages.

<$1> So what's the problem?

<$2> We needed to replace the print head.

<$1> Oh right.

<$2> So that's the problem. <$E> noise of printer in background <\$E>

<$3> <$E> shouting from another room <\$E> Hello.

<$2> <$E> looking at printer manual <\$E> Changing the ink cartridge <?>

<$3> <$E> from the other room <\$E> Change the+

<$1> Changing the ink cartridge yeah. What does it say abou=

<$2> Open the printer cover.

<$1> All right.

<$2> <$E> reading from the instruction manual <\$E> The print head carriage will move
     automatically to the head loading replacement position of the empty print head.

<$1> Right.

<$2> <$E> reading from the instruction manual <\$E> Release only the ink cartridge
     from the print head casing pulling gently outwards the lateral+

<$1> Press the green button first Brian

<$2> That's the black one. No that's fine. If you put that back in+

<$1> There's no print head on it.
```

4 Database texts

Transcription files need to be organised so that source information can be traced. For example, it may be useful to be able to retrieve information such as gender, age, number of speakers, place of birth, occupation, level of education, where the recording took place, relationship of speakers and so on. This information can be stored at the beginning of each transcript as an information 'header' (see Reppen and Simpson 2002: 98–99), or in a separate database, where the information is logged with the file name.

5 Check transcription

Finally, the transcription needs to be checked with the original recording for accuracy.

Stages of building a written corpus

1 Create a design rationale

As discussed above, start with a design rationale. Decide what it is you want to represent and how many texts you need to do this, from how many sources and over what period.

2 Input texts

Depending on what form they are in, written texts may need to be re-typed or scanned. They may already be in electronic format or may be downloadable from the internet, and may have special copyright restrictions on their use. Once they are in electronic form, they need ideally to be saved as 'plain text' files; once again, this will offer the maximum flexibility of use with different software suites.

3 Database texts

Any individual text in a corpus needs to be traceable to its source information (that is, who wrote it, where and when it was published, genre, number of words and so on, especially for purposes of subsequent use in relation to copyright). As discussed above, this can be stored at the beginning of each file (as 'header information') or in a separate database.

1.5   Basic corpus linguistic techniques

Here we overview some of the basic techniques that can be used on a corpus, using standard software such as *Wordsmith Tools* (Scott 1999) and *Monoconc Pro* (2000). Applications of these techniques will be illustrated throughout the book.

Concordancing

Concordancing is a core tool in corpus linguistics and it simply means using corpus software to find every occurrence of a particular word or phrase. This idea is not a new one and many scholars over the years have manually concordanced the Christian Bible, for example, painstakingly finding and recording every example of certain words. With a computer, we can now search millions of words in seconds. The search word or phrase is often referred to as the 'node' and concordance lines are usually presented with the node word/phrase in the centre of the line with seven or eight words presented at either side. These are known as Key-Word-In-Context displays (or KWIC concordances). Concordance lines are usually scanned vertically at first glance, that is, looked at up or down the central pattern, along the line of the node word or phrase. Initially, this may be disconcerting because we are accustomed, in Western cultures, to reading from left to right. Concordance lines challenge us to read in an entirely new way, vertically, or even from the centre outwards in both directions. Here are some sample lines from a concordance of the word *way* using the Limerick Corpus of Irish English (LCIE):

Figure 4: Concordance lines for *way* from LCIE

```
ether in northern Ireland is no different in a way then em what they were desperately
        you see it?  Some of you anyhow?  Now in a way 'What Dreams may come' it's not
        subject to study in college in fact it's a way of life and you find this right
            and how could he present things in such a way that he would persuade people.
ul and the purpose of life is to live in such a way that when you die your soul is
t he was obviously he obviously lived a certain way of live and they wanted to know
    lem that they had to deal with in a different way they couldn't deal with it by
asically in football stadium that's the easiest way to describe it.  There is a large
sking for you ok I find this the most effective way.  Ok now today em you have as well
speculative because there is no evidence either way.  You can't have evidence about
 e theologian starts from the top and works his way down.  The theologian will have
 rts from the ground so it speaks and works its way up.  The theologian starts from
```

Most software allows the number of words at either side of the node word or phrase to be adjusted to allow more of the context to be viewed and you can usually go back very easily and quickly to the source file containing the full text or transcript. Software normally facilitates the sorting of the concordance lines so that we can examine the lexico-grammatical patterns which occur before and/or after the node word. When sample concordance lines for *way* are sorted alphabetically to the left of the screen for example the following patterns emerge:

Figure 5: Sample concordance lines for *way* from LCIE, sorted to the left of the screen

```
ether in northern Ireland is no different in a way then em what they were desperately
        you see it?  Some of you anyhow?  Now in a way 'What Dreams may come' it's not
        subject to study in college in fact it's a way of life and you find this right
            and how could he present things in such a way that he would persuade people.
ul and the purpose of life is to live in such a way that when you die your soul is
t he was obviously he obviously lived a certain way of live and they wanted to know
    lem that they had to deal with in a different way they couldn't deal with it by
asically in football stadium that's the easiest way to describe it.  There is a large
sking for you ok I find this the most effective way.  Ok now today em you have as well
speculative because there is no evidence either way.  You can't have evidence about
 e theologian starts from the top and works his way down.  The theologian will have
 rts from the ground so it speaks and works its way up.  The theologian starts from
```

Another random sample from the concordance lines of the word *way*, sorted to the right of the screen, shows a systematic pattern with *from*:

Figure 6: Sample concordance lines for *way* from LCIE, sorted to the right of the screen

```
 would acquire an unlimited right of way from Abattoir Road to our client's land along
h Hampton magistrates ah just up the way from ah from the Silverstone circuit am the
And then there's one over across the way from Centra.        Oh right.         And
ah oh yeah.          +to come all the way from Frank's house do you know. So it's a
ead here       laughing      all the way from here all the way to the back myself and
     there's a bad test it's a bad go way from it don't bother with it cause it's this
ntion a request that came in all the way from Sweden it it it's sort a it has put a
day and John said he drove the whole way from the top lights to the bottom traffic
            sobbing the whole way from the church to the hotel sobbing
 third last.       Now there's a long way from the third last isn't there to the
h.          Yeah then you can go that way from there as well.        Can we?
```

Because concordance lines can provide many examples of patterns of use, they have application to the language classroom and are now being used in ELT materials. For example, here is an extract from the entry on *there* in *Natural Grammar* (Thornbury 2004: 155), where concordance lines have been adapted for an inductive grammar task:

Figure 7: Extract from *Natural Grammar* (Thornbury 2004: 155)

Exercises

❶ Look at these concordance lines, and identify the
   meaning of *there* in each case. Is it a pronoun (showing
   that something exists) or is it an adverb (saying where
   something is)?

a   **There**'s a bar and a lecture room for guests' use.
b   **There**'d been another quake at 4am, a 6.6 shock.
c   It was only in my third year that I really felt happy
    there.
d   You say **there**'s a certain amount of risk. How much?
e   I was **there** for her birth and it was the most exciting
    thing.
f   But **there**'ll be no alcohol on sale.
g   He was standing **there** with Mrs Kasmin as she tried to
    give him tea.
h   He had been **there** since he left the Pit a year earlier.
i   He was confident **there**'d be no problem. So was I.

Another example is found in McCarthy and O'Dell (2002), where students are invited to look at an extract from a concordance for the word *eye* and to decide which of the occurrences are idiomatic/metaphorical.

Figure 8: Extract from *English Idioms in Use* (McCarthy and O'Dell 2002: 109)

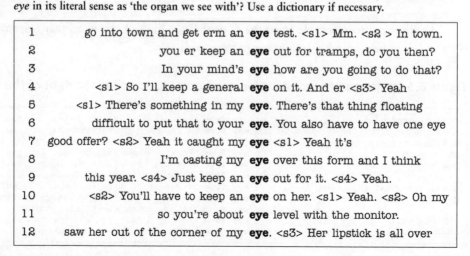

50.4   Here are some random examples from a computer database containing lines from real
           conversations. The figures in diamond brackets, e.g. <s1>, <s2>, mean 'first speaker', 'second
           speaker', etc. How many of the examples use *eye* as an idiom, and how many use the word
           eye in its literal sense as 'the organ we see with'? Use a dictionary if necessary.

1	go into town and get erm an **eye** test. <s1> Mm. <s2 > In town.
2	you er keep an **eye** out for tramps, do you then?
3	In your mind's **eye** how are you going to do that?
4	<s1> So I'll keep a general **eye** on it. And er <s3> Yeah
5	<s1> There's something in my **eye**. There's that thing floating
6	difficult to put that to your **eye**. You also have to have one eye
7	good offer? <s2> Yeah it caught my **eye** <s1> Yeah it's
8	I'm casting my **eye** over this form and I think
9	this year. <s4> Just keep an **eye** out for it. <s4> Yeah.
10	<s2> You'll have to keep an **eye** on her. <s1> Yeah. <s2> Oh my
11	so you're about **eye** level with the monitor.
12	saw her out of the corner of my **eye**. <s3> Her lipstick is all over

Word frequency counts or wordlists

Another common corpus technique which software can perform is the extremely rapid calculation of word frequency lists (or wordlists) for any batch of texts. By running a word frequency list on your corpus, you can get a rank ordering of all the words in it in order of frequency. This function facilitates enquiry across different corpora, different language varieties and different contexts of use. Below, for example are the first ten words from five different corpora (see appendix 1):

Table 1: Comparison of word frequencies for the ten most frequent words across five different datasets

Rank order	1 Shop (LCIE)	2 Friends (LCIE)	3 Academic LIBEL	4 Australian Corpus of English	5 CIC newspaper & magazine sub-corpus
	spoken	spoken	spoken	written	written
1	you	I	the	the	the
2	of	and	and	of	to
3	is	the	of	and	of
4	thanks	to	you	to	a
5	it	was	to	a	and
6	I	you	a	in	in
7	please	it	that	is	is
8	the	like	in	for	for
9	yeah	that	it	that	it
10	now	he	is	was	that

1   Service encounters: a sub-corpus of the Limerick Corpus of Irish English (LCIE) consisting of shop encounters (8,500 words)

2   Friends chatting: a sub-corpus of LCIE, consisting of female friends chatting (40,000 words)

3   Academic English: The Limerick-Belfast Corpus of Academic Spoken English (LIBEL CASE, one million words of academic English[3])

4   Australian casual conversation: the Macquarie Corpus of English (ACE) (one million words of written Australian English)

5   Written British and American English: The Cambridge International Corpus based on a 100,000 word sample of newspaper and magazines from McCarthy (1998: 122–123).

---

[3]   Hereafter, LIBEL CASE will be referred to as LIBEL.

Even from just the first ten words of these corpora, tendencies emerge in terms of genres and contexts of use. The shop (column 1) and casual conversation (column 2) results show markers of interactivity typical of spoken English such as *I, you, yeah* (as a response token), *like, please* and *thanks* (see Carter and McCarthy 2006). Though the academic corpus (column 3) is also naturally-occurring speech, the first ten words lack the interactive markers found in the first two columns. The academic corpus results resemble more the written data from the ACE and CIC (columns 4 and 5). All three share features associated with written language, that is to say the high frequency of:

- articles *a* and *the*, indicating a high instance of noun phrases
- the preposition *of*, suggesting post-modified noun phrases
- *that*, especially in academic corpora, pointing to its multi-functionality, as a subordinator (particularly following report verbs or in *it* patterns) as well as as a relative pronoun in relative clauses
- prepositions *to*, *for* and *in*, suggesting prepositional phrases

Conversely, there is a lack of:

- interactive pronouns *I* and *you*; the only pronoun that figures in the top ten words is *it*, which is referential as opposed to interactive
- response tokens or discourse markers such as *yeah, like, now*

In a number of chapters in this book we will use word frequency lists. In chapter 2 for example, word frequencies will form the basis for identifying the core vocabulary of English for pedagogical purposes in identifying different target levels.

Key word analysis

This function allows us to identify the key words in one or more texts. Key words, as detailed by Scott (1999), are those whose frequency is unusually high in comparison with some norm. Key words are not usually the most frequent words in a text (or collection of texts), rather they are the more 'unusually frequent' (ibid). Software compares two pre-existing word lists and one of these is assumed to be a large word list which will act as a reference file or benchmark corpus. The other is the word list based on the text(s) which you want to study. The larger corpus will provide background data for reference comparison. For example, we saw above that *the* is the most frequent word in the LIBEL corpus of spoken academic English (table 1); if we select one economics lecture from this corpus and generate a word list, we can also see that *the* is again the most frequent word. However, if we compare this economics lecture word list with the larger one from the LIBEL corpus using keyword software (such as that found in *Wordsmith Tools*), it will tell us which words occur with unusual frequency, or 'keyness'. These words are then referred to as the key words.

Table 2: Key words from an economics lecture relative to a general corpus of academic lectures

1	tax	15	higher
2	income	16	percent
3	system(s)	17	rates
4	average	18	ordinary
5	basic	19	sixty
6	rate	20	marginal
7	supply	21	scheme
8	poor	22	labour
9	thousand	23	terms
10	impact	24	cost(s)
11	equity	25	characterised
12	under	26	workers
13	both	27	systems
14	figures	28	negative

Scott (1999) notes the key word facility provides a useful way of characterising a text or a genre and has potential applications in the areas of forensic linguistics, stylistics, content analysis and text retrieval. In the context of language teaching, it can be used by teachers and materials writers to create word lists, for example in Languages for Specific Purposes programmes (e.g. English for pilots, French for engineers), where the key specialised vocabulary can be automatically identified, either from a single text (e.g. an aeronautical training manual) or from a corpus of specialised texts.

Cluster analysis

As chapters 2 and 3 will illustrate, the analysis of how language systematically clusters into combinations of words or 'chunks' (e.g. *I mean, this that and the other,* etc.) can give insights into how we describe the vocabulary of a language. It also has implications for what we teach in our vocabulary lessons and how learners approach the task of acquiring vocabulary and developing fluency. As a corpus technique the process of generating chunks or cluster lists is similar to making single word lists. Instead of asking the computer to rank all of the single words in the corpus in order of frequency, we can ask it to look for word combinations, for example 2-, 3-, 4-, 5-, or 6-word combinations (for further explanation of how this works, see chapter 3). By way of example, using *Wordsmith Tools,* table 3 shows the 20 most frequent 3-word combinations from 10 million words (five million written and five million spoken) of the Cambridge International Corpus (CIC):

Table 3: The 20 most frequent three-word chunks in 10 million words from CIC

	Chunk	Frequency per million words		Chunk	Frequency per million words
1	I don't know	588	11	a couple of	166
2	a lot of	364	12	do you want	159
3	one of the	320	13	you have to	158
4	I don't think	248	14	be able to	157
5	it was a	240	15	a bit of	155
6	I mean I	220	16	you want to	153
7	the end of	198	17	and it was	148
8	there was a	193	18	it would be	142
9	out of the	190	19	do you know	138
10	do you think	177	20	you know what	137

Chapter 3 looks in detail at chunks in spoken and written corpora and at the pedagogical implications of these patterns.

1.6   Lexico-grammatical profiles

A further corpus strategy, when looking at concordance lines, is to create a 'lexico-grammatical profile' of a word and its contexts of use. A lexico-grammatical profile describes typical contexts in terms of:

1 Collocates: which word(s) occur most frequently and with statistical significance (i.e. not just by random occurrence) in the word's environment?

2 Chunks/idioms: does the word form part of any recurrent chunks? Is the word idiom-prone? What types occur (for example, binomials or trinomials such as *rough and ready*, or *ready, willing and able*)?

3 Syntactic restrictions: are there syntactic patterns which restrict the word? For example, are there prepositions that go with the word? What are its typical clause-positions (initial/medial/final)? Are there any tense/aspect restrictions?

4 Semantic restrictions: are there semantic restrictions? For example, the word/phrase is applied to humans only, or is never used with an intensifier.

5 Prosody: 'Semantic prosody' is a term used by Louw (1993) and means simply that words, as well as having typical collocates (for example, *blonde* typically collocates with *hair*, but not with *car*), tend to occur in particular environments, in a way that their meaning, especially their connotative and attitudinal meanings, seem to spread over several words. For example, words might tend to occur overwhelmingly in positive or in negative environments. Stubbs (1995), for instance, shows how more than 90% of the collocates of *cause* are negative, for example *accident*,

cancer, commotion, crisis and *delay*. By way of a positive semantic prosody example, he offers *provide*, which typically collocates with, for example, *care, food, help, jobs, relief* and *support*. Before the advent of computerised language analysis, this phenomenon had never been properly codified in terms of actual usage.

Another example of prosody is seen in the CIC data for the adjective *prim*, where the word seems strongly associated with old-fashioned, frumpy, conservative, mostly female attributes. Figure 9 shows a sample concordance for *prim*.

6   Other relevant or recurring features.

Figure 9: Concordance for *prim* (CIC, 10 million words mixed spoken/written)

```
 1         stuff of sensible office suits and prim 50s ensembles, dogtooth is
 2              You're too        You're too prim and proper to sit in the
 3  girls.         No. But this one's real prim and proper and oh you know
 4   . The young today are not nearly so prim and proper as we were.
 5   o me.     Mm.        So English so prim and proper in the way he
 6   stands either. Mum taught us. We're prim and proper. Mandy, fired up
 7   ed his father-in-law's picture of a prim galleon on frilly sea.
 8   re."    Hallo," said Alma, thin and prim, in a hurry. They must be
 9    delightful part of my life in-that prim, incongruous little parl
10   , thinks you should leave alone the prim little fork that's always
11  day that she died she was a star. A prim Miss Marple lookalike in
12    she blushed furiously feeling all prim. '' So it's powerful stuff t
13   ness,' Bless replied, now sounding prim. The stranger smiled at him
14   roof. Anna thought it looked like a prim woman with its neat apron
15   at their tender leaves. This small, prim woman, devoted to Professor
```

A lexico-grammatical profile is principally drawn from concordance lines, though the frequency and keyness of any item in a particular corpus may also be of relevance. The lines should ideally be sorted and analysed in both screen directions, left and right. Figure 10 (overleaf) shows an example for the word *abroad* using the framework we have just outlined. A lexico-grammatical profile for *abroad*, based on figure 10, would give us the following: Left-screen sorting seems to produce the most visible and productive patterning since *abroad* tends to be phrase-, clause- or sentence-final.

1   Collocates of three or more occurrences: *be, been, go, trip, travel, work*.

2   Chunks/idioms: *home and abroad* occurs three times.

3   Syntax: *abroad* only seems to be used adverbially; no preposition after verbs of motion (*flow, go, shift, travel*); no preposition after *trip/holiday*; only one preposition occurs (*from*). It can be used as a post-nominal modifier (*trip abroad, holidays abroad*).

4   Semantics: *abroad* can be used with static or dynamic verbs; it is never premodified (for example, **very abroad, *far abroad* do not occur). Its most frequent meaning is geographical or political, but there are also examples where it simply means 'in the public domain/out in the open' (lines 30, 33, 39).

5   Prosody: *abroad* is anywhere, not the writer's country or the country in question, often in contrast to the UK or 'home', a place to which people travel for leisure and work and where trade and investment are seen as important; no particular connotations of negativity, but sometimes a prosody of 'difference' or 'exoticness' (lines 15, 22, 25, 48, 49).

Figure 10: Random sample of 60 concordance lines for *abroad*, based on five million words of mixed written texts (CIC)

```
 1   iaspora continues with their activities abroad In the relatively low-tech car i
 2   to ease the curbs on travel at home and abroad. If the reforms really take hold
 3   ervices, to firm leadership at home and abroad; to conditions in which business
 4   s examples of good practice at home and abroad.    Local Authority Involvement
 5    which attracts adults from Ireland and abroad to courses in Donegal on Irish l
 6   well-managed forests in both the UK and abroad.    FSC-certified charcoal is so
 7   deal route for visitors from the UK and abroad. It is easily accessible by rail
 8   n West Germany, 60 % of whose sales are abroad, has no foreigner on board. Elec
 9    companies (about 70 % of its sales are abroad), makes all its Walkmans in Japa
10   new of the murder, although he had been abroad when it had taken place.    The
11   s for the day.    The younger son being abroad, I sent him the news with a litt
12   aking place. The flows of Japanese cash abroad, mainly across the Pacific, are
13    our responsibility to our own citizens abroad, is not an easy question. We can
14   direct investment by Canadian companies abroad. An example of the first was the
15   ay.    He also wore a bored, Englishman-abroad look that suggested he might rat
16   y can get around the rules is to expand abroad rather than at home. Industriali
17   n spent at home to raise incomes flowed abroad instead.    Japan's government,
18   weatshops. Even designs are coming from abroad - from 'cheap' fashion centres l
19   vertising standards, are delivered from abroad every week. The bill is adding t
20   l is being sent into British homes from abroad - and it is subsidised by the Po
21   g in enormous amounts of hot money from abroad by offering high interest to pay
22   s first overseas trip. I would never go abroad, because I'd always heard the ba
23   at deal about it. It means he has to go abroad a lot. He's in Paris at the mome
24   espectfully and indigenously. If you go abroad this summer, support the local c
25   they're fed up with the hassle of going abroad,' said Stan, executive member of
26   hey didn't suffer because she was going abroad.    It all took her longer than
27   t of the chamber of commerce, have gone abroad to avoid arrest. General Noriega
28   y mum and dad. It was our first holiday abroad and we went to Majorca. There wa
29   want" Andrew explains. Regular holidays abroad are also affordable. Florida is
30   on appeared to be the only living human abroad at that ungodly hour. When sa
31   here. About 14 % of JVC's production is abroad, up from 9 % in 1985. JVC's fina
32   ed how many of last year's 183 journeys abroad were necessary.    They included
33   y, £20        ##    There's a big lie abroad and it's about taxes and the wel
34    retire at 30. She has no plans to live abroad, as Morceli has done (in Califor
35   to Amy Johnson, but both are now living abroad and, although they have been con
36   sts.    Success also means selling more abroad. A Russia no longer losing groun
37      to be the case then I'd probably move abroad. But that would only happen if I
38   e caused by the book caused her to move abroad, first to New Mexico where she e
39   . A new, deficit-induced realism is now abroad. This week a draft report by the
40   nds. Who commands the purse, at home or abroad?    That cohabitation did not me
41   itish embassies and other organizations abroad, gathering intelligence in place
42   ed for minimum cover (i.e. third party) abroad.    ADVENTURE and high risk spor
43    the inmates choose to write to penpals abroad. Tito has been writing to a penp
44   eek before he was due to take up a post abroad as a correspondent for a western
45    jewellery boxes which he tries to sell abroad. He also spends a lot of time "t
46    pub with a soldier while I was serving abroad I'd give her such a pasting she
47   technologies will eventually be shifted abroad - but not until the factories no
48   Disorientated and thinking he was still abroad, he shouted: `I'm English like y
49   s checking up on the way they do things abroad,' explained his wife Mavis.    T
50   port is to make it easier when I travel abroad.    Apart from that, I consider
51   ertainly mean that he will never travel abroad again, and inevitably both he an
52   national decline until he had travelled abroad and discovered that, far from be
53   ier in the month I'd made my first trip abroad and came up against another set
54   ay for too long now. His frequent trips abroad had become a fact of her life bu
55   he Children, in the course of her trips abroad; these are located around the bu
56    after six months she resigned and went abroad. Years of exile followed, in Mal
57   Kitty, with Jefferson and Edwina, went abroad for a few months to escape atten
58    apply for a licence for minors to work abroad. That continued until I was eigh
59   who leave the country intending to work abroad for more than a year are deemed
60   there had been mention of a son working abroad, but it had been a long time ago,
```

1.7 How have corpora been used?

Lexicography

Language corpora have many applications beyond language description for its own sake. They are now the standard tool for lexicographers, who use multi-million word corpora to examine word frequency, patterning and semantics in the compilation of dictionaries. This tradition of basing dictionary entries on actual use rather than intuition is not entirely new. In the 1700s, when Samuel Johnson was compiling the first comprehensive dictionary of the English language, he manually collated a corpus of language based on samples of usage from the period 1560 to 1660. Three centuries later, the corpora that lexicographers use are vast, methodical collections of both spoken and written texts; at the time of writing, the Cambridge International Corpus (CIC) has over one billion words. They are constantly added to and facilitate the monitoring of language trends and usage changes. Some publishers also hold learner corpora, for example the CIC consists of over 27 million words of learner writing, 12 million of which are error coded. This provides very useful information about the types of lexical and grammatical errors that are made and in so doing allows for dictionary writers and other materials writers to highlight typical problems. The pioneering work in this area was the *Collins Birmingham University International Language Database* (COBUILD) project. This was set up at the University of Birmingham in 1980 under the direction of John Sinclair. To date it has produced 16 dictionaries and grammars, most influentially the *Collins COBUILD English Language Dictionary* (1987, 2nd edition 1995, 3rd edition 2001, 4th edition 2003) and the *Collins COBUILD Grammar Patterns* series (1996; 1998). It also sparked the design of the Lexical Syllabus (see Willis 1990). All major publishers now provide corpus-based dictionaries.

Grammar

The COBUILD project also had a major influence on grammar. It provided the concept of 'pattern' as an interface between lexis and grammar. How 'pattern grammar' emerged through corpus-based lexico-grammatical research, the debates which surrounded it and its application for language teaching are covered extensively in Hunston and Francis (2000), see also Hunston et al. (1997). Major grammars of English are now corpus-informed (for example, Quirk et al. 1985; Sinclair 1990; Biber et al. 1999; Carter and McCarthy 2006). In recent years, Biber et al. (1999) conducted a seven-year grammar project which led to the creation of their corpus-based grammar of English. It focuses on American and British English and on the four registers of conversation, fiction writing, news writing, and academic writing. This grammar was based on the analysis of a 40 million word corpus of spoken and written texts. Carter and McCarthy (2006) based their grammar on the CIC, at that time consisting of over 700 million words of English, constructed over a ten-year period and still in the process of development. It includes examples from sources such as newspapers, best-selling novels, non-fiction books on a wide range of topics, websites, magazines, junk mail, TV and radio programmes and recordings of people's everyday conversations in a variety of social settings ranging from university seminars

to intimate family conversations. Carter and McCarthy found that it was crucially important in many cases to separate statements made about spoken as opposed to written grammar, and include a CD-ROM where users can access sound-clips for the more than 7,000
example sentences and utterances recorded in the grammar, in the belief that spoken grammar especially needs to be heard and not just read from a page. As in the case of lexicography, corpora have revolutionised how grammar is studied. Corpus tools allow grammarians
to extensively investigate grammatical frequency and patterning, to look in detail at
differences in the use of grammar in different varieties of language, and readily provide contemporary examples of actual language usage. By attesting structures and patterns across a
wide range of speakers and social and geographical contexts (using the database information referred to above for features such as age, gender, educational background, etc.), Carter
and McCarthy were able to include features in widespread spoken usage, even though they
may be frowned upon by traditionalists (see also Carter 1999b, 2005). In chapters 5 and 6,
we look at how corpus-based grammar has forced us to distinguish between patterns which
can be viewed prescriptively (for example that third-person singular present-tense verbs
end in -s) and patterns that are less fixed and need to be viewed probabilistically (we provide a detailed case study of the *get*-passive structure to exemplify this in chapter 5).

Stylistics

In other language-related fields, corpora are also being used. In the area of stylistics,
for example, which is mostly concerned with the study of the language of literature,
Burrows (2002) notes that traditional and computational forms of stylistics have much in
common. Both rely upon the close analysis of texts, and both benefit from opportunities
for comparison. According to Wynne (2005b) corpus linguistics is opening up new vistas
for stylistics, and there are interesting similarities in the approaches of stylistics and corpus
linguistics. Stylistics, he notes, is a field of empirical inquiry, in which the insights and techniques of linguistic theory are used to analyse literary texts, that is by applying systems of
categorisation and linguistic analysis to, for example, poems and prose (see van Peer 1989;
Leech and Short 1981; Louw 1993; Short 1996; Short et al. 1996; Semino et al. 1997; Semino
and Short 2004). A related area of increasing interest in the study of language and literature
is the notion of 'semantic prosody' (Louw 1993), which we mentioned earlier in relation to
lexico-grammatical profiling. Wynne (2005b) tells us several corpus linguists have used evidence of these patterns to study creativity in language, both in fiction and in everyday usage
(Sinclair 1987a, 1987b; Carter 2004; Hoey 2005; Stubbs 2005). The work of Louw is of particular importance for the study of stylistics. His important 1993 paper comes from the lin-
eage of J. R. Firth and Sinclair; it provides a novel methodology for analysing literary texts
through the study of collocations, based on the idea that certain words, phrases and constructions become associated with certain types of meaning due to their regular co-occurrence with the words of a particular semantic category (for a more recent survey see Wynne
2005b).

Translation

Language corpora have considerable application in the area of translation (see Teubert 1996, 2002; Tognini-Bonelli 1996; Zanettin 1998, 2002; Claridge 2000; Serpollet 2002). As noted by Aston (1999), this has been from two main perspectives, descriptive and practical; that is to say descriptive research which looks at corpora of translations, comparing these with corpora of original texts so as to establish the characteristics both peculiar and universal to translated texts (Gellerstam 1996; Baker 1995, 1998; Laviosa 1998). On the other hand, Aston observes, corpora have been looked at as aids in the processes of human and machine translation, and for this purpose he distinguishes between three main types of corpora:

Monolingual corpora

These consist of texts in a single language, which may be either the source or the target language of a given translation.

Comparable corpora

Where monolingual corpora of similar design are available for two or more languages, they may be treated as components of a single comparable corpus. Baker (1995) suggests that comparable corpora have the potential to reveal most about features specific to translated text.

Parallel corpora

These also have components in two or more languages, consisting of original texts and their translations, for example, a novel and its translation in another language. Aston (1999) points to the distinction between 'unidirectional parallel corpora' which consist of texts in one language along with translations of those texts into another language (or languages) and 'bidirectional' or 'reciprocal parallel corpora' which contain four components: source texts in language A and their aligned translations in language B, and source texts in language B and their aligned translations in language A. Parallel corpora exist for several language pairings including English–French (for example, Church and Gale 1991; Salkie 1995), English–Italian (Marinai et al. 1992), and English–Norwegian (Johansson and Hofland 1994; Johansson et al. 1996). Typical applications of parallel corpora include translator training, bilingual lexicography and machine translation.

For further reading about the use of translation corpora see, for example, Johansson and Hofland (1994); Johansson and Ebeling (1996); Sinclair et al. (1996); King (1997); Laviosa (1998); Santos (1998); Salkie and Oates (1999); Santos and Oksefjell (1999); Altenberg and Granger (2002); Salkie (2002); Van Vaerenbergh (2002), among others.

Forensic linguistics

Another area which is increasingly using language corpora as a tool is forensic linguistics, which broadly concerns itself with the use of language in law and crime investigation. Corpora have many applications relative to the diversity of the focus of the discipline itself, which includes the analysis of the genuineness of documents from confessions to suicide notes, authorship identification in academic settings (e.g. issues of plagiarism), ransom notes, threat letters, readability/comprehensibility of legal language, forensic phonetics (e.g. speaker identification), police interview and interrogation data, language rights of ethnic minorities, as well as the discourse of the courtroom setting (see for example Gibbons 1994, 2003; Conley and O'Barr 1998; Shuy 1998; Tiersma 1999; Cotterill 2002a, 2002b, 2003, 2004; Heffer 2005; Tiersma and Solan 2005). Corpora can be used to look at large amounts of courtroom data; for example, Cotterill (2002b) used a corpus of the entire internationally notorious O. J. Simpson trial in the United States. Corpora can be used to compare language patterns; for example, Boucher (2005), in his analysis of features of deceit in recounting, compared a corpus of 200 three- to five-minute discourses where half represented truthful and half inaccurate accounts. He was able to statistically describe significant differences in variables such as hesitation, lexical repetition and utterance length. Authorship and plagiarism are growing concerns within forensic linguistics, for which corpora can prove a useful instrument of investigation (see Coulthard 2004; Solan and Tiersma 2004).

Sociolinguistics

Corpora have also had an impact in the area of sociolinguistics. Their application in this area is not surprising given that many corpora of spoken language, in particular, can be built around sociolinguistic variables such as age, gender, level of education, socio-economic background and so on. Regional variation, for example, can be explored using language corpora. Ihalainen (1991a) looked at variation in verb patterns in south-western British English, while Ihalainen (1991b) compared the grammatical subject in educated and dialectal English in the London-Lund and the Helsinki Corpus of modern English dialects. Kirk (1992, 1999) and Kallen and Kirk (2001) look at languages in contact in the context of Northern Ireland and Irish English, Ulster Scots, Irish and Scots Gaelic using a corpus-based approach. The SCOTS corpus (see Douglas 2003, Corbett and Douglas 2004) offers great potential for sociolinguistic study. It aims to represent the present-day linguistic situation in Scotland eventually representing written and spoken data of Scottish English and Scots, Scots Gaelic as well as non-indigenous community languages such as Punjabi, Urdu and Chinese (see appendix 1).

Age-related research is prevalent especially in the context of teenager language. The Bergen Corpus of London Teenage Language (COLT) (see Haslerud and Stenström 1995; Stenström 1998; and Appendix 1) has provided the basis for numerous studies. Features such as discourse markers have been given particular attention; for example, Andersen (1997a, 1997b) focuses on the use of *like* in London teenage speech. The use of tags is linked to age in a number of studies (Stenström 1997a; Stenström et al. 2002). Hasund (1998) looks at class-determined variation in the verbal disputes of London teenage girls, while Hasund and Stenström (1997) examine conflict talk using a corpus-based comparison of the verbal disputes of adolescent females. Other corpus-based studies on language and gender include Aijmer (1995) which looks at apologies, Holmes (2001) which examines linguistic sexism and Mondorf (2002), a study of gender differences in English syntax.

Taboo language is also looked at using corpora such as COLT and the British National Corpus (see Stenström 1995; Stenström et al. 2002; and Appendix 1). Corpus-based sociolinguistic studies that look at non-standard usage include Stenström (1997b), which again focuses on London teenager usage. Callahan (2004) explores Spanish-English code switching using a corpus comprised of 30 fictional works from 24 Latino authors published in the United States, between 1970 and 2000. Callahan shows that written codeswitching follows for the most part the same syntactic patterns as its spoken counterpart. Her corpus findings also point to the use of non-standard English, which appears in 53% of the corpus in the forms of African-American Vernacular English and certain varieties of New York English. Lapidus and Otheguy (2005), in another New York corpus-based study, look at language contact in the context of English and Spanish. They focus on the use of non-specific *ellos* (English equivalent: *they*). One of Lapidus and Otheguy's main conclusions is that the susceptibility of language varieties to contact influence is primarily at the discourse-pragmatic level. Corpora have had a major influence in the areas of discourse and pragmatics also and throughout this book we will draw on examples of such work.

1.8 How have corpora influenced language teaching?

As we discussed above, the processes of dictionary-making have been revolutionised by the use of language corpora and this obviously feeds into language teaching materials. All major learners' dictionaries of English are now based on constantly updated multi-million word databases of language. Fundamentally, corpora have provided evidence for our intuitions about language and very often they have shown that these can be faulty when it comes to issues such as semantics and grammar. As we noted earlier, we now increasingly base our major grammars, like dictionaries, on large language corpora. The contribution of corpus linguistics, therefore, to the description of the language we teach is difficult to dispute. According to McCarthy (2001: 125) corpus linguistics represents cutting-edge change in terms of scientific techniques and methods and probably foreshadows even more profound technological shifts that will 'impinge upon our long-held notions of education, roles of teachers, the cultural context of the delivery of educational services and the mediation of theory and technique'.

As well as providing an empirical basis for checking our intuitions about language, corpora have also brought to light features about language which had eluded our intuition (e.g. the frequency of ready-assembled chunks; see chapter 3). In terms of what we actually teach, numerous studies have shown us that the language presented in textbooks is frequently still based on intuitions about how we use language, rather than actual evidence of use. While there are often sound pedagogical reasons for using scripted dialogues, their status as a vehicle for enhancing conversation skills has been challenged in recent years (Carter 1998; Burns 2001; Burns, Joyce and Gollin 2001; McCarthy and O'Keeffe 2004; Thornbury and Slade 2006). Burns (2001) notes that scripted dialogues rarely reflect the unpredictability and dynamism of conversation, or the features and structures of natural spoken discourse, and argues that students who encounter only scripted spoken language have less opportunity to extend their linguistic repertoires in ways that prepare them for unforeseeable interactions outside of the classroom. Holmes (1988: 40), for example, looked at epistemic modality in ESL textbooks as compared with corpus data and found that many textbooks devoted an unjustifiably large amount of attention to modal verbs, at the expense of alternative linguistic strategies. Boxer and Pickering (1995) showed contrast between speech acts in textbook dialogues with real spontaneous encounters found in a corpus. Carter (1998) compares real data from the Cambridge and Nottingham Corpus of Discourse in English (CANCODE, see appendix 1) with dialogues from textbooks and finds that the dialogues lack core spoken language features such as discourse markers, vague language, ellipsis and hedges. Gilmore (2004) examines the discourse features of seven dialogues published in course books between 1981 and 1997, and contrasts them with comparable authentic interactions in a corpus. He finds that the textbook dialogues differ considerably from their naturally-occurring equivalents across a range of discourse features including turn length and patterns, lexical density, number of false starts and repetitions, pausing, frequency of terminal overlap or latching, and the use of hesitation devices and response tokens. He looks at dialogues from more recent course books and finds that there is evidence that they are beginning to incorporate more natural discourse features. The *Touchstone* series (McCarthy, McCarten and Sandiford 2005a and b, 2006a and b) is an attempt to show how course book dialogues, and even entire syllabi, can be informed by corpus data. In addition to the conventional four-skills syllabus strands of speaking, listening, reading and writing, the *Touchstone* authors provide a syllabus of conversational strategies, based on the most common words and phrases in the North American spoken segment of the CIC. The strategies recur throughout the four levels of the multi-skills programme and are graded. An example is given in figure 11, where the discourse marker *I mean* is exploited.

Figure 11: Extract from the *Touchstone* series (McCarthy, McCarten and Sandiford 2005a: 49)

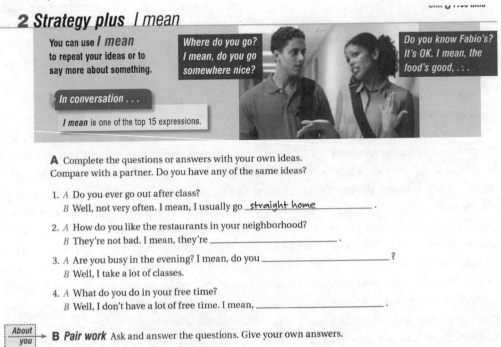

Kettemann (1995) highlights the mismatch between actual language use and the prescription often found in pedagogical grammars that reported speech involves the 'backshift rule' for tenses in the reported speech constructions (see also Baynham 1991, 1996; McCarthy 1998). Hughes and McCarthy (1998) look at the use of past perfect verb forms and find that, across a wide range of speakers in the CANCODE corpus, the past perfect has a broader and more complex function in spoken discourse than hitherto described. Corpus descriptions have also enhanced our understandings of units of fixed phrasing, collocation, and more extended language patterns (Sinclair 1991a, 2003a, 2004; Svartvik 1991; Aston 1995; McCarthy and Carter 2002; Biber et al. 2004; Schmitt 2004; Thornbury and Slade 2006). Throughout the chapters that follow, we will survey and build on relevant findings from corpus research and tease out the implications these have for language teaching.

Corpora of learner languages are a relatively recent, but very important development. Granger (2003), a forerunner in the area, defines a learner corpus as an electronic collection of authentic texts produced by foreign or second language learners. She notes that, in the early 1990s, publishers and academics started, independently but concurrently, to gather and analyse learner data. The International Corpus of Learner English (ICLE, see Granger 1993, 1994, 1996, 1998a; Granger et al. 2002), initiated around that time, currently contains over two million words of writing by learners of English from 19 different mother tongue backgrounds. The writing in the corpus (essays) has been contributed by advanced learners of English as a foreign language rather than as a second language and is made up of 19 distinct sub-corpora, each containing one language variety (English to French, English to German, English to Swedish, etc.). This corpus is error-coded, which allows for invaluable research into typical learner error patterns (see Dagneaux et al. 1996; De Cock et al. 1998). Findings from research into learner corpora can be addressed in materials design, including the development of Computer Assisted Language Learning (CALL) applications. For example, Altenberg and Granger (2001), looking at Swedish- and French-speaking learners, examine the use of high frequency verbs, and in particular use of the verb *make*. As well as looking at the role of transfer in the misuse of these verbs relative to native-speaker norms, they investigate whether learners tend to over- or underuse these verbs and whether high frequency verbs are error-prone or safe. They find that EFL learners, even at an advanced proficiency level, have great difficulty with high frequency verbs such as *make*. They suggest that concordance-based exercises (see Data-driven learning below) can help raise awareness of the complexity of high frequency verbs. Learner spoken data have also been collected, a notable example being the Louvain International Database of Spoken English Interlanguage (LINDSEI) set up in 1995 (see De Cock 1998, 2000). This provides spoken data for the analysis of the speech of second language learners (see also Granger et al. 2002). Numerous other studies have been conducted using learner corpora, including Granger (1996, 1997, 1998a, 1998b, 1998c, 1999, 2002, 2003, 2004), De Cock and Granger (2004), Meunier (2002a, 2002b), Gilquin (2003) and Cosme (2004).

Data-driven learning

Computer Assisted Language Learning (CALL), among many other applications, includes the use of language corpora, where learners get hands-on experience of using a corpus through guided tasks or through materials based on corpus evidence, such as concordance lines on handouts (see Johns 1991a). Here an inductive approach relies on an 'ability to see patterning in the target language and to form generalisations' about language form and use (Johns 1991a: 2). This activity is commonly referred to as 'data-driven learning' (DDL) after Johns (1986 and 1991a). Johns (2002: 108) sees DDL as a process which 'confront(s) the learner as directly as possible with the data', 'to make the learner a linguistic researcher' where 'every student is Sherlock Holmes'. Over the years Johns, among others, has developed the idea and contributed many teaching materials based on the DDL approach (see Johns 1988, 2002; Stevens 1991; Wichmann 1995; Fox 1998; Kettemann 1995; Tribble and Jones 1990; 1997; Flowerdew 1993, 1996; Gavioli 1996; Wichmann et al. 1997; Tribble 2000, 2003; Aston 2001). A basic internet search will bring up numerous homepages dedicated to DDL, which provide many useful links to resources (such as online corpora and concordancers), research findings and materials. Such a search is also evidence of the popularity of DDL among language teachers, many of whom post their materials online and conduct action research into the classroom application of these materials. DDL, like corpus linguistics in general, is not without its critics (see Widdowson 1991, 2000; Prodromou 1996, 1997a, 1997b; Owen 1996; Seidlhofer 1999; Bernardi 2000; see below for further discussion of issues and debates). Many also question the application of DDL to lower-level learners, though some studies provide evidence of its use at lower levels (see Johns 1988, 2002; St John 2001; Kennedy and Miceli 2002).

Chambers, who has been involved in the development of a one-million word corpus of journalistic French (see appendix 1: Chambers-Rostand Corpus of Journalistic French; Chambers and Rostand 2005), provides a number of illustrations of how DDL can be used in the context of teaching French and how it can facilitate the development of learner autonomy (see Chambers and Kelly 2002, 2004; Chambers and O'Sullivan 2004; Chambers 2005; Braun and Chambers 2006; Chambers in press; O'Sullivan and Chambers in press). Chambers and Kelly (2002) note that the pedagogical context of DDL brings together constructivist theories of learning, the communicative approach to language teaching and developments within the area of learner autonomy. Cobb (1997) points to the potential of DDL to provide multiple contextual encounters for the acquisition of new vocabulary. The literature on vocabulary acquisition, according to Cobb, is virtually unanimous on the value of learning words through several contextual encounters (Mezynski 1983; Stahl and Fairbanks 1986; Krashen 1989; Nation 1990). Language learners are advised to read more (see Krashen 1989) so as to facilitate multi-contextual lexical acquisition. In reality, Cobb notes that few language learners have time to do enough reading for natural, multi-contextual lexical acquisition. DDL may have a role in rationalizing and shortening this learning process by providing a rich source of embodiments and contexts from new vocabulary. Empirical studies on the learning benefits of DDL are relatively few, but they do show positive results (see for example Cobb 1997; Turnbull and Burston 1998; Kennedy and Miceli 2001; Lenko-Szymanska 2002). Cobb (1997) reports on his longitudinal study of vocabulary acquisition using concordance line tasks. This study provides interesting examples (with screen shots) of a variety of sequential DDL activities which draw on a specially designed corpus of 10,000 words (comprised of 20 texts of about 500 words each, assembled from the students' reading materials). Figure 12 shows the opening task:

Figure 12: Example of DDL task from Cobb (1997)

Part 1: Choosing a meaning. The learner is presented with a small concordance of four to seven lines, in KWIC format with the to-be-learned word at the centre, and uses this information to select a suitable short definition for the word from one correct and three randomly generated choices.

1 Choosing a meaning

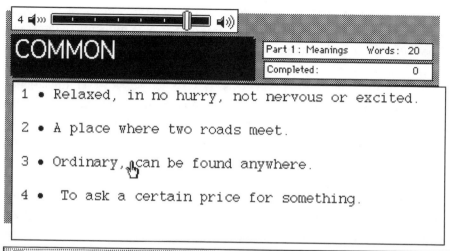

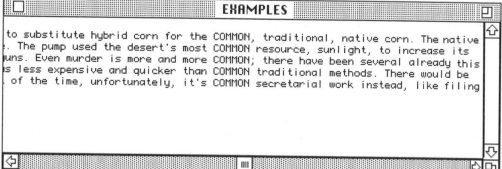

(Cobb 1997, available online http://www.er.uqam.ca/nobel/r21270/cv/Hands_on.html).

1.9 Issues and debates in the use of corpora in language teaching

Authenticity of materials for language teaching and learning

As we have seen, collecting data for use in a corpus means collecting examples of language as it is actually used in authentic contexts. Debate over the extent to which authentic language should form the basis of language courses has been taking place for the last thirty years or so (Canale and Swain 1980; Breen 1983; Van Lier 1996; Rost 2002) but it has been re-energised by the availability of corpus data.

It is often argued that, in language teaching, examples drawn from corpus sources should form the basis for the material used to exemplify the language and that an aim of language teaching should be to produce learners who are able to communicate effectively and competently. In order for this to happen, it is argued further, learners need to experience authentic rather than contrived examples of data; by 'contrived' is meant examples of language that are specially made up or invented for the pedagogic purposes of illustrating a particular feature or rule of the language. One problem is that the terms 'contrived' and 'authentic' have become emotionally charged and in opposition to each other.

The availability of corpus examples has produced a different perspective since we can find in corpora numerous examples of texts that are free-standing, in so far as they are independent of any language learning task. They are in their own authentic context, and they are composed for a particular audience (which tends to be different to that of the language learner). Thus, when they are presented with corpus examples, learners encounter real language as it is actually used, and in this sense it is 'authentic'. However, the language has been wrenched from its original context, and so, in one sense, is 'decontextualised'. This position suggests that as soon as texts are extracted from the context in which they first appeared, are stored in large electronic databases, and are reproduced for the teaching context, they are effectively removed from an authentic environment. The learner, then, has to process such texts with reference to a different context than the one in which they originated, a context which may not reflect his or her communicative goals in the classroom context. Furthermore, one can argue that authentic texts are embedded in particular cultures and may thus be culturally opaque to those outside that (usually western) culture, and that it may, as a result, be next to impossible for learners to 'authenticate' such texts for themselves on this basis. Authenticity should therefore preferably be defined as a relationship between a text and the response that it triggers in its immediate audience (see for example Lee, 1995; Widdowson 1996, 1998). Consequently, there is among many a preference for contrivance and the deliberate use of culturally 'neutral' examples as a more solid basis for a pedagogy that is sensitive to learners' needs. Such contrived texts also allow for material to be more easily graded for learners at different levels of competence. Another non-corpus-based option is to use texts suggested or provided by the learners themselves, which will, by definition, be potentially maximally authentic.

Supporters of the view that there should be more authentic material available in classrooms argue, on the other hand, that naturally-occurring data can be carefully chosen and mediated, that it can be contextualised for the learner, that learners are no different from other human beings, who have a natural proclivity to contextualise language data for themselves, and that the use of such data in the classroom can actually facilitate discussion of cultural background, as well as provide more grounded motivation because the text is so obviously a 'real' example of the target language (Peacock 1997). To deprive learners of such experiences for ideological reasons without consulting them is, in the opinion of the present authors, patronising and self-defeating. Others advance a related argument that tasks can be graded according to the nature of the authentic material (Willis and Willis 1996; Bygate et al. 2001; Willis 2003). The latter position would also seem to be an argument for a more careful pedagogic selection of materials from authentic sources. In our experience, corpora, both spoken and written, do indeed contain many texts that are obscure and culturally opaque, but they also contain numerous texts that are transparent, easily contextualised and interpretable by any mature human being. It is simply a matter of how carefully one selects the material, who the end-users are and what they want and expect from a language programme. For centuries, language teachers have plucked written texts out of the contexts in which they were originally produced and imported them into the classroom, carefully selecting and mediating them for their students; we see the use of corpora in this connection as an example of historical continuity which harnesses the technical possibilities of speeding up searches for useful and usable material. Many teachers are now using the world's biggest corpus, the internet, and its associated search engines, in just this way.

These issues are addressed in several places in this book. Our basic position is that for most pedagogic purposes in most contexts of teaching and learning a language, it is preferable to have naturally-occurring, corpus-based examples than contrived or unreal examples, but always in the context of freedom of choice and careful mediation by teachers and/or materials writers who know their own local contexts. For further reading on the debate that surrounds this see Sinclair (1991a, 1991b), Aston (1995), Carter and McCarthy (1995), Prodromou (1996), Owen (1996), Carter (1998), Cook (1998), Seidlhofer (1999), Widdowson (2000, 2001).

The 'native speaker' and the classroom

Authentic language invariably invokes the idea of language drawn from sources supplied by native speakers and recent research has shown that language learners often regard the approximation to native speaker English as a main goal in the language learning process (Timmis 2002). While the notion of the native speaker of English tends to be used to refer to those whose first language is English, the concept is a complex one (Roberts 2005), as there are, as Rampton (1990) and others have demonstrated, non-native speakers who have great affiliation to a language and are more competent in that language than native speakers. The vast number of different varieties of 'native speaker' English (e.g. American, British, Irish, Australian, South African, Singaporean) means that this notion cannot easily be translated, or modelled, into one particular standard for the language classroom, although international publishers tend to focus on either American or British English as a model.

Whether we are referring to contrived, invented or naturally-occurring samples of English, the choice of a particular variety for the ELT context, even down to fine-grained choices of a particular regional or local variety, is inevitably to some degree a matter of ideology and invariably a political issue. At the same time, it is acknowledged that the proportion of English exchanged daily between non-native speakers is growing rapidly, with an overall increase in globalisation and internationalisation (see Crystal 1997) to the point where non-native users of English far outnumber native speakers of English (Graddol 1998), undermining, for some, any privileging of native speaker discourse.

At the same time this raises the further question whether native-speaker models are the most appropriate basis for language learners, who may predominantly use their L2 to operate in an international, rather than a 'native' context. This state of affairs has led some to propose that English as a Lingua Franca (ELF) is more significant internationally than English as a first or second language and that consequently, corpora of non-native Englishes are needed in order to help us identify the kinds of English crucial to communication in such ELF contexts (see below) and to use such evidence as a preferred basis for classroom teaching and learning (see Medgyes, 1994; Braine 1999; Oda 1999, 2000; Jenkins 2000; Tajino and Tajino 2000; Seidlhofer 2001a; Carter and Fung (forthcoming) for further discussion on native versus non-native speaking teachers).

ELF: English as a lingua franca

Seidlhofer (2001a: 143–4) notes that while learner corpora (see above) have their use as a 'sophisticated tool for analysing learner language . . . some of the data in the learner corpora could also contribute to a better understanding of English as a lingua franca'. Seidlhofer goes on to detail a corpus development which she has championed: The Vienna-Oxford International Corpus of English (VOICE), a collection English as a Lingua Franca (ELF) currently under construction. Here lingua franca is defined as an additionally acquired language system that serves as a means of communication for speakers from different speech communities, who use it to communicate with each other but for whom it is not their native language. It is 'a language which has no native speakers' (Seidlhofer 2001a: 146) (see also Malmkjær 1991; House 1999, 2002, 2003; James 2000). The initial target for the VOICE corpus is to collect around half a million words of spoken data from speakers whose first language is not English and whose primary and secondary education did not take place in English, but who make use of English as a lingua franca (ELF) (see Seidlhofer 2004). In a parallel development, Mauranen (2003) reports on a corpus of ELF in academic settings (EFLA) at the Tampere Technology University, Finland. Its initial target is to collect half a million words of spoken data from two university settings. Both Seidlhofer and Mauranen aim, through empirical investigations of ELF, to show that a sophisticated and versatile form of language can develop which is *not* a native language (Seidlhofer 2001b; Mauranen 2003). Seidlhofer (2001a) argues that this is a much-needed development to fill the conceptual gap between the growing recognition and meta-linguistic discussions about global English and the existence of a codified form which eventually might have pedagogical applications in the identification of the most efficient forms of communication in the domain of ELF. With this in mind, the corpus may establish 'something like an index of communicative redundancy' (Seidlhofer 2001a: 147). Early findings from the VOICE corpus (see Seidlhofer 2004) tentatively identify a number of features which point to systematic lexico-grammatical differences between native-speaker English and ELF, for example dropping the third person present tense 's' (e.g. *she look*), omitting definite and indefinite articles, insertion of prepositions (e.g. *can we discuss about this issue*). These features often involve typical errors which most English teachers would correct and remediate. However, Seidlhofer points out that they appear to be generally unproblematic and do not cause an obstacle to communicative success in ELF. The work of Jenkins (1996, 2000, 2004, 2005) has also been very influential here in relation to the teaching of pronunciation for ELF. She makes a parallel argument relating to ELF phonology. Her research finds that a number of items common to most native-speaker varieties of English were not necessary in successful ELF interactions; for example, the absence of weak forms in words like *from* and *for*, and the substitution of voiceless and voiced *th* with /t/ or /s/ and /d/ or /z/ (e.g. *think* became *sink* or *tink*, and *this* became *dis* or *zis*). Jenkins argues that such features occur regularly in ELF interactions and do not cause intelligibility problems.

Developments in and findings from corpus-based ELF studies further the debate about 'ownership' and function of a language like English and their empirical findings put forward ELF as a pedagogical model which challenges the accepted native-speaker-based norms of EFL. However, great uncertainties remain in this area, not least whether the object of description is a *function* of English rather than a codifiable variety, that is to say a way in which people adapt differently to every different circumstance and make greater or lesser use of their communicative repertoire depending on the exigencies of each individual interaction. Mauranen (2003) confidently labels ELF as a variety, but much discussion is still needed as to what, exactly is meant by 'variety' here. Other problems arise in the (perhaps unfair) equation between a reduced or 'stripped down' ELF syllabus and an impoverished experience of the L2. Indeed, it could be argued that learners of any language always end up producing less than the input they are exposed to, and that if that input itself is deliberately restricted, then even less will be the outcome, and so on. Lastly, the evidence so far as to what exactly ELF is is rather scant, and there is reason to believe that East Asian ELF, for example (e.g. a Chinese speaker interacting in English with a Korean speaker) may be very different from European ELF (e.g. a Danish speaker using English with a Dutch speaker) and we may need to describe many 'ELFs' to get anywhere near an accurate picture of the global uses of English. What the present authors do support, however, is the way native-speaker corpora of spoken language, with all their attendant shortcomings, have sparked a lively if sometimes heated debate as to the most suitable models of English for pedagogy. This is a step forward from the days when southern-England, middle-class English was unquestioned as the pedagogical model in most parts of the world (the situation which pertained when two of the present authors began their teaching careers). We also support the move to build more and yet more useful corpora from a wider range of different settings.

SUEs or Successful Users of English

Rather than continuing to focus solely on the native speaker, we should begin to look much more closely at the notion of the 'expert user' and at ideas advanced by Prodromou and others (Prodromou 2003a, 2005) concerning what he terms SUEs (or Successful Users of English). As we discuss in chapter 4, Prodromou (2005) takes idiomaticity as a paradoxical example of something which, for native speakers, makes life easy, enabling fluent production of deeply culturally-embedded chunks heard and rehearsed since childhood. These same idiomatic chunks seem to place impossible obstacles in the path of the non-native speaker, however proficient. SUEs are highly successful L2 communicators, but they will achieve this goal by strategic use of their resources in ways different from those of native speakers. It makes more sense, therefore, not to see SUEs as failed native speakers, but to look upon all successful users of a language, whether native- or non-native-speaking, as 'expert users'.

A spoken corpus can underline for us how important it is to look closely at what speakers and listeners do, whoever those speakers are, whether they are native or non-native. Such research shows that our ability to interact with others is an important part of what makes us successful users of the language and is, we believe (and this is confirmed by research that is reported throughout this book), what learners of English aspire to know about and do in and with a language, and for the very reason that they know that this is what they do successfully in their first language. We will never meet those needs just by introspecting on what we *think* we say, nor by feeding our learners an impoverished diet of what we think they need based on those intuitions; only by respecting learners' and teachers' choices and aspirations within their own local contexts will we best serve them.

When we do look at what speakers and listeners do, we may not hear native speakers as we might want to hear them or as how we might have learned to expect to hear them. But we do hear real people interacting with one another, working at full stretch with the language, adjusting millisecond by millisecond to the interactive context they are in, playing with the language, being creative, being affective, being interpersonal and, above all, expressing themselves as they engage with the processes of communication which are most central to our lives. It is hard to imagine any learner of a second language not wanting to be a good, human communicator in that second language, whether they are going to use it with native speakers or with any other human beings. Language teaching can only benefit from even closer inspection of such fundamentally human processes. And the road from corpus to pedagogy, upon which we take tentative, sometimes faltering steps in this book, is an essential part of that process.

2 Establishing basic and advanced levels in vocabulary learning

2.1 Introduction

In chapter 1 we outlined some of the basic corpus techniques, including the creation of frequency lists for single words, the generation of collocational statistics, information on the occurrence of clusters, and the use of concordances for the investigation of items in context. One of the most obvious things we can do with the first of these, frequency information, is to ascertain how many words native speakers use, how frequently they have recourse to the individual words they use and how they combine them, and to explore to what extent words have become part of regularly occurring chunks or clusters for the native user. In this chapter we look at some of this evidence and consider how relevant or useful it is for understanding the vocabulary needs of second language learners and for establishing benchmarks by which learners' vocabulary levels can be assessed and evaluated and by which we may come to some general agreement as to what constitutes the various levels of proficiency in vocabulary knowledge.

It is important to state from the outset, however, that just because native speakers can understand a particular number of words and use them in particular ways, it is not necessarily so that L2 learners must be judged solely against native-user standards. In other words, we must not view second language learners as 'failed monolinguals', as Cook (1998) aptly puts it. The native speaker evidence from corpora will be just one piece in the mosaic of the conceptualisation of L2 learners' vocabulary, and whether we call a particular learner a beginner or an advanced user of the L2 will involve more than simply comparing them with competent native users. As we shall see, progress in learning vocabulary involves more than ruthlessly pursuing a native-like vocabulary size, and includes one's ability to work independently, strategic ability and skill in using the lexical resources at one's disposal.

2.2 Frequency and native-speaker vocabulary size

By looking at spoken and written corpora collected from a wide range of users and everyday contexts, we can make fairly reliable statements about how many words are 'in circulation' in everyday communication among native speakers. This is not to say that a corpus of, say, ten million words can capture all the words of a language, and some users will always know obscure and rare words, for all sorts of reasons (e.g. literary words, professional, technical and scientific words, colloquialisms and dialect words), but it will certainly enable us to list the vocabulary of common usage which users are likely to encounter in their daily conversations and in their routine reading of newspapers, magazines, novels, internet texts, etc. If we examine the frequency of words in a large corpus of English, a picture emerges where the first 2,000 or so word-forms do most of the work, accounting for more than 80% of all of the words in spoken and written texts. As we progress down the frequency list, each successive band of 2,000 words covers a progressively smaller proportion of all the words in the texts in the corpus, with many words occurring only a small number of times or, indeed, only once. Figure 1 shows the power of the first 2,000 most frequent word-forms in a mixed corpus of ten million words of English (made up of five million words of spoken data, from CANCODE, and five million words of written data taken from the Cambridge International Corpus, CIC, see appendix 1).

Figure 1: Text coverage in a 10 million-word corpus of spoken and written English

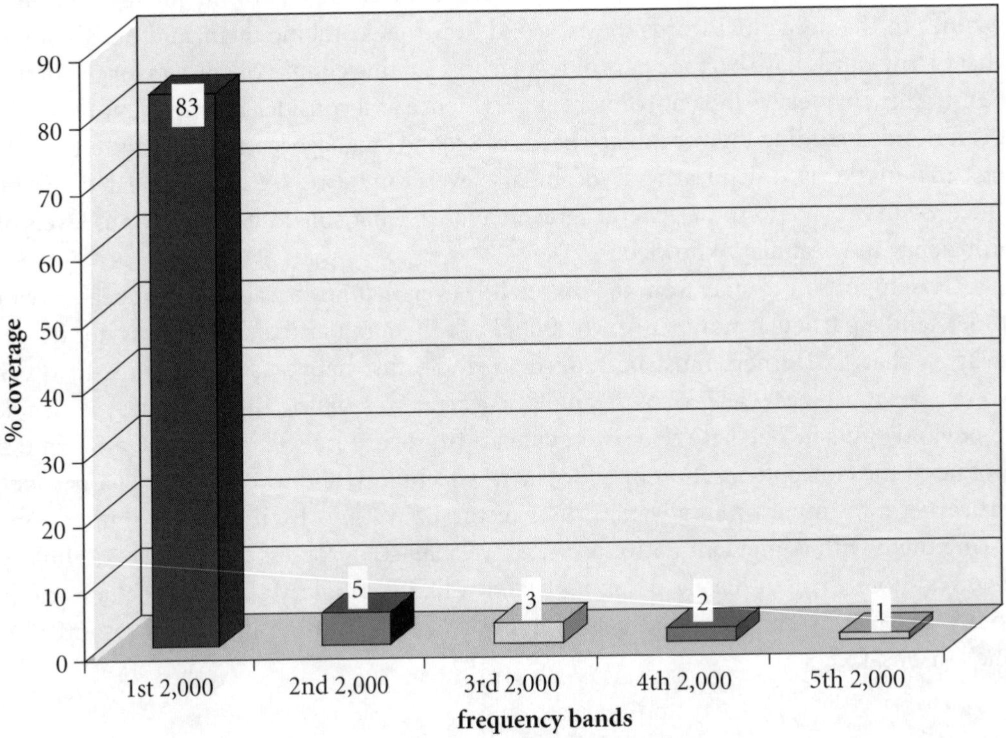

Figure 1 shows the coverage achieved by word-forms, that is to say, the computer considers *look(s)*, *looking* and *looked* as different 'words'. However, the computer software also allows us to bring together semi-automatically the inflected forms of words and treat the combined totals as 'lemmas' (i.e. LOOK would be one lemma composed of the total occurrences of *look(s)*, *looked* and *looking*). There are, however, reasons for hesitating in taking lemmas as our benchmark. Firstly, the process of lemmatisation tends to bundle together all the forms that the computer judges to look similar, for example the quite different nouns *man* and *mane*, or the noun *bit*, which will be conflated with the past-tense form of the verb *to bite*. Conversely, the software often fails to perceive obvious similarities such as *young/younger/youngest*, so, without considerable manual reprocessing of tens of thousands of words, lemmatised counts can be unreliable: the form *bit* as in *a little bit / a bit small*, etc. is vastly more frequent than the past tense of the verb *bite*, but a lemmatised count might suggest the lemma BITE to be very frequent because it conflates all the occurrences of *bit*. Secondly, there is no reason to suppose learners do always make the necessary connections between forms of the same lemma in listening or reading; for example, does the learner necessarily associate the first encounter with *stuck* with the lemma STICK? Will *flown* be associated with FLY, and so on? These are technical questions and, in the last analysis, neither solution is entirely satisfactory. In most cases learners will be able to extrapolate that *look(s), looking* and *looked* are different forms of the same item, and if we do choose to consider lemmas rather than individual word-forms, then the total word-learning burden is considerably less, and the first 2,000 lemmas will typically cover up to 90% of the items in an everyday text.

Whichever is chosen as the benchmark, however, whether word-form or lemma, the picture is strikingly similar, with a hard-working core vocabulary separated from the low-frequency, massive bulk of most of the words of the language. The frequency curve does not decline at a regular rate across the whole of the vocabulary; there is a continental shelf of high-frequency, core items, after which the curve takes a nose-dive into the vast depths of tens of thousands of (relatively) low-frequency words.

2.3 The most frequent words and the core vocabulary

Table 1 (overleaf) shows the 50 most frequent items in a ten-million-word corpus made up of the five-million-word CANCODE spoken corpus and a five-million-word general written corpus sample from the Cambridge International Corpus (CIC). Tables 2 and 3 show the lists separated out into spoken and written forms.

There are differences between the spoken and written, reflected in the high rank of *I* and *you* in the spoken data, along with discourse-marking items (e.g. *well, right*, see below and section 2.4), indicating an overall orientation to the speaker-listener world in conversation. In contrast, the written list shows a greater prevalence of third-person references, prepositions and conjunctions largely representing 'the world out there'. The prevalence of prepositions underlines the common pattern of *noun + preposition + noun* (e.g. *the side of the car, the boy with the red hair, a house near the station*). All of the items are 'functional' rather than lexical; in other words, they have little or no vocabulary content. They are mostly grammar words (pronouns, prepositions, auxiliary and copular verbs, determiners, etc.), but the spoken list also includes items of high frequency in conversational speech (*yeah, er, oh*) which may not always be considered to be 'words' at all. Items such as *well* and *right* are in the spoken top 50 because of the high frequency of discourse markers in conversation, signalling important communicative functions such as responding and boundary-marking (*right*) or shifts in the discourse from expected or predicted directions (*well*) (see chapters 7 and 8). Item 25 in the combined list is *know*, which seems to be more lexical, but it only makes it into the top 30 items by dint of the highly frequent discourse marking chunks *you know* and *(you) know what I mean* (projecting shared knowledge or shared perspectives) (see chapter 3). If we had gone further down the combined list (to 79), we would find *mean*, in the top 100 because of the discourse markers *I mean* (often used to preface an explanation or expansion, or to indicate non-shared knowledge) and *(you) know what I mean*. Indeed, separating out the spoken and written lists shows that *know* climbs to 14, and *mean* climbs to 56, just outside the limit of table 2. The software

Table 1: Most frequent words: 10-million-word corpus (CIC)

	word	frequency		word	frequency
1	the	439,723	26	as	49,697
2	and	256,879	27	at	49,578
3	to	230,431	28	we	46,025
4	a	210,178	29	her	45,574
5	of	194,659	30	had	45,524
6	I	192,961	31	not	44,977
7	you	164,021	32	no	44,541
8	it	150,707	33	what	44,125
9	in	142,812	34	this	43,024
10	that	124,250	35	like	42,297
11	was	107,245	36	all	41,790
12	yeah	86,092	37	mm	41,639
13	he	78,932	38	er	40,923
14	is	75,687	39	there	39,883
15	on	71,797	40	do	39,744
16	for	69,392	41	his	38,420
17	but	64,561	42	well	37,671
18	she	61,406	43	one	36,889
19	they	58,021	44	just	36,275
20	have	55,892	45	if	36,007
21	with	54,994	46	are	35,279
22	be	52,008	47	oh	35,026
23	It's	50,585	48	right	33,598
24	so	50,531	49	or	32,686
25	know	50,307	50	from	31,444

operation of keyword analysis (see chapter 1) confirms that *know, well, right* and *mean* are all statistically significantly more frequent in the spoken corpus. In the case of *know* and *mean*, the corpus is clearly telling us that the core vocabulary includes high frequency chunks, a point we shall return to below. Item 44 in the mixed list (table 1) is *just* (rising to 31 in the spoken-only list, where it is statistically significant), an indication of the high frequency of its hedging function in softened and polite utterances such as *Is there somewhere I can just park the car? / Could you just sign that for me please?* (Hedging is dealt with in detail in chapter 8.).

Table 2: Most frequent words: 5-million-word CANCODE spoken corpus

	word	frequency		word	frequency
1	the	169,335	26	like	33,936
2	I	150,989	27	well	33,930
3	and	141,206	28	what	33,207
4	you	137,522	29	do	32,872
5	it	106,249	30	right	31,551
6	to	105,854	31	just	31,185
7	a	103,524	32	he	30,676
8	yeah	91,481	33	for	29,846
9	that	84,930	34	erm	28,443
10	of	78,207	35	this	28,134
11	in	62,796	36	be	28,089
12	was	50,417	37	all	27,682
13	it's	47,837	38	there	26,478
14	know	46,601	39	got	26,131
15	is	45,448	40	that's	25,691
16	mm	44,103	41	not	25,474
17	er	43,476	42	don't	25,207
18	but	41,534	43	if	24,430
19	so	40,071	44	think	24,300
20	they	38,861	45	one	23,891
21	on	35,914	46	with	22,879
22	have	35,617	47	at	22,194
23	we	35,587	48	or	21,436
24	oh	35,226	49	then	21,420
25	no	35,085	50	she	20,615

Table 3: Most frequent words: 5-million-word written corpus

	word	frequency		word	frequency
1	the	284,174	26	from	21,574
2	to	132,335	27	not	21,554
3	and	125,526	28	they	21,097
4	of	122,903	29	by	20,391
5	a	114,381	30	this	17,577
6	in	84,940	31	are	17,227
7	was	59,454	32	were	16,363
8	it	51,642	33	all	16,240
9	I	50,871	34	him	15,647
10	he	50,007	35	up	15,526
11	that	46,195	36	an	15,431
12	she	41,607	37	said	15,255
13	for	41,606	38	there	14,913
14	on	38,361	39	one	14,525
15	her	36,500	40	been	14,493
16	you	35,773	41	would	14,445
17	is	34,871	42	out	14,337
18	with	33,829	43	so	13,804
19	his	32,535	44	their	13,788
20	had	31,420	45	what	13,646
21	as	30,993	46	when	13,566
22	at	29,026	47	we	13,526
23	but	26,134	48	if	13,313
24	be	26,122	49	me	13,035
25	have	22,805	50	my	12,930

So even this 'lexically empty' brief list is telling us something important about the core vocabulary, especially when it comes to spoken language. The general characteristics of this core vocabulary, therefore, will be an important index of what should be included in a basic syllabus if our aim is to produce good communicators able to do in the L2 what they wish to do in terms of projecting their self-image, creating good relations with their interlocutors, understanding and using the basic grammatical and logical relations that underpin the less frequent vocabulary when it occurs in texts and generally building their proficiency so that new material will be easier to absorb and acquire. Put another way, there are arguments for suggesting that a vocabulary list, defined as a list of non-grammatical meaning-resources, is not necessarily co-terminous with a word list, especially in discourse-based approaches to language description and pedagogy (see Sinclair and Renouf, 1988; Willis, 1990 for further discussion).

All in all, fairly clear categories emerge from the top 2,000 items in the combined spoken/written list which offer the potential for an organised pedagogy (insomuch as few language teachers would ever propose simply working one's way sequentially down the list as a viable methodology for vocabulary building). Those categories are what the next section of this chapter is devoted to illustrating. If, on the basis of general professional consensus, we exclude as a category the closed-system grammar/function words (although we shall return to reconsider them at the end of the chapter) as being the domain of the grammar teacher, the remainder of the 2,000-word list seems to fall into approximately nine types of item, which we shall examine in turn. They are not presented in any prioritised order, and all may be considered equally important as components of basic communication. Where words are given which do not appear in Tables 1–3, they are given a broad-band indication in brackets of their rank within the top 2000 word-forms, as follows: A = within the first 500, B = second 500, C = third 500, D = fourth 500.

2.4   The broad categories of a basic vocabulary

Modal items

Modal items are those which carry meanings referring to the degree of certainty (sometimes called epistemic modality) or necessity (deontic modality). A full list of such items may be found in Carter and McCarthy (2006: 638–678). Clearly the best candidates for such meanings in the 2,000-word list are the closed class of modal verbs (*can, could, may, must, will, should, etc.* – all of which are in band A), but the list contains other, non-grammatical, very high frequency items that carry related meanings. These include lexical modals such as the verbs *look* (A), *seem* (B) and *sound* (B), the adjectives *possible* (B) and *certain* (B) and the adverbs *maybe* (A), *probably* (A), *definitely* (B), *apparently* (B) and *possibly* (C). Some of these may strike teachers as more 'intermediate' level words, and yet their frequency is so high in everyday communication that excluding them from the elementary level would need some other justification (e.g. avoiding duplication of close synonyms and economising on cognitive load). To argue that the domain of modality be expanded beyond the closed-class modal verbs is not a new idea; several linguists have advocated this, based on the frequent occurrence in written texts of a wider range of modal items (Holmes 1988) or on sociolinguistic 'fieldwork' (Stubbs 1986). The corpus statistics underscore this earlier work and provide compelling evidence of the ubiquity of modal items in everyday speech and writing.

Delexical verbs

This category embraces extremely high-frequency verbs such as *do, make, take* and *get* (all band A) in their collocations with nouns, prepositional phrases and particles.

They are termed 'delexical' because of their low lexical content and the fact that their meanings in context are conditioned by the words they co-occur with (e.g. compare *to make a mistake* with *to make progress* or *to make it [to a place]*). In the case of *do* and *get*, a distinction has to be made between their auxiliary-verb functions: *do* in emphatic, negative and interrogative verb phrases and in tags, and *get* in the *have got* (possessive), *have got to* (modal) and *get*-passive constructions, the last being far more frequent in spoken data than in written (Carter and McCarthy 1999; see chapter 5 for more on *get*-passive constructions). One problem associated with the massive frequency of the delexical verbs is the fact that their low lexical content has to be complemented by the lexical content of the words they combine with, and those collocating words may often be of relatively low frequency, beyond the core (e.g. *get a qualification, get jammed, make an appointment*), or may be combinations with high-frequency particles generating semantically opaque phrasal verbs (e.g. *get round to doing something, take over from someone*; see McCarthy and O'Dell's (2004) corpus-informed materials for such phrasal verbs). In language pedagogy, the delexical verbs cannot be taught in isolation, without reference to their collocations, so the task becomes one of ascertaining the most frequent and useful collocating items from lower down in the frequency list, such as *get a job, take something back, make coffee*, etc., which might occasionally involve words from outside of the top 2000, but which are necessary to provide authentic contexts for the learning of the delexical verbs.

Stance words

The core 2,000-word list contains a number of items whose function is to represent speakers' and writers' attitudes and stance towards the content communicated. These are absolutely central to communicative well-being, to creating and maintaining appropriate social relations. They are therefore not a luxury, and it is hard to conceive of anything but the most sterile and banal survival-level communication occurring without their frequent use. The speaker or writer who cannot use them is an impoverished communicator, from an interpersonal viewpoint. The words include *just, whatever, bit, actually, really, quite* (all band A), *slightly, basically, pretty* (all band B), *clearly* (C), *honestly* (D), *unfortunately* (D). Their high frequency (especially in speech) underscores their vital role in communication.

The stance words may variously soften or make indirect potentially face-threatening utterances, or purposively render vague or fuzzy acts of lexical categorisation in the conversation, or intensify and emphasise affective stance towards the content of utterances (these functions are discussed in detail in chapter 8). Some examples from the spoken corpus follow:

(2.1)

[Describing a travel itinerary]

> You fly from Birmingham to Berlin, and then get a taxi **or whatever**, from the airport to the railway station.

(CANCODE)

(2.2)

[Message on an answerphone]

Sue, it's Bob here. I'm **just** ringing up to enquire whether there was any more definite news.

(CANCODE)

(2.3)

[Speaker is recounting how she is having trouble juggling work and other commitments]

It's **a bit** worrying **really**.

(CANCODE)

Discourse markers

The core spoken vocabulary contains high-frequency discourse markers whose function is to organise the talk and monitor its progress. A range of such items has been recognised by linguists such as Schiffrin (1987) and Fraser (1990), and the most common ones occurring in the top 2,000 include *you know, I mean* (both band A when dovetailed with single words), *right, well, so, good, anyway* (all band A), and these occur overwhelmingly in the spoken corpus. Their functions include marking openings and closings, returns to diverted or interrupted talk, topic boundaries and exchange completions (see chapter 8, where they are dealt with in detail). They are, therefore, like the stance words dealt with above, an important feature of the non-propositional elements in any discourse, and, for conversational participants they provide a resource for exercising control. They have an empowering function; their absence in the talk of any individual conversational participant leaves him/her potentially disempowered and at risk of becoming a second-class participant.

There is evidence to suggest that native speakers are poor judges of the all-pervasiveness of such markers in their own talk (Watts 1989), and indeed their frequent use may be perceived by language purists to be a sign of bad or sloppy usage, and yet all the evidence in the spoken corpus is that the markers are ubiquitous in the conversation of educated native speakers. The high-frequency discourse markers also have little lexical content in the conventional sense of the word, and present a problem to language pedagogy, which has traditionally divided teaching into grammar teaching and vocabulary teaching, with items such as discourse markers not fitting happily into either. In short, there is no ready-made pedagogy for this category of items, a point we shall return to in the concluding section.

Basic nouns

Into this category fit a wide range of nouns of very general, non-concrete and concrete meanings, such as *person, problem, life, sort, family, room, car, school, door, water, house* (all band A), *kids, situation, noise, trouble* (all band B), *TV, birthday, silence, theatre* (all band C), *accident, cheese, leader* (all band D), along with the names of days, months, colours, body-parts, kinship terms, other general time and place nouns such as the names of the four seasons, the points of the compass, and nouns denoting basic activities and events such as *trip* (D) and *breakfast* (C).

These nouns, because of their general meanings, have wide communicative coverage. *Trip*, for example, can clearly substitute for *voyage, flight, drive*, and so on. However, interesting problems arise in terms of the closed-set nature of some of these nouns. In any corpus, items apparently belonging to closed sets will not necessarily occur with equal frequency. Figure 2, for example, shows the frequencies of the names of the seven days of the week in the CANCODE spoken corpus.

Figure 2: The seven days of the week in the CANCODE corpus

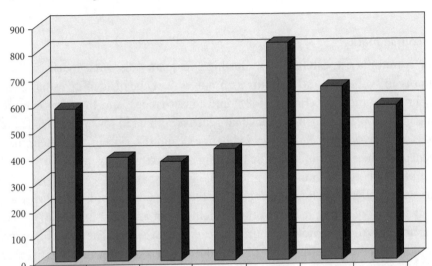

There is a wide discrepancy here, with the weekend days Friday and Saturday achieving nigh on double the frequency of 'low' days such as Tuesday and Wednesday. There may well be cultural reasons for such unequal distribution (in westernised, Christian societies, Monday is considered the start of the working week; Friday and Saturday are associated with the week's end and leisure, etc.), and the corpus can indeed be used as a cultural 'window' for language teaching purposes. However, for the goal of imparting a basic vocabulary of communication, only the most purist of corpus-adherents would propose a pedagogy wherein the basic level classes would only teach five of the seven weekday names, leaving the low frequency Tuesday and Wednesday till later. Thus corpus statistics need to be combined with a notion of psycholinguistic usefulness and the availability (*disponibilité*) of items in the mental lexicon.

Amongst the human body parts, *head* (A), *arm, foot, eye* (all B), *finger, nose*, and *leg* (all band C) all make it into the top 2,000 list, but *knee* and *wrist* do not. In the names of the four seasons, *summer* (B) is more than twice as frequent as *winter* (C) or *spring* (D), and four times as frequent as *autumn*, which lands outside of the top 2,000 list. In the names of countries, *America* (B), *France* (C), *Italy* (D), *India* (D) and *Ireland* (D) make the top 2,000 list (probably reflecting proximity and contexts of British cultural relations), while *Spain, China* and *Canada* fall outside of the list. Once again, pedagogical decisions may override these awkward but fascinating statistics, and most teachers will agree that it makes good sense to teach basic closed sets as completely as is practically possible, and certainly one would want to make sure that any nationality represented in a class of students should be known. However, some closed sets are very large (e.g. all the possible body parts, or the names of all countries in the world), and in such cases, the frequency list is very helpful for establishing priorities.

Two further things that need to be said about the most frequent nouns are the way many of them form part of frequent lexical chunks and the way they can operate as pro-forms and forms which package lengthy strings of information, this latter phenomenon being especially noticeable in written texts. The noun *time* (A) is a good example: its singular form is word number 84 in the mixed spoken/written corpus of 10 million words, with more than 18,000 occurrences. Accounting for part of this total, the expression *all the time* occurs 1,019 times, bringing it into the top 1,000 items, and making it more frequent than everyday single words such as *foreign, east* and *awful* (all band B). Table 4 shows the frequencies of the 10 most common expressions involving *time*. To qualify for inclusion in the top 2,000 forms, single words need to occur approximately 400 times or more; it can be seen here that six of the top 10 achieve this.

Indeed, if we take the spoken corpus alone, *time* occurs 9,223 times, and *all the time* accounts for 756 of these, that is to say 8% of all occurrences; in the mixed corpus, *all the time* accounted for only 5.6% of all occurrences of *time*. *All the time* thus shows a tendency to occur more in speech than in writing.

Other basic band A nouns which are prone to form fixed expressions include *thing(s)* (*the thing is, that sort of thing*, and *things like that*, etc.), *way* (*in a way, in the way, on the way*), *kind* (*kind of, that kind of thing*), *end* (*in the end, at the end, no end of*), *course* (*of course*), *job* (*a good job, have a job to do / doing sth*), *fact* (*in fact, as a matter of fact*), *couple* (*a couple of*).

Table 4: Frequency of expressions with *time*

expression	frequency
all the time	1,019
the first time	834
at the time	733
a long time	657
by the time	583
at the same time	460
in time	323
the last time	238
at a time	216
a good time	127

Some high-frequency nouns are used to refer to whole stretches of information, something particularly noticeable in written texts. These include band A nouns such as *thing, fact* and *idea*, referred to as members of the class of 'general nouns' by Halliday and Hasan (1976), as well as nouns such as *problem* (A), *question* (A), *issue* (C), which have been studied as important 'signal words' in the structure of text-types such as 'problem-solution' texts or 'hypothetical-real texts' (where claims and counterclaims are evaluated). Studies by Hoey (1983; 1991), Francis (1986) and Flowerdew (2003a and b) are important in this respect. An example with *problem* from the written corpus illustrates the phenomenon; the noun phrase *this problem* here encapsulates the whole of the previous sentence and is at the same time an important signal of the problem-solution structure of the text as a whole:

(2.4)

The factories needed iron and coal, but neither of these are found near Lincoln and they had to be transported from elsewhere. **This problem** was solved when the railway was built in 1846.

(CIC)

Example (2.5) shows the noun phrase *the idea* similarly encapsulating the whole of its preceding sentence.

(2.5)

The British are said to be fascinated by the weather and talk of little else when the talk is small. **The idea** may be something out of date.

(CIC)

The list of basic nouns, then, contains names for everyday things, people and ideas, as well as nouns which are prone to form fixed expressions and nouns which do heavy duty in structuring and signalling textual patterns. They are truly at the core of the language.

General deictics

Deictic items relate the speaker to the world in relative terms of time and space. The most obvious examples of deixis are words such as the demonstratives, where *this box* for the speaker may be *that box* for a remotely placed listener, or the speaker's *here* might be *here* or *there* for the listener, depending on where each participant is relative to each other. The corpus, in addition to the demonstratives and *here* and *there*, contains key items with relative meanings such as *now, then, ago, away, front, side* (all band A) and the extremely frequent *back* (in the sense of *opposite of front*, but mostly in the sense of *returned from another place*). *Back* (A) occurs 16,534 times in our ten-million-word corpus, most frequently in the chunks *go/come/get back, the back of (something), at/in/on the back, put/take (something) back*, and is clearly a core word. Similarly being *away* and being *out* are of very high frequency and distinguish two different everyday deictic concepts. Deixis is also encoded in the band A verbs *go* and *come*, and *take* and *bring* (see below), and is a core function reflected widely in the 2,000-word basic list.

Basic adjectives

In this class there appear a number of adjectives for communicating everyday positive and negative evaluations of people, situations, events and things. These include *lovely, nice, different, good, bad* (all band A), *terrible* (B), *awful* (B), *horrible* (C), *brilliant* (C), *excellent* (D), *sad* (D). Questions of near-synonymy are raised, and close observation of actual occurrences in the corpus, and ascertaining how the different adjectives enter into lexico-grammatical patterns, is vital for resolving the issues of what to include and what may be delayed till later stages in the vocabulary teaching and learning operation, etc. *Horrible* and *terrible*, for example, although close in meaning, seem to have a preference for patterning with nouns denoting subjective evaluations of people, things or situations, in the case of *horrible* (e.g. *horrible smell/man*) and more objective situations but not people, in the case of *terrible* (e.g. *terrible earthquake/tragedy*). These are broad preferences, and can only be stated in probabilistic rather than absolute terms, but nonetheless such patterns of preference are evident, and can prove significant in the decision to include both words in a vocabulary syllabus, even though their meanings may seem to overlap (see McCarthy and O'Dell 1999: 48). In other cases, degrees of intensity are involved (e.g. the mid-range *nice* compared with the stronger *lovely*) and it may be advisable to include more than one term for the sake of interpersonal variation, enabling the user to avoid projecting a rather one-dimensional self-image.

One interesting issue relating to basic adjectives (and adverbs, see below) is their frequent occurrence as response tokens in the spoken corpus (see chapter 7 for a detailed treatment). *Great* (A) and *fine* (A) occur very frequently in this function:

(2.6)
[S1 = Speaker 1]
    S1: I'll get back to you in the next ten minutes.
    S2: **Great**.
    S1: All right?
    S2: Thank you.

                                      (CANCODE)

(2.7)
    S1: I'll get them to give you a ring when they get back, okay?
    S2: **Fine**.

                                        (CANCODE)

These important tokens of 'listenership' (see McCarthy 2002, 2003) mark the difference between a respondent who repeatedly acknowledges incoming talk with an impoverished range of vocalisations or the constant use of *yes* and/or *no*, and one who sounds engaged, interested and interesting. The basic adjectives do more, therefore, than just provide a *descriptive* apparatus; they offer the speaker a range of responding functions, and can be used very simply, even at elementary levels of competence, as single-word response tokens, for example, *good* (A), *fine* (A), *great* (A), *wonderful* (B), *true* (B), *excellent* (D). All of these observations are part and parcel of viewing the basic 2,000-word list as a communicative resource rather than just a means of representing the world at the propositional level. Indeed, one might well conclude that for the response-token adjectives, where their response function at least equals and often outweighs their descriptive function (descriptive in terms of the traditional notion of an adjective as an item describing a nominal item, either attributively or predicatively) in terms of frequency, the label *adjective* seems not entirely appropriate, since they evaluate a situation or a whole utterance, and are operating at the level of discourse rather than within the phrase or clause. The same applies to adverbs that occur with high frequency as response tokens, such as *absolutely* (B) and *definitely* (B), suggesting that a contextually determined word-class with the label *response token* or *feedback token* might be more useful as a category for pedagogy. One of the significant insights gained from examining a spoken corpus is that the assumptions we make about word-classes in English (the basic classifications of which were only really established in the eighteenth century) are inadequate to deal with items in everyday spoken interaction such as discourse markers and response items, to name but two common types. Spoken corpora may lead us to fundamentally re-assess the notion of word-classes that we commonly work with.

Figure 3 shows the frequency distribution of basic colour adjectives in the mixed corpus, where considerable variation exists, with *orange* (as a colour rather than a fruit) and *purple* falling outside the top 2,000. *Black* (A) occurs more than six times as frequently as *pink* (D), while *yellow* (C) and *blue* (B) land more in the centre of the list. In a potentially large set (the names of all colours and variations, e.g. *scarlet, turquoise, gold*), the corpus is able to give us useful figures for what to include at the core level.

Figure 3: Occurrences of colour terms per 10 million words (CANCODE)

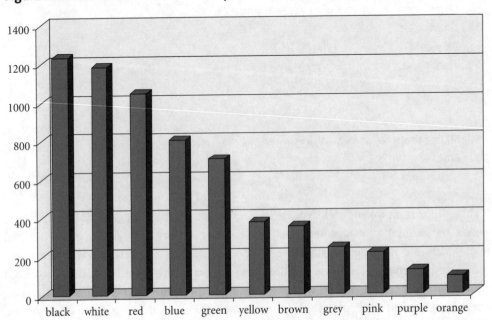

The colour terms do not occur in this distribution for no reason at all. The most common colours are the core ones, black, white and the primary colours red, yellow and blue, with green being a common feature of the physical environment in Britain and Ireland. The commonest colours also figure frequently in fixed expressions and in metaphorical contexts (e.g. *black/white coffee, green politics, out of the blue*, etc.). Figure 4 shows a similar graph for occurrences per 10 million words in a spoken North American corpus (forming part of CIC). Although some of the ordering is different (in the mid-range, *red, blue* and *green*), probably owing to cultural differences, the overall pattern is strikingly similar.

Figure 4: Occurrences of colour terms per 10 million words (North American spoken)

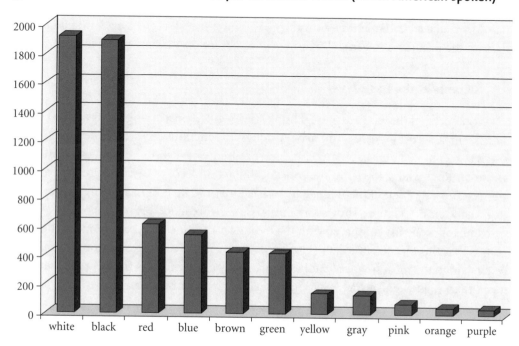

Basic adverbs

Many adverbs are of extremely high frequency, especially those referring to time, such as *today* (A), *yesterday* (B), *tomorrow* (B), *eventually* (C), *recently* (C), those indicating frequency and habituality, such as *always* (A), *usually* (B), *normally* (C), *generally* (D), and those of manner and degree such as *quickly* (B), *suddenly* (B), *totally* (C), *entirely* (D). Also extremely frequent are sentence adverbs such as *obviously* (A), *basically* (B) and *hopefully* (D), which function to evaluate utterances and which reflect speaker stance (see above). This class of word is fairly straightforward, but it should be borne in mind that some prepositional phrase adverbials are also extremely frequent, such as *in the end* and *at the moment* (see below). The raw frequency list hides the frequency of phrasal combinations, and extra investigations are needed to ensure that the most frequent phrasal items are not lost from the basic vocabulary.

Basic verbs for actions and events

Beyond the group of delexical verbs, there are, of course, a number of verbs denoting everyday activity, such as *give, leave, stop, help, feel, put* (all band A), *sit* (B), *listen* (B), *explain* (C), *enjoy,* (C), *accept* (D) and *fill* (D). It is worth noting that the distribution of particular tense/aspect forms may be relevant in considering priorities in the basic vocabulary. Of the 41,389 occurrences of the forms of the verb *say* (i.e. *say, says, saying, said*) in the mixed corpus, 27,236 of these (66%) are the past form *said*, owing to the high frequency of speech reports. With *give*, the picture is different: the simple past form, *gave*, and the past participle *given* are virtually equal, but the base form *give* is more than double the frequency of each of the other two forms. Such differences may be important in elementary level pedagogy, where vocabulary growth might outstrip grammatical knowledge, and a past form such as *said* might be introduced to frame speech reports even though familiarity with the past tense in general may be low or absent on the part of the learner.

2.5   Chunks at the basic level

Chapter 3 of this book explores chunks (i.e. regularly occurring strings of two or more words which seem to possess unitary meanings or functions) in greater detail, but here it needs to be pointed out that many chunks are as frequent as or more frequent than the single-word items which appear in the core vocabulary; indeed, as we saw in section 2.3, some words occur very high in the frequency list because they are part of high-frequency chunks (e.g. *know, mean*). Figure 5 shows for comparison the frequency of some single-word items from the top 2,000 list compared with the frequency of some everyday chunks. What it suggests is that the vocabulary syllabus for the basic level is incomplete without due attention being paid to the most frequent chunks, since many of them are as frequent as or more frequent than single items which everyone would agree must be taught.

2.6   The basic level: conclusion

The ability to generate word lists based on frequency of occurrence is one of the most useful tasks a computer can perform in relation to a corpus. Using a frequency list, we can see that a clear core vocabulary based around the 1,500–2,000 most frequent items seems to emerge, a vocabulary that does heavy duty work in day-to-day communication. However, we have seen that raw lists of items need careful evaluation and further observations of the corpus itself before a vocabulary syllabus can be established for the elementary level. Not least of the problems is that of widely differing frequencies for sets of items that seem, intuitively, to belong to useful families for pedagogical purposes. Furthermore, we have seen that some of the most common items in everyday spoken interaction (e.g. discourse markers and response tokens) defy an easy fit into the traditional word classes of noun, verb, adjective, adverb or interjection. Equally, the list needs to take account of collocations and chunks, as we saw in the case of the delexical verbs, the discourse markers and the basic adverbs. But the list can also be very useful in suggesting priorities and in establishing

Figure 5: Chunks and single items from the top 2,000

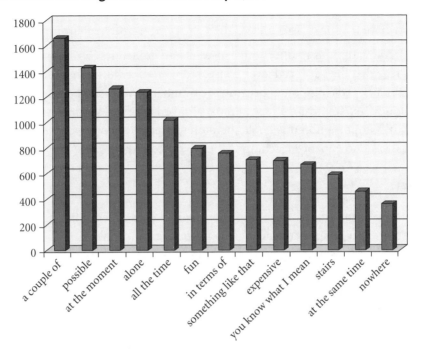

graded information for closed sets consisting of very large numbers of items (e.g. the human body parts). Armed with the complex information a frequency list can give, the teacher, syllabus designer or materials writer can elaborate a more use-centred vocabulary pedagogy at the elementary level and provide useful and usable language items even to very low level learners. Until recently, word lists were derived from intuition or from written text sources only; our ability nowadays to produce lists based on written and spoken data, and to distinguish them where appropriate, considerably enhances our potential for teaching the spoken language more effectively and authentically alongside the well-tried syllabuses for written language.

2.7 The advanced level

Most second language teachers will, at some time or other, be faced with the problem of what, and how to teach at the advanced level. Questions uppermost in their minds are likely to be:

- How many words should advanced level learners be able to understand and/or use?
- Given the impossibility of teaching all the low frequency vocabulary, which words should be included in an advanced level syllabus, or is such a syllabus not even worth contemplating?
- What types of vocabulary knowledge should learners possess at this level?

- How can the language-learning context help learners become independent and autonomous so that they can continue with the vocabulary-learning task after they have left the classroom and the controlled learning environment?

This section attempts to offer some answers and guidelines in response to these challenges. It is true that the advanced level, compared with other levels, has received less attention in vocabulary pedagogy, often because the number of words to be learnt is so vast and their selection so apparently arbitrary (almost all words at this level are, by definition, relatively rare). It is important in this book, therefore, to see if corpus evidence can be brought into the classroom to enhance teaching at the advanced level.

2.8 Targets

We can use corpus evidence to assess how many words a reader/listener needs to know (passively/receptively) to understand a given percentage or proportion of the words in any typical, everyday, non-specialist, randomly chosen written or spoken text. If the desired goal was that 90% of a chosen text should be understood by a group of learners at first encounter without support from course materials, dictionaries, glossaries or direct intervention by the teacher (in other words, that the new word-learning burden should not be more than 10% of the lexical content of the text), then frequency counts suggest that a receptive vocabulary of somewhere in the region of 5–6,000 word-forms will ensure about 90% comprehension for English texts (Carroll et al. 1971; see also figure 1, above). A 5–6,000-word vocabulary entails adding a further 3,000 or 4,000 to the core 2,000 words. This is within the reach of typical learners of English in good educational environments. An example of a pedagogical programme which aims to hold to this ambition is the North American English *Vocabulary in Use* series (see McCarthy and O'Dell 1997, 2001) which is predicated on increments of approximately 2,000 words at each of the levels from Elementary to Lower Intermediate to Upper Intermediate. The targets were derived from a combination of corpus-based quantitative research and feedback from teachers, learners, reviewers and pilot editions of the material.

Achieving 90% coverage of unseen texts would seem, at first glance, to be very effective. However, the remaining 10% of the lexical content will prove a heavy burden for the learner because the words will be of relatively low frequency, but will carry a large amount of specific content meaning. This is because more than 80% of the text will be swamped by the first 2,000 core items, which are rather general in meaning, or are 'delexicalised' (e.g. verbs such as *get, do*; nouns such as *thing, stuff, person*), or are function words (e.g. grammar items, discourse markers). Discussions of the problem of low frequency vocabulary and text comprehension have long acknowledged this conundrum (Richards 1974; Honeyfield 1977). Furthermore, simply providing the missing 10% portions of new texts (either by intensive pre-teaching or explanation during or after the first encounter) will not necessarily foster the independent learning skills that will be needed when learners have left the classroom and continue to meet new words in their reading or spoken interactions. Thus a receptive vocabulary of some 5–6,000 words would appear to be a good threshold at which to consider learners to be at the top of the intermediate level and ready to take on an advanced level programme. Such a programme would ideally have the following aims:

- To increase the receptive vocabulary size to enable comprehension targets above 90% (e.g. up to 95%) for typical texts to be reached.
- To expose the learner to a range of vocabulary at frequency levels beyond the first 5–6,000-word band, but which is not too rare or obscure to be of little practical use.
- To inculcate the kinds of knowledge required for using words at this level, given their often highly specific lexical meanings and connotations.
- To train awareness, skills and strategies that will help the learner become an independent vocabulary-learner and user who can continue the task for as long as (s)he desires.

2.9   The vocabulary curve

Increasing the receptive vocabulary size to a point where 95% comprehension is possible does not, as we have seen in figure 1 above, simply mean adding another 2,000 words to the 5,000 or 6,000 possessed by good upper-intermediate learners, since the vocabulary frequency curve falls off dramatically after the most frequent words, to a point where almost everything is very low frequency indeed, even in massive corpora. It is a chastening fact that the nearer one attempts to approach native-speaker vocabulary levels, the bigger the gap seems to be between what is known and what needs to be known. Figure 1 showed the increments in comprehension offered by adding further 2,000-word bands to the core 2,000 word-forms, based on a combined spoken and written corpus of ten million words of everyday texts. The leaps required to go from zero to 90% to 95% and to 97% (highly-advanced, expert-user level) were not evenly spaced.

A 5–6,000-word upper intermediate vocabulary would seem to offer around 90% comprehension. Adding another 4,000 word-forms (from the 6,000 to 10,000 word level) accounts for only a 3% gain in coverage, and the next 6,000-word increment (from the 10,000- to 16,000-word level, not shown in the graph) only brings with it a meagre 2% gain, and so on. These figures are approximate and are taken, at this level, as excluding basic function words (non-lexical words). Depending on the type of texts and their degree of specialisation, totals of 1,000 words either side of these figures may not be unusual. The figures are, though, based on word forms rather than lemmas, as discussed in section 2.2. The probably much greater ability to predict the meaning of inflected forms from a base-form of a word at the advanced level does, of course, mean that the actual new word learning burden will be considerably less, but the general pattern of very low frequency for most forms in the advanced arena still holds, and progress towards native-speaker levels of comprehension will be slow, however one looks at the picture.

Any optimism about successful and innovative pedagogy at the 90% text coverage level should be tempered by the reality that every tenth word in a typical unseen text will be new to the learner, and this will likely be extremely de-motivating: there will simply not be enough known words to support the guessing, inferring and deducing of meaning of the new words. No learner can be expected to look up one word in every ten in a dictionary and still remain motivated at the end of reading a 500-word text (50 look-ups). Hu and Nation (2000) support the argument that a 90% text comprehension level is insufficient for a learner-reader to gain adequate access to the text's message. Nation (2001:147–8) further argues that for full, pleasurable engagement with the meaning of a text, comprehension in the region of 97–98% must be the desired threshold, which is without doubt something that the average learner even at the 5,000 or 6,000 word level can only achieve with greatly simplified or very carefully selected material. The 95% comprehension level brings the learner much closer to a full engagement with the content of an unseen text: in such a circumstance, 1 in 20 words will still be new, but the co-textual and contextual support, and the motivation to look up new words will be considerably greater. Carver (1994) suggests that native users of English operate at a 99% level of comprehension with average reading materials; clearly second language learners cannot easily achieve that kind of level in a short time, but the 95% level (9–10,000 word-vocabulary perhaps) is probably achievable in tertiary level education with extensive reading programmes and intensive vocabulary teaching materials designed to focus on a useful range of words at the 6–10,000 word-band level and fostering strategies for dealing with unknown words. Research also suggests that vocabulary gains may be quite impressive (up to 2,500 new words per year) if the learner is in a native-speaker environment, for example, on a study abroad programme, as reported by Milton and Meara (1995), or adopts a more specialised focus, for example, academic vocabulary (Coxhead 2000), where up to a 10% leap in comprehension can be gained simply by learning small, carefully chosen academic word lists consisting of fewer than 1,000 common core words. Notwithstanding, the 6–10,000 general word level would appear to be a zone where gains in comprehension are still worth pursuing; we have not yet reached the vast plain of extremely rare vocabulary that offers little in terms of overall return on the investment of learning every new word encountered.

2.10 The 6,000 to 10,000 word band

Isolating the 4,000 word-forms which occur between frequency ranks 6,000 and 10,000 in our 10-million-word spoken and written corpus is a straightforward matter. That list cannot be presented in its entirety here, but its content and flavour is the subject of the broad description and discussion below.

Figure 6 shows how these words are distributed in terms of frequency of occurrence in the 5-million-word written corpus (the written corpus is chosen here as it is more likely that new vocabulary at this level will be encountered in extensive reading than in spoken encounters). It can be seen, for example, that 461 of the words occur more than 60 times in the corpus, but that over 3,000 of the 4,000 or so only occur 40 times or fewer. However, the

Figure 6: Frequencies in the 6–10,000 word bands (5m word-written corpus)

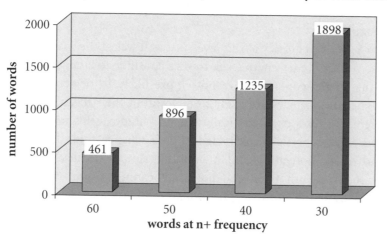

frequency curve is relatively smooth, with even the words in the 8–10,000 word rank occurring with sufficient frequency for them not to be condemned as rare or useless: 30 or 40 occurrences are usually sufficient for robust patterns of form and meaning to emerge in concordance output. It must be noted, nonetheless, that in the same corpus, even the bottom 100 of the core 2,000 items occur more than 250 times, so the frequency rates are very relative.

Figure 6 shows frequency of word forms. Frequency of form, however, provides an incomplete picture as regards meaning. So, in the case of this English corpus, although the word *spine* occurs in the 6–10,000 word list, not all of its meanings are 'part of the human body', and metaphorically extended meanings such as 'part of a book where the binding is attached' or 'main vertical item in a network' (as in 'spine of a national network of cycle routes') occur. This illustrates the fact that *spine* may well have been learnt as a body-part at the intermediate level and as part of a natural, psychologically-motivated set, independently of its frequency, along with other body-parts, as we discussed in the section on basic vocabulary, but the teacher or materials may need to revisit it at the advanced level in its extended meanings. Indeed, much advanced level vocabulary pedagogy will be concerned with dealing with less frequent, extended and metaphorical senses of words, and new psychological sets may be forged which are at odds with raw frequency. For example, *spine* forms part of a set with *jacket/cover* as belonging to the field of 'books'. New associations will need to be forged, as in table 5:

Table 5: Expanded associations of *spine*

existing learner set	new learner set	existing learner set
spine	**spine**	**jacket**
head	**jacket**	trousers
back	binding	shirt
thigh	cover	skirt
neck, etc.	frontispiece, etc.	sweater, etc.

The expansion of such associations and the forging of new networks are seen as a central aspect of being an advanced learner or user by researchers such as Wolter (2001, 2002), and Wilks and Meara (2002).

Another important aspect of frequency at this level, just as it was at the basic level, is the occurrence of chunks. At the 6–10,000 item level, chunks continue to emerge as more frequent than many of the single words, but are now more likely to be semantically opaque, idiomatic ones. Their frequencies are likely to be low, but their meanings challenging, and their occurrence in texts psychologically salient: paradoxically, rarity often increases salience. Learners and teachers alike, attracted by their salience, find them interesting and colourful, and often motivating and memorable simply because they are unusual. The phrasal verb *show up*, with its several idiomatic meanings, occurs more than 100 times in our mixed corpus, and the idiomatic phrase *on the spot* occurs 37 times, bringing both into the frequency levels of the single-word 6–10,000 word list. Because such expressions are inherently less frequent, language pedagogy will need to broaden its scope at this level and make a wider trawl of the frequency list or increase the size of its corpus to include idioms of lower than 30 occurrences. *Peace and quiet*, for instance, occurs 24 times, and is typical of many binomial structures with frequencies of between 10 and 30 in the present corpus (see the concordance in Figure 8 below). Account has to be taken, too, of widely divergent frequencies in the spoken and written segments of the corpus taken separately. For example, the two idiomatic expressions *stumbling block* and *it just goes to show* have widely divergent frequency in speech and writing, but a corpus greater in size than the present 10 million-word one is needed to demonstrate this fully. Figure 7 is therefore based on the addition of the 10-million-word spoken element of the British National

Figure 7: *stumbling block* and *it just goes to show* in speaking and writing

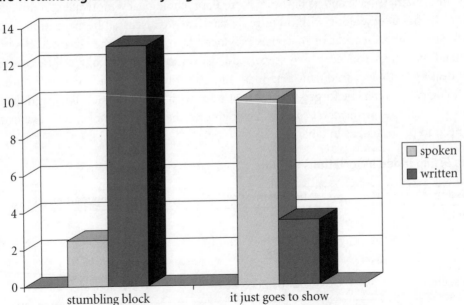

Corpus (see appendix 1) to the present corpus (figures are occurrences per 10 million words):

The overall conclusion regarding the vocabulary of the advanced level frequency bands must be that, as at the basic level, the single-word frequency list alone is not sufficient and must be supplemented by chunks, by a careful distinction where appropriate between spoken and written vocabulary, and by psychological and commonsense considerations.

Collocations (two-word combinations whose component words, unlike chunks, may or may not occur immediately adjacent to one another; see chapter 1) are also a major and by now uncontroversial aspect of advanced level vocabulary knowledge, but learners may have to be explicitly introduced to the importance of collocation via awareness-training, since many language learners, even at higher levels of attainment, see vocabulary-learning as largely a matter of confronting single words. One may conclude that collocations, along with semantically transparent and opaque, idiomatic chunks, form the main component of the multi-word lexicon and that the multi-word lexicon is at the heart of advanced level lexical knowledge, given that the challenge at this level is as much to do with grappling with observing recurrent collocations and chunks (which will most often consist of words already known individually) as it is with simply pushing for a (never-ending) linear increase in the vocabulary size based on single words never seen before.

2.11 **Meanings and connotations**

One characteristic of words at the low frequency bands was mentioned above: their proclivity to occur in sub-senses and extended/metaphorical meanings. Another characteristic is a tendency to display connotations and degrees of nuances and subtlety which the core 2,000 items generally operate independently of; words like *table, hand, blue, cup, water*, etc. are typically learned through their core, high-frequency meanings at the elementary level and it would be regarded as wasteful of precious time to explore at leisure their cultural or more obscure connotations (e.g. *blue mood* or *blue pencil* [the latter referring to censorship]). Words in the 6–10,000 word band seem less capable of innocent, neutral use, and a great deal of focus will necessarily be on the connotations of words in their typical contexts of occurrence, over and above grappling with semantic issues. The expression *peace and quiet* (18 occurrences in 5 million words of written texts), already mentioned above in the context of chunks, is a case in point. Figure 8 (overleaf) shows a concordance for *peace and quiet*. It is notable that it is not neutral in its use, but is characteristically associated with contrastive contexts, where someone seeks, needs or finds peace and tranquillity in contrast to some other (negative) situation where noise or lack of peace and tranquillity is / has been problematic.

Thus, for example, in the case of wanting to make a neutral statement that one loves to live in the country because it is peaceful and tranquil, *peace and quiet* may not be appropriate, implying as it does a contrast which the speaker/writer may have had no intention of making. This is typical of the lexical issues that have to be tackled at the advanced level,

Figure 8: Concordance for *peace and quiet* (5m words written)

```
 1      recognise the need for a little visual peace and quiet occasionally.
 2    ning every skirmish on the streets. For peace and quiet the walker
 3    ded to share a vacation in the relative peace and quiet of Beirut.
 4    d only contacted the police to get some peace and quiet because her
 5    men who wish to while away the hours in peace and quiet with a rod and
 6    d-of-term exams to study for an' I need peace and quiet for a while.
 7    k by the possibilities they offered for peace and quiet, writing to
 8    ss Price used to come here for a bit of peace and quiet, ' Tom remarked
 9    t. It is the penalty, perhaps, for such peace and quiet. Some years
10     long as I can have my beer and eggs in peace and quiet. He looked up,
11    , charming beaches and countryside, and peace and quiet. And the dog
12     go in, when all we wanted was a bit of peace and quiet. He didn't ant
13    set resort 18 months ago hoping to find peace and quiet. Instead she
14    always was when she was having a bit of peace and quiet. She had on an
15    eft London for a while to convalesce in peace and quiet. Sean felt a
16    l yourself with a long-term poultice of peace and quiet. Squadron-
17    nd we did nothing, Inspector. We wanted peace and quiet. We had no wish
18    beauty treatments, exercise classes and peace and quiet. She found
```

since the connotations of words and their characteristic environments of use seem to operate more forcefully (their *semantic prosody*, after Louw 1993; Sinclair 1991a; see also chapter 1). Alexander (1985), who sees phraseological knowledge as one of the key issues in learning and using vocabulary at the advanced level, observes that for metaphorical idioms the kind of knowledge needed is overlaid by cultural connotations. The advanced learner, then, may be seen as possessing, amongst other qualities, an interest in and an ability to grapple with extended meanings and connotations, and not just the possession of a vast, receptively recognised word list.

2.12 Breadth and depth

What the corpus-based investigation outlined in this chapter suggests is that the quest for an ever larger and larger vocabulary reflects a rather one-dimensional view of advanced level achievement. A focus simply on linear increase in vocabulary size (or vocabulary *breadth* as it is often termed) produces diminishing returns as far as text coverage is concerned; there is evidence anyway that learners' vocabularies are far from stable and may fluctuate up and down, with words known at one point in time forgotten at a later point (Meara and Rodriguez Sánchez 1993). What needs to happen alongside the increase in breadth is an increase in *depth* of knowledge, i.e. the knowledge of the various aspects of use of a word, including, beyond its formal properties, its collocations, its sub-senses, and its semantic prosody. Such knowledge ultimately contributes to the learner's ability to create associations between words and to place them meaningfully within various networks in relation to other words (Meara 1996; Henriksen 1999; Haastrup and Henriksen 2000). Depth of knowledge is not simply a second-best to ever-increasing breadth: Qian (2002), for instance, found that vocabulary depth was as significant as vocabulary size in predicting performance on academic reading. And since the vocabulary learning task is open-ended and impossible to complete in a typical institutional programme, the implication is that the advanced level should also be defined by the extent to which the learner is able to operate independently with a set of skills and strategies for processing and using new vocabulary. Such a learner may not in fact have a massive vocabulary, but may be better equipped to use and explore the vocabulary of the target language than one who simply adds more and more words without building an integrated lexicon and without developing that 'learner agency' so often discussed in sociocultural theory (Lantolf and Appel 1994a, 1994b), which can enable the learner to surpass instructional intervention and become a better, self-regulated learner. Independence is often conflated with 'autonomy'; in most cases of interaction (especially face-to-face speech) individuals do not operate autonomously but effective learners exploit the support of their environment, their interlocutors and other resources, and they can do so independently of any pedagogical intervention[1].

We are now in a better position to confront the aims of an advanced vocabulary learning syllabus sketched out in section 2.8, above. The corpus-based investigation has provided useful answers to some of the quantitative issues and in part offered guidelines for the more qualitative issues.

To push the vocabulary size towards comprehension targets above 90% for typical texts seems feasible, and involves ultimately aiming for a 9–10,000-word receptive vocabulary. The advanced learner can be expected to come to the task with anything from 4–6,000 words already known, presenting a learning target of around 4–5,000 words to achieve good, fluent reading levels. Most teachers will recognise, however, that 5,000 words is an impossible target for direct classroom teaching as such, and its achievement will depend on motivated work out of class, including extensive L2 reading, training of learning strategies which will be available both during and after formal/institutional learning, and, in ideal situations, some time spent in an L2 native-speaking environment. The other, best option, is to encourage learners to specialise. The example mentioned above was specialisation in academic vocabulary, but specialisation of any kind can produce dramatic results, whether it be reading cookery books or gardening books, or pursuing the vocabulary of music, business or politics, whatever one's personal interests are. And one may safely speculate that with the increased motivation provided by reading texts about things one is truly interested in will come benefits for the general vocabulary breadth and depth.

In terms of exposing learners to a vocabulary drawn from frequency levels beyond the first 6,000-word band, corpus-based techniques come into their own, since, even at lower levels of frequency, it is possible to generate word lists which differentiate low frequency items from extremely rare items. One proviso which needs repeating here relates to the mismatch between frequency of occurrence and the powerful, natural tendency of the mind to learn associated sets of items which can be retrieved as wholes, as well as the notion of psychological saliency, which may generate the curiosity and motivation to learn even rare items such as idioms. On this last point, the corpus size may need to be expanded in order to generate sufficient occurrences of salient but infrequent items so that relevant patterns of use can be observed.

---

[1]   We are grateful to Elana Shohamy of the CALPER Project at the Pennsylvania State University, USA, for raising the point about autonomy versus independence.

Words at the lower frequency levels tend to bring with them more sub-senses and extended meanings, and more obvious cultural connotations, in the sense that high frequency words can be, and usually are, dealt with at lower proficiency levels in terms of only their core, most frequent meanings – a sensible way of tackling the polysemic nature of most words in graded learning, in the view of Lennon (1990). Connotations and recurrent collocations can be usefully traced using concordance evidence. The issue of chunks also comes into play, and corresponding questions about the distribution of expressions in speech versus in writing.

To develop awareness and skills that will stand the learner in good stead for becoming an autonomous vocabulary-learner is a question of developing activities alongside the actual learning of words which introduce to the learner notions such as collocation, metaphor, connotation, etc. For example, in the case of English, many learners have an awareness of idioms of the 'verb + complement' type (*hit the sack, carry the can, jump on the bandwagon*), but probably few are aware of the pervasiveness in everyday language of binomial idioms (*rough and ready, part and parcel, out and about, down and out;* see also chapter 4). Explicit focus on such items may be necessary to tune the learner's antennae to be receptive to new ones when they are used both in and out of class, and to foster learner agency and independence. Vocabulary skills include ways of maximising learning opportunities during interaction (e.g. asking for paraphrases, probing the meaning of unfamiliar items with one's interlocutor, etc.). Vocabulary skill also involves being able to retrieve synonyms to create conversational flow and elegant variation in written text production. In this conversational extract from the CANCODE corpus, note how the speakers vary their ways of essentially saying that someone was 'in love' (indicated in bold); such a skill is a marker of the advanced user of vocabulary, someone who has created the necessary network of associations between the various items rather than just storing them as an atomised list in the memory.

(2.8)
[Two middle-aged male teachers are gossiping about a female ex-colleague.]

> S1: There was this guy that she was really **madly in love with** that went on and ended up working on an oil rig somewhere
> S2: Really
> S1: Oh yes she really was really loyal, **very struck on** him
> S2: **Smitten**
> S1: **Smitten with** him, had he, had he asked her at that particular time, er, I think she would have probably married him

(CANCODE)

In the final analysis, the classroom or course materials will only be able to traverse the surface of the vast iceberg of low frequency vocabulary and the onus will be on the learner him/herself to achieve the goals, but the goals are achievable given the right strategies and motivations.

In sum, neither the basic nor the advanced level vocabulary programme need be a haphazard free-for-all where planning and organisation simply dissolve into the fog of tens of thousands of unknown words. The basic level learner needs to achieve the target of covering the core items as fast as possible so that more effective, independent learning and use of the language can emerge. On the other hand, the advanced level learner will not be defined simply by his/her vocabulary size vis-à-vis native speakers, but rather more by his/her ability to develop depth of knowledge and the tools and strategies to pursue vocabulary learning and use independently. With a combination of corpus-based insights and strategic training for learners who will have to complete the task for themselves, we may go at least some way towards presenting a vocabulary level pedagogy worthy of the word *programme.*

3   Lessons from the analysis of chunks

3.1   Introduction

In chapter 2, although we focused primarily on single words, we also made occasional mention of the status of chunks as an element of the lexical competence of Successful Users of English (SUEs) (see chapter 1), noting that some chunks (e.g. *a couple of, at the moment, all the time*) were every bit as frequent as ordinary, everyday single words such as *possible, alone, fun, expensive*. Our argument was that, ideally, corpus information on chunks should be dovetailed into the information on single words in order to get a full picture of what needs to be learnt at the various levels of vocabulary attainment.

The title of this chapter is ambiguous. Corpus analysis, as we have seen, is relatively easy and straightforward when the computer is asked to search for and list single words. However, when we expand our search criteria to look for recurrences of more than one word (i.e. pairs and trios of words and even larger groupings), things become more complicated, and there are lessons to be learned about how we describe the vocabulary of a language, as well as implications for what teachers teach in their vocabulary lessons and how learners approach the task of acquiring vocabulary and developing fluency. But first we shall consider how the traditional view of vocabulary, where vocabulary means all the single words of a language, has changed over the years, especially in light of corpus analysis.

3.2   The single word

Until recently, in the study and description of vocabulary, the single word has been widely considered to be the basic unit of meaning and the main focus in the study of vocabulary acquisition in second and foreign language learning. There is no denying that single words form a substantial part of the vocabulary of English and that the word is perceived in language teaching as the basic unit to be acquired. Words, after all, carry important grammatical characteristics such as the ability to show number, person, tense, word-class, etc. For this reason, chapter 2 was dominated by consideration of single words. Other units consisting of more than one word, such as phrasal verbs, compounds and idioms, are often treated as items belonging to higher levels of proficiency, to the extent that imaginary textbook titles such as *The absolute beginner's book of idioms*, or *Beginner-level phrasal verbs* sound discordant with our pedagogical experience. There are, of course, exceptions to this: greetings and other everyday expressions (e.g. *How are things? See you tomorrow. Thanks very much.*), specialised functional phrases (e.g. *Happy New Year. Good luck.*), common prepositional phrases (e.g. *at the weekend, on the first of May*), and high-frequency compounds (e.g. *bus stop, whiteboard*) are generally taught and acquired even at very elementary levels. The single word has served us well, and will continue to do so, as we hope chapter 2 has demonstrated. But linguists have also, for a long time, been interested in how words combine as pairs in collocations (see Halliday 1966; Sinclair 1966) and how groupings of more than one word often have unitary meanings and specialised functions (Bolinger, 1976; Pawley and Syder 1983). The advent of corpus linguistics has enabled linguists to verify these earlier, mainly intuition-based notions in actual, attested language use on a large scale, and the ease with which currently available software can compute statistics about collocation (see chapter 1) means that teachers can often become their own researchers, even in such a complex area.

3.3 Collocation

One of the most important developments in the study of vocabulary has been the neo-Firthian approach to word meaning. Firth (1935) argued that the meaning of a word is as much a matter of how it combines with other words in actual use (i.e. its collocations) as it is of the meaning it possesses in itself. So, in the Firthian view, *bark* is part of the meaning of *dog*, and vice-versa, by dint of their high probability of co-occurrence in texts (Firth 1951, 1957). *Dog* and *bark* collocate significantly, *cat* and *bark* are not likely to do so to any significant extent. Collocations are not absolute or deterministic, but are probabilistic events, resulting from repeated combinations used and encountered by the speakers of any language. We say *bitterly disappointed* in preference to (but not the absolute prohibition of) *sourly disappointed* (there is nothing to stop, say, a poet using this unusual collocation); tea is usually *strong*, but cars are *powerful*, and so on. Some forty years ago, both Halliday (1966) and Sinclair (1966) foresaw the development of computational analysis of texts as a way of getting at the common collocations of a language, and both, in different ways, have fulfilled that vision, especially Sinclair (1991a, 2004). The automated study of collocation has shown that not only the rarer words, such as *auburn* and *rancid*, form preferred collocations. *Auburn hair* (but not **auburn car*) and *rancid butter* (but not **rancid bread*) do indeed illustrate the case that words are strongly attracted to one another in what may appear to be arbitrary ways. However, it is the collocations of the banal, everyday words that are most difficult to light upon by intuition alone which computers have been very good at teasing out. We are all familiar with the situation in class where we fall back on the statement 'that's just the way we say it', when faced with an awkward question from a student about why something is expressed the way it is, and often, what we are really explaining is a strong statistical preference which can be powerfully demonstrated by the use of corpus data. The answer, in the final analysis, is still that collocation shows us 'the way we say it', but we can gain considerable confidence as teachers if we can present something as a widespread and frequent collocation rather than a one-off occurrence in the particular text we are working with.

Common verbs such as *get, go, turn*, and so on display distinct preferences for what they combine with. Things *turn* or *go grey, brown, white*; people *go* (but not **turn*) *mad*, *insane, bald, blind.* The notion of collocation therefore shifts the emphasis from the single word to pairs of words as integrated chunks of meaning and usage, and collocation has now become an accepted aspect of vocabulary description and pedagogy (e.g. Lewis 2000; McCarthy and O'Dell 2005). Clearly, for the learner of any second or foreign language, learning the collocations of that language is not a luxury if anything above a survival level mastery of the language is desired, since collocation permeates even the most basic, frequent words.

Corpus software, when it searches for collocations, compares the *predicted* likelihood (based on the corpus size and the frequency of each single word) that two words will occur in the same environment with their *actual* occurrence in the same environment. The computer can then say whether something is occurring in a way we might expect (e.g. *the* before a vast number of nouns), or in a way we would not expect, and with statistical significance (e.g. the adjective *crucial* appearing alongside *role*). Most software packages do this automatically, at the click of a mouse for any particular word in the corpus.

3.4   Strings of words in corpora

Developments in corpus linguistics have convinced many linguists that vocabulary is much more than what Chomsky (1965: 84) called the 'unordered list of all lexical formatives'. Studies of large corpora by linguists such as Sinclair (1991a, 2004) have shown lexis to have a far more central role in the organisation of language and the creation of meaning than was generally previously conceived. A corpus can reveal the regular, patterned preferences of the language users represented in it, speaking and writing in the contexts in which the corpus was gathered. A big, general corpus can show how large numbers of language users, separated in time and space, repeatedly orientate towards the same language choices when involved in comparable social activities. And what corpora reveal is that much of our linguistic output consists of repeated multi-word units rather than just single words. Language is available for use in ready-made chunks to a far greater extent than could ever be accommodated by a theory of language which rested upon the primacy of syntax, as the transformational-generative (TG) tradition did.

Pursuing this radical view that it is lexis, rather than syntax, which accounts for the organisation and patterning of language, Sinclair (1987a, 1987b, 1987c, 1991a), based on his lexicographic work, argues that there are two fundamental principles at work in the creation of meaning. He calls these the 'idiom principle' and the 'open choice principle'. The idiom principle is the central one in the creation of text and meaning in speech and writing. The idiom principle holds that speakers/writers have at their disposal a large store of ready-made lexico-grammatical chunks (that is to say, the grammar of such chunks is preformed as part of their lexical identity, rather than vice-versa). Syntax, the slots where there are choices to be made (the open choice principle) far from being primary, is only brought into service occasionally, as a kind of 'glue' to cement the lexical chunks together.

Sinclair (1996a) sees meaning and form as working hand in hand: different senses of a word will typically be manifested in different structural configurations. For example, in the Cambridge International Corpus, out of 100 examples of the string of words *be touched by*, only 14% have the meaning 'experience physical contact', while 86% have a non-physical meaning (e.g. emotionally affected by, tinged with, affected by human activity), and, in turn, 80% of these non-physical senses have the meaning of 'emotionally affected by'. At the very least we can say there is a strong correlation between the occurrence of *touch* in the passive voice and non-physical (typically emotion-related) senses. The delicate relationship between syntax and lexis extends the original notion of collocation to encompass longer strings of words and includes their preferred grammatical configurations or 'colligations' (see also Mitchell 1971). Collocation and colligation together produce unitary, meaningful strings or chunks of language which are stored in the memory (see also Bolinger 1976) and which give substance to the idiom principle. Chunks are ready for use at any moment and do not need re-assembling every time they are used. Thus we can also partly account for the notion of 'fluency', a term frequently used to describe smooth, effortless performance in a language but one that is often only loosely defined.

Biber et al. (1999) call the kinds of strings we shall examine in this chapter 'lexical bundles' (see also Biber and Conrad 1999), though, unlike Sinclair's approach, Biber and his associates tend towards a more purely quantitative model of bundles, with less attention in the first instance to the relationship between form and meaning. Bundles are defined as recurrent strings of words, delimited by establishing frequency cut-off points, for example, that a string must occur at least 10 times per million words of text (or 20 times in the case of Cortes 2002), and must be distributed over a number of different texts, to qualify as a bundle. The process of finding the strings is purely automatic, which has advantages and drawbacks. The advantage is that the process is objective, and can pick up frequent chunks not easily brought to light merely by introspection or intuition. But it also means that a bundle might consist of (a) fragmentary strings which nonetheless are highly frequent such as *are to my*, *this one for*, (b) frequent, syntactically incomplete but meaningful strings such as *to be able to* or *a lot of the*, examples offered by Cortes (2002), and (c) more obviously semantically and pragmatically 'whole' expressions such as *on the other hand* and *as a result*.

Once again, the process of discovering bundles or chunks in corpora is a relatively easy task for corpus software. In the simplest terms, the computer opens a 'window' of a desired number of words (set by you, the user, for example, three words, or four words) and then searches through the corpus. If the window is three words, the computer looks at words 1, 2 and 3 of the text it begins with, then 2, 3 and 4, then 3, 4 and 5, and so on, through the millions of words of running text. At the end of the operation, the computer produces a list of three-word clusters/bundles/chunks which occur over and above the minimum cut-off point set by the user.

We can generate a list of chunks for the whole of a big corpus to get some idea of the general distribution of chunks. However, linguists and applied linguists who have investigated lexical bundles generally argue that bundles operate as important structuring devices in texts and are register- (or genre-) sensitive. Oakey (2002), for example, demonstrates that commonly recurring chunks such as *it has been [shown/observed/argued] that*, which are used to introduce external evidence in writing, are differently distributed across three genres, while Biber et al. (2004) demonstrate the different occurrences of chunks in university textbooks and classroom teaching. Furthermore, the use (or non-use) of lexical bundles by second-language learners has been considered a useful yardstick for the comparison and evaluation of learner competence vis-à-vis native speaker competence (see De Cock 1998, 2000; see also Granger 1998c). Meanwhile, Spöttl and McCarthy (2003, 2004) have used lexical chunks to investigate processing strategies and relationships across the several lexicons of students learning a third language. In short, comparisons of chunks across different data sets can reveal interesting 'fingerprints' of particular text-types, modes of communication or groups of users.

3.5   Phraseology and idiomaticity

It would be wrong, however, to suggest that corpus linguists have made all the running in the understanding of multi-word vocabulary. Developments in corpus linguistics have been paralleled, over the years, by non-corpus-based research into multi-word lexical units. The field of phraseology and the study of idiomaticity have contributed much to our understanding of multi-word vocabulary units, both in the West and (at the same time, but often unknown to Western linguists) in the former Soviet Union (see Kunin 1970; Benson and Benson 1993). Linguists interested in phraseology and idiomaticity have for a long time worked comfortably within frameworks not dominated by syntax.

In the research literature on idioms, discussion usually revolves round the semantics, the syntax, the cross-linguistic differences and the universality of opaque idiomatic expressions (Makkai 1978; Fernando and Flavell 1981), which, by and large, are relatively rare in occurrence in everyday conversation (e.g. idioms such as *pull somebody's leg* or *fly off the handle*). However, that is not to deny their interest for teachers and learners. Many aspects of language are fascinating and curious in themselves, and teachers and learners know that oddity and unusualness can often be more enjoyable, learnable and memorable than the more anodyne, utilitarian elements of everyday language, and we shall return to the traditional kinds of opaque idioms in the next chapter. But there has also been useful and illuminating research into what might be called the ordinary idioms of every day: conversational routines and rituals, gambits and discourse markers, and this has involved a recognition of the multi-word nature of such items (see Coulmas 1979, 1981a and b). However, few idiom researchers have gone so far as to examine idiom use in naturally-occurring spoken data, an exception being Strässler (1982), and more recently Powell (1992).

McCarthy (1998) listed different formal and functional types of idiomatic expression which were found through manually searching the CANCODE spoken corpus, the data on which much of the material in this book is based. McCarthy's purpose in that categorisation was to show that a wide range of idiomatic fixed expressions are present in everyday native-speaker conversation, both formally and functionally, perhaps a wider range than that suggested by the traditional emphasis on 'verb + object' idioms (e.g. *kick the bucket, pass the buck*) in language teaching. We take this aspect of the discussion much further in chapter 4.

The study of multi-word units has also focused on how they develop pragmatically specialised meanings in regular contexts of use (e.g. Bolinger 1976; Cowie 1988; Nattinger and DeCarrico 1992; Lewis 1993; Howarth 1998). Multi-word expressions have also come under the scrutiny of sociolinguists and conversation analysts, whose purpose is to assess the social significance of the moment of placement and use of particular linguistic items. Drew and Holt (1998), for instance, show that idiomatic expressions are used regularly at points of topic-transition and as periodic summaries of conversational gist. This work spotlights the non-random occurrence of idiomatic expressions and strengthens the claim of this chapter, and the next, that examining multi-word phenomena in corpora can teach us important lessons about the nature of human interaction.

As is often the case in linguistics, different terminology has been used over the years to describe the phenomena of multi-word vocabulary or chunks. Labels include 'lexical phrases' (Nattinger and DeCarrico 1992), 'prefabricated patterns' (Hakuta 1974) 'routine formulae' (Coulmas 1979), 'formulaic sequences' (Wray 2000, 2002; Schmitt 2004), 'lexicalized stems' (Pawley and Syder 1983), 'chunks' (De Cock 2000), as well as the more conventionally understood labels such as '(restricted) collocations', 'fixed expressions', 'multi-word units/expressions', 'idioms', etc. Whatever the terminology, all seem to agree that multi-word phenomena are a fundamental feature of language use. 'Off-the-peg' vocabulary enables fluent production in real time, and would seem to be at least as significant as single-word vocabulary when it comes to investigating either the semantics or the pragmatics of language. Indeed, it is hard to imagine any language not being produced (at least in part) in a ready-assembled manner (see Bolinger 1976), so we are not talking of a quirky phenomenon of English. What is much more complex and difficult to resolve, nonetheless, is the question of how easily the non-native learner or user can assimilate the multi-word fluency of the native-speaker or SUE. We return to this question below in discussing Prodromou's research.

One could reasonably posit that an over-emphasis in language teaching on single words out of context may leave second language learners ill-prepared in terms of both the processing of heavily-chunked input such as casual conversation, and of their own productive fluency. Wray, whose recent work on what she calls 'formulaic sequences' (which include idioms, collocations and institutionalised sentence frames; see Wray 2000, 2002), stresses that both formally and functionally, formulaic sequences bypass the analytical processes associated with the interpretation of open syntactic frames in terms of both production and reception (compare once again Sinclair's contrast between the idiom principle and the open choice principle). Wray also notes that utterances may be formulaic 'even though they do not need to be' (Wray 2000: 466), in the sense that they *can* be generated by the rules of open syntax and vocabulary selections to fill the syntactic slots (she gives as an example *it was lovely to see you*). Their formulaic nature comes from their recurrence and established colligations coinciding with their pragmatically specialised functions (in the case of *it was lovely to see you*, typically as a follow-up message after spending pleasurable time with someone).

In this chapter, we want to shift the balance away from the more semantically opaque multi-word expressions, the traditional 'idioms' (which will feature more prominently in chapter 4) and will focus instead on some of the most common chunks in everyday talk. As with most high-frequency phenomena, their core contribution to language use is subliminal and not immediately accessible to the intuition of the native speaker or SUE. In this chapter, therefore, we allow the first steps in the process of examining recurrent everyday chunks to be done automatically, by a computer count of recurring characters and spaces. This has both advantages and disadvantages, as we have already suggested, and as the next section will show, with concrete examples. We shall base our analyses primarily on spoken data, since, as we argued in the preface, there is ample work available on written texts and it is one of our central aims in this book to help to redress the imbalance between spoken and written studies.

3.6 **Looking at corpus data**

As elsewhere in this book, this chapter uses the five-million-word CANCODE spoken corpus. For further details of CANCODE and its construction, see McCarthy (1998) and appendix 1. As we said earlier, computer software can retrieve recurring strings of words, but its output will include strings which, in many cases, lack any syntactic or semantic integrity and just seem to be gobbledegook, as well as strings that display integrity of some kind and strike us as items of ordinary usage. Computers in their present state cannot distinguish between strings which recur but which have no psychological status as units of meaning (e.g. the fragment . . . *to me and* . . . occurs more than 100 times in CANCODE) and those units which have a semantic unity and syntactic integrity, even though they may be less frequent (e.g. the everyday modal expression *as far as I know* occurs with less than half the frequency of . . . *to me and* . . .). This difficulty has led some researchers to settle for incorporating fragmentary strings (e.g. Altenberg 1998; De Cock 2000) into their definition of chunks even where these include sub-phrasal and sub-clausal strings (De Cock offers as examples *in the* and *that the*), alongside pragmatically meaningful sentence-frames such as *it is true that* . . . In the present chapter we shall focus only on those items in the automatically extracted strings which display pragmatic integrity and meaningfulness regardless of their syntax or lack of semantic wholeness, a task which involves us in manual inference and qualitative interpretation of the automatically generated data (see below).

The procedure we followed for extracting the recurrent strings from CANCODE was to generate rank-order frequency lists of two-, three-, four-, five- and six-word sequences for the entire five-million-word corpus. For practical reasons, a frequency cut-off point has to be established, and for the present purposes, an occurrence of at least 20 times in the five-million-word corpus was the criterion for inclusion, that is to say four times per million words. This compares with Biber et al.'s (1999) cut-off figure of 10 times per million and Cortes' (2002) figure of 20 per million. Our figure is more liberal mainly because of the low occurrence of six-word chunks (only 18 being generated at the necessary 20 or more occurrences in five million words). Six-word recurrent chunks are of very low frequency in CANCODE, and it does appear that six is a practical cut-off point beyond which such chunks seem to be extremely rare. Only one chunk of seven words occurs more than

Figure 1: Distribution of strings in excess of 20 occurrences (CANCODE)

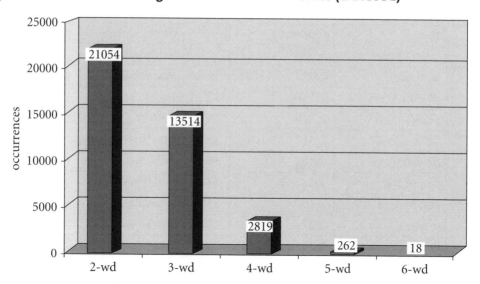

20 times: *but at the end of the day* (on the 'magic' number of seven as a psychological limit for the mind to process, see Miller 1956). The lists for the smaller combinations were, predictably, much longer. Figure 1 shows the comparative distribution of two-, three-, four-, five- and six-word chunks which occur more than 20 times, and it can be seen that there is a very sharp fall-off between the three-word chunks and the four-word chunks, and an even sharper drop between the four- and five-word chunks. It should be mentioned that, in these counts, contracted forms such as *it's* and *don't* are considered as one 'word', since the computer is counting characters and spaces only.

Tables 1 to 5 show the top 20 items in each list for 2–5-word chunks, and all of the 6-word chunks.

Table 1: Top 20 two-word chunks

	item	frequency		item	frequency
1	you know	28,013	11	I was	8,174
2	I mean	17,158	12	on the	8,136
3	I think	14,086	13	and then	7,733
4	in the	13,887	14	to be	7,165
5	it was	12,608	15	if you	6,709
6	I don't	11,975	16	don't know	6,614
7	of the	11,048	17	to the	6,157
8	and I	9,722	18	at the	6,029
9	sort of	9,586	19	have to	5,914
10	do you	9,164	20	you can	5,828

Table 2: Top 20 three-word chunks

	item	frequency			item	frequency
1	I don't know	5,308		11	you want to	1,230
2	a lot of	2,872		12	you know what	1,212
3	I mean I	2,186		13	do you know	1,203
4	I don't think	2,174		14	a bit of	1,201
5	do you think	1,511		15	I think it's	1,189
6	do you want	1,426		16	but I mean	1,163
7	one of the	1,332		17	and it was	1,148
8	you have to	1,300		18	a couple of	1,136
9	it was a	1,273		19	you know the	1,079
10	you know I	1,231		20	what do you	1,065

Table 3: Top 20 four-word chunks

	item	frequency			item	frequency
1	you know what I	680		11	a lot of people	350
2	know what I mean	674		12	thank you very much	343
3	I don't know what	513		13	I don't know whether	335
4	the end of the	512		14	and things like that	329
5	at the end of	508		15	or something like that	328
6	do you want to	483		16	what do you think	312
7	a bit of a	457		17	I thought it was	303
8	do you know what	393		18	I don't want to	296
9	I don't know if	390		19	that sort of thing	294
10	I think it was	372		20	you know I mean	294

Table 4: Top 20 five-word chunks

	item	frequency			item	frequency
1	you know what I mean	639		11	and all that sort of	74
2	at the end of the	332		12	I was going to say	71
3	do you know what I	258		13	and all the rest of	68
4	the end of the day	235		14	and that sort of thing	68
5	do you want me to	177		15	I don't know what it	63
6	in the middle of the	102		16	all that sort of thing	61
7	I mean I don't know	94		17	do you want to go	61
8	this that and the other	88		18	to be honest with you	59
9	I know what you mean	84		19	an hour and a half	56
10	all the rest of it	76		20	it's a bit of a	56

Table 5: Six-word chunks (all)

	item	frequency
1	do you know what I mean	236
2	at the end of the day	222
3	and all the rest of it	64
4	and all that sort of thing	41
5	I don't know what it is	38
6	but at the end of the	35
7	and this that and the other	33
8	from the point of view of	33
9	A hell of a lot of	29
10	in the middle of the night	29
11	do you want me to do	24
12	on the other side of the	24
13	I don't know what to do	23
14	and all this sort of thing	22
15	and at the end of the	22
16	if you see what I mean	22
17	do you want to have a	21
18	if you know what I mean	21

Table 6: Top 20 North American English three-word chunks

	word	frequency		word	frequency
1	I don't know	3,617	11	I want to	668
2	a lot of	2,107	12	I mean I	660
3	you know what	1,002	13	a little bit	657
4	what do you	909	14	you know I	632
5	you have to	870	15	one of the	581
6	I don't think	813	16	and I was	568
7	I was like	797	17	I have a	560
8	you want to	788	18	do you think	539
9	do you have	767	19	you have a	527
10	I have to	716	20	and then I	513

The tables exclude repetitions such as *you, you, you,* which often occur as hesitant starts, reduplicated responses such as *no, no, no* (although we recognise that these may indeed be relevant to some kinds of conversation analysis) and non-lexical vocalisations (e.g. *er, er*). The lists were then used as the basis for analysis and interpretation, firstly in terms of identifying integrated, meaningful units, and then in terms of what those units can show us about everyday conversational interaction.

The North American spoken segment of the CIC corpus presents similar evidence across the range of chunks. Table 6 shows the top 20 North American three-word chunks from a two-million-word sample. The chunks are strikingly similar to those in the CAN-CODE data, with some variation in sequence and some different items (e.g. *a bit of* in the British data, and *I was like* in the American data).

To illustrate just how distinctive these chunks are, in line with our earlier statements about register- and genre-sensitivity, it is useful to look at the chunks one finds in a written corpus. Table 7 shows the top 20 three-word chunks from five million words of mixed written CIC data for comparison.

Table 7: Top 20 three-word chunks (written)

	item	frequency		item	frequency
1	one of the	1,886	11	it would be	671
2	out of the	1,345	12	in front of	655
3	it was a	1,126	13	it was the	643
4	there was a	1,083	14	some of the	621
5	the end of	1,045	15	I don't know	604
6	a lot of	785	16	on to the	602
7	there was no	753	17	part of the	600
8	as well as	737	18	be able to	596
9	end of the	691	19	the rest of	577
10	to be a	672	20	the first time	567

Compared with the spoken chunks in table 2, what has disappeared almost entirely here (except for *I don't know*) is the speaker-listener world of *I* and *you,* and instead we have a 'world-out-there' representation, dominated by impersonal constructions, determiner phrases and prepositional relationships. The spoken chunks are, therefore, providing us with some sort of fingerprint of everyday conversation. A fuller comparison of such chunks, as well as chunks in academic data, may be found in Carter and McCarthy (2006: 828–837).

3.7   **Interpreting the data: chunks and single words**

The first thing we shall do is try to gain a perspective on how the high-frequency chunks compare with the frequency of single words in the corpus, something we partially did in chapter 2. An exhaustive count is beyond the scope of this chapter, but some indicative examples are offered to support the overall understanding of the place of chunks in a description of vocabulary.

Only 33 items in the single-word frequency list for CANCODE occur more frequently than the most frequent chunk (i.e. more frequently than the number one *you know*, which occurs 28,013 times). On the basis of our British English evidence, we may reasonably posit that *you know* is one of the most frequent items in the lexicon (this finding is borne out in spoken American English corpora too).

A selection of two-word chunks which occur with greater frequency than some common, everyday single words is given in figure 2. This chart may be compared with figure 5 in chapter 2.

Figure 2: Two-word chunks and common single words

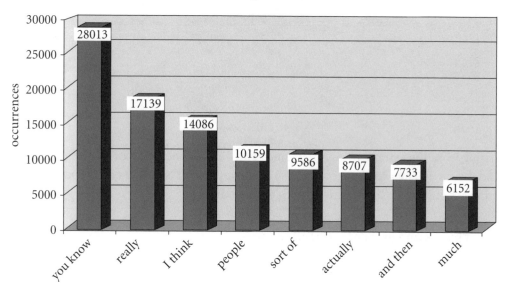

Individual chunks will be discussed below. Figure 3 (overleaf) shows examples of three- and four-word chunks which occur more frequently than some common everyday words which would uncontroversially be considered part of the core vocabulary of English, as we demonstrated in chapter 2.

The graphs suggest that vocabulary lists which consist only of single words risk losing sight of the fact that many high frequency chunks are more frequent and more central to communication than even very frequent words. However, the question remains whether the chunks in the tables and figures should be considered as units of any kind or simply as statistical phenomena reflecting inevitable recurrence of a finite number of words in the vocabulary. In short, should something like *and then* be merely viewed as a co-occurrence

Figure 3: Three-, four- and five-word chunks and common single words

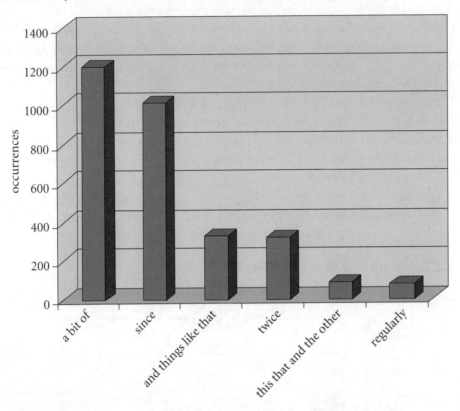

arising from the extremely high frequency and weak collocability of its component words and their inevitable repeated collision in the corpus, or do such co-occurrences reveal anything about how we communicate with one another?

3.8   Chunks and units of interaction

The notion of pragmatic integrity

Many of the chunks listed in the tables and figures above are syntactic fragments, i.e. they do not constitute complete syntactic units such as phrases or clauses. These include *in the, and I, of the* and *do you* in the two-word list, *one of the* and *I think it's* in the three-word list, *the end of the* and *a bit of a* in the four-word list, and so on. Conventional grammars would certainly dismiss these as incomplete structures. That is not to say that all models of grammar would reject such phenomena: emergent grammar, as epitomised in the work of Hopper (1998), considers fragments to be important clues as to how interaction unfolds and how grammar emerges rather than being pre-existent in interaction. There is no absolute reason why we should exclude syntactically fragmentary strings from consideration when evaluating their interactive role. For instance, *I think it's* is indicative of the ubiquity of *I think* as a hedge prefacing evaluations of situations likely to be referred to by pro-form *it*. *I think* is number 3 in the two-word list, occurring more than 14,000 times. *A bit of a* may be considered similarly: speakers routinely downtone utterances with *a bit (of a)* (e.g. *it's a bit late, it was a bit of a mess*), and *a bit* occupies rank number 24 (with a frequency of 5,341) in the two-word chunk list. Thus, although an expression like *a bit* may be semantically fairly 'empty', and although it may be grammatically dependent as a quantifier, it has become pragmatically specialised as a downtoner, and thus possesses pragmatic adequacy and integrity. It is perhaps more helpful to see these grammatically incomplete strings as 'frames' to which new, unpredictable content can be attached:

		mess
		problem
It was	**a bit of a**	*performance*
		hassle
		nuisance
		bargain

where the main constraint seems to be a preference for collocating with negative situations. The notion of a frame does not depend on any grammatical requirements, and it can be seen how frames are very useful in generating fluent performance. Other chunks seem less pragmatically specialised (e.g. *it was, what do you, in the middle of the*) and their occurrence is probably due to repeated events in the content world as opposed to those in the speaker-listener world. For example, the chunk *an hour and a half* is number 19 in the five-word list; this may simply reflect the fact that people frequently make references to time and duration, and especially in multiples of 30 minutes. We would argue, then, that it is in pragmatic categories rather than syntactic or semantic ones that we are likely to find the reasons why many of the strings of words are so recurrent, and in the idea of chunks as *frames* that we will find the most pedagogically useful 'handle' on chunks for vocabulary teaching and learning. By 'pragmatic categories' we mean the different ways of creating speaker meanings in context. Such categories would include discourse marking, the preservation of face and the expression of politeness, acts of hedging and purposive vagueness, all of which refer to the speaker-listener world rather than the content- or propositional world.

Discourse marking

Some of the most frequent chunks have discourse-marking functions. These include:

you know
I mean
and then
but I mean
you know what I mean
do you know what I mean
at the end of the day
if you see what I mean

You know is the most frequent chunk of all, and is an important signal of (projected or assumed) shared knowledge between speaker and listener, as well as being a topic-launcher (Östman 1981; Erman 1987). It is ubiquitous in everyday informal conversation, as extract (3.1) exemplifies:

(3.1)

S1: **You know**, our Gregory he's only fifteen but he wants to be a pilot.

S2: Does he?

S1: Now he couldn't get in this year to go to Manchester, **you know**, on that erm course that they do, experience course thing.

S2: Work experience.

S1: But he's going for next we= next year.

S2: Oh yeah.

S1: Work+

S3: Oh yeah.

S1: +experience yeah. And this time he's been to erm Headingley, coaching, doing a bit of coaching with the young kids **you know**.

(CANCODE)

The extended chunks *(do) you know what I mean* have a similar function of signalling shared knowledge. *I mean*, on the other hand, is used when shared knowledge cannot be assumed or when the speaker needs to reformulate what (s)he is saying (Erman 1987):

(3.2)

[In a sports equipment shop]

S1: Are there any tennis racquets you'd recommend? Erm I need the medium price range.

S2: Medium price.

S1: Yeah.

S2: What are you looking= What sort of price range are you looking at?

S1: Erm well not too expensive.

S2: **I mean**, they start at m= about fifteen pounds and they go up anywhere to about three hundred quid.

S1: Oh right. Probably under a hundred pounds cos it's not+

S2: Okay.

S1: +professional.

S2: Is it for yourself?

S1: Yeah.

S2: **I mean**, the decent racquets, you've got you've got a *Head* . . . seventy nine.

S1: Yeah.

(CANCODE)

The overlap of components within the longer chunks *(do) you know (what) (I mean)* partly account for the extreme high frequency of *you know* and *I mean*, but it is their core function in the monitoring of the state of shared knowledge which gives both the shorter and longer versions their pragmatic integrity. Likewise, *and then* is extremely frequent in narratives as a marker of time sequence (as previously mentioned), while *at the end of the day* typically has a summarising function. (For further discussion of the relational function of discourse markers, see chapter 8.)

Face and politeness

Speakers use indirect forms to soften speech acts such as directives (e.g. commands, requests, suggestions, etc.) in order to protect the face of their addressees, and the chunks reveal common everyday frames for such acts. Indirectness is also important in the polite and non-face-threatening expression of attitude, opinion and stance. Speakers work hard to protect the face of their interlocutors, wishing to neither demean them nor restrict or coerce them (see Brown and Levinson 1987). Chunks which function in this way include:

do you think
do you want (me) (to)
I don't know if/whether
what do you think
I was going to say

Examples (3.3) and (3.4) show these in action:

(3.3)
[Discussing the priorities for preserving lives in the British National Health Service, and whether age should be a factor]

    S2: I thought it was shocking.
    S1: Mm. **Do you think it** would have made any difference if she was say eighty years of age instead of a teenager?
    S2: Well I think that er anyone's attitude should be to save life irrespective of age.

                                  (CANCODE)

(3.4)
[At a travel agent's]

    S1: Did you want to take out insurance?
    S2: Erm I'd like to ask about it but **I don't know if** I want to do that today.
    S1: Okay.

                                    (CANCODE)

The utterances containing the chunks can be perfectly well formed with more direct language, for example *Would it have made any difference . . .?* (example 3.3); *I don't want to do that today* (example 3.4), but the presence of the chunks plays an important role in the mutual protection of face and the smooth, sensitive and sociable progression of the conversation. Once again, it is pragmatic function rather than syntactic or semantic wholeness, and the availability of the chunks as frames, which is most relevant.

Another important aspect of face-protection and politeness is hedging. Some of the most frequent chunks have a hedging function, i.e. they modify utterances to make them less assertive and less open to challenge or rebuttal (see chapter 8 for a detailed treatment of hedging). These include:

I think
sort of (North American spoken English shows a preference for *kind of* in this function)
a bit (of a)
I don't know
I don't think
to be honest with you

Examples (3.5) and (3.6) illustrate these functions:

(3.5)
> S1: That's fine Jess. Are there many to do?
> S2: No.
> S1: No. I've got an appointment in Healdham at five fifty so I'm going to have to leave you know **sort of** shortly after three.
>
> (CANCODE)

(3.6)
> S1: I went to college in the spring
> S2: Mm.
> S1: and sat the exam in June and passed it.
> S2: Mm.
> S1: But it was basically er an E-E-C update on the new regulations. **To be honest with you** it was pret= pretty easy I thought but you know s= some people have to fail I suppose and some do it you know.
>
> (CANCODE)

Vagueness and approximation

Salient among the high-frequency chunks are markers of purposive vagueness and approximation. Vagueness is central to informal conversation, and its absence can make utterances blunt and pedantic, especially in such domains as references to number and quantity, where approximation rather than precision is the norm in conversation (compare that with technical and scientific discourse, where precision is usually sought after and admired). Vagueness also enables speakers to refer to categories of people and things in an open-ended way which calls on shared cultural and real-world knowledge to fill in the category members referred to only obliquely (see Chafe 1982; Powell 1985; Channell 1994; O'Keeffe 2003; Evison et al. 2007). Such tokens include:

a couple of   *(and) this that and the other*
and things like that   *all the rest of it*
or something like that   *(and) all this/that sort of thing*
(and) that sort of thing

Examples from the corpus show the chunks in action:

(3.7)

[At a travel agent's]

> S1:   And what about er local taxis **and things like that**? Are they included or are they extra?
>
> S2:   Er everything is included apart from any sort of top up insurance you may want.
>
> (CANCODE)

(3.8)

> S1:   She said, 'We've just come out here. We've just bought an apartment here.'
>
> S2:   Mm.
>
> S1:   And she said, 'We've come out to furnish it and buy the furniture **and this that and the other**.'
>
> (CANCODE)

In examples (3.7) and (3.8) it would be clearly conversationally inappropriate and absurd to list all the items implied by the vague tokens; speakers need only allude to the shared cultural knowledge and may assume their listeners can fill in the detail. Once again, the vague tokens exhibit pragmatic specialism and play central interactive roles, even though their grammar is incomplete and dependent. In chapter 8, we look in detail at vague language.

3.9   Conclusions and implications

Not all of the recurrent strings we have listed can be, or need to be, accounted for in terms of pragmatic integrity. For example, repeated strings such as *on the*, *it was a*, and so on are probably best explained either by their semantics (e.g., core spatio-temporal notions) and by the frequency of acts such as describing location or narrating the past. However, by exploring the uses of the chunks in the spoken corpus, it is apparent that amongst the most frequent (the top 20 in each case), there are a considerable number which have clear, common pragmatic functions in the organisation and management of conversation and the speaker-listener relationship. What the chunks show is the all-pervasiveness of interactive meaning-making in everyday conversation and the degree to which speakers constantly engage with each other on the interactive plane. The addition of these chunks to the vocabulary list of any language should not be seen as an optional extra, since the meanings they create are extremely frequent and necessary in discourse, and are fundamental to successful human interaction. The chunks support Sinclair's notion of the idiom principle at work, and are best viewed as being evidence of single linguistic choices rather than assembled piece by piece at the moment of speaking. They make fluency a reality.

Lessons of the second type

We feel we have learnt some lessons about how vocabulary is organised through our analyses of common chunks. But what about the other type of lesson, what we do in class, and how students can be helped to learn and use these chunks in a natural way? Some of the issues raised by this chapter include:

- Chunks seem to be a badge of native-speaker identity. Why should learners who do not necessarily wish to sound like native speakers bother with them?
- If the use of ready-made chunks is central to fluency, how can they be presented and practised in language classrooms and teaching materials?
- How do learners typically process chunks when they encounter them?
- How can learners become aware of chunks and recognise potential chunks when they listen or read?

Chunks as a mark of the native speaker

Research by Prodromou (2005) suggests that the speech of native speakers can be distinguished from the speech of advanced non-native Successful Users of English (SUEs) by, amongst other things, the presence or absence of common chunks. Prodromou argues very persuasively that core chunks such as *sort of* and *you know* membership speakers within cultural communities and project a 'deep commonality' amongst interlocutors which the learner or even the highly successful non-native user may not wish to claim nor has any reason to claim. Prodromou is not advocating the enforced metamorphosis of expert users into native speakers; nor are we. The lesson here may be that receptive mastery is more important than productive repertoire. But the issue is twofold: firstly, we believe that those students who *do* wish to push forward towards near-native fluency should be given appropriate exposure to and practice in the use of chunks. Certainly in terms of social integration (e.g. students living and attempting to integrate in the L2 environment), it would seem that those who integrate more successfully are likely to acquire and use chunks more naturally, a claim for which Adolphs and Durow (2004) present some evidence. But secondly, even those whose espoused goal is to 'be themselves', and not simply to ape native speakers, may wish to consider the implications of engaging in conversation without the use of the highly interactive tools which the common chunks represent – it may be that we end up precisely *not* 'being ourselves' in the target language and may be presenting quite a false image of ourselves and a stereotyped image of our culture. Most important, we believe, is to air such issues in the language classroom so that students can make informed choices, and not to prejudge them.

Chunks and fluency

One of the features of chunks not discussed above, where the evidence has, of necessity, been the purely printed evidence of corpus output on a computer screen, is that chunks have phonological unity; put simply, they need to be said fast and all in one go. Typically, chunks occupy a single intonation unit (or 'tone unit', separated here by //, characterised by one strong stressed syllable, marked here in bold capitals) and the rest of the chunk is much reduced:

// he's **SHY** // *you know what i* ***MEAN*** //
// they sell **JEW**ellery // *and* ***THAT*** *sort of thing* //
// the **ROOM** was // *a* ***BIT*** *of a* // **MESS** actually //

Choral or private repetition, increasing the speed at each repetition, with practice in reducing the non-stressed syllables, can be a useful way of drilling chunks so that they become imprinted in the memory as 'musical' items. Then, in actual use, it can be stressed that it does not matter how slowly and carefully the rest of the utterance is, or needs to be, constructed. Provided the 'chunk' is said fast, the utterance will sound natural; the opposite, a fast message with a slow chunk, will sound completely unnatural and non-fluent. The appropriate use of a smooth, quickly uttered chunk can transform even a lower level speaker's fluency. The challenge of saying chunks at ever-increasing speed can also be an enjoyable interlude in a vocabulary lesson.

Although chunks can be drilled for speed in isolation, it goes without saying that it is a good idea to incorporate them into sentences and longer utterances for more sustained practice. Presentation of chunks in spoken language can most naturally be done by raising awareness of them through listening and noticing activities. Practice can also take the form of re-inserting chunks into dialogues from which they have been removed. The adult English language course *Touchstone* (McCarthy, McCarten and Sandiford, 2005a and b, 2006a and b), whose entire syllabus is corpus-informed, encourages students to listen and notice how chunks are used in the creation of conversational utterances and then to link together utterances using an appropriate chunk. In the example from *Touchstone* in figure 4 (overleaf), one of the common functions of the chunk *I mean*, to link the parts of a two-part utterance, is presented and practised. In the B-exercise, *I mean* is used in its natural context in a controlled utterance-building activity.

Processing chunks

Spöttl and McCarthy (2003) found that students interacting with chunks presented to them in edited contexts from the CANCODE corpus tended to focus on a 'strong' lexical verb or noun in or near the chunk in attempting to process the meaning of unfamiliar chunks. Furthermore, there was no evidence in their study that chunks in one language are readily associated with equivalent chunks in the learner's L1 (or other languages the learner may have). This suggests that building awareness of chunks could capitalise on the presence of strong lexical items where the chunk includes them, and that some cross-linguistic comparisons with learners' L1s might help them to see how their own language uses chunks and that they are not a peculiarity of English or any other language. However, chunks often contain no 'strong' lexical item, and may be made up of lexically 'light' items or entirely consist of grammatical items (e.g. *this, that and the other*), and such cases may require explicit direction towards and greater focus on the surrounding text to find clues to meaning.

There is evidence that the use of chunks 'frees up' the cognitive processing load so that mental effort can be allocated to other aspects of production such as discourse organisation and successful interaction (Girard and Sionis 2004). In that sense, chunks liberate the learner and allow a degree of automaticity to take over in both comprehension and production.

Figure 4: Extract from *Touchstone* (McCarthy, McCarten and Sandiford, 2005a: 48)

Wray (2000) stresses the non-analytical nature of formulaic language in native speaker competence. Attempts by teachers and textbooks to encourage the analysis of chunks by learners are, in Wray's words, 'pursuing native-like linguistic usage by promoting entirely *un*native-like processing behaviour' (p. 463, her emphasis). This is certainly the case. However, Spöttl and McCarthy (2003) offer two counterweights to this: (1) there is psycholinguistic evidence that, even among native speakers, at least some degree of literalness or at least metaphoric awareness is retained in the processing of figurative expressions (Gibbs 1986; Gibbs and O'Brien 1990), suggesting that even the most 'frozen' of chunks, such as idioms and stock metaphors, retain something of the meaning of their individual items which is potentially available to users. Learners may be even more inclined to analyse chunks than native speakers, and may see it as an important part of the learning process. Receptive mastery may indeed gain from an occasional analytical approach. (2) Classrooms *are* places where conscious analysis of social phenomena of all kinds can occur, unlike the world outside the class, where the same phenomena are primarily experienced first-hand and are often only made sense of in post-facto reflection and informal analysis. One might also add that the more the learner has successfully acquired a repertoire of chunks, the easier it becomes to reflect and analyse them at a later stage, so that certain aspects of grammatical acquisition may flow from the knowledge and use of chunks, rather than vice-versa.

It is also worth noting that chunks may not necessarily be acquired in an 'all-or-nothing' manner (Schmitt and Carter 2004: 4); in other words, the absorption and learning of the meaning and appropriate use of a chunk may be gradual and only apparent over time and after a number of exposures, just as with grammatical structures or single words.

Awareness raising

The most salient chunks, because of their curiosity and rarity, are the low-frequency idioms (see chapter 4), and learners often find it easier to recognize these rather than some of the more transparent, high-frequency ones. Underlining or colour-highlighting patterns which are frequently repeated in texts and dialogues may be one way of raising awareness of useful chunks, and encouraging students to record whole chunks in their vocabulary notebooks may raise awareness of their usefulness as frames that can be used with a potentially large number of utterances. Listening activities are perhaps the best way of awareness raising, especially since in naturalistic listening passages, common chunks will be spoken rapidly and will punctuate content. Several listenings to the same passage can be carried out: some for content, others purely for noticing chunks.

A final word needs to be said about the status of chunks vis-à-vis the more opaque idiomatic units that have traditionally been studied. In the absence of corpus evidence it is difficult to introspect on what one says. It is much easier to introspect on what one writes, and, additionally, introspection is more likely to light upon the colourful, the curious, the rare, precisely because such items are psychologically salient. Hence it should not surprise us that, with few exceptions, pre-corpus studies of multi-word units focused on idioms, phrasal verbs, compounds and so on, either as colourful curiosities or, in the pedagogic domain, a perverse and difficult characteristic of English for learners to struggle with. Meanwhile the banal, hidden, subliminal patterns of the everyday lexicon stubbornly resisted exposure. Corpus analysis enables us to circumvent many of the difficulties in retrieving such patterned occurrences, but the automatic retrieval of recurrent strings is only the beginning, and a good deal of inferential analysis is still necessary to see meaning in the lists spewed out by the computer. And indeed, in the case of opaque idioms, automatic analysis serves us even less adequately, and it is to this problem that we turn in the next chapter.

4 Idioms in everyday use and in language teaching

4.1 Introduction

In chapter 3 we examined the ubiquity of chunks in everyday spoken language, focusing on the high-frequency chunks which oil the interpersonal wheels of conversation. We argued that such chunks have often not been given the status they deserve as an important part of the vocabulary. However, some chunks are quite low in frequency and quite opaque in terms of their meaning, and yet have long been favoured by pedagogy; these are usually called idioms. Everyone loves idioms, teachers and learners alike. They offer a colourful relief to what can otherwise be a rather dull landscape of grappling with difficult grammar rules, learning new word lists, doing tests, and so on. Publishers are aware of this and offer materials specially devoted to idiom-learning, and there are good learners' dictionaries of idioms available for English, including corpus-based ones. A search through the back issues over decades of important language teaching journals such as *ELT Journal* and *TESOL Quarterly* will reveal continual mention of idioms, usually as part of vocabulary teaching or the teaching of language and culture, and mostly not seen as anything special or peculiar in the language teaching repertoire, albeit a challenge. However, in a book by one of the authors of this book (McCarthy 1998), it was noted that there was a shortage of information on how idioms are actually used in everyday communication, and it was argued that better information on actual use might benefit pedagogy. McCarthy offered spoken corpus examples in an attempt to remedy that lack of perspective; here we take the question further and offer more corpus evidence, and, in addition, look at teaching applications. We offer this chapter as a progression of the work reported in McCarthy (1992), McCarthy and Carter (1994) and McCarthy (1998).

We also consider the question of whether idioms, because of their cultural resonance and their status as 'badge of membership' of the speech communities from which they spring, have any place in a world where English is often used as a lingua franca and/or by learners and expert users (or SUEs) who may have no desire to claim membership of the native-speaker culture.

In our earlier research, we used the word 'idiom' to mean strings of more than one word whose syntactic, lexical and phonological form is to a greater or lesser degree fixed and whose semantics and pragmatic functions are opaque and specialised, also to a greater or lesser degree. This overlaps, of course, with the characteristics of a number of the everyday chunks we looked at in chapter 3, many of which, although they form part of our most ordinary everyday language, are, nonetheless, 'idiomatic' in the sense that their forms are unpredictable and the relationship between their form and meaning is not always one-to-one (e.g. *on the other hand, this that and the other, all the rest of it, thank you very much*). We focused on high-frequency chunks in chapter 3 because they are usually the ones least amenable to retrieval from intuition, but which corpus software can reveal because of their regular recurrence. In this chapter, however, we shall confine our attention to the other end of the spectrum: items which have, traditionally, been included in intuition-based language teaching materials probably just because they are low-frequency but very colourful and, consequently, psychologically more salient and accessible to expert users than the frequent, everyday chunks. These are the opaque 'idioms' beloved of language teaching, such as *kick the bucket* (= die), *hit the sack* (= go to bed), and so on. These are fixed and relatively inflexible in form and word-by-word analysis fails to yield their unitary meaning. The questions we want to raise in this chapter are: Are the intuition-based materials a good reflection of language use in terms of what actually occurs in a corpus and what the functions of such items are? And how far can the automated processes of corpus analysis assist us with items which are, of necessity, low frequency and unpredictable?

An example of a string of words where all elements are fixed is the expression *part and parcel*. The string must have that particular word-order, include those and no other words and be said as one single tone-unit (/²PART and ¹PARcel/). Its meaning is fixed and not transparent, in this case meaning 'a necessary and unavoidable part of some experience'. Other expressions may be more flexible. The expression *to pass the buck* (meaning to pass the responsibility for something to another person when one should accept responsibility oneself) can be rendered in the passive voice and has a noun form which derives from it (*buck-passing*), both of which are attested in the Cambridge International Corpus:

(4.1)

The buck was already **being passed** again before we had even started.

(CIC)

(4.2)

. . . managers and subordinates are too close together in experience and ability, which smothers effective leadership, cramps accountability, and promotes **buck passing**.

(CIC)

Here there is greater syntactic flexibility. McCarthy (1998) argued that the line where highly idiomatic expressions gave way to transparent and unrestricted syntactic constructions was rather hazy, but that a somewhat blurred definition of idioms had advantages as well as disadvantages. One advantage was that it allowed a lot more types of expressions to be included amongst idioms apart from the well-researched 'verb + complement' expressions like *pass the buck, swallow one's pride, grasp the nettle*, etc., and idiomatic phrasal verbs (e.g. *look up*, meaning 'to improve'). Some of the types McCarthy (ibid) listed are well attested in everyday usage. They included prepositional expressions such as *after a fashion, off the wall*; binomials and trinomials such as *high and mighty, mix and match, lock, stock and barrel* (see Norrick 1988; Fenk-Oczlon 1989; Wang 2005 for further examples and discussions); frozen similes such as *as mad as a hatter, as black as your hat* (see Tamony 1982; Norrick 1986), possessive *'s* phrases such as *the lion's share*; and idiomatic noun compounds such as *whitewash, belly-full*. The list was further extended to include idiomatic speech formulae and discourse markers, such as *mind you, to crown it all, how's tricks?*, cultural allusions, quotations, proverbs, slogans, catch phrases, and so on (see also Alexander 1984). Some of the idiom-types were identified by their syntactic configuration, others simply by their degree of pragmatic specialisation (e.g. the speech routines and discourse markers; see chapter 8 for more on discourse markers and routines). Other scholars have suggested dividing the cline of idiomaticity differently; Yorio (1980), for example, distinguishes between idioms as semantically opaque items and routine formulae, defining a routine formula as 'a highly conventionalized pre-patterned expression whose occurrence is tied to a more or less standardized communication situation' (p. 434), giving *it's not what you think* as an example.

McCarthy (1998) proposed that idiomatic expressions were not merely colourful alternatives to their literal counterparts, but that they encoded important cultural information and often performed discourse roles that could best be observed in real data. Idiom selection seemed not to be random and unmotivated. Written corpus research, showing idioms functioning as evaluative devices, often found in authorial comment segments in texts, seemed to underline this view of idioms as non-random (Moon 1992). McCarthy (ibid) focused on spoken data, and here we take that research on these colourful, low-frequency idioms in spoken language further.

4.2 Finding and classifying idioms

Since computers do not know what an idiom is, automatic retrieval of idioms using conventional software is only partially possible, despite recent advances in the recognition of syntactic patterns involving idiom-prone words (see Volk 1998 for a discussion of the difficulties and some solutions), and the exploitation of latent semantic analysis (put simply, the likely absence of semantically related words within and surrounding the idiomatic expression; see Degand and Bestgen 2003). One can generate lists of recurring chunks, as we did in chapter 3, but such lists are massive and still have to be sifted manually to decide which items can be classified as idioms and which not, and the lists do not provide contextual information – one still has to call up the contexts to fully research the idioms. One can also simply load a pre-compiled dictionary of idioms and ask the computer to search for their occurrences in the corpus. However, this necessarily presupposes that the dictionary has already recorded all the idioms in common circulation, which may not be so, and, again, one still has to bring up the contexts to research the items properly.

Certain everyday words do seem to be 'idiom-prone', probably because they are the foundations of basic cognitive metaphors. These would include parts of the body (*eye, shoulder, hand, nose* and *head* all generate a number of idioms), money (the metaphor that living is akin to spending money can be seen in idioms such as *money talks, put your money where your mouth is, the smart money*, and so on), light and colour (*be in the dark, shed light on, give the green light, have green fingers*, etc.) and other basic notions. A corpus can be searched productively simply by starting with such basic words. The word-form *face* has 520 occurrences in CANCODE, and a reading of the 520 concordance lines yields no less than 15 idiomatic expressions, of which the following occur three times or more:

let's face it	20
on the face of it	10
face to face	6
keep a straight face	4
face up to	4
till you're blue in the face	3
fall flat on one's face	3
shut your face	3

So, although the process of analysis is not entirely automatic, much can be gained by doing searches on basic, everyday words.[1]

However, a corpus does contain extended examples of the usage of its speakers and writers, and we should not forget that we can also read its entire texts, however time-consuming and, at times, tedious this may be. We therefore chose files at random from the CANCODE spoken corpus and a same-sized sample of conversations from the North American segment of the CIC, and read through the conversations as continuous texts, noting each idiomatic expression as we encountered it. This, and our subsequent procedure, was similar to that followed by Simpson and Mendis (2003). After finding 100 idioms in each of the British and American datasets, we then attempted to classify them according to their syntactic and pragmatic functions in context. This is only a partial solution to the problem but does give us a useful window into idioms in their actual contexts of use.

The opaque idioms fell into the following categories (with examples of their realisations):

1　Clausal expressions evaluating people's actions and personal states (*look down one's nose at sb* (BrE), *give sb a hard time* (AmE))
2　Clausal expressions evaluating things and events (*make sense, it's a small world* – in both datasets)
3　Names for people (*man/woman of the world* (BrE), *sugar daddy* (AmE))
4　Names for things and events (*pub crawl* (BrE), *small talk* (AmE))

---

[1]　We are grateful to Susan Hunston for encouraging us to explore the use of idiom-prone words in the corpus.

5 Discourse routines and interjections (*there you go* (BrE), *here's the thing* (AmE))
6 Miscellaneous adjectival, adverbial and prepositional expressions (*by and large* (BrE), *top notch* (AmE))

The complete lists of 100 items for each dataset are given in appendices 2 and 3.

The strongly evaluative nature of idioms comes out in the list of 100 items. Even the miscellaneous syntactic types show this (e.g. *by and large, as deaf as a post, till you're blue in the face*). A number of the expressions can be seen to support discourse functions such as marking staging-points in conversations (*here's the thing, let's face it, there you go*).

Here is an example of *here's the thing*, signalling an important point in the discussion:

(4.3)
S1: What about the French Canadians? Do they celebrate Independence Day?
S2: Well I mean **here's the thing**. I mean there is certainly a city of Montreal parade.

(CIC North American)

The lists also show considerable variation in the transparency of the expressions, with some being relatively transparent or easier to decode with minimal contextual cues (*put a stop to, get the message, it's a small world*), while others provide few or no clues as to their meaning (*take the Mickey, be hung over*). As we suggested earlier, there is no hard and fast cut-off line between what we are here calling 'idioms' and the common, everyday chunks we examined in chapter 3.

Relatively few analysts have attempted to describe idiom use in naturally-occurring spoken data, but those that have (Strässler 1982; Norrick 1988; Drew and Holt 1988 and 1995; Powell 1992) have all underlined the evaluative role of idioms and their discourse functions, which we return to below in section 4.5.

4.3 Frequency

The next procedure was to investigate the total frequency in the whole of the CAN-CODE corpus and the whole of the CIC sample for each item in the 100-item lists. It turns out that frequency varies greatly, with expressions such as *there you go, figure sth out, (not) make sense, once in a while, how come* and *fair enough* enjoying hundreds of occurrences, while about 20% of all the items occur only once. The two lists are comparable. Figure 1 (overleaf) shows the distribution of items in the different functional classes for the two datasets.

To get a handle on what these frequencies might mean for pedagogy, it is worth noting that any item occurring 10 times or more would find its place in the top 7,000 items if dovetailed into the lemmatised list of single-word items in CANCODE (for an explanation of lemmatisation, see chapter 2, p. 32). Any item occurring 20 times or more would find a place in the top 5,000 items in the CANCODE single-item list. 5,000 to 7,000 words is often seen as a realistic range for the receptive vocabulary size of high intermediate to advanced level EFL students (Hever 1997; Waring 1997; see also chapter 2

Table 1: 20 idioms occurring 10 or more times (from the CANCODE 100 idiom list)

	idiom	occurrences		idiom	occurrences
1	fair enough	240	10	good god	44
2	at the end of the day	221	11	be/have a/some good laugh(s)	41
3	there you go	209	12	the only thing is/was	41
4	make sense	157	13	good grief	38
5	turn round and say	139	14	keep an/one's eye on	37
6	all over the place	75	15	half the time	34
7	be a (complete / right / bit of a / absolute / real) pain (in the neck/arse/bum)	73	16	up to date	30
			17	take the mickey	25
8	can't/couldn't help but/ -ing	69	18	get on sb's nerves	24
			19	how's it going	21
9	over the top	53	20	along those lines / the lines of	20

Table 2: 20 idioms occurring 10 or more times (from the 100 North American idiom list)

	idiom	occurrences		idiom	occurrences
1	figure sth out	348	11	piss sb off	53
2	once in a while	278	12	ahead of time	50
3	(not) make (any) sense	276	13	put up with sth	44
			14	be sick of sth	43
4	(no) big deal	179	15	make fun of sb	40
5	screw up	151	16	stay away from sth	40
6	oh my gosh!	149	17	it all comes/came down to	40
7	how come …?	111			
8	oh boy!	71	18	throw up	35
9	freak out	56	19	what's up with …?	30
10	get over sb/sth	54	20	I'll be darned!	30

of this book). It would therefore seem reasonable to suggest items in our lists occurring 10 or more times, and any other idioms which can be shown to occur with such frequency, as possible targets for study if teachers and learners decide they want to explore a set of native-speaker idioms at the upper intermediate or advanced level. The top 20 items from the CANCODE 100 list are shown in table 1; those from the American sample in table 2.

Figure 1: Functional types in BrE and AmE (random sample 100 items each)

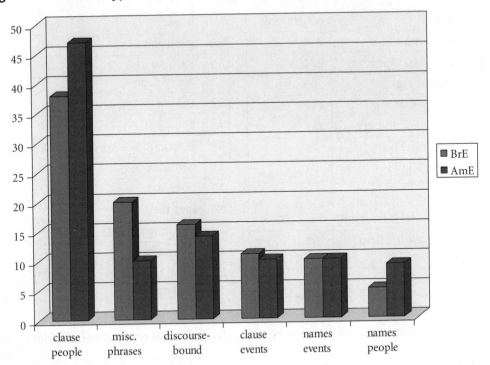

The lists (in tables 1 and 2) certainly offer a variety of types over and above the traditionally favoured clausal ('verb + complement') types and includes prepositional expressions, discourse routines, interjections, nominal compounds and a trinomial expression (*left, right and centre*), offering a rich menu of different types for study. We should bear in mind, though, that this is a random list and not necessarily an accurate cross-sectional picture of idioms in spoken British/Irish and American English, but it does seem to capture something of the richness and variety of idioms in everyday native-speaker conversations, and is preferable, we would argue, to lists drawn up entirely on the basis of intuition, where the colourfulness and consequent psychological salience of some expressions may blind us to their low frequency and limited usefulness, and where only an impoverished range of formal types may be represented.[2]

4.4 Meaning

We began by saying that idioms are characterised by degrees of opacity of meaning, with prototypical examples being quite opaque (e.g. *take the Mickey, be hung over*). There are certainly many idioms of this kind, where, in the absence of contextual clues, there is no

---

[2] The only occasion the old favourite idiom *kick the bucket* occurs in the CANCODE corpus, for example, is in an informal university English language seminar, where it is discussed as an example of the fixedness of idioms!

way of decoding the unknown expression by examining its constituent parts. However, there are two considerations which appear in the literature that suggest that apparently opaque meaning may offer an opening to good pedagogy. The first is the often partial literalness of expressions and the ability of the mind to 'image' literal meanings and to go from them to possible figurative interpretations. These include those which Yorio (1980) refers to as 'recoverable' images, giving as examples expressions such as *bumper to bumper* and *shake hands* (see also Lazar 1996; Boers and Demecheleer 2001). Where there are similarities in the basic concepts across languages, the interpretation of figurative expressions can be expected to be easier (Charteris-Black 2002). Horn (2003) further relates degrees of transparency of interpretation to potential for syntactic flexibility, offering a useful link between form and meaning reminiscent of the discussion of Sinclair's approach to form and meaning in chapter 3, section 3.4.

A second consideration, the literature on cognitive metaphors suggests that basic metaphors, often universally comprehensible, underlie many idiomatic expressions; for example, the idioms *let the cat out of the bag* and *spill the beans* share the underlying metaphorical construct of the human mind as a 'container', from which thoughts/information can be released suddenly and involuntarily. There is also evidence to suggest that such metaphors may be activated by key words in the idioms (Tabossi and Zardon 1993). McGlone et al. (1994) suggest that speakers do not ignore the non-idiomatic meanings of individual words in idiomatic expressions, and that even in opaque idioms literal meanings of component words are in some sense activated, or at least are potentially available. Underlying metaphors, Gibbs (1994) and Gibbs and O'Brien (1990) argue, partly enable language users to make sense of idiomatic expressions (see also Kövecses and Szabo 1996). We referred to this argument briefly in connection with the debate over the wisdom of analysing the everyday chunks examined in chapter 3.

But meaning, as always, is best apprehended in context, and in actual contexts of use one can observe relevant aspects of semantic and pragmatic meaning. A case in point is the expression *be a (complete / right / bit of a / absolute / real) pain (in the neck, etc.):* of its 73 occurrences in the CANCODE corpus, 52 refer to things and events and situations, while 21 refer to people. The expression *(let sth.) wash over sb.*, on the other hand, is only used with non-human subjects referring to events and situations. Knowing whether an idiom typically refers to people and things or only to one or the other is clearly an important aspect of knowledge of the expression and is best observed in context. Good dictionaries of idioms encode such information for the user, based on large-scale observations of corpora. But corpora also enable us to immerse ourselves in longer contexts and thus to observe functional aspects of idioms, such as who uses them and when. This is typically done by expanding concordances to include long segments of texts or whole texts.

4.5 Functions of idioms

McCarthy (1998) gave examples of idioms functioning in various generic patterns, such as the characteristic 'observation-comment' pattern, where speakers make an observation about some phenomenon in the world and then evaluate it, with idioms typically occurring in the evaluative segment:

(4.4)

S1:   Well I thought you were gonna go on holiday.

S2:   +yeah. The thing – well I don't think I'm gonna do that now cos none of us can get together at the right time when we want to do it. Which **is a pain in the arse**.

(CANCODE)

(4.5)

[An informal discussion about a book the speakers have read]

S1:   Yet it made a lot of political statements as you were saying, a lot of comments [S2: Mm. Yeah. Yeah.] on even the way the world is today.

S2:   Today. Yeah. I thought that.

S3:   +But I I just felt the whole book was written **tongue in cheek**. I think that was, that was initially his whole point he was just laughing at us. He's **taking the Mickey**.

(CANCODE)

(4.6)

S1:   There's no fast food.

S2:   There's just nothing really nice.

S3:   There's not that many [name of popular restaurant chain] around either.

S2:   No there's only one on um Route twenty-two across from=

S3:   Yeah.

S1:   It's terrible.

S2:   Yeah. And then I was thinking, go and get a sandwich.

S1:   Yeah.

S2:   And then by the time I go to and find a parking spot.

S1:   **You're starving to death**. Yeah.

(CIC North American)

In examples (4.4), (4.5) and (4.6) we have three cases of factual observations or claims, followed by evaluative comments, with idioms performing their characteristic function of evaluation. It is worth noting that in two of the three cases, the comment/evaluation is performed by a speaker other than the one who makes the initial observation. This illustrates the important interactive functions idioms can perform, creating and reinforcing interpersonal relations, projecting informality, camaraderie and social bonding. It also underscores the fundamental characteristic of conversation as jointly created, a point we return to in later chapters.

(4.7)

[Speaker 1 is recounting a story about her car windscreen wipers breaking down]

S1:   Colin erm fixed it sort of you know disconnected the windscreen wipers and that was like in the first week. [S2: Mm mm.] So now it's started raining a bit more I thought I'm gonna have to get it sorted you know. Cos I ended up walking when it's not raining you know and and, no, sorry, I've ended up walking when it's raining rather than the other way round.

S2: Yes. Yeah. Yeah. Yeah. Which **doesn't really make sense** does it.

S1: No. So I thought I'm gonna get this sorted.

(CANCODE)

(4.8)

[Speaker 1, a teacher, is recounting a story about an irritating colleague]

S1: Yeah. This morning he had them first lesson and I had them second and he'd actually come back down into the staff room before the bell had gone.

S2: Mm.

S1: And I just said to him, I tried to be nice, and I just said to him 'Oh have you finished now?' Meaning have you finished with the lesson+

S2: Yeah.

S1: +so I'll go up. And I just said 'Oh have you finished?' He said 'Finished what?' [S2: (laughs)] I said 'Well I meant have you finished your lesson.'

S2: Oh your maths department sounds brilliant with him and Mr Higgins.

S1: (laughs) Oh he's just **driving me round the bend**.

(CANCODE)

Examples (4.7) and (4.8) show typical narrative functions. McCarthy (1998) distinguished between the 'event line' and the 'evaluation line' in narratives, with idioms signalling the evaluation line, as can be seen in (4.7). (For further examples see McCarthy and Carter 1994: 111).

Another context where idioms occurred was in the evaluative elements of narratives (after Labov 1972), where tellers and listeners often use idioms to evaluate the events in terms of their emotive or moral impact and to round off the story in its 'coda' (the end-segment which brings tellers and listeners out of story time and back to real time). Example (4.8) shows an idiom appearing in the coda, where the teller switches back to present time and uses an idiom to round off the story. McCarthy (1998) noted that narrative codas are a particular example of the more general phenomenon of summing up gist at points along the way in a discourse, offering 'formulations' or paraphrases of where participants feel they have got to and judgements of the general significance of what has been said so far (Heritage and Watson 1979). Examples (4.9) and (4.10) illustrate this summarising function of idioms:

(4.9)

S1: I actually went last weekend with, my father was in town and we went and looked at used cars around town. Uh, and I, you know, I found like a nineteen eighty-four Regency Ninety-eight with only forty-six thousand miles on it and that was pretty good condition, uh.

S2: Yeah.

S1: But I also found a nineteen eighty Volvo, uh, station wagon+

S2: Right.

S1: +that was in just super condition. I mean there's not a dent on the outside body, the inside is clean it's had the same owner for years.

S2: Right.

S1: It, it has about eighty thousand miles on it but that's all right, you know, the engine's in excellent shape and I think it would last me probably another fifty or sixty thousand miles.

S2: Yeah.

S1: So, I guess **I'm kind of in limbo** waiting to see what the insurance is, you know, company is going to do, to see whether or not I can get one of these cars.

(CIC North American)

(4.10)

[Speaker 1 has been encouraging Speaker 2 to keep looking for a job in her area.]

S1: Keep, **keep an eye on it**.

S2: Yeah.

S1: To see what comes up. Because good jobs do come up in Bradford occasionally. Might just tempt you.

S2: Okay.

S1: All right.

S2: All right then.

S1: So **keep an eye on it**.

(CANCODE)

Other general conversational contexts where idioms are found were also noted by McCarthy (1998) and by Powell (1985, 1992), including more creative aspects of idiom usage, the 'unpacking' of idioms and word play, a point we return to in chapter 9, section 9.7 (see also Fernando 1996; Carter and McCarthy 2004).

4.6 Idioms in specialised contexts

We argued in chapter 3 that common chunks were sensitive to registers and genres, and would thus expect the same to be true of the low-frequency opaque idioms. Here we consider the occurrence of idioms in more specialised contexts, and focus on two areas, spoken business English and academic English. Neither context is immediately associated with the occurrence of idiomatic expressions in most people's minds, perhaps owing to the early days of ESP/LSP in the 1970s and 1980s, where the focus was often on the more informational/transactional functions of language at the expense of the interpersonal. However, there is no shortage of idioms in business and academic data. Using the one-million-word CANBEC spoken English corpus (see appendix 1), McCarthy and Handford (2004) observed how the discussion of problems among business colleagues was often given an informal flavour in an atmosphere of camaraderie by the use of idioms. The business data in CANBEC is predominantly about problem-solving and consensus making (e.g. striking deals, deciding on courses of action), and the occurrence of idioms often supports these core goals. An example from the data illustrates this, where evaluations of people's roles in creating and solving problematic issues is foregrounded:

(4.11)
[Recorded at an internal meeting between the technical manager and a technician in a British internet service provider company.]

S1: Okay. So we know full well the account manager's not gonna tell them cos the account manager **doesn't give two hoots**. All right. So the next person it comes from is DLM who send the customer a fax and I know DLM haven't been doing that because they they realize that they're gonna **get it in the neck** from the customer. Cos the customer will see a thing which says 'Right let's do a concrete example.' So let's say a customer says be on site by nine.

S2: Yeah.

[1 min]

S1: For this and of course the overtime will just be deducted from= Well either the over-time'll be deducted from the account manager or somehow Componet'll just pay this which I can't believe will happen.

S2: Yeah.

S1: Yeah? So it'll get deducted from the account managers which means the account managers'll **be up in arms** but then tough. Cos **the buck's gotta stop somewhere** and I don't see why it should stop with well I don't see why it necessarily should stop with BJE.

S2: Yeah.

S1: Well it's been on the agenda. And I mailed you about it. I mailed the whole team about it. Cos in your= Well either way it's got to be resolved.

S2: Yeah.

S1: Cos it's a **it's a pain in the arse for everybody** at the minute.

S2: I know I know. I know.

S1: All right?

S2: Yeah.

(CANBEC)

Such data raises similar issues for the LSP context to those which native-speaker casual conversation data do for the teaching of general spoken English, that is to say a high degree of intimacy and in-group membership is projected by such idiomatic usage. Many students of business English may never find themselves in such chummy native-speaker environments or indeed ever doing business with native speakers at all, yet nonetheless conducting their affairs in English. As always, the use or rejection of such material in any individual pedagogical context should be left to teachers and learners to decide, especially in the business domain, where students are likely to be mature individuals perfectly capable of making their own decisions as to what they wish to study. The point is that the specialised corpus offers the opportunity to explore business cultures and to see how idiomatic language is exploited in characteristic ways, albeit in a context where such study may not have as its goal the acquisition and use of such language.

A similar case can be made for academic English, though here perhaps the need to confront the actual language used is usually more pressing, since so many students travel to study and live in countries where English is a native language. Simpson and Mendis (2003), using the 1.7 million-word MICASE corpus of spoken academic English (see appendix 1), found that idioms were distributed across all types of academic disciplines and situations, with no particular concentrations in any one context, and that idioms constituted a 'not-insignificant feature of the lexical landscape of academic speech' (p. 427). Idioms occur in the MICASE data with a variety of functions, including the observation-comment function already mentioned in this chapter, as well as description, paraphrase and other functions. Simpson and Mendis (ibid.) offer a list of useful idioms for the spoken academic contexts and in their list one can see how many of the idioms serve the description and evaluation of knowledge and its transmission, with items such as *bottom line, the big picture, come into play, get a grasp of, get to the bottom of things, go off on a tangent,* etc.

Following up on Simpson and Mendis' study, Murphy and O'Boyle (2005) performed a similar analysis on 20 hours of data from the one million-word LIBEL Corpus of Academic Spoken English (see appendix 1). Murphy and O'Boyle found overlaps with MICASE in both forms and functions (e.g. both corpora had *bottom line, down the line, come into play, hand in hand, thumbs up, get a handle on, take one's word for it*), and found 37 idioms in their 20 hours of data, distributed fairly evenly across monologic and dialogic data, as were the idioms in MICASE. Murphy and O'Boyle additionally found idioms such as *on the same track, lose track of (the meaning), both sides of the same coin, the other side of the coin, part and parcel, the nitty gritty, take on board,* again showing the relationship between the construction and transmission of disciplinary knowledge and the informality and interpersonal and cultural bonding projected in the use of these idioms. If it is true that idioms do project a high degree of interpersonal closeness, then it is further worthy of note that the monologic academic data seem to be as interpersonally charged, at least in this respect, as dialogic contexts, in both studies.

Examples from the spoken academic data segment of CIC showing the use of some of the idioms mentioned are given here. All three examples strike friendly, informal notes in what are otherwise formal contexts. (4.12) is a law lecture, perhaps typically conceived of as a rather dry, impersonal affair, (4.13) is a seminar on politics where the seminar leader obviously feels a necessity to bring the students to the nub of the issue in a non-threatening way, and (4.14) is an individual consultation where, again, the dissertation supervisor projects a more informal relationship leading up to telling the student to get on with the work:

(4.12)
[From a lecture on contract law]

To what extent are terms and contracts between business controlled by the Act?' Now w= how would you answer that? [long pause] Well, er you need, you know you have to **get a handle on** er saying to what extent are terms and contracts between business. Well erm what sections of the Act I mean is the Act designed and is its application dependent on whether contracts are between businesses or whether they're between businesses and consumers or not?

(CIC)

(4.13)

[From a politics seminar]

No. It's You've actually all around the point. You're scattered around the point. The critical point is they devalued because. You're telling me what happened when they devalued like structural adjustments all that. Let's just **get down to the nitty gritty**. They devalued because of huge IMF pressure on France to cut the currency link. The IMF have been saying These countries are in the mire. They can't repay debt. They're never going to get anywhere.

(CIC)

(4.14)

[From a one-to-one PhD supervision]

Student: You have to have something to talk. This is you have to feel that what you're saying is worth=

Supervisor: Yeah. Is worth saying.

Student: Yeah.

Supervisor: Cos otherwise we can all bluff. And we know+

Student: I know

Supervisor: +we're, we're professional at bluffing. And we we can we can build castles+

Student: [laughs]

Supervisor: +on nothing. And and we do it every day in our teaching **somewhere down the line**.

Student: Mm.

Supervisor: But then when you want when you've actually got to put words down and it's gotta be solid that's when=

Student: Mhm.

Supervisor: Good. Right. Get on with it then.

(CIC)

The two studies of spoken academic data and the study of spoken business data seem to suggest that using specialised corpora focusing on particular discourse communities can produce insights into how idioms are used to create and reinforce particular cultures and types of relationships within the members of those communities. In support of this, we may note that Wenger (1998) points to the importance of jokes, stories, lore, idioms and metaphors, which become the routine ways of confronting problems in institutions and which help to construct and solidify communities of practice. Idioms have been shown to be created among small groups or those with shared interests (for example, see Gibbon 1981), right down to partnered couples, where intimacy is often accompanied by private lexicons of expressions (see Hopper et al. 1981).

4.7 Idioms in teaching and learning

In a pioneering investigation of a substantial non-native-user spoken English corpus, Prodromou (2005) raises fundamental questions about what he calls the 'paradox' of idiomaticity: the very thing which, for native speakers, promotes ease of processing and fluent production (Fillmore 1979) seems to present non-native users with an insurmountable obstacle. Try as they may, many advanced SUEs (see chapter 1 and Prodromou 2003a and b) still have problems with idioms, even when they have mastered most other aspects of the language system. And Prodromou is not alone in adducing evidence of these high-level difficulties; many studies have shown under-use of idioms amongst learners and other non-native users in comparison with native-speaker data, or avoidance of idioms in favour of single-word or other more literal alternatives, or errors in form and function (Bahns et al. 1986; Kellerman 1986; Hulstijn and Marchena 1989; Yorio 1989; Arnaud and Savignon 1997; De Cock 1998, 2000; Altenberg and Granger 2001; Meierkord 2005).

Several problems seem to lie at the root of the apparent 'deficit' (a term used guardedly here) in idiom-learning and use as opposed to the impressive levels of grammatical and non-idiomatic lexical proficiency in English which many SUEs achieve. Firstly, because of their varying degrees of syntactic and lexical flexibility, and because of their often specialised pragmatic attributes, idioms are, simply, difficult to get right. Secondly, as Irujo (1986) pointed out, idioms, even when correctly produced, can sound strange on the lips of non-native users. One often hesitates to use idioms in a foreign language even if one knows them; it is as if one is claiming a cultural membership and identity one has no right to or does not wish to lay claim to. In this situation, there can be no question of a 'deficit' of any kind. Thirdly, as Prodromou convincingly shows, idioms do not just 'pop up' in native-speaker speech; rather they occur as part of:

> . . . a more extended and diffuse phenomenon that generates subtle webs of semantic, pragmatic and discourse prosodies. It is through these situated webs of signification that L1-users achieve fluency and the promotion of self rather than in the manipulation of isolated idiomatic units *in vacuo*.
>
> (Prodromou 2005: 2)

Prodromou also refers to 'networks of semantic, discourse and pragmatic prosodies' (ibid.: 295). The CANBEC business data in example (4.11) above well illustrates this notion of a 'situated web' or network of meanings in the way idioms weave in and out of the talk alongside other pragmatic markers and serve to structure the problem-solving episode while creating a particular type of relationship and collegiate bond for the participants.

Such appropriate, contextualised use, embedded in the native user's lifetime experience of socio-cultural practices, cannot simply be 'picked up' in a language course, however intensive and however authentic the data learners are exposed to. Native speakers may well be taught spelling, pronunciation and grammar and aspects of formality during their years of schooling, but they are generally not *taught* the appropriate use of idioms; it is a long-term 'priming' (Hoey 2005) of the items which builds in the native user over many years. There are several possible pedagogical conclusions which can be drawn from these three militating factors.

The first conclusion might be not to bother with idioms at all, since (a) they are simply too much of a formal obstacle and it may be better to focus on learning and using the many thousands of single words which can largely do the same job, at least from the viewpoint of propositional meaning and (b) for many, interpersonal and socio-cultural meaning will be a (useless or unnecessary) luxury. Provided the learning community of teachers and students are content with this, then such a choice should be respected. We might, at this point, however, still make a useful distinction between the needs of learners and the desirability of increased language knowledge and awareness among teachers during teacher education (see Liu 1998).

A second option is to question the input–output metaphor that informs a lot of thinking about language learning. Partly due to the dominance of utilitarian approaches to language learning from the 1970s onwards, the more traditional, belletristic approaches to language learning (which typically included literary and cultural studies) have slipped into the twilight in many areas of the world. But there is still undoubtedly a place in many educational contexts for learning about the colourful, cultural aspects of language and for observing cultures as they live through their words and actions, without any presupposition that the goal is short-term or even long-term lexical acquisition or production. There is indeed room for 'play' in language, the sheer enjoyment of handling words and expressions, uttering them and sharing them. Such a non-utilitarian view of language learning also opens the door to allowing the non-native learner to appropriate idiomatic expressions and make them their own. As Kramsch and Sullivan (1996) argue, learners may be encouraged to 'acquire correct and idiomatic forms of English, but then use these forms with the poetic licence of the non-native speaker' and 'create their own context of use according to the values cherished in their national, professional-academic, or institutional culture' (p. 210). In situations which are not threatened by the sanctions of tests and consequent risk of failure, such explorations can be motivating, enjoyable and creative. And where non-native speakers use idioms, with whatever degree of departure from the native-speaker norm, as long as comprehensibility for the target listeners is not impaired, there should be no necessary censure or labelling of 'error'. A recent example, on the junior version of the annual *Eurovision Song Contest*, broadcast primarily to a non-native-speaking European audience in English and French, was seen in the programme anchor's reference to 'being back on tracks', after the restoration of a break in the show's continuity. British native-speaker usage only permits singular *track* here, but in situations such as this, what Weinert (1995: 195) refers to as 'faulty grammatical rules' that seep into conventionalised language usage need not be seen as problematic at all (Prodromou 2005 gives further examples of non-native variations on native-speaker norms).

A third recourse is to engage in the teaching of idioms based on sets of relatively more frequent ones, ones which non-native users are at least likely to hear and see when confronted with native-speaker data, whether it be printed or electronic media, or films, TV and popular music, especially in an age of increasing global availability of such material. If this be the choice, then we would argue that basing one's evidence on a spoken corpus would be most likely to offer the best preparation for what the learner is likely to hear. In this respect, we would support the kinds of language awareness activities and exposure to corpus data (albeit edited and in longer extracts than just single concordance lines) which Simpson and Mendis (2003) have shown to be both usable and popular with their students. Simpson and Mendis (ibid.) and Murphy and O'Boyle (2005) show that it is possible to extract useful lists of the most frequent idioms from their specialised corpora. In these specialised cases the dividends in terms of increased comprehension and motivation are likely to be tangible, but the same will probably also be the case with more general spoken data.

Language awareness means discussing, perhaps through one's own language and looking at data, why idioms are being used and by whom (for example in advertising texts, where idioms are often used to project a friendly, informal relationship between the advertiser and the potential customer, a situation more likely to be conducive to successful sales). The role of the first language in terms of either positive transfer or idiom-avoidance is a complex one, but there is some evidence that, in the mental processing of collocations, formulaic sequences and idioms in a second language, the first (or third or fourth) language plays a role (Nesselhauf 2003; Spöttl and McCarthy 2004). Some materials on teaching idioms draw on transfer, or lack of it, between languages, for example McLay (1987), which offers speakers of some European languages cues in their L1 to assist them in choosing the appropriate English idiom (see figure 2).

The more contexts observed, the more likely it is that greater insights will be available as to what idioms are and what they are for. The discussion may indeed range from whether such items are worth studying, or whether they may be worth learning for receptive purposes, or whether they may be worthy of serious attention in the same way that other vocabulary is. Unless teachers and learners find themselves in the unenviable position of being forced by the curriculum to study idioms, language awareness sessions open the way to making informed choices.

The importance of looking at idioms in context has benefits for the awareness of recurrent formal features too, as Coulmas (1981a) has argued. In this chapter, we have suggested that a wide variety of idiom types are in everyday circulation in native-speaker English; seeing these in actual contexts of use will give a better feel for their distribution than simply studying a list of idioms. Lattey (1986) suggests organising the contexts in which idioms occur on the basis of recurrent pragmatic functions (for example, interaction of speaker and listener, speaker and outside world, positive evaluations and negative evaluations of people and phenomena, etc.), rather as our data sampling and categorisation suggested. McCarthy and O'Dell (2002), using a database of idioms extracted from the

Figure 2: Extract from *Idioms at Work* (McLay 1987: 54–55)

9. Complaining or Commiserating

a. **pull the wool over other people's eyes**
b. **a stab in the back**
c. **pay lip service to**
d. **fed up to the teeth with**
e. **get away with murder**
f. **That's below the belt.**
g. **talk behind (his) back**
h. **take (someone) for granted**
i. **fob (someone) off**
j. **isn't pulling (his) weight**

THAT'S QUITE A STAB IN THE BACK

MPHFF!!

HITTING BELOW THE BELT

Fill in the blanks with the best idiom from the list above. Use the equivalents below each situation to help you. Answers at the back of the book.

1. I know what I'd do to those kids next door if they were mine.
    I agree. They're completely out of hand.
    It's high time their parents did something. They let them ____
    _____ .
    Young parents are all the same these days. Anything goes as far as they're concerned.

    do bad things without being punished
    s'en tirer impunément   *salirse con la suya*
    sie erlauben ihnen alles   *lasciare fare totto quello, che vogliono*

2. I'm (1) _____ Linda Brown; the boss thinks she's a great worker because, whenever he's around, she really tries to impress him. But when he's not there she doesn't do any work at all.
    I hate people like that who try to (2) _____, but I suppose one of these days he's going to find out the truth.

    (1) annoyed by someone's behaviour over a long period of time
    (2) deceive someone into thinking well of them
    (1) par dessus le tête   *(1) hasta las narices*
    (2) jettent de la poudre aux yeux de quelqu'un   *(2) engañar a alguien*
    (1) ich habe die Nase gestrichen voll mit   *(1) averne fin sopra i capelli*
    (2) einem Sand in die Augen streuen   *(2) gettare fumo negli occhi*

54   55

Cambridge International Corpus, in their self-study materials for idioms, organise contexts around typical conversational areas (e.g. *dealing with problems, reacting to what others say*), as well as more notional, metaphorical and topic-oriented areas (e.g. *necessity and desirability, colour, weapons and war*). Figure 3 (overleaf), an extract from their book, attempts to build practical pedagogy around the observation-comment function discussed in this chapter, where a second speaker typically uses an idiom to comment on something in the first speaker's utterance. The follow-up exercise then gives students the opportunity to produce similar comment-utterances using idioms, in response to stimulus utterances.

Wright (1999) includes sections on metaphors in the organisation of the contents of his teaching material for idioms. These include animal metaphors (see also Nesi 1995), metaphors based on parts of the body, and various other categories, including conceptual metaphors such as *Life is a journey* and *Business is war*. Given the discussions on the role of metaphor in the mental processing of idioms, this would seem to be a laudable approach with great potential for increasing language awareness and improving comprehension (see Boers 2000, who also suggests classroom activities).

Replicating in the classroom and in materials, however artificially, the contexts in which idioms typically occur is likely to be more motivating to learners than decontextualised attempts to understand and remember these tricky items, not least because in actual contexts idioms often contain their own paraphrases or at least many clues as to their meaning. We have seen, for example, that idioms occur naturally in narratives, and so help-

Figure 3: Extract from *English Idioms in Use* (McCarthy and O'Dell, 2002: 38)

15   Reacting to what others say

A   Complete phrases

possible stimulus	response	meaning of response
I understood everything he said to me in French. I was just pretending not to.	Really? **You could've fooled me!**	You do not believe what someone says about something that you saw or experienced yourself.
Josh adores cowboy films!	**There's no accounting for taste(s)!**	You can't understand why someone likes or doesn't like something.
Are you prepared to hand in your notice to stop them going ahead with their plans?	Yes, **if all else fails!**	If all other plans do not work.
What do you think of the Labour candidate in the election?	**The lesser of two evils,** I suppose.	It is the less unpleasant of two bad options.
How did we get into this terrible position?	**One thing just led to another.**	A series of events happened, each caused by the previous one.
It was such a stupid thing to say to her.	I know. **I'll never live it down!**	You think that you have done something bad or embarrassing that people will never forget.
My boss just congratulated me on my report. Should I ask him for a pay rise now?	Yes, go on. **Strike while the iron is hot.**	Do something immediately while you have a good chance of success.
How are you going to live on such a small salary?	I don't know – **one way or another.**	You are not sure exactly how yet, but it will happen.

ing learners incorporate idioms into their own personal narratives and histories may assist in acquiring at least receptive competence. Encouraging learners to connect idioms with their own personal experiences (Bergstrom 1979), or any kind of personalisation, is widely considered to be a good aid to learning. One can begin with skeletal narratives and then work on them to add, where appropriate, idiomatic expressions. McCarthy, McCarten and Sandiford (2006b: 100) build idioms into a narrative and suggest grouping the idioms according to different stages of the story as an aid to learning. All this can be done in a context where it is understood that the object of the exercise is not necessarily productive use outside of the class, but rather the building of receptive knowledge, the fostering of memorability and the development of language awareness.

Earlier we mentioned that idioms, with all the socio-cultural baggage they bring with them, might have no place in a world where English is used as lingua franca (ELF). However, some things need clarifying. It has yet to be demonstrated that ELF exists as a *variety* of English rather than as a *function* of the use of English, which responds to every context differently (rather in the way that people adapt their language for use with small children or animals). The assumption that ELF is a variety brings with it several common inferences: that the variety is in some way a 'reduced' form of the native variety, that the reduced repertoire can inform a consequently reduced syllabus, and that idioms are likely to be one of the features that can be dispensed with. If it could be shown that ELF is a variety (or, more likely, a series of varieties manifesting differently in different parts of the world) and that the variety or varieties was characterised by an idiom-free, efficient lexicon, then there may be good arguments for de-emphasising idioms. Here, once again, there would be no question of talking about a 'deficit'. But if we are in fact talking about a function of English, then there would seem to be no a priori reason to 'reduce' anything; users would make their own choices from their available repertoire of forms, just as any normal person does when adapting to any context. Much research still remains to be done in this area, and until satisfactory evidence can be brought to bear on the nature of ELF, the jury must remain out, though recent research by Roberts (2005) suggests that there is no obvious lack of orientation to interpersonal meaning in ELF situations. We need more information on how ELF users achieve interpersonal harmony and construct human relations, and what part, if any, idiomatic expressions play in such interactions. In the meantime, what seems to persist, despite the healthy and vigorous debates, is teachers' and learners' natural curiosity towards and interest in idioms, and it is in the service of that positive interest that corpus-based studies can best make their contribution by providing evidence of the forms and functions of idioms in use. This chapter has shown that there are no easy answers as to how we get from corpus to classroom in the case of idioms, but the corpus evidence does suggest, both formally and functionally, ways in which idioms might be incorporated into teaching in a manner which better reflects their actual use and which can engage students with this area of language without necessarily pressuring them into using a type of vocabulary which displays such a strong claim to native-speaker ownership.

5 **Grammar and lexis and patterns**

5.1 **Introduction**

Throughout this book so far we have discussed how corpus evidence can be used to draw attention to features and patterns of words that may not always be noticed by relying on our intuition, however extensive this may be. For example, we have seen in chapter 1 how information from the concordances for words such as *bargain* or *way* may display patterns that tell us about the key partnerships a word has with other words, about the most frequent prepositions it takes or about the kinds of idiomatic functions revealed by its usage. We have also seen that, although we conventionally regard words as single items, they habitually occupy the territory of other words or of strings of words. Sometimes these patterns, if they occur regularly, force us to speak of common collocations, idiomatic expressions and chunks (see chapters 2, 3 and 4). In this chapter, we take an important next step and consider the ways in which words combine to form particular grammatical patterns. A corpus can once again assist us in this endeavour.

A corpus can tell us different things about grammar. It can extend our understanding of traditional grammatical notions and categories, in particular by giving us more information about the distribution of these categories (see below the example of *'s not* and *isn't*) or, for example, across specific spoken and written registers of the language (Biber et al. 1999, is a very good example of this latter kind of information). Because corpus software is especially adept at identifying patterns associated with individual words, it can help us to isolate grammatical points that are particularly associated with certain words, (see the example of *yet* below). Or a corpus can indicate important links between grammar and lexis (Sinclair 1990, 1996b, 1998 offer many good examples). A corpus can do this in different ways. For example, a corpus can highlight an unusual or unexpected grammatical environment for particular lexical items such as the word *border* (see below), and it can illustrate different semantic and attitudinal associations between lexical words and grammatical words. And a corpus can also provide more information about a key form and underline lexico-grammatical and semantic patterns associated with the form. The study of the '*get*-passive' form in this chapter is an example of this latter feature.

This chapter examines a range of these examples and others related to them. We begin by looking at concordance lines for an individual word that sits on the border of grammar and lexis. Let us consider the concordance lines in Figure 1 for the word *yet* taken from CANCODE.

Figure 1: Concordance lines from CANCODE for *yet*

```
        <$2> Yeah. We haven't got any answer yet We'd like it trimming. <$E> laughs
   the wedding.        <$2> I haven't got any yet. Em <$069> Janet looked lovely <\$06>
 but we haven't made er any arrangements yet it's sort of er a bit too early yet
 ?     <$1> Sorry?      <$2> Has FX arrived yet?       <$1> Who is this?      <$2> MX's f
  be in.      <$2> They haven't arrived as yet.       <$1> <$=> It is a whole <\$=> it
  yet?      <$1> No not a price breaker as yet. Just their own winter programme.
 ame in. <$E> laughs <\$E> Erm but er as yet it's not available in every store.
 ll over the place. Em we haven't got as yet a timetable to show you as to what's
  haven't come have they?      <$2> Not as yet. No. Normally about two weeks before
 . Well I said I don't know the story as yet.      <$2> Mm.      <$1> <$=> I said But
 . But they're not putting anybody up as yet because they have an appeal launch r
 ms. Er that's still not p= er set up as yet though. Erm we're gonna do something
 n't managed to mark any of your work as yet but I I promise I'll have it back to
 Manda are you ready for your assessment yet?      <$F> I think so yeah.      <$1> I'
  Anyway you obviously haven't gone back yet so <$=> erm I won't be er <\$=> you
 t know. <$G?>       <$1> Oh he's not back yet.      <$2> No.      <$1> Oh right.      <
 eeks ago. And he he hasn't written back yet. So <$E> laughs </$E>      <$1> No. Mm
 G?>.      <$4> Have you changed your bank yet?      <$3> My turn. <$E> sighs <\$E>
    <$1> Bye. Cheers.       <$3> Won't be yet until I've <$013> lost <\$013> a lit
 <$2> Have you seen Beauty And The Beast yet?      <$1> No I was wanting to go.
 p to see me every year. She hasn't been yet. And she and I like to trip out on a
 tomorrow.      <$6> No. No. Not for a bit yet.      <$3> Good.      <$6> We we thought
```

These sample lines show us that in uses of *yet* a negative environment is very common and that *as yet* is a commonly recurring pattern in this environment (the negatives and *as yet* are marked in bold in figure 1). At the same time, however, we might also note that this negative pattern does not seem to be frequent in the case of questions. So in treating the word *yet* in a dictionary entry or learning about its syntactic use as an adverb in a grammar, we would probably want to include these kinds of examples and, by examining more concordances, in the process begin to provide a more complete picture of how *yet* is used.

Another example is the distribution of the contracted negative forms of the present tense of the verb *be*. The authors of the *Touchstone* adult language course (McCarthy, McCarten and Sandiford 2005a) needed to decide whether to prioritise the form *(s)he isn't* or the form *(s)he's not*. The corpus used for *Touchstone* (the North American spoken segment of CIC) showed the distribution given in table 1, below:

Table 1: Frequencies of *he's not, he isn't, she's not, she isn't* from CIC (North American English segment)

form	frequency	form	frequency
he's not	704	he isn't	18
she's not	476	she isn't	15

What emerged was an overwhelming preference for the *'s not* form after pronouns, with the *isn't* form being common after full noun phrases (e.g. *The classroom isn't ready yet.*). It seemed clear, then, that this was useful information for both teachers and learners, and so it was directly presented in the student's book (figure 2).

Figure 2: Extract from *Touchstone* (McCarthy, McCarten and Sandiford 2005a: 25)

3 Grammar Yes-No questions and answers; negatives

Am I late?	Yes, you are.	No, you're not.	You're not late.
Are you busy?	Yes, I am.	No, I'm not.	I'm not busy.
Is he tired?	Yes, he is.	No, he's not.	He's not tired.
Is she strict?	Yes, she is.	No, she's not.	She's not strict. (My boss **isn't** strict.)
Is it hard work?	Yes, it is.	No, it's not.	It's not hard work.
Are we late?	Yes, we are.	No, we're not.	We're not late.
Are they nice?	Yes, they are.	No, they're not.	They're not nice. (My co-workers **aren't** nice.)

About you ➝ Write *yes-no* questions. Then write true answers. Ask and answer the questions with a partner.

1. you / shy ?
   __Are you shy?__   __Yes, I am.__
2. this class / easy ?
   _____   _____
3. the teacher / strict ?
   _____   _____
4. the students in this class / lazy ?
   _____   _____
5. your neighbors / nice ?
   _____   _____
6. your friends / outgoing ?
   _____   _____

In conversation . . .

People use **'s not** and **'re not** after pronouns.
   She**'s not** strict.
   They**'re not** nice.

Isn't and **aren't** often follow nouns.
   My boss **isn't** strict.
   My co-workers **aren't** nice.

The above patterns are significant. Knowing such patterns is an important part of the lexico-grammatical competence of a speaker and attention is being increasingly focused on such patterns in teaching and reference materials for language learners. Conventionally, materials for language learners and books on language treat vocabulary and grammar as separate. Dictionaries are dictionaries and deal with words; grammars are grammars and deal with grammatical structure. The study of large corpora makes us question these conventional divisions and helps us see how grammar and lexis interpenetrate and overlap in all kinds of ways (see, in particular, Sinclair 2004 for a range of examples). We discuss this symbiosis further below.

5.2   The example of *border*

In addition to the patterns of frequency noted above, there are also larger patterns that operate in ways that involve both lexico-grammatical and semantic patterns and these are even harder to identify by means of intuition. For example, if we ask a group of students or teachers what is meant by the word *border*, most would probably say that it meant 'the edge or boundary of something'. They would probably also say that the word was both a noun and a verb. As a verb they would probably say further that it had various inflections that embraced the forms *bordered, borders, bordering* and would probably conclude that there was no real difference in the meaning of these various inflections of the verb.

However, an examination of the word *border* in the 100-million-word British National Corpus (BNC) reveals some interesting patterns.

Table 2: Frequencies of patterns of *border* in the BNC

	BNC frequency	x + on
border	8,011	89 (1%)
borders	2,539	84 (3%)
bordering	367	177 (48%)
bordered	356	99 (28%)

Table 2 shows that the forms *border* and *borders* are the most frequent forms from the word family and closer inspection reveals that these are mostly noun forms (singular and plural). However, when these individual forms are studied in patterns, the picture changes. One salient pattern involves the phrase *border* + the preposition *on*. The corpus calculations show that the preposition *on* occurs rarely with the nouns *border* and *borders* but co-occurs frequently with the verb forms *bordering* and *bordered*.[1]

However, the grammatical patterns are not the whole story and simply learning these patterns will only take a learner so far. When we consult a corpus and look more closely at the patterns displayed by the word *border*, it is underlined for us that there are other co-occurrences. As Sinclair (2003a) points out in his reading of concordance lines for this word, we see that there are patterns that are semantic and not simply grammatical. That is, the different combinations produce different meanings. The nouns *border* and *borders* refer literally to 'edges' and 'boundaries', but the verbs *bordered on* and *bordering on* (which account for almost three quarters of the instances of the item 'border') display meanings that are more figurative.

Table 3: Distribution of figurative meanings across *border* forms and patterns

form	figurative sense
border	very rare
borders	very rare
bordering	71%
bordered	75%

[1] Our thanks to Norbert Schmitt (Schmitt 2006) for the calculations here.

Examples include:

(5.1)

His passion for gardening **bordered on** the neurotic.

(BNC)

(5.2)

Their approach to the match was very thorough, **bordering**, in fact, **on** the illegal.

(BNC)

Further corpus searches (sorting only the first few words in an alphabetic order) show the following collocates as complements of *bordered on / bordering on*:

arrogance	*bad taste*	*contempt*
apathy	*blackmail*	*conspiracy*
alcoholism	*carelessness*	*cruelty*
antagonism	*chaos*	*cynicism*

It will be seen that these figurative meanings share a semantic pattern, what Sinclair (1991a, 1996a, 2003a, 2004) and Louw (1993) term 'semantic prosody' (see also chapter 1). There is a distinct preference for collocation with words which indicate something that is undesirable, and often a state of mind that is undesirable.

These lexico-grammatical patterns are systematic and they go beyond a straightforward grammatical description which shows a structure of *noun phrase + be + bordered/bordering + on + noun phrase*. The pattern-based description tells us much more about how particular distributions in the use of the words involve particular meanings. The grammatical patterns entail semantic patterns that learners of the language also need to know (see Schmitt 2006 for further discussion and see also discussion of the phrases *peace and quiet* and *be touched by* in Chapter 2, as well as examples in Willis 2003). Sinclair 1996b and 1998 are major lexico-grammatical studies of this significant phenomenon.

We should also underline here that the pattern of *something + bordered/bordering on + something undesirable* is not an invariable rule. However, it is the case that the pattern is predictable, and therefore probable. The issue of structural, deterministic rules and probabilistic patterns is one that we now consider more fully in the next section.

5.3   Grammar rules and patterns: deterministic and probabilistic

The general lay person's perspective is that grammar is about unchangeable rules of speaking and writing. But not all 'rules' given by grammarians are of the same kind. Some rules are deterministic, that is, they are rules which always and invariably apply. For example, the definite article always comes before the noun (we say *the camera*, not *camera the*), or indicative, third person singular present tense lexical verbs always end in *s* (we say *she sings*, not *she sing*). Other rules are probabilistic, that is to say, they state what is most likely or least likely to apply in particular circumstances. For example, in the overwhelming majority of cases, a relative pronoun (e.g. *who, which, that*) must be used to refer to the subject of a relative clause:

(5.3)

> We spoke to a man **who had photographed** The Beatles in New York.

(CANCODE)

However, *who, which* or *that* may be omitted, especially after a *there* construction, examples of which we find in CANCODE:

(5.4)

> There was a garage in the town rented bicycles.
> (*or* There was a garage in the town which/that rented bicycles)

(CANCODE)

It is not a rule that in such structures the relative pronoun must be omitted, but it can be omitted. It is a pattern that can be selected; and corpus evidence underlines that it is chosen in more informal contexts in both speaking and writing. There are thus deterministic rules about the pronouns *who, which* or *that* (e.g. that *who* refers to animate beings, not things). But there are also probabilistic rules concerning their use. It is probable, in most cases, that the relative pronoun will be used, but when a user chooses to omit it, the likelihood is high that the context of use will be informal. In this book, we acknowledge the practical usefulness of structural rules, but also argue throughout for the importance of patterns that are probabilistic, since they are based on observations of what is most likely and least likely in different contexts in real spoken and written data, and what learners are most likely to read or hear, especially if they experience native-speaker usage. We also recognise that pedagogic accounts of these kinds of patterns need to be addressed and that, rather than simply learning what is correct and incorrect, it can be difficult for learners of a language to come to terms with the idea of choices and probabilities.[2]

---

[2] Itkonen (1980: 338) makes a contrast between 'correct sentences' and 'factually uttered sentences', which illustrates an important principle of probabilistic grammars. Such grammars need real corpus data to verify their claims, as we have attempted to show in this chapter. Probabilistic grammar has a considerable history: Halliday (1961: 259) saw the fundamental nature of language as probabilistic and not as 'always this and never that'. Halliday has resorted to corpus evidence to ratify his view. His concern has been with how frequently the terms in binary grammatical systems (e.g. *present* versus *non-present*) actually occur in relation to each other, and he concludes that the statistics of actual occurrence are 'an essential property of the system – as essential as the terms of the opposition itself' (1991: 31). Nesbitt and Plum (1988) also take a predominantly quantitative line in their study of the distribution of clause complexes in real data, and are interested in what is more likely or less likely to occur, rather than what may possibly occur. See also Aarts (1991) and Leech (1991) for further discussion along such lines.

5.4   The *get*-passive: an extended case study

There are also many other lexico-grammatical patterns that are differently distributed between informal spoken and formal written English and which contract different meanings when used in these different environments. Using evidence from a sub-corpus of 1.5 million words of everyday, informal, spoken British English in CANCODE, we now explore a key feature of English grammar: the passive voice. We devote a case study to this form because it is a core grammatical pattern that manifests both structural rules and variable contexts of meaning and use from which speakers and writers can select. We explore corpus-based frequencies in structure and pattern with particular reference to how the *get*-passive is used in informal spoken British English, contrasting it with the standard passive form. Our corpus sample contains 139 *get*-passives of the type *X get + past particle (by Y)*: for example, *Our letter got lost by the chief clerk.*

5.5   Previous studies of the *get*-passive

One early study of the *get/be* contrast in passive voice usage (Hatcher 1949) noted that the co-occurrence of the *get*-passive with an explicitly stated human subject (or 'agent') was quite unlikely, though impersonal or depersonalised agents might occur (the term 'agent' is another term for the entity which acts in a clause). Hatcher did not base her statements on a corpus, but did conclude that *get* will be used only for the two types of events just treated: those felt as having either 1) fortunate, or 2) unfortunate consequences for the subject. Our corpus evidence suggests, contrary to Hatcher, that human subjects are present, but that the association of the *get*-passive with unfortunate consequences is relevant. Figure 3 shows some sample concordance lines from the CANCODE sub-corpus.

Here we see that a pattern emerges where the *get*-passive relates to things happening to a human subject that may not be desired or intended and that the outcomes of actions

Figure 3: Concordance lines of *get*-passive from CANCODE

```
you heard of anybody any neighbours who got  broken into recently? I know
        any extra precautions since the car got  broken into last time? Er well I
        he jilted her at the altar. So so she got  brought up by her grandmother
she's been a bit nervous ever since we got  burgled once Yeah. That was a
        done that so I suppose I could have got  caned. Yeah. And as you've gone
   ol for being honest. Mm. You know he     got  called an idiot for being honest.
              yeah. To the machines. They all got  deported in the end didn't they
know it didn't seem much point. No. All got  deported I think. Every one of
            mm. And this chap actually he he got  done for either the drugs. Cos it
     that should have been white but it got  dyed grey in the wash and my
        yeah. Anyway tell us about when you got  er picked up. About the hitch
randmother not her real mother then she got  jilted at the altar by this fellow
        and she was saying that they she they got  kerb crawled her and her friend
        the Social from the Job Centre. I got  led up the garden path a fair few
suppose and some do it you know. Em I got  offered a job about three weeks
        then all of a sudden they em got they got  raided by the police. Mm. And shop
        and told you about them. Mm. tuts.    Got  ripped off didn't I.
```

are commonly problematic or adversative. A full description of the passive voice, including the use of the standard *be*-passive, would therefore need to account for these attitudinal or interpersonal functions on the part of the speaker.

This argument is illustrated further by Lakoff (1971), who also centres the discussion more firmly on speaker attitude. Lakoff's study was not corpus-based, and it additionally focuses on the relationship between the surface (grammatical subject) of the clause and the logical subject. The *be*-passive is more concerned with the logical subject, and the *get*-passive with the surface subject, such that *he got killed* focuses on *he* rather than who killed him (tying in with the unlikelihood of the occurrence of an explicit agent). Such a view is in no way in conflict with one that sees the *get*-passive as an attitudinal marker, since the attitude in *get*-passive utterances in our data is indeed normally directed towards the fate or condition of the grammatical subject (sometimes referred to in the literature as the 'patient' to contrast with the actions and doings of an 'agent'). Granger (1983), using a 160,000-word sample from the Survey of English Usage corpus (see appendix 1), finds statistical support for the lack of focus on agency: of nine *get*-passives, only one has an explicit (in this case indefinite, non-human) agent, a figure which tallies reasonably well with the number of such agents in our own, almost ten-times larger sample from CANCODE.

The views outlined above would suggest that agency is always secondary in passive utterances; in the *get*-passive case, where agency is usually implicit, there would seem to be a further downgrading of the agent and consequent highlighting of the patient (and event). More recently, in a corpus-based study along the lines of this case study, Collins (1996) has provided large-scale evidence of *get*-passives and their occurrence in a corpus of 5.25 million words. Although larger than the present corpus, Collins' corpus is a mixed spoken and written one, and the fact that Collins isolates 291 'central' *get*-passives (i.e. one per 1,800 words), compared with our 139 (i.e. one per 1,080 words) is probably a reflection of the lower probability of occurrence of *get*-passives in written texts. Collins, following Quirk et al. (1985: 167–71), prefers to think of a 'passive gradient' on which varying degrees of agentivity are manifested. Collins also discusses possible restrictions on the occurrence of *get*, in sentences such as *Paddy got known to be an IRA sympathiser* (though some corpus evidence might suggest caution in forbidding such utterances), and it is clear that some sentences, to say the least, sound highly unlikely with *get*-passive instead of *be* (e.g. factual information statements such as *The steam engine got invented in the nineteenth century* and truly stative passives such as *The house is/*gets surrounded by fields.*) As well as examining the question of a gradient of passive meanings related to different forms, Collins' paper offers a useful description of the different distributions of the *get*-passive across different varieties of English. However, although Collins notes the importance of providing corpus evidence for the *get*-passive, his paper is purely descriptive, and he does not put his findings to the service of any wider implications for grammatical description, unlike the present study.

We thus have, to date, a variety of studies both non-corpus-based and corpus-based which have homed in on various aspects of the *get*-passive, but all of which seem to be agreed that the form is closely related to *be*-passives, with a different focus on agent, event and patient, and with some marking of attitude, however achieved.

5.6 *Get*-passives and related forms

The *get*-passive is thus difficult to pin down to any one structural configuration, and a range of forms occurs with closely related meanings. In our case study, we shall focus on type **a** constructions (see Table 4 below), which Collins (1996) also found to be of central importance and of the highest frequency in his corpus. But before we turn to our more specific focus, it is worth considering how the various passive forms relate to one another as potential alternatives. Table 4 shows types **a** to **g**, with 'passive' alternatives where these are possible, or, in the case of **g**, with an active equivalent too.

Table 4: Range of structural configurations of *get*-passive and their passive alternatives

type	example	alternative(s)
a	**He got killed** trying to save some other man.	*He was killed* trying to save some other man.
b	You see, if ever **you get yourself locked out**	You see, if ever *you are locked out*
c	**Rian got his nipple pierced** and it was so gross.	i *Rian had his nipple pierced* and it was so gross. ii *Rian nipple was pierced* and it was so gross.
d	**She got me to do a job for her,** fencing.	*She had me (to) do a job for her,* fencing.
e	**The tape seems to have got stuck.**	i *The tape seems to have become stuck.* ii *The tape seems to be stuck.*
f	Right we've got to **get you kitted out**	i Right we've got to *have you kitted out* ii Right we've got to *kit you out*
g	**They've had the phone cut off.**	i *Their phone's been cut off.* ii *They got their phone cut off.*

The alternative to **a** seems to neutralise the attitudinal signalling of original **a**. The **b** alternative removes the marking of agency/responsibility of the grammatical subject in original **b**. The **ci** alternative retains agency and seems to differ from original **c** only in degree of formality, while **cii** neutralises agency and is ambiguous between description of a state and reporting of an event. The **d** alternative is like **ci**, apparently affecting degree of formality only. The **ei** alternative likewise affects formality, but the **eii** alternative removes the emphasis on *change* of state. Original **f** is ambiguous between speaker as agent and some other party as agent; alternative **fi** retains this ambiguity, **fii** removes it, with speaker clearly as agent. Original **g** is ambiguous as to the volitional involvement of the patient; **gi** removes patient involvement, while **gii** retains it, still ambiguously, and less formally.

There is thus every reason to conclude that *get-* (and *have-*) 'pseudo-passive' constructions carry meanings on a 'cline of passiveness', or the 'passive gradient' that Gnutzmann (1991) refers to. Choices of construction clearly involve presence and/or absence of (potential) participants, degree of active involvement of those participants (or put another way, degree of 'passivity'), a differentiation between events and changes of state, and an as yet unspecified difference between *be* and *get*.

The complexity of passive and pseudo-passive forms in English is amply illustrated by the consideration of the various alternatives, and what is clear is that speakers may mark agency and involvement of participants in various ways, and that a range of syntactic choices is available. Why such a range of choice should exist can best be explained by seeing the grammar as offering the speaker different perspectives and positions from which to report events; such perspectives not only influence the information-structure of messages, but also the interpersonal interpretation of speaker stance and attitude, and the degree of perceived formality. Type **a**, however, is more specifically problematic, since the choice between *be* and *get* seems purely attitudinal. It is to this we now turn in greater detail, deferring for the moment but recognising at the same time the importance for this book of the question of how lexico-grammatical choices are presented to language learners.

5.7 Core *get*-passive constructions in the CANCODE sub-corpus

Verbs and contexts

The CANCODE 1.5-million-word sample contains 139 type **a** *get*-passives, from which strongly patterned regularities emerge. 124 of the 139 examples refer in some way or another to what we have termed 'adversative' contexts, i.e. a semantic prosody that is perceived by the conversational participants as unfortunate, undesirable, or at least problematic. A number of these include verb phrases that are inherently adversative in their semantics, for example:

get arrested
get flung about in the car
get killed
get locked in/out
get lumbered [= landed with an unpleasant job]
get picked on
get sued
get burgled
get intimidated
get criticised
get beaten

get penalised
get stopped (by the police)
get nicked [= stolen]
get done [for fraud; done = charged]
get kicked off

Some typical contexts follow:

(5.5)

> S1: Was it the electricity that killed him?
> S2: No no it was the pylon.
> S1: The impact . . . I mean he'd have **got flung about** in the car, wouldn't he? Probably broke his neck.

(CANCODE)

(5.6)

['The halls' are student halls of residence]

> S1: Oh God that is a nightmare. Cos like loads of them aren't there, all, like they **got** like **kicked off the halls**.
> S2: Mm I know. Trouble is they're all too interested in like drinking and socializing.

(CANCODE)

But inherent properties of the verb are not decisive in the choice of *get*-passive, as Sussex (1982) notes in critiquing Chappell's (1980) semantic classification, and as example (5.7) demonstrates with the verb *pay*, where any 'adversativity' can only be seen to attach to the fact that *pay* is negated. Nor is it entirely obvious that the absence of payment is 'unfortunate' in this case:

(5.7)

> S1: She's got a book published.
> S2: Really.
> S1: And she's got a contract. She's, actually she **didn't get paid for it**, her her
> S3: Her payment is shares in the company, book company

(CANCODE)

A small but interesting number of instances in our corpus are like this, referring to neither inherently fortunate nor unfortunate events, for example:

(5.8)

[A customer in a village shop has just realised that the shopkeeper has remembered a neighbour's fish order but forgotten her own order of fish for her cat. She addresses the neighbour humorously]

> So **you got remembered and our cat got forgotten**

(CANCODE)

(5.9)

[Students talking about upcoming hectic social timetable]

    S1: **I've got invited to the school ball** as well

    S2: Are you?

    S3: Don't really fancy it

                                     (CANCODE)

In (5.8) and (5.9), the circumstances are not inherently negative, but they are problematic for the speakers choosing the *get*-form, who make this quite clear in the co-text. Other (but even fewer) examples (accounting for less than 5%) are clearly seen as fortunate/good outcomes by the speaker, for example:

(5.10)

[The speakers are talking about S2's past successes as a tennis player]

    S1: And were those like junior matches or tournaments or county matches?

    S2: Er both county and er, well I played county championships and lost in the finals the first year and er **I got picked for the county** for that and then so I I played county matches pretty much the same time.

                                       (CANCODE)

Get, therefore, seems to act as an attitudinal marker, coinciding mostly, but not exclusively, with verbs where the attitude is marked towards obviously unfortunate events, but equally capable of marking any event simply as noteworthy or of some significance to the speaker, including the relatively small number of cases where that significance is one of *good* fortune. The speaker's stance is contained neither in the main verb nor in *get*, but is negotiated in the context. *Get* overlays the potential alternative *be* with a stance-signalling function. But stance is a more expressive, interpersonal and pragmatic feature of the discourse and cannot simply be explained in terms of grammatical structure.

Frequency of verbs

In the corpus sample of 139 type **a** *get*-passives, one verb occurs with a frequency strikingly greater than all others: *pay*. *Pay* occurs 20 times, while its nearest rivals, *tell* and *ask*, occur only five and four times respectively, with most other verbs occurring only once or, in the case of *burgle*, *give*, *treat* and *beat*, three times, and *injure*, *intimidate*, *push*, *kill*, *tell off* and *distract*, twice. Some typical contexts for *pay* follow:

(5.11)

    S1: Paperboys **get paid** £13 a week.

    S2: Mm, that's good.

                                       (CANCODE)

(5.12)

[Speaker 1: is complaining about people who have an easy time. MP = member of the British parliament]

    S1: MPs' holidays for one, they **get paid** for going on holiday for about six weeks you know.

    S2: Mm, yeah, yeah.

    S1: There's that many MPs, we don't really need them.

(CANCODE)

Payment, or lack of it, and how much people earn is, in most societies, a matter of interest, debate, and, not infrequently, of criticism, wonder, pleasure and annoyance. It should not surprise us, therefore, that attitude is often strongly marked in utterances to do with money and payment. Whether marking approval or disapproval, stance is highlighted in the frequent co-occurrence of *pay* with *get*-passives. If *be*-passives are the canonical form (i.e. the passive norm), and *get*- the marked form, then it is worth noting that, in the case of *pay*, the corpus sample offers 20 cases of *get*- with only slightly more (24) cases of *be*-passives. In the next rank of frequency (*tell* and *ask*), it should not surprise us either that speakers' choices to report what they are told and asked should be marked as noteworthy in some way and reflective of the speaker's stance.

Adverbials

It was noted above that the occurrence of adverbials with *get*-passives was problematic, since adverbial focus on the verb might serve to de-focus from the subject. This is generally true, and the only adverbials that occur in our data sample, apart from negating particles and adverbials with verbs which must have adverbial complementation (e.g. *I got treated differently*), are *actually*, *nearly*, and *really*, all of which have an intensifying or focusing role (as opposed to denoting manner, place, time, etc.). For example:

(5.13)

    You can **actually get done** for it. (done = arrested/charged in court)

(CANCODE)

(5.14)

    I **nearly got picked on**, but I didn't say yes or no.

(CANCODE)

(5.15)

    Nothing ever **really gets followed through**.

(CANCODE)

The general lack of adverbials and the presence of only these few reinforce the view that type **a** *get*-passives focus mainly on the subject, sometimes on the event, but rarely on the agent or the manner in which the action or event occurs. It may also be noted here that no adverbials occur in medial position between *get* and the main verb past participle, unlike *be*-passives, where this is not uncommon (e.g. *She was slightly coerced into it; It was actually destroyed*).

We conclude this case study by returning to some of our other types of structures and see how they occur in ways that highlight their interpersonal meanings just as the type **a** *get*-passives have done. Example (5.16) shows three different choices of perspective on the verb *frame*, concluding with a type **g** structure:

(5.16)

[Speakers are discussing some photographs]

    S1: I'm afraid I can't afford **to frame them**, but erm . . .

    S2: But do you **want them framed**?

    S1: I'd love to **have them framed**.

    S2: Well if that's the case then the next time we come [S1: Yeah] we'll take them with us [S1: Mm] and then we'll **have them framed**.

(CANCODE)

In speaker 1's first turn, the simple active is chosen, and agency is ambiguous, though likely to mean 'I cannot afford to pay someone else to frame them', which would be a challenge to speaker 1's positive face (self-esteem) in Brown and Levinson's (1987) terms. Speaker 2's response equally avoids explicit mention of agency, thus preserving face (consider the possible alternatives: *Do you want to have them framed? Do you want them to be framed?*, both of which do or could carry implications of outside agency). Speaker 1 then openly admits a desire to have an outside agency perform the task, and speaker 2 agrees. Interpersonal equilibrium is maintained, face is preserved, by strategic choices of perspective upon patient and agent. Key grammatical choices are made that are interpersonally significant. Such choices, once again, enable speakers to position themselves in relation to the message, and illustrate the delicacy of the interpersonal meanings of the passive gradient.

5.8 **Discussion**

It is thus once again necessary to distinguish between 'deterministic' grammar and 'probabilistic' grammar. Deterministic grammar deals with structural prescription (e.g. that *be-* and *get*-passives are always formed with the past participle of verbs, rather than the base-form or *ing*-form). Such determinism enables grammars of languages to be codified in a relatively straightforward way, and has served teachers and learners, as well as linguists codifying the language, well for centuries. Probabilistic grammar consists of statements of what forms are most likely to occur in particular contexts of use, and the probabilities may be stronger or weaker. Probabilistic grammars need real corpus data to substantiate their claims, but statistical data alone are insufficient; evaluation and interpretation are still necessary to gauge the form-function relationships in individual contexts, from which probabilistic statements can then be derived. In the case of our type **a** *get*-passives, the probabilities are that *get* will occur in informal contexts when speakers are marking attitude, most probably that attitude denoting concern, problematicity in some way, or, at the very least, noteworthiness of the event, *as judged by the speaker*, beyond its simple fact of occurring. Indeed, no deterministic statement about when speakers will choose *get* instead of *be* can be made; judgements about adversativeness, problematicity, noteworthiness, etc. are socio-culturally founded and are emergent in the interaction rather than immanent in the semantics of verb choice, or of selection of voice or aspect. This brings us squarely back to our other types of pseudo-passives, **b** to **g**. The passive gradient itself cannot be prescribed deterministically; choices of structural configuration, as represented by types **b** to **g**, depend on how the speaker cares to position the subject, event and (possible) agents and circumstances relative to judgements about perceived responsibility, involvement, and affective factors connected with the results of events. A much more detailed account of *get*-passives – on which this case study is based – can be found in Carter and McCarthy (1999).

Get-passives and related structures are, needless to say, not the only grammatical features to display strong interpersonal meanings (see chapter 8). McCarthy and Carter (1997) account for so-called 'right-dislocated' elements (e.g. **He's a rugby fanatic, Brian**) in a similar way, using spoken corpus evidence, and McCarthy (1998) investigates a number of grammatical features including speech reporting, tense and aspect, and idiom selection from a similar perspective. The present case study has attempted to use corpus evidence to state more precisely the contextual conditions in which the *get*-passive and related forms occur and taken a step forward in the understanding of how a grammar of English might be formulated to take fuller account of attitudinal factors and of how speakers and writers can make expressive choices from the grammar to make more interpersonal meanings. Of course such factors are not, as we have seen, easily captured by structural rules and this returns us to questions raised above concerning structures, choices and probabilities.

5.9   Grammar as structure and grammar as probabilities: the example of ellipsis

Grammar as structure means: what rules does one have/need to know in order to construct a sentence or clause appropriately? An example of a structural rule would be that the determiner *none* must be followed by *of* (*none of my friends*, as opposed to **none my friends*). On the other hand, grammar frequently involves ellipsis, which is the choice not to use words that can otherwise be understood from the surrounding text or from the situation. For example, the ellipsis of the understood subject noun or pronoun in expressions such as *looking forward to seeing you*, *don't know* and *think so* is largely the speaker's/writer's interpersonal choice. Interpersonal refers to choices which are sensitive to the relationship between the speaker/writer and the listener/reader (see chapter 8). In such a case as this, grammar as choice means: When is it normal to use ellipsis? Are some forms of ellipsis more likely to be used in spoken than in written modes? What kinds of interpersonal relationships does it project between speakers and listeners? Are the forms linked to greater or lesser degrees of intimacy and informality? (See also Ricento 1987; Thomas 1987; Greenbaum and Nelson 1999; Wilson 2000; Aarts 2001; Carter 2005.)

Once again, such occurrences are probabilistic, are contextually interpreted, and display subtle variations among viable alternatives. An interpersonal grammar, if such is desirable (and we would argue that our corpus evidence suggests that any other type of description is inadequate), needs to be stated in probabilistic terms. This does not weaken such a grammar; on the contrary, it lends strength to the enterprise of examining grammar in context, which many grammarians, especially those working within the field of discourse grammar, are currently engaged in, and offers the possibility of harnessing the full power of computerised corpora.

5.10 **Conclusions and implications**

In this chapter we have drawn attention to the implications of different grammatical choices and how this gives the user opportunities to observe and learn about these choices in relation to particular contexts in which the language is used.

From the point of view of the learner, structural rules need to be learned and internalised. Interpersonal meanings depend more on probabilities, and learners need to develop habits of observation, assessing when, why and how they might make choices from the possibilities within the language in order to convey particular meanings. The examples drawn from Carter, Hughes and McCarthy (2000) (see figs. 4–7 below) underline the importance of assisting learners to develop habits of observation of language in use so that they notice usage, become more aware of the choices and probabilities that exist and are more conscious of where rules stop and choices begin. It is a process in which teaching materials attempt to promote greater autonomy on the part of the learner. The examples focus on raising and developing consciousness of key uses of ellipsis and, following our case study above, differences and distinctions between various forms of the passive. The examples are derived directly from evidence provided by a corpus that may not otherwise have been observed.

The examples from *Exploring Grammar in Context* (figs. 4–7) illustrate a number of key points in the teaching of grammar that go beyond structures. Corpus analysis with its inclusive consideration of grammatical structures, semantic prosodies and patterns of probabilities entails changes in classroom methodologies for language learning. Pattern drills based on *P P P* (presentation, practice, production) are still needed to reinforce and automatise structure, but complementary methods are needed to support learners in making choices. Carter and McCarthy (1995) propose a parallel *I I I* teaching sequence which builds on illustration, interaction, induction, which may help learners better internalise and appreciate relationships between patterns of language and purposes and contexts.

Figure 4: Extract from *Exploring Grammar in Context* (Carter, Hughes and McCarthy 2000: 165)

---

2 Ellipsis in narratives

Look at this story which Amy tells her friend Barbara.

- Is there much ellipsis in it?
- Would you normally expect to use a lot of ellipsis when telling an informal story like this one?

[Two cousins are remembering a journey. Yarmouth, Norwich and Fareham are towns in the Eastern part of England.]

Amy: I remember that journey. We went from Yarmouth, when we had the car, and we went into Norwich, and there's a ring road round Norwich, and this road to Fareham was off this ring road. Well, we turned right, if you remember.

Barbara: Oh I can't remember.

Amy: And we went right round this ring road, I bet we did twenty miles, and when we came back it was the next one on the left to where we'd started.

Observations

- Ellipsis is a natural part of conversation, but is mainly used when the speakers do not expect or want a strong focus on what they are saying.
- In narratives such as the one above it would be unusual to see much ellipsis because the speaker wants the listeners to concentrate on the story. Ellipsis also functions when the speaker can assume knowledge on the part of a listener. Telling a story usually involves giving listeners **new** information.

D Follow-up

- Write a dialogue about three friends who are planning an evening out. Where would ellipsis be natural? Try to include one of the following somewhere in your dialogue.

    don't know   haven't been there   too far/expensive   seen it

    If possible, act out your dialogue with two close friends. Do you feel natural using these expressions? If so, why? If not, why not?

- If you want more practice exercises, do the Further exercises at the end of Unit 24.
- If you want further details of points relating to this unit, go to the Reference notes on pages 226–31.

Figure 5: Extract from *Exploring Grammar in Context* (Carter, Hughes and McCarthy 2000: 162)

---

1 Simple patterns of ellipsis in conversation

Look at the following extracts from conversations.

- Mark places where you think ellipsis is used at the start of clauses.
- List the words which you think could be added in a more formal context, and try to categorise them according to grammatical structure. ⚷

a) A: Want another coffee?
   B: Yes, thanks.
   A: Like some more cake as well?
   B: Yes, please. But it'll make me fat.

b) A: Did you knock on the door?
   B: I did. Nobody at home.

c) A: Seen Mike lately?
   B: Yes, I saw him last night actually.

d) A: Heard the joke about the monkey and the glass of beer?
   B: Don't you remember you told me it last week at the party.

Figure 6: Extract from *Exploring Grammar in Context* (Carter, Hughes and McCarthy 2000: 99)

---

2 Typical uses of *get*-type passives

Get-passives are often used as alternatives to standard passive forms. The following passives, which are all formed with the verb *get* + past participle, have been collected from actual conversations.

- Do the passives have anything in common?
- Are there any exceptions?
- What kinds of events were people talking about? ⚷

got flung about the car   got killed   got locked out   got lumbered*

got criticised   got picked for the team   got sued   got promoted

got burgled   got beaten   got intimidated

Figure 7: Extract from *Exploring Grammar in Context* (Carter, Hughes and McCarthy 2000: 99)

---

3 Choosing between different passives

a) In the following extracts from recorded conversations both *get*-passives and passives formed with *have* + object + past participle are found.

■ **What differences do you notice in the way the two passive constructions are used?** ⚬⚊

i) [A married couple, Jill and Matt, are discussing with a friend, Carol, the hurricane-like storms which hit Britain in 1987.]

Jill: Remember those gales when our roof was blown off?

Matt: Yes, by that massive gust.

Jill: Then the pipes got frozen up and we had three plumbers come in to repair it all.

Carol: And they never even put out weather warnings.

As exemplified in *Exploring Grammar in Context*, the aim is to provide a text in which particular forms are *illustrated*, tasks which actively involve the learner in noticing features through *interaction* and then to invite the learner to *induce* the patterns of usage. It offers an approach that is essentially inductive and complements the more deductive approaches that are generally (though not exclusively) better suited to teaching and learning more deterministic structures. It also leads into further activities in which learners then extend the induction by producing language in a series of self-study exercises, which can then be checked and monitored by learners themselves. Over the past two decades, research into the value of such consciousness-raising, especially in relation to the teaching and learning of grammar, has been growing steadily (Rutherford and Sharwood-Smith 1988; Fotos and Ellis 1991; Odlin 1994; Ellis 1998; Hewings and Hewings 2005).

The difficulties of helping learners at all levels to move from awareness of structures as right or wrong, to choices from along a gradient of possibilities, to an assessment of what is probable in one context rather than another should not be underestimated. A number of questions are inevitably raised by such processes. These include questions about:

- the level at which learners might begin to work with grammar more inductively
- the part played by corpus samples as illustrative examples (to what extent should learners search the corpus themselves?)
- the role of metalanguage in the classroom, including corpus analysis metalanguage
- the balance between language awareness, which is more passive and receptive, and knowledge, which is more active and productive

- the extent to which learners may be disconcerted by answers to some exercises being indicated as possible/probable answers rather than definitive answers, and so on (see also Dagut 1985; Fox 1998).

And because, reinforced by corpus evidence, we have emphasised the interaction of grammar, vocabulary and meaning, there are further questions for publishers about how much information about grammatical probabilities should be provided in dictionaries and how much information about the typical behaviour of lexical patterns should be given in grammars. Beyond the language classroom as a site for language learning, too, there are also issues raised for the teaching of interpretative skills through grammatical choices and how corpora may be utilised in the service of a more critical linguistic perspective on texts, especially texts here in which the passive voice is central to that end (see O'Halloran and Coffin 2004).

We do language learners and students of language a disservice if we fail to recognise the significance of the patterns revealed by modern multi-million-word corpora. The information has provided us with more evidence than ever before about differences and distinctions between spoken and written usage, as well as between more formal and informal options. Patterns of grammar and lexis are at the heart of these uses.

6 Grammar, discourse and pragmatics

6.1 Introduction

In the last chapter we looked at the interface between lexis and grammar. Building on this, we consider here the ways in which using corpora can promote a better understanding of the relationship between grammatical patterns and their contexts of use. We will set out to show that grammatical choices are rarely arbitrary and that pragmatic factors often account for particular ways of using grammar. As with so much of this book, we shall base our evidence on spoken corpora, largely because research into spoken grammar is still in many ways relatively young and overshadowed by research into the grammar of written language. To illustrate our points, we take three common structures and look at how they are used in everyday conversation, with occasional reference to their use in writing, for comparative purposes. The three structures are non-restrictive (or non-defining) *which*-clauses, *if*-clauses and *wh*-cleft clauses.

6.2 Non-restrictive *which*-clauses

This section is very much based on research by Tao and McCarthy (2001). They looked at the distribution and functions of non-restrictive *which*-clauses in two spoken corpora. They used a one-million-word sub-corpus of CANCODE and a 160,000-word sample of the Corpus of Spoken American English (CSAE). The CSAE project was undertaken at the University of California, Santa Barbara (see Chafe et al. 1991; see also appendix 1), and is composed of recordings made in a variety of settings, with a focus on casual conversation. Its transcriptions are quite narrow, based on the notion of intonation unit (Chafe 1987, 1994; Du Bois et al. 1993); essential interactional features of talk and prosody are all represented. The CANCODE transcripts are broader, though they do indicate overlaps and 'latched' turns (when one speaker's turn immediately follows another's, without any pause at all; see chapter 1).

Most language teachers will be aware of the distinction between 'defining' and 'non-defining', otherwise known, respectively, as 'restrictive' and 'non-restrictive', relative clauses (Carter and McCarthy 2006: 566). The two clause-types convey two different types of information. Defining/restrictive information specifies something or someone (usually a noun or noun phrase) by separating it from other members of a class. For example, (6.1) below specifies which oil tanker the speaker is referring to (i.e. the particular one that caused pollution off Alaska).

(6.1)

Work has begun to refloat the oil tanker **which caused pollution off Alaska.**

(CIC)

The information about the tanker is essential for appropriate interpretation; it *defines* or *restricts* which tanker the speaker is referring to, hence the term 'restrictive' relative clause, or as it is sometimes called, 'defining' or 'identifying' (e.g. Eastwood 1994: 356; Swan 2005: 479). Here we shall retain the term 'restrictive' when referring to the linguistic literature, since it is the preferred term there, but also use 'defining', since it is a more widely used term in language pedagogy.

In (6.2) below, the information about the job is not essential to interpret the utterance; the information about where the job was is, in a sense, 'extra'. The sentence would be perfectly interpretable without it. It may be helpful, relevant or important information, but its function is not to identify the job being talked about within a set of jobs:

(6.2)

He was going to leave because he got offered another job, **which was in York in fact.**

(CANCODE)

In terms of Grice's (1975) conversational maxims, listeners judge what is said in relation to the maxims of quantity, quality, relevance, and manner, and in cases such as (6.2) the listener judges why the non-identifying information is introduced and what relevance it may have. Relative clauses like those in (6.2) are called 'non-defining', 'non-restrictive' or 'non-identifying'.

A further interesting type of non-defining clause is sometimes referred to as a sentence *wh*-clause, where the information in the *wh*-clause refers to the whole sentence or utterance:

(6.3)

I dialled a different number. But I didn't get a dialling tone, **which was a bit odd.**

(CANCODE)

Jespersen (1909: II, 109–114) refers to these as 'continuative' relative clauses, and one test for them is the possibility of substituting a main clause with *and* (i.e. in this case: '*But I didn't get a dialling tone, **and that was a bit odd.***'). Nonetheless, as Tao and McCarthy (2001) noted, the terms 'restrictive', 'non-restrictive', etc. originated in grammatical descriptions based either on intuitive data or on mostly written sources, and show a concern more with the semantics of information transfer rather than with the interactive side of grammar. In traditional grammars, the influence of interactive factors is often given very low priority or is even considered beyond the scope of 'grammar' altogether. Spoken corpora, however, enable us to observe and take into account co-textual and contextual information which may support a description not focusing solely on information exchange, but one which also incorporates interactional features, recognises the presence and contributions of more than one speaker where this occurs and shows us how speakers use grammar to create and maintain interpersonal relations.

6.3   Previous studies of *which*-clauses

McDavid (1977) was an early example of a corpus-based investigation of the distribution and use of relative clauses with *which* in the one-million-word written Brown corpus (Kucera and Francis 1967; see also appendix 1), focusing on the environments and the types of writing in which such clauses were most frequent. A little later, Cornilescu (1981) noted that restrictive clauses were typical after nouns modified by words such as *any, no* and *every* (e.g. *Any person who tries to escape will be shot.*), while non-restrictive clauses typically occurred after proper names (e.g. *William Brown, who I think you've met, is getting married next week.*) (see also Thorne 1988). Cornilescu also called on the evidence of intonation to underline the difference between restrictive and non-restrictive clauses, though Tao and McCarthy (ibid) observed that the evidence of their corpora was by no means conclusive on that score. Based on the Lancaster/IBM Spoken English Corpus (see appendix 1), Yamashita (1994), looked at the positioning of restrictive and non-restrictive clauses, and noted the influence of end-weight: non-restrictive clauses are more likely to occur in sentence-final position, owing to the fact that they often convey lengthy, complex information. Depraetere (1995, 1996) also looks at such clauses from an informational standpoint. Depraetere (1995) argues that, although both restrictive and non-restrictive clauses give relevant information, in a restrictive clause the information is to be found in the same information unit as its referent (i.e. as a modifying clause in the noun phrase), but in a non-restrictive clause, the information is contained in a separate information unit. This helps to explain why the non-restrictive type lends itself to being 'tagged on' to an utterance of one speaker by another speaker (see below). Depraetere (1996) further reports that non-restrictive clauses are more likely to convey foregrounded information, and that such information is interpreted as to its implications (just as we noted with reference to Grice's maxims, above).

Tao and McCarthy (2001) found that most of the non-defining *which*-clauses in their data were of the continuative type; out of almost 700 examples, more than 500 (just over 70%) had a continuative function. They also found that many of the examples were evaluative and that the verb following *which* was overwhelmingly the copula *be* in various forms (*is, was, are, would be,* etc.), with an overwhelming bias toward the present tense. Equally noticeable were the many discourse markers and modal expressions immediately following *which*. Tao and McCarthy then subjected more than 200 of the samples to detailed analysis and concordancing.

6.4   Concordance analysis of *which*-clauses

Tao and McCarthy identified three broad functional categories for non-defining *which*-clauses. These they called 'evaluative', 'expansion' and 'affirmative'. Evaluative clauses give the speaker's opinion, attitude or stance towards the immediately preceding utterance(s). Expansion clauses contain additional information projected by the speaker as topically relevant, i.e. about the just-mentioned person or thing, or as a projection of the anticipated informational needs of the listener. Affirmative clauses confirm that an event referred to in the previous utterance has / has not happened, is / is not happening, or will / will not happen. The types were distributed roughly as follows: evaluative clauses were the majority, expansion clauses were next (just half of the number of evaluative ones) and affirmative clauses were a small class, accounting for less than 4% of the sample. Furthermore, almost 90% of the evaluative clauses had the continuative function. Typical of evaluative clauses in CANCODE are the following; additional features to be commented on below are in bold:

(6.4)

[Speakers are talking about how much money people spend on presents for their children]

S1: Like if they don't spend two hundred pound on them you know it's not enough, *which I think is silly*, but that's the way of things today I suppose, it's all money.

[later in the same conversation, different speaker]

S2: Em a cousin of mine she spends five hundred pound on each child, *which **I think** is bloody ridiculous*.

(CANCODE)

(6.5)

I'm cooking this meal tonight, *which **I mean** I don't mind at all*, but I'm just such a bad cook.

(CANCODE)

(6.6)

[Speaker is talking about the formation of a folk-music group]

And so we, we got together, got a repertoire together and actually the first gig we did was the Cambridge Folk Festival, *which **actually** wasn't very clever at all to do a thing like that as your first performance*.

(CANCODE)

(6.7)

[Discussing someone's choice of university]

S1: Actually I think from what I've heard about all the prospectuses about erm the universities, that Amsterdam sounds good but isn't actually quite as good as it looks on paper. Because I've heard, I mean Susanna said some of the courses weren't actually in English that you might think and things like that, [S2: **Mm.**] *which is **obviously** a bit off-putting if you don't know Dutch, it's a bit difficult*.

(CANCODE)

In bold are the discourse markers and modal items which are so typically found in the continuative clauses. A good many of them also follow immediately on from some sort of acknowledgement or response token by another speaker, a point we shall return to below.

In Tao and McCarthy's data, the discourse markers and modal items included *I think / thought / don't think* (30 occurrences), *you know* (10 occurrences), *I mean, actually, of course, really, just, fair enough, hopefully, probably, evidently, seem, I suppose, I'm not sure, would* (12 occurrences), *will, could, may, must*, and *might*, all of which reinforce the evaluative nature of the *which*-clauses.

As stated above, the other two types of *which*-clause, expansion and affirmative, represented a minority of Tao and McCarthy's data. Some examples from CANCODE are given here. (6.8) and (6.9) are of the expansion type, where extra information, considered relevant by the speaker, is given. (6.10) and (6.11) are of the affirmative type, where the speaker states that something is, was, or will be so.

(6.8)
[Speaker is recounting the narrative of a book]
> And er Ned pulled Nell out of the car and they sat there on top of the car, **which was nearly up to the top with water**.

> (CANCODE)

(6.9)
> I've looked, there's water leaking out the bottom of the radiator, **which is making the smell and re-dirtying this bit of mat again** and so I've had to wrap it all round erm with the cloth.

> (CANCODE)

(6.10)
> So he says 'Well we'd better go back to the hospital again for some more tests, **which basically is what I've done**.'

> (CANCODE)

(6.11)
> S1: See you at the meeting then.
> S2: Yeah. Four o'clock. Yeah.
> S1: And I shall bring my cheque book if I remember.
> S2: Yeah.
> S1: **Which I probably won't**.
> S3: I'll remind you.

> (CANCODE)

However, even these extracts have something of an evaluative overtone about them, and this often seems to be the case. However we classify such clauses, we are left with the conclusion that evaluation is certainly the most frequent context for non-defining *which*-clauses, rather than just giving 'extra information'.

Tao and McCarthy (ibid.) also noted interactive patterns occurring across speaker turns. A typical pattern was one of a first speaker making an assertion which was acknowledged by a second speaker and then followed by a *which*-clause by the first speaker. Example (6.12) shows this pattern:

(6.12)

> S1: But we were gonna leave Rob's car+
> S2: Yeah.
> S1: +in Manchester.
> S2: Right. I'm with you. Yeah.
> S1: So that we could pick it up on the way back.
> S2: Yeah. Right. Right. Right.
> S1: **Which seemed a good idea at the time.**

(CANCODE)

The speaker may add another *which*-clause to a previous one, without any overt linking:

(6.13)

[Speaker is talking about essay grades; 'two-one' means the upper part of a grade two]

> S1: And he's told me that he gave me sixty five for it **which is two-one**.
> S2: Mm.
> S1: **Which is a good two one really.**

(CANCODE)

Another pattern was where a second speaker tagged on a *which*-clause to the turn of a first speaker:

(6.14)

[Speaker 1 is talking about a problem with car windscreen-wipers]

> S1: Colin erm fixed it sort of you know disconnected the windscreen wipers and that was like in the first week. So now it's started raining a bit more I thought I'm gonna have to get it sorted you know. Cos I ended up walking when it's not raining you know and, no, sorry, I've ended up walking when it's raining rather than the other way round.
> S2: Yes. Yeah. Yeah. Yeah [laughs]
> S3: **Which doesn't really make sense does it?**

(CANCODE)

(6.15)

[Speakers are planning a family holiday, and discussing train and ferry times]

> S1: It leaves, it gets in at ... I'm sure I said the night crossing.
> S2: You said twelve till ten.
> S1: No that's coming back twelve o'clock, coming home midday but that one the one going out it gets in at seven in the morning.
> S3: **Which is fine isn't it?**

(CANCODE)

The second speaker may add a *which*-clause even when the first speaker's turn ends with a *which*-clause:

(6.16)
[Talking about public speaking and the problem of 'drying up']
    S1: So you don't want to sort of dry up and not know what to say, **which is what will happen.**
    S2: **Which always happens to me.**

(CANCODE)

A second speaker may add a *which*-clause and then the first speaker may come back with another *which*-clause:

(6.17)
[Talking of the problems of keeping a business going at a bad time]
    S1: Is there any way you could sort of prop the business up or er you know take=
    S2: Not at the moment.
    S1: Mm.
    S2: Not without having to go heavily into debt on a on a mortgage on a remortgage or+
    S1: Mm.
    S2: +have a personal loan.
    S1: Mm.
    S3: **Which is the one thing we don't want to do.**
    S2: **Which at the moment none of us can afford.**

(CANCODE)

There is, therefore, considerable flexibility here as to who may use *which*-clauses and when. Written texts have far greater restrictions, require special kinds of punctuation and linking, and are usually single-authored. Of note too is the fact that Tao and McCarthy found no instances of a listener disagreeing with or challenging the evaluation in the *which*-clause, although clearly such an option is always available. Such clauses seem to play an important role in conversational convergence. Overall, then, corpus evidence seems to suggest that, in everyday conversation, non-defining *which*-clauses, especially the continuative type, occur in contexts of evaluation, and are highly interactive in that they enable speakers to share evaluations, either following an acknowledgement or through joint production of the grammatical pattern. This suggests that, for pedagogy, we may wish to separate the typical written contexts of their use from their typical spoken contexts, and that a focus on function, not just form, will be very useful in enabling authentic contexts to be introduced during the presentation and practice stages of learning such patterns. And, as always, before the formal presentation stage, we would advocate an awareness-raising stage during which the same kind of awareness may be offered to learners which we as researchers can gain from corpus-based observation, whether that stage be through data-driven learning (see chapter 1) or by some other means of confronting authentic contexts.

6.5 *If*-clauses

The corpus work we report here is based on that of Farr and McCarthy (2002), who compared Farr's 60,000-word POTTI (Post-Observation-Teacher-Training Interactions; see Farr 2005) corpus of post-observation teacher trainer-trainee feedback sessions with CANCODE. Farr and McCarthy began by observing differences in frequency per million words of three hypothetical items (*if, maybe* and *perhaps*) in POTTI as compared with a 2.6-million-word sub-corpus of everyday socialising interactions from CANCODE and the spoken academic portion of CANCODE (approximately 340,000 words). The comparisons were made on the hypothesis that the trainer-trainee interactions would probably share some features of academic tutorial sessions but also features of everyday conversation, given the desire to create an informal and non-threatening environment in which (experienced) teachers and their trainers could exchange their thoughts. Figure 1 shows the differences in the three corpora.

Figure 1: *If, maybe* and *perhaps* in POTTI and CANCODE (**CNC soc** = socialising, **CNC acad** = academic)

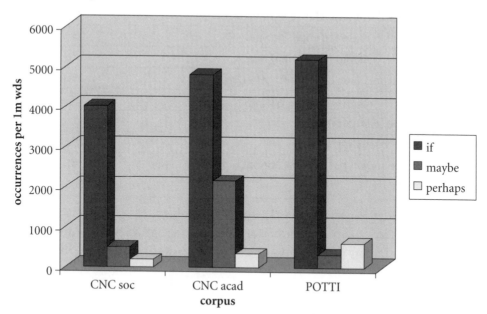

Further investigation showed that the uses of *if* in POTTI were not dominated by the classic three types of conditional clauses familiar to most English language teachers, often know as first, second and third conditionals (Carter and McCarthy 2006: 748). Farr and McCarthy found that, in POTTI:

- A wide range of patterns (more than 30) occurred with *if*. These were highly flexible structures, adaptable to conditions of use.
- The most frequent pattern was (*if*-clause) *if + present simple (main clause) present simple or progressive*, sometimes called *zero* conditionals or *real* conditionals (see Carter and McCarthy 2006: 749, and examples below).
- Three of the non-traditional patterns were more frequent than type 3 conditionals.
- The top 10 patterns accounted for more than half of the total of all *if*-patterns. The three traditional conditional types accounted for fewer than half of the occurrences of *if* shown in table 1 below.
- The raw data were superficially messy and difficult. Embedded and multiple subordinate clauses were often attached, changes of subject occurred, unexpected tense and aspect combinations were found and it was often difficult to isolate a main clause to which a particular *if*-clause was subordinate.
- The majority of *if*-clauses were uttered by the teacher trainers rather than the trainees.

Table 1: *If*-clauses in POTTI

If sequences (if + subordinate clause + main clause)	occurrences
if + present simple + present simple/progressive	55
if + present simple + modal (traditional type 1)	28
alternative *if* structures (not falling into other types)	25
if + past simple + modal (traditional type 2)	23
if + present simple + imperative	11
if + past simple + past simple	10
if + past perfect + modal perfect (traditional type 3)	8
Total	160

The results for all *if*-clauses in POTTI were as in table 1.

On closer observation of concordances it could be seen that many of the trainers' *if*-clauses occurred to modify or hedge in some way directives to the trainees. Some examples follow.

(6.18)

Bite your tongue a little bit **if you have to**.

(POTTI)

(6.19)

If you need to do that then make sure that you move within a certain space.

(POTTI)

(6.20)

> So just be careful **if you want to promote discussion**.

(POTTI)

(6.21)

> **If you're good at organising things** make sure your discussions are organised and that will suit you better.

(POTTI)

(6.22)

> Yeah I mean get them involved quickly **if they do come in late**.

(POTTI)

(6.23)

> Just try to to make a conscious effort to do that **if you feel they're not responding**.

(POTTI)

(6.24)

> **If you're teaching that class** don't feel obliged to explain everything to her.

(POTTI)

Equally, the trainers' directives were often hedged within an 'if I were in your place' context:

(6.25)

> **If I were to teach this** I would simply say 'You've got a list of words here, pick the four that you don't know the difference between.'

(POTTI)

(6.26)

> **If I were to do this exercise** I would approach it from an elicitation point of view.

(POTTI)

(6.27)

> **If I were to teach this lesson** I wouldn't see me getting beyond those two either.

(POTTI)

(6.28)

> **If I were to do it** I would go with giving good clear instructions.

(POTTI)

Many of the 'alternative' *if*-patterns (i.e. those which could not be classified into the other types in table 1) were grammatically anomalous in traditional terms but apparently made perfect sense to the participants in the interaction. (6.29) is one such example:

(6.29)

> Trainee: Because sometimes I think like **if you had to be putting on a performance then I get really on edge**, you can, like other people, you know, like some people naturally love to be out in front and like doing it, showing, I don't think I do.
>
> (POTTI)

Probably the reason why such anomalies are adequately communicative is that the POTTI interactions spend a good deal of their time drifting in and out of *irrealis* worlds, exploring what could have been, what might have been, what was not, or what should have been, rather than what actually happened in the lesson observed. There is also a certain amount of tension and real-time pressure which might account for the apparently 'unstructured' sequences. In this situation, the *if*-patterns of many different kinds provide an overarching hedged context which enables the trainers and trainees to explore ideal and desired states in a non-threatening way, especially when it comes to directives for how to solve current problems and how to act in future lessons. Example (6.30) shows just how important the *irrealis* mode is, realised not just through the use of *if*, but also via modal expressions, negation and vagueness (relevant words are in bold).

(6.30)
[S1 = Trainer, S2 = Trainee]

> S1: Okay so you're saying you **would like to have** devoted **a bit** more time to that?
>
> S2: I th= I think I= you know it **could have been** useful but you know I think that given the time I had you know I mean it was a a complete exercise I mean.
>
> S1: It **wasn't sort of** left hanging mid air **or anything** [S2: No.] it was fine yeah okay but **if you were to** do it again essentially that's what you're saying **you might** [S2: Yeah.] tighten up at the beginning and leave more time for=
>
> S2: Yeah I mean certainly I mean the the very fi= the **sort of** introduction was a, was very slow you know I **wasn't** getting a lot of response I **wasn't** asking the right questions **maybe, I don't know whether**, it's just, it's funny, it, I, with that class I mean I found with most of the classes when you go back again it's a case of being more relaxed really . . .
>
> (POTTI)

If is a versatile word, and not just in the POTTI corpus. Carter, Hughes and McCarthy (2000: 70–78) present a wide range of corpus-informed patterns with *if*, and offer practice activities and exercises exploring the different choices.

6.6 *Wh*-cleft clauses

We finally turn to consider *wh*-cleft patterns. Here we are concerned with examples such as the following. We start with some typical written examples.

(6.31)

[About relations between the Soviet political leader, Molotov and US President Truman]
Not normally a sensitive man, Molotov protested against Truman's tone, but he had little difficulty understanding the message: American policy had changed. **What he could not discern** was whether American objectives had changed.

(CIC)

(6.32)

[From a newspaper horoscope]
You aren't usually emotionally derailed, so put irrational fears behind you and try to get to the heart of the problem. **What matters** is proving to others that you have more courage than them.

(CIC)

(6.33)

[About Pascal, the seventeenth-century French philosopher]
Exactly how Pascal goes about treating these data so as to perceive and to produce a distinctive kind of logical sequence is **what we now need to examine**.

(CIC)

The first two examples are canonical *wh*-cleft clauses, while extract (6.33) is of a type often called reverse *wh*-cleft (because the *wh*-clause comes after the verb, as the complement rather than as the subject of the clause). Such clauses are normally held to signal some kind of focus, emphasis or contrast, as can be seen in the three extracts above (see also Kim 1995; Carter and McCarthy 2006: 786). *Wh*-clefts have also been posited as signalling the most important information in a written paragraph (over and above the traditional explanation of paragraph-initial 'topic' sentences; see Jones and Jones 1985). *Wh*-clefts are often contrasted with *it*-clefts (e.g. *It was the plate* that got broken, not the mug.), with which they share many characteristics, but by which they are not always substitutable (see Delin 1990 for corpus-based examples of *it*- and *wh*-clefts and a discussion). Unlike many other areas of grammar, *wh*-clefts have been the subject of several corpus-based studies, both written and spoken, and much insight has been gained into their functioning in relation to presupposed and new or salient information (e.g. Collins 1987, 2004; Geluykens 1988; Weinert and Miller 1996).

Here we examine *wh*-clefts in a one-million-word socialising sub-corpus of CAN-CODE to see if everyday conversation, the most frequent communicative activity, supports or challenges conventional descriptions. Since the first person pronoun *I* was found to be the most frequent word to follow *what* in our corpus, we searched initially for the string *what I . . . .*, which generated 654 occurrences. Of these, 319 (slightly under half) were cleft constructions of some sort (the rest being mostly reported clauses, such as 'You know *what I mean*'). Of these 319, the biggest single group (170 examples, or more than half) were what are often called the *demonstrative* type, exemplified by utterances such as 'That's *what I want*' (cf. 'I want that'), 'This is *what I was wondering*' (cf. 'I wondered this'), etc., where a demonstrative pronoun is the subject (Weinert and Miller 1996; Miller and Weinert 1998: ch. 6). These clauses, which refer back to something already said, often function to pause the discourse in some way, either to highlight something, to comment on it, to paraphrase or expand upon it or to shift the topic. By far the most frequent contexts involve mental process verbs such as *That's what I* + forms of *mean, think, wonder, want* and speech reporting verbs such as *That's what I* + forms of *say, tell*. Extracts (6.34) and (6.35) illustrate these types.

(6.34)
[Talking about hair]

> S1: I think Laura's looked nicer before she went to the hairdresser's. [pause] No.
> S2: Yeah. I don't know. I=
> S1: It looks different. I don't know+
> S2: It looks different.
> S1: +whether it does her any good.
> S2: Yeah. **That's what I mean.** Cos I think it looks better when it's tied back than when it's loose cos otherwise it's just too much.
> S2: Yeah. Big hair makes her look a bit bigger.

(CANCODE)

(6.35)

> S1: You'd have thought he'd have actually listened to my answerphone message wouldn't you?
> S2: Well **that's what I thought.** Have you changed the message?
> S1: Yeah it says, 'Hi it's Martin. Sorry I'm out for a run. Bye'.

(CANCODE)

The remainder of the 319 examples of *what I . . .* clefts cover a wide variety of types. One prominent type is what we might call 'prefaces', which precede a statement in order to highlight it or signal it as newsworthy in some way. These prefaces often take forms such as *What I might do is . . ., What I (really) like about X is . . ., What I couldn't understand is/was . . ., What I find is . . .,* where the *wh*-clause typically creates a bridge with the previous utterance(s) and refers forward to an up-coming message which the speaker projects as newsworthy in some respect:

(6.36)
[Speaker 1 is talking about her teaching job]

> S1: I want to keep it.
> S2: Yeah.
> S1: Yeah.
> S2: Mm.
> S1: And **what I really like about it** is meeting people from all over the place+
> S3: Yeah.
> S1: +you know really different backgrounds and cultures. I think it's, I love it you know.

(CANCODE)

(6.37)

[Speakers are talking about an area in the south of England]

    S1: I'd love to see it in the summer.

    S2: Lovely.

    S3: Oh in summer it's beautiful. Er Alice's mum and dad they, they loved going around there.

    S1: **What I didn't realize** was that there are all these little canals and+

    S3: Oh yeah. Yeah.

    S1: +it's just like, almost like the fen land.

(CANCODE)

In many ways, these spoken uses of *wh*-clauses reflect the kinds of textual signalling they often provide in written texts. For example, in written texts, the demonstrative type often has an encapsulating role vis-à-vis the preceding text, while the canonical *wh*-clefts perform a bridging role, leading into some new matter (Prince 1978; Collins 2004):

(6.38)

[Magazine article about competition in the computer industry]

    Of course, the competition must learn to take care of itself: **that is what competition is all about**.

(CIC)

(6.39)

    He obviously looked ill, but **what I found terrible** was the look of starvation on his emaciated body and face.

(CIC)

However, the spoken corpus also offers a considerable number of items which are syntactically anomalous but which perform clear communicative functions. These are most typically occasions where the copula *be* is not present, as in (6.40) to (6.42):

(6.40)

    What I'll do I'll phone Sam up and say, 'Have you done it yet?'

(CANCODE)

(6.41)

[Speaker 2 is talking about revisiting her old school]

    S1: Ah. Why, is it sort of, like, how many years since you left?

    S2: Well I don't know. But erm **what I first thought**, 'ah yeah you know, go to that have a bit of a laugh and that and see what+

    S1: Yeah.

    S2: +everyone's turned out like.'

(CANCODE)

(6.42)

[Speaker 1 is discussing offers of university places based on alphabetic grades (e.g. two grade As, three grade Bs) obtained in school-leaving examinations]

S1: But what I should have done, what the s= what the teachers at school were trying to encourage me to do was take my Manchester offer which was three Bs+

S2: Mm.

S1: +and then take the Leicester one as like a back up.

S2: Yeah.

S2: **But what I did** I took the Manchester one as three Bs as my first offer.

(CANCODE)

It is questionable whether we gain anything by suggesting that these are examples of ellipsis and that the listener 'fills in' a missing form of the verb *be*. Rather, it makes sense to view such clauses as chunks, in the way we have discussed in chapter 3, acting as a kind of frame or headline for the upcoming discourse. Indeed, there is good evidence to suppose that speakers themselves regularly consider *wh*-clefts to be frozen chunks, even ones with copula *be*, in the attested phenomenon of the 'double *is*' (Bolinger 1987; McConvell 1988; Massam 1999; Carter and McCarthy 2006: 148). The 'double *is*' often occurs with expressions such as *the thing is, the problem is, the trouble is*, etc., where the first *is* characteristically bears more stress than the second. However, it also occurs frequently with *what*-clefts. Some examples follow:

(6.43)

[Speaker 2 is having trouble with a piece of sewing]

S1: So where is the difficulty?

S2: **Well the difficulty is is** in getting+

S1: The dimensions to fit then isn't it.

S2: +getting a straight line and getting right angles and getting them both exactly the same size.

(CANCODE)

(6.44)

[Speaker 1 is expressing worries over the opening of a drive-through fast-food outlet nearby]

S1: Erm what it might do it might end up with people throwing polystyrene boxes through our front window.

S2: Er yes

S1: But you see **the thing is is** like they buy it in the drive-through and then drive along for a bit and eat it whilst they're driving.

(CANCODE)

(6.45)

S1: Harry and I were just going It might get better. And we're thinking It might get better next week. But=

S2: Mm. Right.

S1: And he's just, **all he does is is** seduce women.

S2: Fool around with different women. Yeah

(CANCODE)

(6.46)

[Speakers are discussing accountancy book-keeping entries]

S1: Yeah. But it's a manual, manual entry isn't it.

S2: Yeah.

S3: Now. **What you've got to remember is is** are we gonna need that as a straightforward for shares and deposits.

S2: And loans.

(CANCODE)

(6.47)

S1: **What I find funny is is** pictures of cars with great big balloons attached to their roofs. Driving on methane were they instead of petrol?

S2: I don't know. I don't remember that now.

S3: I think I've seen that.

(CANCODE)

(6.48)

S1: **What I can't understand is is** why is it, why has all this come out all of a sudden?

S2: After all these years.

(CANCODE)

Further examples of the double *is* with *what*-clefts are given in figure 2, a concordance of *what* + *x* + *is is*.

Figure 2: *What + x + is is* (CANCODE)

```
 1   Speaker 4: <$=> Well it's like er <\$=> What I can't understand is is why is <$
 2   lights on ever.    <$?M> Yeah.    <$?M> What I find funny is is pictures of car
 3   t kind of thing.    Speaker 1: But <$=> what I </$=> what I'm thinking of is is
 4   no. I I mean <$=> I think <\$=> I think what I'm getting at more is is erm just
 5   ng.    Speaker 1: But <$=> what I </$=> what I'm thinking of is is there could
 6   ne thing at this point that is that erm what I've done here is is really nothin
 7   hing?    Speaker 3: Well really speaking what it all boils down to is is what we
 8   s oh blimey <$G?> It doesn't mean that. What it means is is now I've made you a
 9   $2> <$=> He's got to <\$=> <$=> Well no what they've said is is he's got to erm
10   e of the the simple er principles about what we believe is is the way in which
11   t and <$G?>    Speaker 2: <$G?> in fact what we can start doing is is clearing
12   redit. <$G?> credit.    Speaker 1: Well what we could do is is reject this eith
13   ve paid it in. Er everybody pays it in. What we're saying is is that there isn'
14   3. <$=> Yeah or you can have <\$=>. Wh= what you could do is is erm if I <$=> i
15   se well well if it costs <$G1> you know what you do is is just a small part of
16   .    Speaker 2: and National Insurance. What you have been paying for is is whe
17   stics it's the microscope isn't it. And what you want is is the two to be broug
18    the sort of wider dimension. I suppose what you're saying is is entirely true.
19   r 2: Mm.    Speaker 3: I mean basically what you're trying to do is is trying
20    <$?M> <$E> laughs </$E>    Speaker 2: What you've got to remember is is are we
```

These are just a few of the occurrences of *what*-clefts with double *is* in CANCODE, and what they seem to suggest is that the speakers perceive of the clefts as chunks, in other words they are not synthesising them afresh each time; they are routine formulae, frames upon which important content is hung.

Overall, we may observe that the *what*-clefts, like the *which*-clauses, are strikingly found in contexts of evaluation, where speakers project their attitudes and stances. These highly interpersonal contexts are magnified in the spoken corpus because of the face-to-face nature of the discourse.

6.7   **Bringing the insights together**

What do we learn from our investigation of these three patterns? They do seem to have a good deal in common when we look at them in corpora. The three patterns have in common, we would argue, the following:

- They embody structures whose description, like so much of grammar, has been dominated by invented sentences and/or observations of use in written texts. All three structures present a different and more varied picture of their forms and functions than that which would be obtained solely by looking at written examples. Additionally, such forms may also display flexibility and variation depending on the variety of English being considered (for example, see Newbrook 1998 on the wide variability of relative clauses in different varieties of English around the world).
- They display variety and flexibility in use: the *if*-clauses show variations of tense and aspect patterns, the *which*-clauses have a proclivity to occur as follow-ups to listener acknowledgements, to be strung together without linking, to occur as part of jointly-produced clause-complexes, and the *what*-clefts can be used as ready-made chunks, and without being integrated into the conventional clause structure.
- They realise important interpersonal functions: the *which*-clauses overwhelmingly serve to evaluate and encode attitude and stance, and project conditions for conversational convergence. The *if*-clauses project a non-threatening context in which possible remedies can be sought and directives issued by the authority figure in a friendly, informal and collaborative way. The *what*-clefts 'headline' information considered salient or newsworthy by the speaker and also express stance and attitude.

Moreover, all three patterns seem to depart from canonical grammatical 'rules' in some way and display a detached, almost fragmentary nature that defies the normal requisites of syntactic integration within tight sentence patterns that characterise formal writing. Such uses have lent support to those who advocate the theory of 'emergent' grammar, where structure is not seen as a pre-ordained system through which discourse realises its communicative intent, but rather, the opposite: grammar is always 'deferred', temporally negotiable, and is always emergent from the exigencies of discourse, moment by moment. Language is seen 'as a kind of pastiche, pasted together in an improvised way out of ready-made elements' (Hopper 1987: 144–5. See also Hopper, 1998).

6.8 **Corpus grammar and pedagogy**

The implications of looking at common, everyday structures in spoken corpora are complex and not suggestive of easy, straightforward application. What we find in spoken corpora is messy, variable, anomalous (at least in terms of conventional 'rules') and embedded in the moment-by-moment contingencies of face-to-face interaction. However, we would propose the following as guidelines for language teachers keen to follow what corpora suggest about spoken grammar.

- Spoken grammatical patterns often reveal a flexibility of form that means that learners need be less subject to the stresses of constructing 'well-formed sentences' when engaging in conversation in L2. The cognitive demands of speaking in real time are heavy enough, without having to stop to make everything conform to what we find in writing. Teachers and, above all, oral examiners should take this into account when listening to learners performing, and, with enough exposure to authentic listening texts, learners might ultimately acquire a more relaxed attitude to their use of grammar in spoken contexts, especially informal, conversational ones.

- Constant exposure to and practice in the use of the prefabricated chunks with which communication is forged, whether those chunks be complete lexical phrases or the kinds of 'frames' we have seen in this chapter, may be more useful than dissecting and analysing those chunks. Analysis can come later, when fluency in use has been established. We have already discussed this in some detail in chapter 3.

- Awareness of what one is likely to hear (especially if interacting with native speakers or expert users) is always helpful. Listening to spoken grammar, whether in naturally occurring recorded conversations or in media broadcasts and films, along with noticing tasks, can raise awareness. This kind of listening is often best carried out as 'listening *for* something' rather than 'listening *to* something'. More advanced learners can be encouraged to spot 'anomalous' clauses in their listening, 'anomalous' in the sense that they may violate the rules the learners have been taught (e.g. for conditional sentences with *if*) and then to discuss why the clauses are different from the written norm, and whether changing them to conform to the written norms would have any consequences for meaning or interpersonal relations.

- The POTTI corpus is a specialised corpus of interactions between teacher trainers and trainees. It shows how grammar is sensitive to particular contexts and how special genres develop their own grammatical conventions which emerge from the demands of particular types of interaction. We might expect the same kinds of grammatical conventions to apply to other special contexts, and indeed they do, as we show in chapter 10 of this book (e.g. the high incidence of the verb *need* in spoken business interactions). Learners wishing to focus on their special needs should be given the opportunity to work with the typical grammatical patterns which characterise the special contexts in which they work or study, and, above all, given noticing activities to spot just the types of grammatical patterns which recur in their special genres.

- Grammar pedagogy should see structural choices as strategic acts with important interpersonal consequences. The authors of the *Touchstone* series attempt to capture this notion of strategic choice in their presentation and practice activities for *wh*-clefts, part of which is reproduced here. The exercise is based on a conversation which the students have already listened to between a group of young people about the best way to go about choosing a career, where opinions and stance are central to the exchange of ideas:

Figure 3: Extract from *Touchstone* (McCarthy, McCarten and Sandiford, 2006a: 119)

Unit *12* Careers

2 Grammar *What clauses and long noun phrases as subjects*

What clauses and long noun phrases introduce important information. They are often the subject of the verb be, which can be followed by a word or phrase (noun, adjective, or verb), or by a clause.

What clauses	*Long noun phrases*
What you need is lots of information.	**The main thing you need** is information.
What my friend did was interesting.	**Something my friend did** was interesting.
What I would do is talk to people.	**The best thing to do** is (to) talk to people.
What I'm saying is (that) you need to choose a career you'll really like.	**The good thing about that** is (that) you end up with a job you love.

A Once you've chosen a career, how do you go about getting your dream job? Choose the best expression on the right to complete each sentence.

1. I think _the first thing to do_ is to get some work experience. _____ is contact a company I was interested in. You know, _____ was good. She started out in the mail room at a newspaper and ended up as a reporter.

   what I would do
   ✓the first thing to do
   what my friend did

2. You know, _____ is go to a job fair. _____ is to meet the recruiters. They sometimes interview you right there, and _____ is you might get hired immediately.

   the main reason to do that
   one thing you can do
   the good thing about that

3. Well, _____ is a good résumé. _____ is get mine done professionally. _____ is that you can make a really good first impression.

   what you really need
   the advantage of that
   what I'd do

4. You know, _____ is ask all my friends and family if they had any personal contacts. _____ is that they might be able to help you get an interview. _____ is good contacts.

   the main thing you need
   the good thing about that
   what I'd do first

The teacher's book for *Touchstone* additionally offers further information about the occurrence of *what*-clefts in the corpus used in the creation of the course (the North American spoken segment of the CIC), as illustrated in figure 4.

Figure 4: Extract from *Touchstone* (McCarthy, McCarten and Sandiford, 2006c *Language Notes*, Unit 12).

> *Use*
>
> The *What* clauses and long noun phrases as subjects help to highlight or give extra emphasis to the ideas expressed in the complement.
>
> When a verb phrase follows *be,* the verb is usually the base form, even if the *What* clause or noun phrase contains a modal verb or a verb in a tense such as the simple past (e.g., *The first thing I would do is **talk** to people.; What my friend did was **call** some companies.*).
>
> *Corpus information*
>
> *Verb forms in the verb phrase complement*
>
> In conversation, when the *What* clause or noun phrase subject includes *to* + verb, the verb in the complement is usually the infinitive, or *to* + verb (e.g., ***The best thing to do** is **to talk** to people.*).

This general principle of observing contexts in a corpus, devising a classroom activity which reflects those contexts, and providing backup information about forms and functions for the users of the material can be applied to any grammatical structure.

Having underlined the need for observation and listening for the types of patterns we have highlighted in this chapter, we still cannot give easy answers to the issues of how positively or negatively teachers and (mature) learners might react to grammar that seems anomalous and, in some cases, downright wrong (e.g. the double *is*), and what should be done about such data. It is possible, however, with more mature and interested groups of learners, to discuss processes of language change, and how these often begin with apparent violations of rules, and how it is the informal spoken language which tends to lead the way with respect to grammar. Above all, pedagogy needs to address the issue of expectations and prejudices which are firmly rooted in experience of the written language by exposing learners to the richness and variety of spoken language and opening windows on to the immense grammatical variety we find therein.

7 Listenership and response

7.1 Introduction

As we have seen in several of the previous chapters, some lexical items are many times more frequent in spoken language than in written language. For example, figure 1, below, compares the occurrences of *right* per million words across spoken and written corpora.

Figure 1: Frequency of *right* across spoken and written corpora (BNC = British National Corpus; Brit newsp = British newspaper corpus of CIC)

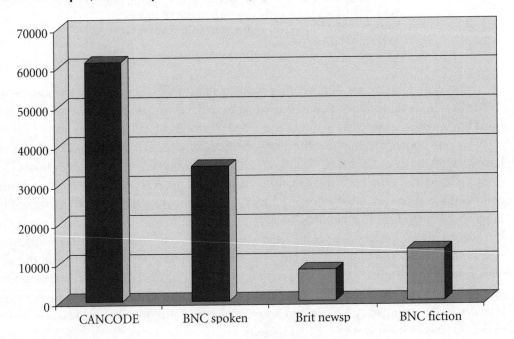

When we seek the reason for this striking difference, what we find is that *right*, in the spoken language, has important discoursal functions, including the marking of boundaries (see Sinclair and Coulthard 1975; see also chapters 8 and 11) and as tokens of listener response, as in extract (7.1), where *yeah* and *right* both serve to acknowledge the incoming talk:

(7.1)

[Giving driving directions: 'the M6' is a motorway in Britain]

  S1: Tell me the best way to get to your showroom?

  S2: If you come up the M6 to junction forty-four.

  S1: **Yeah**.

  S2: Come off at junction forty-four which is the main road coming into Carlisle and we are about half a mile down that road on the left hand side.

  S1: **Right**.

  S2: There's a pub just before us called The Coach and Horses.

                             (CANCODE)

In this chapter we focus on a common feature of spoken interaction which accounts for discrepancies between spoken and written corpus frequencies of the kind illustrated in figure 1, and which involves words such as *yeah* and *right*, along with many others, which we shall call 'listener response tokens'. Conversations typically contain listener responses in the form of short utterances and non-verbal surrogates (e.g. head nods) (see Fries 1952; Kendon 1967; Yngve 1970; Oreström 1983; Maynard 1989, 1990; 1997; Tottie 1991; Drummond and Hopper 1993a, 1993b; Gardner 2002). These signals are produced by the listener, according to Kendon (1967), as an accompaniment to a speaker, and he suggests that there is some evidence that the speaker relies upon these for guidance as to how the message is being received. Let us consider a further example from the Limerick Corpus of English of how *yeah* functions, in this case in an extract from a radio phone-in:

(7.2)

[Here an elderly caller is explaining how, when she was young, a local woman used to do home ear-piercing using a thick darning needle, olive oil, some string and a cork.]

  Caller: The way this was done was a Scottish lady who lived across the road from us.

  Presenter: **Yeah**.

  Caller: And she would soak some grey wool. A length of grey wool in a saucer with olive oil.

  Presenter: **Yeah**.

  Caller: And then she'd thread it through an extremely large darning needle.

  Presenter: **Yeah**

  Caller: Then there was a cork held together . . . and she just threaded the needle with the wool straight through your ear and into the cork . . .

                              (LCIE)

In extract (7.2) above we see that the presenter wants to signal that she is listening and that she wants the caller to continue telling her story, but she does not want to take over the speaking turn (or the 'floor'). To achieve this she uses short response tokens that keep the conversation going (in this case, *yeah*). Tottie (1991: 255) provides an apt metaphor for this phenomenon, saying that these tokens 'grease the wheels of the conversation but constitute no claim to take over the turn'.

In this chapter, we will look at the different forms and functions of such response tokens and examine how a corpus can aid their analysis in different contexts. Their relevance to pedagogy will be examined in terms of how we need to re-assess our notions of teaching 'speaking' and 'listening' to accommodate this basic interactional phenomenon within a model that takes into account the active, responsive role that listeners have in conversation. We shall refer to this role as 'listenership', and we will consider good listenership to be something which is both natural and desirable for efficient spoken communication, thus extending the notion of fluency to accommodate joint production between speaker and listener(s). We put forward the term 'confluence' to refer to this.

In the research literature, response tokens go by many names, often varying according to discipline. Yngve (1970) introduced the term 'backchannel' to refer to the 'short messages' that a speaker receives while holding the floor (1970: 568) and this term is widely used. Fellegy (1995) uses the term 'minimal response', which comes from the body of research into language and gender (see Zimmerman and West 1975; Fishman 1978 and Coates 1986), while Roger et al. (1988) use the term 'listener response'. In this chapter, we will use the term 'response token' as an umbrella term to refer to the many vocal, verbal and non-verbal non-floor-holding devices that a listener may use to respond to the floor-holding message in a conversation. It is worth noting that this term refers to the discourse function of these lexical items rather than their word-class identity as adjectives or adverbs etc.

Mott and Petrie (1995) point out that response tokens are the antithesis of interruptions. Duncan and Niederehe (1974) note that they project an understanding between speaker and listener that the turn has not been yielded, but they also note that it is often difficult to identify the boundary between brief utterances and proper turns, where the 'listener' becomes the 'speaker'. The problem, however, is more for the analyst than the actual conversational participants, who, in real-time conversation, will draw on prosodic features, facial expressions, gestures and so on to interpret whether an interlocutor is trying to take the floor or display listenership in a given context.

7.2   Forms of listenership

Response tokens are often divided into 'minimal' and 'non-minimal' tokens, though the distinction is not necessarily clear cut (see below). It is also worth noting that spoken corpora, for the most part, have been based on transcriptions of audio recordings and so they usually fail to capture non-verbal response tokens such as head nods and shoulder shrugs.[1] Usually minimal responses are defined as short utterances (for example *yeah*) or non-word vocalisations (such as *mm, umhum*) while non-minimal response tokens are mostly adverbs or adjectives (for example *good, really great, absolutely*) or

---

[1] However, recent multi-media corpus projects may be able to obviate this problem by the use of synchronised video records alongside the conversational transcript; see, for example, Reder et al. (2003), Carter et al. (2006).

short phrases / minimal clauses (such as *you're not serious, Is that so?, by all means, fair enough, that's true, not at all*).

Minimal response tokens

Extracts (7.3) and (7.4) show examples of minimal response tokens:

(7.3)

> S1: . . .and I am sure this is not only happening in Lincolnshire it's happening in probably every town in Great Britain.
> S2: **Mm.**
> S1: So it's an issue but obviously we can devote time to it in terms of um the general thing+
> S2: **Mm.**
> S1: +without the specifics+
> S2: **Mm.**
> S1: +who what why when where.
> S2: **Mhum.**

(LCIE)

(7.4)

[Paula Abdul is a pop singer]

> S1: I loved Paula Abdul.
> S2: **Yeah.**
> S1: That's her, isn't it?

(LCIE)

Non-minimal response tokens

Extracts (7.5) and (7.6) show examples of non-minimal response tokens:

(7.5)

> S1: I wouldn't have minded giving an apprenticeship to that lad here on the site cos he was a good strong worker so he was. . . . he was a polite young fella too.
> S2: **Is that right?**
> S1: She had a tough job with them she brought up those two kids herself. Her marriage broke down there a long time ago.

(LCIE)

(7.6)

> S1: Jack rang last night and he's going to come round and discuss the boiler.
> S2: **Lovely.**

(CANCODE)

As we can see from (7.7) and (7.8), non-minimal response tokens may be pre-modified by intensifying adverbs, which add further emphasis:

(7.7)

[Woman talking about giving birth]

    S1: Dick was very excited cos at one point they asked for hot towels.

    S2: Oh.

    S1: Just like the movies. So he skipped off down the corridor to get the hot towels.

    S2: Oh **jolly good**.

(CANCODE)

(7.8)

[Discussing tenancy problems in rented accommodation]

    S1: Isn't there something in your tenancy agreement about it? You have a written agreement don't you?

    S2: **Most definitely**.

(CANCODE)

Clustering of response tokens

Both minimal and non-minimal response tokens can occur in pairs or clusters:

(7.9)

    S1: . . . you know it reminds me of am the play and ah.

    S2: Mm.

    S1: And the character in the play is not+

    S2: I don't know.

    S1: +someone I'd kind of identify with+

    S2: Yeah that's true that's true but I wonder if that's a cultural sort of+

    S1: **Yeah mm**.

    S2: +I don't know I had the same question for Rosemary . . .

(LCIE)

Carter and McCarthy (2006: 190–191) note that clustering is particularly evident when a topic is being closed down or at a boundary in the talk when another topic is introduced. Such pairs function both to signal a boundary *and* to add satisfaction or agreement or simply to express friendly social support. Occasionally, triple response tokens occur (example (7.11)).

(7.10)

[Speaker 1 is a waiter and speaker 2 is a customer in a restaurant]

    S1: If you need some more just order some more. All right.

    S2: **Right. Fine**.

    S1: Okay. Thank you.

    S2: Thank you.

    S1: You're welcome.

(CANCODE)

(7.11)

[Couple asking permission to look at a disused railway line]
>S1: It went through, it goes through. Straight, straight on.
>S2: **Right. Wonderful. Great.** Can we look round then?
>S1: Yes certainly.
>S2: Thank you.

(CANCODE)

Negation of response tokens

Absolutely, certainly and *definitely* may be negated as response tokens by adding *not*:

(7.12)

[Speaker 1 is considering buying a CD player for the first time]
>S1: . . . but then I'd have to go out and buy lots of CDs wouldn't I.
>S2: Well yes. I suppose you would.
>S1: There's no point in having a thing if you can't play them. Haven't got any.
>S2: **Absolutely not. Absolutely not.**

(CANCODE)

(7.13)

[Discussing the difficulty of studying in the evenings after working all day in a day job]
>S1: Seven o'clock in the evening after a day at work is not really quite what you need is it?
>S2: No.
>S1: Hm.
>S2: **Definitely not.**
>S1: No.

(CANCODE)

7.3 Response tokens across varieties of English

It is interesting to use a corpus to compare how forms vary across language varieties. For example, below we compare the frequency of *yeah* in different varieties of English, including a non-native corpus of English conversations (SUE in figure 2).[2] This leads one to question why the London-Lund Corpus (LLC) data has so few *yeah*s and this may be explained by the type of data that it contains. The corpus is made up of part dialogue (casual conversations and public discussions) and part monologue (some spontaneous and some prepared in advance in writing) (see Svartvik 1990 for details, and appendix 1). Because many of these contexts are less vocally interactive (or not at all in the case of

---

[2] The non-native speaker data come from a corpus of Successful Users of English (SUEs) which consists of spoken interactions between SUEs, both native and non-native speakers of English (see Prodromou 2003a, 2003b, 2005). The results shown here, for which the authors are very grateful, have been provided by Luke Prodromou and are based on 150,000 words of non-native-speaker interactions only (see also chapters 1, 4 and 9).

monologues), the opportunity for using listener response tokens is less. This type of variation is borne out when we look at the frequency of *yeah* in the Corpus of Spoken Professional American English (CSPAE). Here we find just 43 occurrences per million words. This corpus consists of recordings of more formal interactions: White House press conferences and university academic council meetings (see appendix 1).

Figure 2: Occurrences of *yeah* across a range of spoken corpora
(CANCODE = British English, WSC = Wellington Spoken Corpus, New Zealand English; LCIE = Irish English; COLT = Corpus of London Teenage Language; SUE = Successful Users of English corpus; LLC = London-Lund Corpus, British English; see appendix 1)

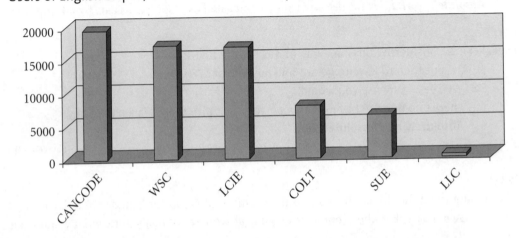

McCarthy (2003) looks at non-minimal response tokens in two corpora: a 3.5-million-word sample of the 5-million-word CANCODE spoken corpus and a similar-sized North American spoken sample of the Cambridge International Corpus, giving a total corpus of approximately seven million words. He finds the forms shown in figure 3 to be the most frequent in these corpora of spoken British and American English.

Figure 3: Most common forms of non-minimal response tokens: British and American English

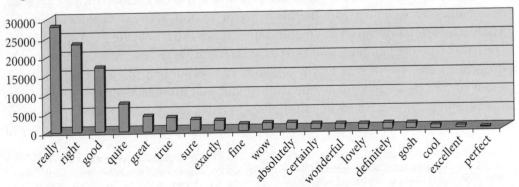

McCarthy (2002) compares the frequency of key response tokens in British and American spoken English (figure 4).

Figure 4: Comparison of non-minimal response tokens: British and American English

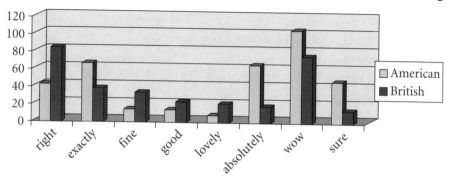

However, looking at a discourse feature such as listener response in such a large amount of data can give an homogenised picture where the most common items 'float to the top'. When using a corpus to examine discourse, it is also worth taking a small amount of data where the conversational conditions can be accounted for as much as possible and examining it more closely. For example, an analysis of non-minimal response tokens in a sub-corpus of the Limerick Corpus of Irish English consisting of just 20,000 words of conversations between young Irish female friends chatting in cafes, pubs and in their homes generates the following forms (figure 5):

Figure 5: Non-minimal response tokens: 20,000-word sub-corpus of LCIE; young females

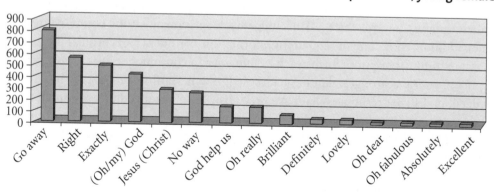

Notable in this Irish English data is the use of religious references which expose a socio-cultural dimension to how language is used in context. One example from this corpus is extract (7.14) below, where two girlfriends are gossiping about an ex-boyfriend who one of the girls spotted in a local night club after they had broken up; we see *God help us*

used mockingly to mean 'how pathetic'. Note also the other religious references in the extract and the use of different minimal and non-minimal response tokens to keep the conversation going:

(7.14)

S1: Was he was delighted with himself, he was? (laughing)

S2: He was thrilled . . . thought he was a king. (laughing)

S1: **Ah God help us.**

S2: And am he rang John Murphy that night and I think they went out . . . in Limerick.

S1: **Isn't he right?**

S2: No rest for the wicked.

S1: **Jesus indeed.**

S2: But tell us this what d'you mean you felt awful sorry for him?

S1: I just I don't know I was kind of looking going Jesus we're all going our own way like.

S2: **Yeah.**

S1: . . . He had his new suit on God help us (laughing) he looked lovely his new shiny shoes (laughing) I think he was . . . upset.

S2: Yeah Helena was saying that alright.

(LCIE)

7.4   Functions of response tokens

Many studies address the functions of response tokens. For example, Fellegy (1995) concludes that the functions of minimal responses can be considered both grammatical and social. Maynard's (1989) cross-cultural study of Japanese students conversing with American counterparts identified the following functions: continuers, display of understanding of content, support towards the speaker's judgement, agreement, strong emotional response, minor addition, correction or request for information. Gardner (1997) profiles the functions of certain minimal response forms such as *mm hm* as a continuer; *mm* as a weak acknowledgement; *yeah* as a stronger, aligning acknowledgement. Gardner (2002) goes into substantial detail on listener responses that have previously been put together as minimal types of responses such as *mm, mm hm* and *yeah*. Antaki et al. (2000) look at response tokens in the context of interviews (they use the term 'high-grade assessment' for items such as *brilliant*) (see also Antaki 2002).

Continuer response tokens

Continuer response tokens are facilitative in that they maintain the flow of talk. As their name suggests, they encourage the current speaker to continue. Many researchers have identified this function of listener response and usually minimal response tokens are associated with it (see Schegloff 1982; Maynard 1989; Gardner 1997, 1998, 2002). Speakers perceive them as floor-yielding signals that mark the addressee's desire for the talk to continue. By looking at concordance lines for a minimal response token such as *mm*, we find that it is surrounded by ongoing utterances rather than being part of a turn itself (figure 6):

Figure 6: Sample concordance lines of *mm* from LCIE

```
riginally there was four of us. Mm. Running it am Barry Murphy w
ere was nothing outside Dublin. Mm. You know and the idea then w
e making transmitters for them. Mm. So when the whole steam step
       They see it as competition. Mm. You see.          Competition
ey probably have less interest. Mm. In the ideals of community r
   they know their task they're+ Mm. +not so preoccupied with th
you know they tear it to bits+ Mm. +with all their questions s
uld        get local programmes. Mm. And they'd
 thi=        great in your head. Mm. But actually when you sit do
ted this thing up in my garage. Mm. And em playing records on a
       thirty clubs came in now. Mm. We elect okay these thirty c
to thirty-six year old bracket. Mm. You know.          So you wer
ure at this stage I would say. Mm. And you decided to to chang
t through this with you or not. Mm. But the board of direct
 o those sort of things anyway. Mm. I mean I know sometimes whe
```

Extract (7.15) is an extract from an interview between a researcher and the director of a local radio station taken from LCIE. Notice how the researcher S1 frequently provides continuer response tokens in the form of *mm* to show that she is listening and that she wishes the interviewee to keep the narrative going:

(7.15)

S1: Why did you want to start it? Was it from the radio perspective?

S2: Well 'twas basically from the radio perspective because we saw an opening that ah radio in this country ah you know right up until recently was very when I say archaic it was mostly run by Dublin.

S1: **Mm.**

S2: And ah there was nothing outside Dublin.

S1: **Mm.**

S2: You know and the idea then was starting to catch on in em in England.

S1: **Mm.**

S2: Ah with the independent ah radios starting to open up around the same time and ah listening to those here. Because like you could receive a lot of these here on the medium wave.

S1: Of course right yeah.

S2: You know ah you know ah I was struck by the idea and a lot of other fel= people I'm sure were struck by the same idea about the success.

S1: **Mm.**

S2: Of the of the community radio of the actual local radios . . .

(LCIE)

Extract (7.16) is an example of a group of friends talking about shopping. Here again we see *mm* functioning as a continuer:

(7.16)

> S1: . . . you know when you think of something you want to have.
> S2: **Mm.**
> S1: And you haven't seen them in the shops.
> S2: **Mm.**
> S1: . . . I sort of visualised what I wanted and then erm I went down Superdrug with Rebecca and we popped in and I thought Ooh. They're the ones I want.

(CANCODE)

Convergence response tokens

When we scrutinise corpus examples more closely, we find that response tokens are frequently found at points of convergence, that is where participants agree, or simply converge on opinions or mundane topics and this leads them collaboratively to negotiate topic boundary points where a topic can be shifted or changed. Convergence can also be followed by a conversational closure point.

In the example from a conversation between female flatmates (7.17), we see that the topic (a great night out that the friends had together) has run its course and it is collaboratively rounded off with the non-minimal response token *You never know*. Notice also how this phrase is a recycling of a phrase from the previous turn, which makes for a very symmetrical ending point at which participants move on to a new topic:

(7.17)

> S1: Yeah. We haven't had a night like that for a while have we?
> S2: No. Must have another one.
> S1: Silly night. (laughs) What?
> S2: Must have another one.
> S1: Well I think we will.
> S2: Wednesday.
> S1: Mm. Lifts the spirits.
> S2: Mm. **You never know** we might be able to get a new recruit.
> S1: (laughs) **You never know.**
> S2: (laughs)

(CANCODE)

As well as helping to bring about topic changes, these tokens are often found in closings as they allow conversations to come to a collaborative end. Observe how the radio presenter uses them and other markers of agreement in the closing of a phone call in extract (7.18) below from an Irish radio phone-in:

(7.18)

[The presenter and the caller are chatting about the merits of clip-on earrings:]

Presenter: And aren't they grand?

Caller: Yes they're very very handy.

Presenter: **Yeah.**

Caller: But they're not as secure as having them in your ear.

Presenter: **This is true. This is true.**

Caller: You know you could lose them easily.

Presenter: **That's true.** OK Tess well thanks for talking to us thanks very much.

Caller: Right thanks very much. Bye.

Presenter: All the best. Thank you indeed bye bye bye bye.

(LCIE)

McCarthy (2003) notes that non-minimal responses tokens sometimes cluster in consecutive series across speakers, providing multiple signals that a conversation is about to be terminated while at the same time consolidating interpersonal relationships. He observes that they often occur together with other markers of closure (such as *thanks*), checks, confirmations and greetings and that clustering is especially frequent in telephone conversations where there are often pre-closing and closing routines (7.19).

(7.19)

[Telephone call concerning a printing order]

S1: Do you think it needs editing?

S2: Erm I shouldn't think so.

S1: **Good. Brilliant. Okay, well** I'll be round to pop it up.

S2: **Okay.**

S1: Pick it up today.

S2: **Okay** Jack.

S1: Have you got the compliment slips?

S2: Yes.

S1: On all er=

S2: They they look very good.

S1: **Great.**

S2: Yes.

S1: **Fabulous.**

S2: **All right.** [laughs]

S1: Okay. Thanks for that.

S2: **Okay** Len.

S1: **Cheers.**

S2: **Bye.**

(CANCODE)

Convergence response tokens seem to do more than just signal turn-yielding listenership and a desire for the narrative to continue. Signalling agreement or converging on mundane topics is a form of interactional bonding between speaker and addressee and convergence response tokens help maintain good speaker relations by reinforcing commonality. In this way, we can say that they carry a relational value (see chapter 8 on relational language).

Engagement tokens

This type of response token functions very much at an affective level. They signal the addressee's enthusiasm, empathy, sympathy, surprise, shock, disgust etc. at what the speaker is saying without taking over the turn. It is also indicative of the addressee's high level of engagement with the content of the speaker's message. These tokens are typically non-minimal responses and common items include *brilliant, absolutely, wow, cool, gosh, really* and short phrases such as *that's tough, that's true, you're not serious, Is that so?* In example (7.20) below an engagement token is used to express the addressee's delight at what her friend is saying:

(7.20)
[Speaker 2 is talking about how she will spend the summer with her boyfriend in Edinburgh. 'Debenhams' is a well-known British department store; 'CV' refers to curriculum vitae or résumé]

S1: What are you going to do about a job?
S2: I don't know. He says that it's going to be like Killarney and that I should get one easily enough and I've been in contact with Debenhams and they told me to send over my CV.
S1: **Brilliant** Mary **brilliant.**

(LCIE)

In this example from a family chatting, the addressee signals his surprise:

(7.21)
S1: Len Mitchell? He's the bursar isn't he? Len Mitchell?
S2: Is he? Is he?
S1: He's the director.
S2: **You're not serious!**
S1: Yeah.
S2: Len Mitchell? In the choir?
S1: Yeah yeah.

(LCIE)

This type of response token functions at a much higher interactional level than continuer tokens. They not only signal a desire for the speaker to continue, they also communicate the addressee's affective response to the speaker's message.

Context-specific functions

Some response tokens are strongly associated with particular contexts. McCarthy (2003) for example notes that *fine* most typically occurs in the making of arrangements and reaching decisions, and that *certainly* most typically occurs in reply to a request for a service or favour:

(7.22)

    S1: Okay. I'll see you a bit later then.
    S2: **Fine**.
    S1: In the morning, whenever.

                       (CANCODE)

(7.23)

[To a waiter]

    S1: Can I have the bill please?
    S2: Yes, **certainly**.

                       (CANCODE)

McCarthy also notes that in example (7.23) one cannot use other tokens such as *definitely*, underlining the context-sensitivity of response token choice. The tokens are not merely an undifferentiated list of alternatives. This is also the case in example (7.24), from a radio phone-in:

(7.24)

    Caller: Marian may I come in there for a moment please.
    Presenter: **Certainly** yes.
    Caller: There are a tremendous amount of do . . .

                       (LCIE)

McCarthy (2003) also notes that adjectives such as *excellent, fine, great, good, lovely, right, perfect* offer positive feedback to the speaker and often mark the boundaries of topics where speakers express their satisfaction with phases of business such as making arrangements, agreeing on courses of action, and marking the satisfactory exchange of information, goods and services:

(7.25)

[At a travel agent's]

    Assistant: There you go. There's your ticket. And your accommodation there. Insurance, and just some general information.
    Customer: **Excellent. Right**.

                       (CANCODE)

(7.26)

[Speaker 1 is a dealer and speaker 2 is a customer in a car spare parts depot]

    S1: I'll get one of the lads in to come and do it for you.
    S2: **Lovely**.

                       (CANCODE)

In data from service encounters in LCIE, we find similar use of response tokens at points of transaction:

(7.27)

Customer:	Have you a car wash here?
Shop assistant:	We have yeah out the back. Hot wash.
Customer:	I pay for it here don't I?
Shop assistant:	Yeah.
Customer:	**Grand.**
Shop assistant:	(sound of till)

(LCIE)

O'Keeffe and Adolphs (in press) found that in radio phone-in recordings, some context-specific response tokens existed in relation to marking the receipt of information. In particular they found that *right* was used by the presenter to indicate that adequate information had been received and so the topic could be moved on, or ended (they frequently occur at points of closure). They also note that these tokens are usually marked by falling intonation (marked with ↓ below):

(7.28)

[The caller has been explaining why he got a tattoo]

Presenter:	Did any member of your family object?
Caller:	Ah no my wife was all for it actually. She was.
Presenter:	**All ↓right.**
Caller:	She was getting tired of listening to me [laughs] talking about it and 'I must do this I must do this'. I mean in fairness to the tattoo parlours they're all very clean they all have certificates now I mean you must be eighteen and some of them will ask for ID. I mean if you look under the influence of drink or drugs they'd just turn you around and show you the door you know.
Presenter:	**↓Right.**
Caller:	I mean it's changed from the time when maybe that lady is thinking about sailors and criminals you know. I think it may be. She may have a bias but as a mother maybe she's entitled to it.
Presenter:	[laughs] **↓Right** okay okay. **Right** Emmet thank you very much indeed for that.

(LCIE)

These response tokens have a highly organisational function and are more associated with asymmetrical discourse where one speaker has managerial power over the flow of the discourse. Not surprisingly they are quite common in radio data and are considerably less frequent in casual conversation data. The findings of Adolphs and O'Keeffe (2002) support this. They took three small sub-corpora of 20,000 words each from (1) radio phone-ins, (2) young female friends chatting from LCIE and (3) young female friends chatting from CANCODE (a total of 60,000) and compared the percentage of occurrence of this type of response token across the three datasets.

Figure 7: Percentages of information-related transactional tokens across radio phone-in, LCIE and CANCODE sub-corpora

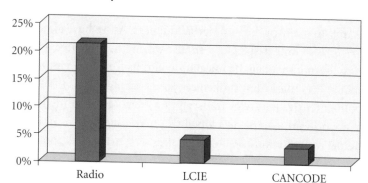

7.5 Conclusions and implications

Now that we are at the stage in the book where we are using corpora to investigate beyond the word, chunk or grammatical pattern, that is, looking at discourse in corpora, it is timely to look at some pointers for anyone interested in looking at discourse features using a corpus in order to create materials or use with their students:

- Large corpora can generate wordlists and concordance lines based on many millions of words of spoken language. In looking at a spoken discourse feature it is often very insightful to start by comparing our findings from spoken data with those from written corpora. As we found at the very outset of this chapter, if there is a high discrepancy between spoken and written results then, this is likely to point to the item in question having some important spoken discourse function.
- When we identify an item that seems to have some 'spoken significance', it is valuable to follow up by comparing findings across different spoken corpora. This will illuminate the degree to which the item may be universally used in English of different varieties. Comparing different types of corpora also allows for the identification of certain situational factors; for example, something which occurs in different varieties of conversational English, but which has a low occurrence in corpora made up of more institutional interactions, can be seen as an item which is specific to casual conversation.
- We have also found here that in looking at a discourse feature, concordance lines are very useful. They show us systematic patterns of use and then when we look more closely, we are able to see links between certain forms and specific discourse functions. We would also argue for the need to look beyond frequency to actual examples. By isolating sub-corpora of manageable sizes, it is possible to look very closely at how certain conversational conditions affect patterns of use and, very importantly, one can see the impact of socio-cultural factors at play as evidenced above in the sub-corpus of young Irish female friends chatting (figure 5). In chapter 8, the use of specialised contextualised corpora will be explored further.
- A more specific point, that this chapter indirectly raises in relation to looking at spoken corpora so as to better understand how we use language, is that spoken corpora

cannot always give us the full picture of interaction. In most spoken corpora to date, conversations are usually recorded in audio, rather than audio-visual format; a person who usually was not present at the conversation then transcribes them, and so we miss out on many of the non-verbal nuances. As we have alluded to above in the case of *right* as a context-specific response token, there is often a link between the form of the response token, its intonation and its function. Unfortunately, intonation is not always marked in spoken corpora (simply due to the enormous expense and labour-intensive nature of transcription). Digitally recorded audio-visual corpora are beginning to be developed where transcription is linked to a recording of the actual conversation (see Reder et al. 2003; Carter et al. 2006).

Getting down to specific implications for pedagogy resulting from this chapter, firstly, we have made the case here that response tokens form part of what constitutes the core spoken vocabulary (see chapter 2), but not only on the basis of their statistical frequency. We argue that while the corpus tells us that these items are very frequent in spoken English, it is their function that is even more core; that is, their central role in constituting an 'interaction'. Without response tokens, interactions would very often fail because speakers would perceive their message as not being well received. Without response tokens, conversations, even the most business-like and utilitarian ones, would be lacking in terms of the social relationship between the speakers. That is, an interaction without response tokens may achieve its goal, but it may not achieve any level of relational bonding between interactants (see chapter 8). To illustrate this, table 1 looks at example (7.19) again, where two colleagues are talking; in the right-hand column (B) we have removed the response tokens:

Table 1: Comparisons: response tokens versus no response tokens

A: with response tokens	B: without response tokens
S1: Do you think it needs editing?	S1: Do you think it needs editing?
S2: Erm I shouldn't think so.	S2: Erm I shouldn't think so.
S1: **Good. Brilliant. Okay, well** I'll be round to pop it up.	S1: I'll be round to pop it up. Pick it up today. Have you got the complement slips?
S2: **Okay.**	S2: Yes.
S1: Pick it up today.	S1: On all er=
S2: **Okay** Jack.	S2: They they look very good.
S1: Have you got the compliment slips?	S1: Thanks for that.
S2: Yes.	
S1: On all er=	
S2: They they look very good.	
S1: **Great.**	
S2: Yes.	
S1: **Fabulous.**	
S2: **All right.** [laughs]	
S1: **Okay.** Thanks for that.	

As we can see, B achieves its goal on a very basic level, but the interactants do not gain anything in terms of social relations from the interaction, which is in contrast to version A where the goal of the interaction is achieved, and, the participants simultaneously increment their working relationship (see chapter 8 on relational language). We can say that A is socially more successful than B.

Relating all of this back to pedagogy, if it is our goal to assist our students in becoming successful communicators in English, then listenership is a very important area that has to be addressed. The classroom as a site of interaction (as chapter 11 will discuss in detail) is not the most suitable as a model for response token use. Teachers do most of the responding and their response tokens are generally evaluative in nature (e.g. *right, not quite, okay, very good*). Having access to real spoken data is very important therefore and corpora of spoken language are certainly a viable option. Moving from specific to general, we make the following concluding points in relation to response tokens, listenership and pedagogy.

- Listenership, no more than speaking or listening, is not a totally new concept for our students. They 'do' it all the time in their first language. This is a good starting point in the classroom, that is to look at the forms used in a corpus of the learners' first language(s). Apart from helping to raise awareness as to the concept of listenership itself, finding out more about these forms serves some other sound pedagogical purposes. Firstly, it is often the case that while a form may have an equivalent in another language, it does not mean that it is directly transferable in all instances. For example, *claro* in Spanish, *bien sûr* in French and *of course* in English may seem like equivalents, or patterns of use might seem to be transferable such as *sí sí sí* in Spanish and *yes yes yes* in English (Amador et al. 2005). In both of these examples, there is no direct relationship. In fact, it would lead to a pragmatic error to transfer these directly; for example, the use of *of course* as a response token in English could suggest arrogance, or the reduplication of *yes* in the form *yes yes yes* may unintentionally convey impatience. This may be an opportunity to get your students to work on corpora of their own language as a starting point to exploring how these high frequency items differ in their use as response tokens across languages.
- A more general point is that to be good at communicating and interacting, learners need to be able to show listenership and engagement just as much as they need to be able to make a point, tell a story, comment on the world around them, and so on. This forces us to reappraise our models for teaching speaking and listening to incorporate 'listenership'. Teaching of speaking traditionally focuses on developing fluency and teaching of listening refers generally to improving learners' receptive skills. Listening classes are most often where comprehension is tested, and this is also a standard part of international exams in English. Here we are advocating that both speaking and listening as skills need to incorporate listenership by moving to a bi-directional model of communication. Rather than looking just at speakers' transactional competence (their ability to 'get the business done' in conversation), we need to address interactional competence. Rather than asking

students to listen and respond in writing to an aural stimulus, listenership needs
to be incorporated. In order to practise and test listenership we need to structure
classroom and testing materials around asking students to listen, respond and
react appropriately to what they hear. In the context of developing the skill of
listening, a new paradigm is therefore needed, one that goes beyond listening
comprehension and incorporates the listening process, including *response*.

- Another notion familiar to all language teachers, which can be held up to question, thanks to the kinds of insights gained in this chapter, is that of fluency in
the context of developing speaking skills. This tends to be judged by the solo performance of an individual speaker. A socio-culturally embedded notion of conversation sees speakers as supporting one another, in other words as 'scaffolding'
each other's performance, in Vygotsky's terms (Vygotsky 1978), in the case of the
examples in the present chapter, by exploiting the repertoire of response tokens.
The conversation, and its flow, is seen as a joint responsibility, and our perception of fluency is much influenced by the cooperatively created flow of talk,
rather than just the talent of one individual speaker. The notion of fluency has its
roots in linguistic qualities related to lexico-grammatical and phonological flow
created by individual speakers, in the ability of participants to converse appropriately on topics, and so on (see Fillmore 1979), but we argue that it is enhanced by
the degree of interactive support each speaker gives to the flow of talk, helping
one another to be fluent. A great deal of what fluency really is would seem to be
missed by judging a speaker on monologic performance alone, or through an
oral examination where assessors hold back from responding in the way normal
human beings would, or building measures of fluency according to solo perform-
ances of read-aloud speech analyzed by speech recognition software which
counts speech rates, pauses, etc. (e.g. Cucchiarini et al. 2000). What we actually
observe in the interplay between initiation and response is a confluence, jointly
produced, and we offer the term 'confluence' in preference to the monologic
notion of fluency. The joint production model of fluency is a much more stu-
dent-friendly concept upon which to build classroom and testing materials. In
the context of testing this poses many challenges and would mean moving away
from monologic speaking tasks based on pictures or written prompts to a situation where confluence can be tested as part of joint production, involving at least
two participants.

8 Relational language

8.1 Introduction

In chapters 2 and 3 we took a systematic look at the core words and chunks in English and this showed us that many of the most frequent items in the spoken corpora had pragmatic functions in the organisation and management of conversation and in the speaker-listener relationship, particularly in terms of maintaining good relations. These high frequency words and chunks illustrate the pervasiveness of interactive meaning-making in everyday conversation. They also point to the degree to which speakers constantly engage with each other on the interactive plane. Many of the items that we identified in chapters 2 and 3 fell into the broad functional categories shown in table 1 (overleaf).

In order to understand these features better, we introduce the notion of *relational* versus *transactional* language. When we talk about relational language, we are referring to language which serves to create and maintain good relations between the speaker and hearer, as opposed to transactional language, which refers to the exchange of information between speakers (i.e. the propositional content of the conversation). However, we are not saying that all language can be strictly divided into either relational or transactional types. Relational episodes can be found in what are ostensibly transactional interactions and vice versa. Iacobucci (1990), who looks at customer calls to a phone company concerning billing queries, provides interesting insights into the importance of 'apparently relational-oriented talk' (p. 97) integrated with the transactional tasks. For example, Iacobucci's informants often seemed to give unnecessary explanations and background information about their purpose in ringing the billing company. These are clearly shown to be not merely interpersonally motivated, but strategic elements in the achievement of the caller's transactional goal. Cheepen (2000: 289) notes that even in the most extreme examples of 'interactional' and 'transactional' dialogues, we are likely to find 'cross-over features between task-direction and person-direction'. For example, (8.1), (8.2) and (8.3) are three very brief encounters recorded in an Irish shop. On the surface, these encounters are transactional yet relational language is interwoven (see bold script).

Table 1: Summary of functional categories with pragmatic functions from chapter 2 and 3

category	examples (see chapters 2 & 3)	corpus examples
Discourse marking	*right, well, so, anyway,* *You know* *I mean* *And then* *But I mean* *You know what I mean* *Do you know what I mean* *At the end of the day* *If you see what I mean*	. . . I remember when I was young when I was younger *you know* er where I come from *you know* . . . (WSC) S1: if nothing else we can find the road *if you know what I mean* S2: yeah but two hundred numbers is a is a big street S1: it's two hundred and seventy it's actually almost more three hundred numbers it's basically three hundred numbers (WSC)
Face and politeness	*Do you think* *Do you want (me) (to)* *I don't know if/whether* *What do you think*	right okay um *do you think* Maori is for Maori people only or for all New Zealanders? (WSC) [as opposed to the more direct form interrogative form *Is Maori for Maori people only or for all New Zealanders?*]
Vagueness and approxima- tion	*just, whatever, basically,* *quite, pretty,* *a couple of* *And things like that* *Or something like that* *(And) that sort of thing* *(And) this that and the other* *All the rest of it* *(And) all this/that sort of thing*	It's *a bit* worrying really. (CANCODE) . . . do you want a sleeping bag *or something* in case it's cold? (WSC) S1: I kind of got the bug to travel, to travel around more and to move around and live in different places. S2: Uh-huh. S1: Went over to Italy and lived with my brother over there for *a couple of* years. (CIC North American spoken segment)

(8.1)
[A customer S2 approaches the counter with four scones]

    S1: Four scones **is it?**
    S2: Yes yeah and those. [till rings up price] **Thanks**. [customer hands over money]
    S1: **Now that's lovely.**
    S2: **Thanks.** [sound of plastic bags]
    S1: **Bye now.**
    S2: **Bye.**

(LCIE)

(8.2)

> S1: **You don't sell stamps do ye[1]?**
> S2: We do.
> S1: **Ah can I have**=
> S2: How many do you want?
> S1: Four **please**.
> S2: **Now** one twenty please.
> S1: **Thanks a million.**
> S2: **Thanks.**
> S1: **Thanks.**

(LCIE)

(8.3)

> S1: **Can I have** a bag of potatoes **please**?
> S2: The four ninety nine bag **is it**?
> S1: Yes **please**.
> S2: Seven eighty three **so please**. [sound of till] **Now thanks very much. Coolish isn't it?**
> S1: **So it is shur[2]. Tis grand. Tis great shur tis kind of dry**.
> S2: **Now thanks a lot**.
> S1: **Last of all is there any** lad around that **would** lift it?
> S2: **Oh right** I'll get someone for you
> S1: **Okay**
> S2: **Now** see the lad there he'll lift them in for you.
> S1: **+Okay dear thank you very much.**
> S2: He's actually outside.
> S1: **Fine dear thanks**.

(LCIE)

If we remove the relational language from these interactions, they still function, but in a very robotic way because they are purely transactional.

Here are extracts (8.1), (8.2) and (8.3) without relational language:

(8.1a)

Encounter 1

> S2: Four scones?
> S1: Yes yeah and those. [till rings up price] [S1 hands over money] [sound of plastic bags]

---

[1] *Ye* is commonly used as the plural form of *you* in Irish English.
[2] *Shur* is used in Irish English as a pragmatic booster meaning *for sure* to *to be sure.*

(8.2a)

Encounter 2

S1: Do you sell stamps?

S2: We do. How many do you want?

S1: Four.

S2: One twenty.

(8.3a)

Encounter 3

S1: a bag of potatoes

S2: The four ninety nine bag?

S1: Yes.

S2: Seven eighty three. [sound of till]

S1: Is there a lad around that will lift it?

S2: I'll get someone for you. See the lad there he'll lift them in for you. He's actually outside.

What the three encounters show us is that while we could interact in a purely trans-actional way, especially at a shop counter where a transaction is expected, we very often modify our language so as to attend to the relational side of the interaction. That is, we try to create and maintain good relations with our interlocutor. Table 2 summarises the fea-tures of relational language in extracts (8.1) to (8.3).

Table 2: Summary of relational language features used in extracts (8.1) to (8.3)

feature of relational language	example
conversational routines • thanking • leave-taking • requestive routines	*Thanks, thanks a million* *bye now, bye* *Can I have . . . please?*
small talk	*Coolish isn't it?*

hedging
 • hedged syntactic structures
   – negative declarative + tag question
 	
   – noun phrase + tag
   – vague interrogative + hedging modal verb *would*
	You don't sell stamps do ye?
	 [unhedged version: *do you sell stamps*,
	 even less hedged: *I want stamps*]
	 Four scones, is it?
	 is there any lad *around* that *would* lift it?

discourse markers	*now, ah, oh, Last of all, right, okay*
vagueness and approximation	*Coolish, any lad around, tis kind of dry*
vocative use (endearment form used)	*dear*

As we have discussed in other chapters in this book (for example in relation to fixed expression in chapters 3 and 4), the question of whether features such as relational language should be taught is really for teachers and learners to decide. Many of the items are core spoken vocabulary (see chapter 2) and so it is legitimate to argue that they can be learnt as vocabulary items or as part of discourse strategies, but equally they may be rejected as something that a non-native user might not be comfortable with. Nonetheless we feel that, as core features of English, all learners need, at a minimum, a passive understanding of these high-frequency items.

8.2 Conversational routines

As noted in chapters 3 and 4, formulaic utterances can extend from multi-word chunks to discoursal routines. Wray (2000: 466) points out that utterances may be formulaic 'even though they do not need to be'. In other words, they can be generated by the rules of open syntax and vocabulary selections to fill the syntactic slots (for example: *It was lovely to see you*). Such utterances are formulaic because of a combination of their recurrence, established colligations and their pragmatically specialised functions. In this chapter, we hope to show how interesting examples of pragmatic specialisation can be found when we look at small corpora of data from specific social interactions. These patterns might not become obvious when they are part of a large corpus. Patterns emerge in these small specialized datasets because they are linked to very specific socio-cultural contexts of use. These patterns become pragmatically specialised over time. For example, in a corpus consisting of calls to an Irish radio phone-in programme, the phrase *thank you very much indeed for talking to us* has a pragmatic specialisation for the presenter at the closing of the calls, which has become routinised in this show:

Figure 1: Concordance lines from a corpus of Irish radio phone-in (*Liveline*) closings

```
  listen thank you very much indeed for talking to us. Thank you for
         thank you very much indeed for talking to us. Okay thank you.
 Richard thank you very much indeed for talking to us.
 Donelly thank you very much indeed for talking to us and thank you Una. Thank you. All
  Dowell thank you very much indeed for talking to us. Thank you Marian
   Brian thank you very much indeed for talking to us. Right you are Marian.
    Anne thank you very much indeed for talking to us. Thank you.
```

Listeners to the show become familiar with this call-closing pattern and this familiarity also has a relational function, in that it generates a sense of pseudo-intimacy (see O'Keeffe 2006). In a very different context, a corpus of service encounters at an electrical shop (a sub-corpus of CANCODE), we find the two-word chunk *you've got* within the top ten two-word items. When we explore this through concordance lines, we find that it has acquired a pragmatic specialisation within the shop encounter in the context of selling/demonstrating a product to a customer. For example:

(8.4)

> Sales person: . . . **you've got** the separate oven and things like that.
>
> Customer: Yeah. But clean= cleaning's important isn't it?
>
> Sales person: Oh yeah. Yeah. Definitely it is. So here **you've got** you see **you've got** your microwave level. **You've got** your grill. Your grill one two three levels . . . Erm then **you've got** your microwave grill.
>
> Customer: Yeah
>
> Sales person: And fan. So again+
>
> Customer: Gosh.

(CANCODE)

Concordance lines show more examples from the sub-corpus. Notice the tendency towards the pattern *you've got your*. The merits of this phrase as a selling device are obvious as the customer is positioned interactively (Davies and Harré 1990), through pronoun use, as the owner of the product.

Figure 2: Concordance lines of *you've got* from service encounters (CANCODE)

```
a twenty two zoom on that one. Here you've got a sixteen digital.   <$2> On this Sharp's on
your video.    <$2> Yes.    <$1> So you've got a video.    <$2> Right.    <$1> I'm sure you
   $1> Right. Well you'll find that you've got a fader on the top here to zoom in and out.
oker. Right?    <$2> Yes.    <$1> So you've got er an ordinary cooker at home. That is the
    <$2> I see.    <$1> <$=> Where you've got erm. You see you can't see it all on here. T
<$1> Yep. That's it. Yeah. And then you've got everything here. As it shows you on this on
one. Right? And you just use it. So you've got.  It's a nice size. It's a point nine which
deo. Okay?    <$2> Right.    <$1> So you've got naturally pause stop play rewind fast forwa
hirty pound.    <$2> Yes.    <$1> So you've got quite a lot more on there. <$=> Wide stable
<$1> +different type of cooking. Now you've got the oven+    <$2> Yeah.    <$1> +as it would
se <$=> it's got you know it's it's. you've got the separate oven and things like that.   <
ay. So you could say on a normal one you've got thirty two zoom so it's still better than th
eah. Yeah. Definitely it is. So here you've got you see you've got your microwave level. You
.    <$1> All right. I mean <$=> you you've got your you <\$=> you'll have an auto s= switch
?.    <$1> Then you go up from this. you've got your Panasonics. Right? Which is giving eve
on the other side of it. Right? Then you've got your <$G3> fader right?    <$2> Yes.    <$1
   Sort of r= really <$G3>.    <$1> you've got your new Sharp. I know Sharp does <$G?>.
o here <$=> you've got <\$=> you see you've got your microwave level. You've got your grill
d things like that.    <$1> <$=> You you've got your <\$=>    <$2> Sort of r= really <$G3>.
<\$=> Oh. <$E> laughs <\$E> Erm then you've got your microwave grill.    <$2> Yeah.    <$1
```

The term 'conversational routines', after Coulmas (1981b) and Aijmer (1996), is often used to refer to chunks of language that are found to recur in spoken interactions. When we look at examples from a large spoken corpus, broad social routines are reflected in chunks such as *how are you? I'm sorry, could I have, thank you.* Though these are more generic compared with the examples above, they are nonetheless bound to specific communicative domains (Carter 1987) such as greetings, apologies, requests and thanking (see also Yorio 1980; Fónagy 1982). Alexander (1984) puts these routines under the general heading of 'discoursal expressions', within which he further categorises them as 'social formulae'. These items are seen as part of the continuum of fixed expressions (Alexander 1984):

← idioms – proverbs – stock   – catch   – allusions/ – idiomatic – discoursal expressions →
                      phrases   phrases   quotation   similies   (including social formulae)

In chapter 4, we categorise such discourse routines, along with interjections, as situation-bound idioms; again this is part of a cline of fixedness (for further discussion of fixedness see chapters 2, 3 and 4). Here we are interested in these chunks because they comprise part of the core words and chunks in English and have specific pragmatic functions in terms of organising the speaker-hearer relationship and maintaining good relations within it. From our multi-word list (see chapter 3), there are quite a number of possible routines that we could look at (as illustrated in table 3).

Table 3: Conversational routines

random example of routinised patterns from CANCODE	conversational routine
Hey, Hiya, hello, hi there, How are you	greeting
See you later	leave-taking
welcome, thank you very much, thank god for that, thank goodness for that, thank you ever so much, thanks for your help.	expressives (or acknowledgements) such as: apologizing, appreciating, complimenting, condemning, congratulating, regretting, thanking, welcoming.
Would you like to, do you want, do you want some, I'd love to, that's a nice idea, that would be lovely,	commissives such as promising, offering, inviting
how would you feel about, have you got, would you be willing to, you've got to, you're supposed to, you'll have to, you'd be better off	directives such as commanding, instructing, suggesting, advising, warning, requesting

In this section we look at how a corpus can help us better understand the pragmatic importance of a frequently recurring chunk, which is understood as part of a conversational routine. We have chosen a less obvious example to focus on: the chunk *Are you sure?*

When we explore concordance lists of this chunk in CANCODE, we find that many of its occurrences relate to the seeking of clarification:

(8.5)

> S1: Has he got a drink problem?
> S2: Yeah. He has got a drink problem+
> S3: **Are you sure?**
> S2: +she told me that.
> S4: Ah.

S2: Yeah. He drinks all the time.

S1: Does he?

S2: Mm

(CANCODE)

However, it also occurs as part of the routines of offering and requesting. These speech acts have caused much debate in terms of their categorisation (see Clark and Lucy 1975; Bach and Harnish 1979; Gibbs 1979; Edmonson and House 1981; Blum-Kulka and Olshtain 1984; Blum-Kulka et al. 1989; Brown and Levinson, 1987; Aijmer 1996; Márquez-Reiter 2000). Here we place them under two broad speech act categories, 'commissives' and 'directives' respectively (after Searle 1976; see Carter and McCarthy 2006: 680). Commissives are acts where the speaker commits to a course of action associated with acts such as guaranteeing, offering, inviting, promising, vowing, undertaking. Directives are acts where the speaker intends to make the hearer act in a particular way, associated with acts such as asking, challenging, commanding, daring, forbidding, insisting, instructing, permitting, requesting. In CANCODE, we found that the chunk *Are you sure?* was part of the routine of offering, particularly food. Within this routine re-offers of food are frequently made using *Are you sure?* (a distinction is sometimes made between 'ritual' and 'substantive' re-offers, see Goffman 1971; Schneider 2000, 2003; Barron 2003, 2005). For example:

(8.6)

S1: Tea or coffee?   *offer*

S2: Ooh coffee please.

S3: Nothing for me thank you.

S1: **Are you sure?**   *re-offer*

S3: Yeah no thanks.

(CANCODE)

(8.7)

S1: There's a little bit more pasta there. Would you like it Hannah?   *offer*

S2: I'm full thank you.

S1: **Are you sure?**   *re-offer 1*

S2: Yeah.

S1: Absolutely sure?   *re-offer 2*

S2: Honestly.

(CANCODE)

In these examples, the chunk *Are you sure?* enacts a social routine (or *ritual* within Goffman's 1971 terms; see also Schneider 2000) and has become pragmatically specialized, protecting the negative face of the hearer. It also gives the hearer a chance to opt out of refusal without loss of face:

(8.8)

S1: **Are you sure** you don't want anything to drink Cora?
      There's a load out there.   *offer*

S2: No. I'm grand.
S1: **Are you sure** now?   *re-offer*
S3: Yeah. [unintelligible utterance]
S2: All right. I'll have one.   *acceptance*
S1: Okay. Fine.

(CANCODE)

We also find the chunk *Are you sure?* in the context of the speech act of requesting. Here it is also used relationally to soften the imposition of the request on the hearer even though the request has been acceded to:

(8.9)

S1: . . . Would it be all right if we left some of our stuff here?
S2: Oh that's fine. Yeah.
S1: **Are you sure?**
S2: Yeah. Yeah.

(CANCODE)

In extract (8.10), we see an extended routine where *Are you sure?* is employed twice along with *Positive?, Yeah? Is that okay?, Is that all right?*

(8.10)

S1: . . . em what was I gonna say. Em am I still all right to come round?
S2: Yeah course you are.
S1: **Are you sure?**
S2: Yes.
S1: **Positive?**
S2: Yes.
S1: **Yeah?**
S2: (laughs)
S1: Yeah.
S2: Yes.
S1: Okay. Em cos I'm going to try and get out of here for about half eleven **is that okay?**
S2: Mhm.
S1: **Is that all right?**
S2: Yeah.
S1: **Are you sure?**
S2: Yes.

(CANCODE)

If we compare this chunk across two other spoken corpora, representing Irish English and New Zealand English (LCIE and WSE, respectively), we find similar patterns in the Irish data, but with far more instances of its use in re-offers (33% of all occurrences of *Are you sure?* in LCIE relate to re-offers, almost all relating to food):

(8.11)

S1:	Do you want tea John?	*offer*
S2:	No.	
S3:	**Are you sure** John?	*re-offer*
S2:	Yeah I'm fine thanks.	
S1:	Yeah do you want some of this bread?	*modified re-offer*
S3:	No I'm alright.	

(LCIE)

(8.12)

S1:	. . . will you have a cup of tea?	*offer*
S2:	No thanks.	
S1:	**Are you sure** do you want a bag of Taytos[3] or something?	*re-offer + modified re-offer*
S2:	No thanks.	
S1:	**Are you sure?**	*re-offer*
S2:	No I have to be back for around six.	

(LCIE)

All of the uses of *Are you sure?* in the New Zealand spoken corpus relate to the seeking of further clarification in relation to the offer. In a two-million-word conversational sample of the spoken data of the North American segment of CIC, we find a similar predominance of requests for clarification, for example:

(8.13)

S1:	That big enough?	
S2:	Uhuh.	
S1:	**Are you sure?**	
S2:	Certain.	

(CIC)

This adds weight to those who assert, contrary to Searle (1969), that speech acts, and the strategies and linguistic means available for their realisation, are not universal, but are bound by particular cultural contexts of use (see Fraser and Nolen 1981; Wierzbicka 1985; Fukushima and Iwata 1987; Blum-Kulka 1989; Olshtain 1989; Kasper 1992; Barron 2003, 2005).

8.3   Small talk

In example (8.3) (see p. 161) from the shop encounter, we saw that the shop assistant and the customer engaged in some chat about the weather:

S2:	. . . Coolish isn't it?
S2:	So it is shur. Tis grand. Tis great shur tis kind of dry.

---

[3]   *Tayto* is an Irish brand of potato crisps.

Small talk such as this is a very common relational feature of conversation and something which occurs frequently in a corpus of casual conversation (see Eggins and Slade 1997; McCarthy 2002, 2003). However, *small* talk, as Candlin (2000) warns, should not be confused with unimportant talk. It has an important socio-relational function.

This type of talk was first identified as *phatic communion* by Malinowski (1923, reprinted 1972). His definition cast it in a rather negative light, as a mode of communication which could establish human bonds or communion 'merely' by talking (Coupland 2000). As noted by Coupland (2000), this definition created a legacy whereby small talk was dismissible as 'aimless, prefatory, obvious, uninteresting, sometimes suspect and even irrelevant, but part of a process of fulfilling our intrinsically human needs for social cohesiveness and mutual recognition' (Coupland 2000: 3) (see also Turner 1973; Leech 1974; Wolfson 1981, for examples of negative perceptions of small talk).

More recent reassessments of non-transactional talk, for example Coupland et al. (1992) who build on Laver's work (e.g. Laver 1975), see phatic exchanges as a type of talk that should not be relegated or seen as in some way communicatively deficient. As McCarthy (2000) notes, Laver's work was important, in that he saw phatic exchanges not only as constructing and consolidating social relations, but as strategic mechanisms for creating transitions into and out of transactional talk. Thus, McCarthy (2003) points out, small talk is not something that just sits in the gaps between transactional episodes, but actually facilitates them and enhances their efficiency; it threads them into socially recognisable fabrics which constitute our everyday spoken genres (e.g. service encounter, job interview, etc.). A number of studies have looked at the role of small talk in different contexts, for example Schneider (1989) looked at small talk during hotel check-ins (see also Schneider 1988); Komter (1991) focused on job interviews, where he finds that small talk plays an important role at the beginning of an interview; Ylänne-McEwen (1997) examines the strategic role of small talk in the task of buying and selling in a travel agency (see also Coupland and Ylänne-McEwen 2000); Farr (2005) shows how small talk is used at the start of a post-observation teacher training interaction (this is discussed in chapter 11). Holmes (2000), who looks at 121 hours of workplace interactions in four government departments, concludes that the distinction between business talk and small talk can be difficult to draw and she offers the following continuum, which reflects the cline along which small talk occurs (figure 3):

Figure 3: The small talk continuum from Holmes (2000: 38)

core	work	social	phatic
business _____	related _____	talk _____	communion
talk	talk		

$\leftarrow$ -----S M A L L T A L K ----- $\rightarrow$

Holmes comments that small talk in the workplace functions like knitting, which can be easily taken up and easily dropped. It is 'a useful and undemanding means of filling a gap between work activities' which 'oils the social wheels' and is 'flexible, adaptable, compress-ible and expandable'(2000: 57). This is borne out in the context of this next extract, from a casual conversation between friends. Here we see how small talk is seamlessly interwoven as part of the ongoing business of talk. It is indexical of how the participants orient towards each other relationally as close friends or, as noted by McCarthy (2000) and Tracy and Naughton (2000), how small talk gives voice to social identities and relationships:

(8.13)

S1:   That taxi driver was always telling me
      how his wife was a TEFL teacher.

S2:   No way.

S1:   And she was also a real= she worked
      for the county council but she also
      had a degree from like Trinity.

S3:   Does TEFL mean anything?

S4:   Teaching English as a foreign language.

⎫ ongoing narrative

S2:   **That's a gorgeous top where did you get that?**

S1:   **You got it in Gas didn't you cos you showed**
      it to me the last time. I saw a lovely kind of army
      top in Gas it was a shirt right but it was a bit
      revealing it was crissy crossy from here to there
      but it was lovely on but it was about eighty euro
      and I was like it's going into the summer.

S2:   **And for a top as well you know jeans yeah**
      definitely but.

S1:   **Yeah well I would have worn it if= I probably would**
      have bought it if it was the start of the whole craze
      maybe if it had been winter you probably would have
      gotten more wear out of it cos of you know the whole
      army thing.

⎫ small talk topic 1

S4:   *I'll bet you there is no tea left and Ethel is the*
      one who wanted tea.

S1:   *No it's a big teapot and they're small cups.*

S4:   *We hope.*

S1:   *Yeah there's tea and it's grand strong tea.*

⎫ small talk topic 2

(LCIE)

Part of the relational value of small talk is linked to topics that recur such as weather talk, which is seen as 'safe'. Coupland and Ylänne-McEwen (2000) look at weather talk in two corpora collected in travel agencies in the Welsh city of Cardiff (in differing time periods). The weather, they propose, is a neutral topic, accessible to all participants, non-person-focused and uncontroversial. Or, as Robinson (1972, 1985) notes, the weather is well suited to filling out moments in social interaction when speakers are avoiding other problems, merely maintaining a conversational flow (see Coupland and Ylänne-McEwen 2000). Romaine (1994: 23) sees talk about the weather as more a British phenomenon, where the weather is a safe impersonal topic that can be discussed between two strangers who 'want to be friendly but not too friendly'. Kuiper and Flindall (2000), however, found that the weather was the most frequently raised topic in their study of New Zealand check-out interactions. Coupland and Ylänne-McEwen (2000) point out that, especially in Britain, weather is unpredictable and often does not live up to our expectation and so its constant state-of-change makes it ideal for comment, as this extract from a hairdressing salon shows:

(8.14)

> Hairdresser: It's a lovely day isn't it. Mm.
> Customer: It's lovely.
> Speaker 3: [unintelligible]
> Hairdresser: Too nice to be inside.
> Customer: I know. [unintelligible]
> Hairdresser: Yeah. [laughs] It's it's nice enough really isn't it to sit in the garden.
> Customer: It is.
> Hairdresser: Mm.
> Customer: Yeah. Mind you. It were my day off yesterday. And it was lovely yesterday.
> Hairdresser: It was. Yeah.
> Customer: So that's all right.
> [nine turns later]
> Hairdresser: Thing is you it's hard to think about it coming snow again isn't it+
> Customer: Yeah.

(CANCODE)

McCarthy (2000), using data from CANCODE, looked at small talk episodes in the context of two extended service encounter (the hairdresser's and a driving lesson), where participants were forced into a physically close and mutually captive encounter. He shows how phatic, relational and evaluative episodes were an indispensable aspect of two types of encounters. Even though the hairdresser and driving lesson encounters differ, he notes the similarity in patterns of non-transactional talk and this leads him to conclude that the small talk episodes are something participants worked hard at, and are not something just tossed in for good measure. He confirms their relational role in the construction and consolidation of ongoing commercial relationships and their contribution to the mutual assurance that service was being delivered appropriately.

8.4 Discourse markers

Discourse markers are considered part of a broader class of pragmatic markers within the grammar of spoken English (Östman 1981; Owen 1981; Erman 1987; Schiffrin 1987, 2000; 2001; Fraser 1988, 1990, 1998, 1999; Finell 1989; Redeker 1990, 1991; Jucker 1993; Aijmer 1996, 1997; Brinton 1996; Lenk 1998; Andersen 2000, 2001; Norrick 2001; Macaulay 2002; Carter and

McCarthy 2006; Carter and Fung (forthcoming)). Pragmatic markers are items which mark speakers' personal meanings, their organisational choices, attitudes and feelings. Apart from discourse markers, they include stance markers, which express speakers' attitudes and positions, hedges (see below), which enable speakers to make their utterances less assertive, and common interjections, which encode speakers' affective reactions. Discourse markers are defined as words and phrases outside of the clause structure, that function to link segments of the discourse to one another in ways which reflect choices of monitoring, organisation and management exercised by the speaker. They have a number of communicative functions including the marking of responses in conversation (see chapter 7) and organising discourse through the marking of shifts and boundaries in ongoing talk. The most common discourse markers in everyday informal spoken language are single words such as *anyway, cos, fine, good, great, like, now, oh, okay, right, so, well*, and phrasal and clausal items such as *you know, I mean, as I say, for a start, mind you*. In chapter 2, we found that items such as *well* and *right* were within the top 50 most frequently occurring words because of their high frequency as discourse markers in conversation. A corpus–based description of the forms and functions of discourse markers is provided in Carter and McCarthy (2006: 207–222). Here we focus on the relational aspect of discourse markers.

Discourse markers as monitors

When we speak, we orient towards our listener(s) and constantly monitor what we are saying and how it is being received. Discourse markers have an important role in this. Firstly, they are commonly used to mark reformulations, where the speaker has not selected the most appropriate way of expressing things and is adding to or refining what they say with a more apt word or phrase, or else drawing attention to a word or phrase. The following are some of the most common such markers: *as I was saying, as it were, I mean, if you like, in other words, not to say, so to speak, strictly speaking, to put it another way, well* (see Carter and McCarthy 2006: 220–221 for a more extensive list). Extract (8.16) is from the North American segment of CIC:

(8.16)

    S1: We both+

    S2: Okay.

    S1: +have the same kindred spirits.

    S2: Really?

    S1: We are definitely soul mates **so to speak**.

    S2: Right.

                                                   (CIC)

We can also find examples in writing:

(8.17)

    In specific areas such as space exploration, computer science, and popular music, an author can expect many young readers to have a considerable (**not to say** a remarkable) amount of existing knowledge.

                                                   (CIC)

Another important monitoring function of discourse markers is their use in relation to shared knowledge. As we noted in chapter 3, *you know* is the most frequent chunk of all, and is an important signal of (projected or assumed) shared knowledge between speaker and listener, as well as being a topic-launcher (Östman 1981; Erman 1987). Carter and McCarthy (2006) note that two of the most common discourse markers are *you know* and *(you) see*. Both of these signal that speakers are sensitive to the needs of their listeners and are monitoring the state of shared knowledge in the conversation. *(You) see* projects the assumption that the listener may not have the same state of knowledge as the speaker:

(8.18)

> **You see**, since I've damaged my back in that fall, I find it difficult to climb the stairs without help.
> [Speaker cannot assume the listener knows this.]

(CANCODE)

(8.19)

> You do it like this. Cut the branches right back, **see**, then cut them into smaller pieces.

(CANCODE)

You know projects the assumption that knowledge is shared or that assertions are uncontroversial, and reinforces common points of reference, or checks that the listener is following what is being said:

(8.20)

> S1: Yeah, my mom's always trying to help me, **you know**.
> S2: Yeah.

(CIC North American)

Discourse markers are also used to mark shared knowledge. In this way they are central to a process which binds participants in a conversation as they constantly mark, monitor, and project shared knowledge and shared space. In example (8.21), a friend is relating a sad tale about a man who went into debt, lost his family and ended up homeless. We see how discourse markers here have a binding effect for the speakers, who use them to draw on shared knowledge and a shared sense of empathy:

(8.21)

> S1: . . . he thought it would be best if he wasn't living with his family. Then the husband and wife obviously split up.
> S2: Oh.
> S1: And then+
> S2: How sad.
> S1: +**you know** he he went with friends obviously for a drink to **you know** drown his sorrows.
> S2: Yeah.

S1:   And ended up+

S2:   On the street.

S1:   +on the street. And she doesn't know where he is or anything.

S2:   Could've just cracked. **Well** it must have been he did crack.

S1:   **Well** yes. Yes.

S2:   Because everything collapsed round him. He was obviously a very responsible chap. He [unintelligible] bread-winner.

S1:   He was fine. **I mean** no different from the rest of us

(CANCODE)

This tale could have been told without the use of discourse markers, but it would have lacked the ties to the speakers' shared world. The discourse markers place the speakers relative to the sad tale. They converge on an understanding of how it could have happened to anyone.

8.5   Hedging

Definitions of hedging abound (see Lakoff 1972; Brown and Levinson 1978; Rosch 1978; Fraser 1975, 1980; Rounds 1982; Hübler 1983; Channell 1990; Clemen 1997; Markkanen and Schröder 1997; Schröder and Zimmer 1997). The term was coined by Lakoff (1972: 195) where it was used to refer to the semantic concept of how certain words 'make things fuzzier or less fuzzy'. Within a pragmatics paradigm (see Brown and Levinson 1978), hedging is viewed interactionally in terms of how the use of certain words or phrases can mitigate the directness of what we say and so operate as face-saving devices (see Channell 1990; Clemen 1997; Markannen and Schröder 1997). Carter and McCarthy (2006) include hedges within the category of 'pragmatic markers'. 'Speakers are often careful not to sound too blunt and assertive', they say, 'and a variety of markers exist to hedge (i.e. to express degrees of uncertainty) and to be less assertive' (Carter and McCarthy 2006: 223). Take the following example:

Hedged utterance:

And I was up all night **like** Wednesday and I **just I think** I'm **just a bit kind of** dazed from the whole experience.

(CIC North American)

Unhedged utterance:

And I was up all night Wednesday and I'm dazed from the whole experience.

The corpus example, which contains six hedges (*like, just* (twice), *I think, a bit* and *kind of*) attends to the potential face threat for the hearer. The unhedged example does not and so could offend the hearer. The terms *mitigating* and *downtoning*, which are often used in relation to hedging, capture the function of the hedges in this example: they *downtone* the force of the utterance and they *mitigate* against any potential threat to face.

Hedges come in many forms (see Biber et al. 1999; Carter and McCarthy 2006), the most common of which are summarised in Table 4.

Hedging can vary relative to context. Some situations demand more hedging than others. For example, there is more at stake when we are talking to our boss than when we are chatting with a family member. This is borne out if we search a corpus for some of the

Table 4: Summary of the most common forms of hedges (examples from LCIE)

form	example
modal verbs and verbs with modal meaning (*believe, feel, guess, imagine, reckon, suppose, think*), especially when used with the pronoun *I*	*I **guess** the bus service isn't too good, is it?*
nouns	*there is a **possibility**, the **thing** is*, etc.
adverbs • degree adverbs • restrictive adverbs • stance adverbs	*quite, really, relatively, necessarily* *just, only* *of course, actually, kind of, sort of, really, maybe*
syntactic choices • choice of question form • double negative • evaluative relative clause insertion	***And would you have thought** you were very close to him?* [as opposed to: *And **were you** very close to him?*] *it's not that I'm not afraid . . .* vs. *I am afraid* *You got them to do this cross-group reporting **which was a good idea** but the time was the problem*
features of 'onlineness' adjustments (false starts, repetitions, etc.)	*And **will you would you** like to go **sort** of on a sun and sea holiday with him this year?*

most frequent hedging items across different types of data. Farr et al. (2002) exemplified this context sensitivity of hedging when they conducted a comparative word frequency count for the ten most frequent hedging items in LCIE: *just, really, actually, probably, I think, a bit, kind of, sort of, you know, I suppose.* They compared how these forms varied in frequency as hedges across the following contexts: family conversations, teaching practice feedback, calls to a radio phone-in show, conversations at the counter of a shop and female friends chatting. They found the distribution shown in figure 4:

Figure 4: Frequency distribution of hedging items in LCIE (per million words) (Farr et al. 2002)

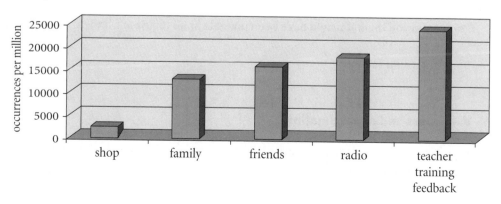

As we can see from these data, the least amount of hedging was found in shop encounters. This is perhaps explained by the lesser need to protect face in service encounters, where a customer and a server do not know each other, and where they are interacting within transactional roles. Nonetheless, there is a degree of hedging in such encounters, for example *I'll just have a receipt,* where *just* is used as a hedge to lessen the imposition of a request for a receipt. The next least hedged context was found to be in the family settings. Here, as Clancy (2002, 2005) notes, the family relationship is fixed and so needs less attention to save face as a result (see also Blum-Kulka 1994, 1997a, and 1997b). In the CANCODE sub-corpus of conversations between family and friends CANSOC, we found also that *just* is commonly used with directive acts (figure 5):

Figure 5: Sample concordance lines for *just* in CANSOC

```
<$2> Can't you just keep your hair out of your eyes.
     Yes. If we just lay them over so they're overlapping a bit on the blades like that.
        <$1> Just lean on them. <$2> It doesn't matter.
Why don't you just leave earlier. But it only takes ten minutes to get here.
    t.    <$3> Just leave it Steve.      <$?M> <$E> laughs </$E>    <$3> <$=> Take take
  ah.    <$?F> Just leave it there.      <$?F> Oh.    <$E> briefly unintelligible <\$E>
ear okay let's just leave it <$G2>    <$2> Hi.    <$3> Hello.    <$2> I think <$G?>
  <$1> And then just leave it on your on your thing.    <$2> +and they leave
    $=>    <$3> Just leave it till Saturday morning. <$G?>    <$6> No. I'll do it tomorrow
it on.    <$1> Just leave it on.    <$5> <$G?>.    <$1> What do you think of the poem
Just mate just just let go. <$H> No problem. <\$H>    <$2> Oh we had a great night
go after this. Just let him get out the way.    <$1> I've gotta look for something for my
<\$E>.    <$1> Just let it go son. <$H> <$=> Put it <\$=> <\$H> Put it on the bed. <$E>
no just just just let it flow you know.    <$1> Emphasis required. Er    <$2> Just a
    just <\$=> Just let Maisie out. I think she's just off. Won't be a second.    <$?F>
> Yep.    <$7> Just lift her up a little bit.    <$5> <$G?>    <$7> That's it.    <$3>
```

Note, however, that *just* can also be an intensifier in directives, depending on intonation. The institutional contexts of radio discourse and teacher training post-observation feedback contain a relatively high degree of hedging and this correlates with the speaker relationship. The speaker relationships are asymmetrical yet the power role holder (the teacher trainer and the radio presenter) wishes to downtone her power and to seem encouraging to the trainees and the radio listeners and callers respectively. An example from Farr's data (see Farr 2005) illustrates this in the context of criticism:

(8.22)

Trainer: **Do you think it would have been possible at all** to **just** leave them work through them all?

Trainee: **I would say so.**

(LCIE)

8.6   **Vagueness and approximation**

Vague language is another pervasive feature of spoken English. Like hedging, its use softens expressions so that they do not appear too direct or unduly authoritative and assertive. Carter and McCarthy (2006: 202) tell us that it is an important feature of interpersonal meaning and includes words and phrases such as *thing, stuff, or so, like, or something, or anything, or whatever, kind of, sort of.* Vagueness is motivated and *purposeful* and is often a mark of the sensitivity and skill of a speaker (Powell 1985; Channell 1994; Carter and McCarthy 2006). There are times where it is necessary to give accurate and precise information in many informal contexts; however, speakers prefer to convey information which is softened in some way. For example, (8.23) is an extract from a sales presentation from the CANBEC spoken business English corpus where an important point is being made, but where the speaker regularly inserts hedges and monitors of shared knowledge (as discussed above):

(8.23)

> . . . **I mean I think** there is often a tendency to keep introducing new varieties things with new features but like I say what you can end up with with is a is a very unwieldy set of products that you offer. And sometimes you need to say 'Right. Let's go back to the core sellers and cut out these that **you know** we've we've added on to our our product mix but really they're **just** we've **just** got **kind of** peripheral sales for those'. [pause]. And finally you've got **this thing of** increasing or reducing consistency. [pause] **I think** sometimes firms end up they've diversified too much and then they decide 'Well we're gonna cut back down to our our core business'. So those are are really **kind of** the key areas of product mix management. . . .

> (CANBEC)

Vague language is defined in a number of ways. Franken (1997) distinguishes between 'vagueness' and 'approximation' (see also Carter and McCarthy 2006), while Channell (1994) restricts the definition of vagueness to 'purposefully and unabashedly vague' uses of languages. Chafe (1982) puts vagueness and hedging together into the category of 'fuzziness', all of which are seen as 'involvement devices' more prevalent in spoken rather than written language.

Here we are interested in the relational side of vague language and the two main functions of vague language in this respect are:

- to hedge assertions or to make them fuzzy by allowing speakers to downtone what they say; this is often done through approximation.
- to indicate assumed or shared knowledge and mark in-group membership because the referents of vague expressions can be assumed to be known by the listener; this is especially achieved through the use of vague category markers using items such as *and things like that, and that kind of thing.*

Approximation

Being absolutely precise, especially in spoken language, can come across as being pedantic and so speakers frequently introduce approximators to downtone what might otherwise sound overly precise; for example, adverbs and prepositions are most commonly used for this purpose (Carter and McCarthy 2006: 203–205).

I'll see you **around** six.

There were **roughly** twenty people turned up.

I had the goldfish for **about** three years.

In extract (8.24), from CANBEC, we see how the speakers approximate using vague quantifiers:

(8.24)

> S1: . . . I didn't want to do that if then we were going to get a big tax bill from it and we+
>
> S2: Yeah.
>
> S1: +couldn't afford to pay it.
>
> S2: Yeah. How much is that? How much is in the rental account then assuming you've had no drawings out of that have you?
>
> S1: No no drawings at all.
>
> S2: You've just let it build up.
>
> S1: There's **about** two thousand.
>
> S2: But we're now don't forget **a couple or three** months into the next year.
>
> S1: Yeah. Yeah it's **round about** two thousand.
>
> S2: Yeah.
>
> S1: **About a couple of** months in advance now.
>
> S2: Yeah.
>
> S1: So that's handy.

(CANBEC)

The second relational function that we focus on here is the use of vague category markers (VCMs) to indicate assumed or shared knowledge and mark in-group membership. VCMs are most typically, but not exclusively, found in clause-final positions and often consist of a conjunction and a noun phrase (for example, *and/or that sort of thing*). In the literature, they go by different terms such as: 'general extenders' (Overstreet and Yule 1997a, 1997b); 'generalized list completers' (Jefferson 1990); 'tags' (Ward and Birner 1992); 'terminal tags' (Dines 1980; Macaulay 1991); 'extension particles' (DuBois 1993); 'vague category identifiers' (Channell 1994; Jucker et al. 2003); and 'vague category markers' (O'Keeffe 2003, 2006; Evison et al. 2007). Consider extract (8.25), from a casual conversation between friends:

(8.25)

[Friends are talking about the possibility of going to a health farm]

> S1: +we said at one point 'Wouldn't it be great to go to a health farm'. And I said 'I'm sure Sarah's been'.
>
> S2: Well the reason I liked Inglewood was that it's it was totally sort of unpretentious.
>
> S1: Yeah.
>
> S2: It wasn't all+
>
> S1: Yeah.
>
> S2: +**designer tracksuits**+

S1:   Yeah. Yeah.
S2:   **+and that kind of thing**.
S1:   Yes. I think I'd I would.
S2:   There was er you know a fair cross section of people there.

(CANCODE)

Speaker 2 creates a category which did not exist before they spoke in any pre-fabricated form: *designer tracksuits and that kind of thing*. Vague categories are regularly established in this way in conversations between participants who have shared knowledge which they can draw on. Speaker 2 created this ad hoc category (see Barsalou 1983, 1987) because she knew that her friend would know what she meant. Speaker 1 did not seek clarification as to what was meant. The reference is also a marker of shared cultural knowledge. The set has a finite range and is drawn from a British context. Speaker 2 is referring to a set of people who wear designer clothes, come from a higher social class and interact in glamorous social networks, a group that neither participant feels part of. The vague category thus has a relational value in that it reinforces the shared knowledge and close relationship of the interlocutors. Vague categories ask the hearer to construct the relevant components of the set which they evoke and promote the active co-operation of the listener (Jucker et al. 2003). The meanings of vague categories are socio-culturally grounded and are co-constructed within a social group that has a shared social reality.

Some more examples of vague category markers (VCMs) are given here from CAN-CODE and the spoken North American segment of CIC:

(8.26)
[Speaker is talking about various people's jobs]
   And my husband travelled for his father, selling **and that sort of thing**.

(CANCODE)

(8.27)
   And then she's got like a nice living room. It's like table and chairs and **that kind of thing**.

(CIC North American)

(8.28)
S1:   So when you go there it's everything's covered.
S2:   Hm.
S1:   Transportation and ticket fees **and so on and so forth**.

(CIC North American)

In order to use VCMs successfully, speakers must have expectations about what their co-participants know, and such expectations are negotiated within social space. Within a socially defined group, VCMs become a tool for creating short-cuts and by looking at these short-cuts we can get an indication of the nature and degree of shared knowledge which is held within a socially defined group (Evison et al. 2007). There is a further example in (8.29) overleaf.

(8.29)

[From a business meeting]

S1: Again well it's is is er is a big town. Ninety thousand people would you believe live there. Down between Bournemouth and Weymouth. And what we've got there is if you turn . . . that way up it says Lyndon shopping centre at the bottom. And that is er a full shopping centre which is . . . you've got all the usual culprits in there.

S2: Mm.

S1: Marks and Spencer Debenhams British Home Stores **all that kind of thing**.

(CANBEC)

The ad hoc category created here refers to a British type of shop, of a certain size, one which is usually considered to be a high street store and an anchor tenant in the context of a shopping centre. The participants share this understanding and there is no requirement for speaker A to provide an exhaustive list, nor to say what is not included, like a local butcher or cake shop. However, there is obvious relativism here culturally. McCarthy et al. (2005) looked in detail at how VCMs functioned in academic discourse as a means of constructing a sense of shared space within which learning takes place. Here is in an example from the LIBEL corpus (see appendix 1) where a lecturer is negotiating shared space, in the sense expounded by Vygotsky (1978), for whom social relationships, language use, thought and cultural activity share the same creative space (see chapter 11). Notice also how the use of markers of shared knowledge, *you know, do you know what I mean* (as discussed above), serve along with the VCM, to invoke this shared space in (8.30), indicating the relational importance of creating this commonage in the context of learning:

(8.30)

[drama lecture]

Yeah aam well there there has been this there has been a massive dichotomy in drama education over the last forty fifty years where aam I suppose traditionalists process drama is by its nature. It's not just about drama it's quite it's an emancipatory form **you know** it's about aam discovery learning. It's about active learning. It's it's **you know** it would have taken **you know** in theoretical terms it would have taken its lead from **playwrights like** Brecht but also from **people like** Paulo Freire **and stuff like that. You know** it's about freedom. It's about discovering aam and it's not so much about the drama okay at least that's how people in theatre have viewed it **do you know what I mean?** Whereas the traditional side of things the tradition of mainstream drama and theatre feel that what we should be doing in terms of drama is we should be going in teaching people about theatre history and we should be teaching them about how drama works about who were the great playwrights were aah what a monologue is how do you mime **and so on and so forth**.

(LIBEL)

8.7   Conclusions and implications

Here we have focused on the functions of many of the most frequently recurring words and phrases in spoken English based on our earlier studies of words, chunks and idioms (chapters 2, 3 and 4, respectively). Their pervasiveness in spoken language has a number of implications. In relation to corpus data and corpus investigation, we conclude with the following points.

- As we noted in chapter 7, by looking at frequency lists in a corpus, these items become obvious in terms of their frequency. However, it is necessary again here to go beyond the list itself to see how they are functioning. What appears to be an adjective or adverb may for the most part be functioning at a discourse level, for example, as a discourse marker, outside of the clause structure. Going beyond the word list to look qualitatively at concordance lines and stretches of discourse also brings to light how these high-frequency words and fixed phrases can often function as part of conversational routines, which, as in the example of *Are you sure?* (as part of the routine of ritual offers), may not be immediately obvious. This is also the case when we look at small corpora of specific interactions such as the sales example in the electrical shop, where we found the pragmatically specialised use of *you've got*.
- Looking at a corpus also tells us that, in many cases, items are high frequency because of their discourse function rather than by virtue of their traditional word class. Perhaps a broader model is needed for how we view word classes. We have no problem talking about a verb that can also be a noun (or vice versa, for example, *rebel, record, knife*). Perhaps we should also view discourse markers in the same way. Then we could say that '*right* most commonly occurs as a core discourse marker in spoken English. It is used to organise discourse openings and closing, raise topics, mark responses and when it is used in asymmetrical interactions, it is used by the power-role holder. It is also used as an adverb and adjective . . .'

As we have seen in this chapter, so many of these high-frequency items are central to interaction and this makes them difficult to ignore as vocabulary items. Let us consider some pedagogical implications from this chapter.

- The items which we have looked at in this chapter relate to how speakers in the real time of online speech orient, monitor, manage, modify and soften their message so as to relate to the hearer. This, as we have seen, is as much a part of purely transactional discourse, as it is part of conversations between friends, though it may vary in degree and nature. This makes a compelling argument for not neglecting this area of language when teaching. As we have discussed elsewhere however, learners may choose to reject such items or never actively use them, but nonetheless we argue that language learners need to be made aware of their role in spoken English (and in any other languages to which they pertain). They are not something that can be cast aside as only being needed when native speakers interact. As we have frequently seen here, there is a high degree of crossover between interactional and transactional language and this carries teaching implications in the context of professional discourses which native and non-native speakers engage in. We have shown numerous examples here from academic and business English contexts and shown how features such as vagueness and hedging are socially valued in these situations.

- Many of the examples that we looked at in this chapter came from small sub-corpora, or specialised corpora (shop encounters, academic lectures, radio interactions, teacher education feedback sessions, business meetings). If we had looked at mega-corpora, many of the features would not have shown up or may not have been as apparent. By isolating sub-corpora of specific contexts of interaction from very large datasets, we can get a very concentrated picture of how language use becomes specialised in its context of use and how lexico-grammatical patterns become routinised.

- This creates a compelling case for using small specialised corpora in the context of teaching Languages for Specific Purposes. By way of illustration, if we look at a high frequency verb such as *go* in CANBEC, a one-million-word corpus of business interactions, we find many examples of the pattern *going forward:*

Figure 6: Sample concordance lines for *going forward* in CANBEC

```
that it couldn't actually see our forecast going forward it could only see what we'd
 the present day. It couldn't actually see going forward. So with erm the requirements
this+           That's good.          +year going forward.           Mm.          That's
     we're hoping they'll be back       and going forward we can actually reduce the
ually need to make sure that your forecast going forward is actually  correct which then
is that it won't generate as much revenue  going forward. It doesn't have the right level
```

The term is used as an alternative to *in the future,* but it only occurs in the context of business interactions. On one level, this is a matter of specialised vocabulary use, but the broader pedagogical implication is that this is a phrase which marks in-group membership. By looking at this sub-corpus of specific interactions, we have been able to identify this fixed pattern which is, to paraphrase Kuiper and Flindall (2000: 185), part of the 'culture' within this type of discourse. In this sense, it has a relational value for the users. If you can use this phrase, you can belong more within the 'business culture'. This goes beyond whether the user is a native or a non-native speaker. The use of an in-group marker such as *going forward* has more to do with belonging or not belonging. This is just one of countless examples of routinised language use within specific contexts which a carefully chosen sub-corpus can show up either through hands-on discovery-based use or through teacher-led tasks. It also illustrates the importance of specialized corpora for materials writers in the area of Languages for Specific Purposes.

- On a number of occasions, we have alluded to the cultural relativity of these features of relational language and this brings up the issue of cross-cultural communication and the importance of pragmatic awareness in language teaching. Using small specialised comparative spoken corpora across different languages means that we can take a close look at language use cross-culturally in specific socio-cultural contexts. We can examine closely, for example, how speech acts compare, how shop encounters differ, the degree to which people hedge and how they hedge across languages, and so on. As Dash (2004) notes, it is important that language teachers have an understanding of pragmatics and of the implications for teaching it, particularly in the L2 classroom, so that students can be better equipped to avoid cross-cultural communication problems (or pragmatic failure, see Thomas 1983). However, for this to be fully realised as a pedagogical strategy, we ideally need audio-visually aligned spoken corpora.

9 Language and creativity: creating relationships

9.1 Introduction

This chapter extends the theme of relationship building and language use explored in the last chapter, by exploring how creativity and language play in spoken language contribute to interpersonal involvement between speakers. In the context of spoken language, we see creativity as something which is achieved collaboratively by speakers, and thus it is highly relational. We start by reflecting on the relationship between language and creativity, moving beyond description in linguistic terms to reflect on the implications for pedagogy. It must be said that, while much research has been undertaken at the interface between language and creativity, less thought and less empirical investigation have been devoted to classroom applications. The ideas suggested at the end of the chapter, where we look at whether pedagogic strategies can be developed to make such language use more widespread in the language classroom, are necessarily tentative though we argue that they provide a strong basis for development. In discussing such moves from corpus to classroom, we also return to questions raised in our introduction about the role of native and non-native Englishes, the expectations surrounding different uses of English by different expert users and, in particular, we discuss what may happen to interpersonal relationships between speakers when different kinds of creative language use are mobilised.

9.2 Spoken language and creativity

We begin by examining a typical instance of language extracted from CANCODE and describe what is creative about it. Researchers working with CANCODE have been unable to ignore the pervasive instances of word play and creative language use in many parts of the corpus and have begun to investigate these phenomena further (Adolphs and Carter 2003; Carter 1999a; Carter 2004; Carter and McCarthy 1997, 2004). This research takes a different direction to most accounts of creativity which normally pursue the topic in relation to canonical written text, often drawing on traditions of creativity and composition theory (Nash and Stacey 1997). Drawing on and extending analysis in Carter (2004) and (2006), the corpus research reported here allows us to question the significance of terms such as 'figures of speech' (which are, ironically, rarely illustrated with speech examples) and to challenge notions that terms such as *literariness* can only be reserved for contexts of writing.

Creative speech in action: an example on a Sunday afternoon

Extract (9.1) is typical of many such instances from CANCODE. Two main features are manifest in the extract (as they are in many other extracts): 'pattern-forming choices' and 'pattern-reforming choices'. What are these patterns? What do they do? Pattern-forming in this extract mainly involves repetition across speaking turns. For example:

(9.1)

[Three extracts from a conversation recorded on a Sunday afternoon (see also extract (9.2) for the extended extract), involving female students around the age of 20 who share a house, talking freely among themselves on no fixed topic. In the first extract they comment how nice it is that one of them comes home on Sundays at the end of the weekend, when she is normally away from the house.]

1 S1: [laughs] cos you **come home**
   S2: I **come home**
   S3: You **come home** to us
2 S1: Sunday is **a really nice day** I think
   S2: **It certainly is**
   S1: **It's a really nice relaxing day**
3 S1: I reckon **it looks better like that**
   S2: And it was another **bit** as well, another dangly **bit**
   S1: What, attached to
   S2: The top **bit**
   S1: **That one**
   S2: Yeah. So it was even
   S1: Mobile earrings
   S3: I like **it like that. It looks better like that**

(CANCODE)

Here the pattern-forming involves both verbatim phrasal and clausal repetition and repetition with variation (for example, the addition of the word *relaxing*). The patterning with variation includes both lexical and grammatical repetition (the repetition of the word *bit* or *like* – in its different grammatical realisations as verb and preposition – as well as repetition of the deictic *that*), pronominal variation and phonological variation (for example, *bit/better*). Repetition is by means of word, phrase, clause and phonetic pattern. Pattern-forming tendencies normally involve expected language forms that are reproduced rather than departed from.

Pattern-forming choices do not normally draw attention to themselves in the same way as pattern-reforming choices. In the case of 'pattern-reforming' choices speakers draw attention to the expected sequence of patterns by reforming and reshaping them. In extreme versions of reforming a more radical position can be created by the 'reform' in which co-conversationalists may be prompted to pleasure and laughter as well as to positive (and negative) stances and evaluative viewpoints. Pattern-reforming can often make our routinised 'normal' view of things appear strange or disturb or upset it, and thus generate new or renewed perceptions. There are risks connected with pattern-reforming as others may not understand or appreciate what is being said or done and some speakers will be averse to such risks.

The most marked example of pattern-reforming in the 'Sunday afternoon' conversation in extract (9.1) involves metaphoric and associated word play and occurs, most markedly, in the word *mobile* which is metaphorically linked with the word *earrings*. There is a pun on the meaning of 'mobile' (with its semantics of movement) and the fixture of a mobile – either a brightly coloured dangling object which is normally placed over a child's bed to provide distraction or entertainment or else which is a piece of moving art. Here is a fuller version of the conversational extracts in (9.1):

(9.2)
[Extended extract as for (9.1)]

 1 S1: I like Sunday nights for some reason. [laughs] I don't know why.
 2 S2: [laughs] Cos you come home.
 3 S1: I come home+
 4 S2: You come home to us.
 5 S1: +and pig out.
 6 S2: Yeah yeah.
 7 S1: Sunday is a really nice day I think.
 8 S2: It certainly is.
 9 S1: It's a really nice relaxing day.
 10 S2: It's an earring.
 11 S1: Oh lovely oh lovely.
 12 S2: It's fallen apart a bit. But
 13 S1: It looks quite nice like that actually. I like that. I bet, is that supposed to be straight?
 14 S2: Yeah.
 15 S1: I reckon it looks better like that.
 16 S2: And it was another bit as well. Was another dangly bit.
 17 S1: What . . . attached to+
 18 S2: The top bit.
 19 S1: +that one.
 20 S2: Yeah. So it was even.
 21 S1: Mobile earrings.
 22 S3: I like it like that. It looks better like that.
 23 S2: Oh what did I see. What did I see. Stained glass. There w=, I went to a craft fair.
 24 S1: Mm.
 25 S2: C=, erm in Bristol. And erm, I know. [laughs] I went to a craft fair in Bristol and they had erm this stained glass stall and it was all mobiles made out of stained glass.

26 S1: Oh wow.

27 S2: And they were superb they were. And the mirrors with all different colours, like going round in the colour colour wheel. But all different size bits of coloured glass on it.

28 S1: Oh wow.

29 S2: It was superb. Massive.

Let us now look more closely at the extract. There is a lot of pattern-forming here. As researchers such as Tannen (1989) observe, pattern-forming functions in particular to make people feel more together. The pattern-forming features here also have a more cumulative effect and create conditions in which speakers grow to feel they occupy shared worlds, in which the risks attendant on pattern-reforming creativity are reduced and in which intimacy and convergence are actively co-produced. These relationship-reinforcing shared worlds and viewpoints are created not just by the repetitions and echoes we have highlighted but also in a number of ways: for example, by means of supportive minimal and non-minimal response tokens (see chapter 7), such as *Oh lovely, oh, lovely, Yeah yeah* (lines 6, 11, 14); by means of specifically reinforcing interpersonal grammatical forms such as tags: *They were superb, **they were*** (line 27) and: *They do, **don't they***, and by means of affective exclamatives: *oh wow* (line 28). The exchanges are also impregnated with vague and hedged language forms (e.g. *fallen apart a bit, the top bit, I reckon, for some reason, I don't know why*), and a range of evaluative and attitudinal expressions (often juxtaposed with much laughter) that further support the informality, intimacy and solidarity established. These are typically, spoken, interactive forms of language, often dismissed as irrelevant to language study, or as mere dysfluency, or by most grammars of English as simply non-standard. Of course, most grammars of English are based on written examples so we find ourselves in a circle we cannot easily break out of but must if spoken language is to be properly recognised and described.

Pattern-reforming has, however, more than a relationship-reinforcing function, even when it involves pattern-forming creativity. For example, in an earlier phase of the 'Sunday' conversation (extract 9.3) two of the women deliberately take on parodic voices by mimicking low-prestige accents and concerns, in the process indirectly co-producing an ironic, humorous reflection on their own needs. The repetitions here draw attention to the effects produced:

(9.3)

['They', in the first turn, refers to a type of cake being offered by one of the women; 'fag' means cigarette in this context.]

S1: Well they would go smashing with a cup of tea wouldn't they.

S2: Oh they would.

S1: [in mock Cockney accent] **Cup of tea and a fag**.

S3: [in mock Cockney accent] **Cup of tea and a fag missus**. [reverts to normal accent] We're gonna have to move the table I think.

The chorus-like repetition by speaker 3 of speaker 1's parody and her addition of *missus* underlines the collaborative nature of the creative humour, a point to which we shall return. The women perform the temporary speech roles of 'working-class London (Cockney-speaking) women'. Other examples of pattern-reforming are also more directly interpersonal. There are less overtly displayed instances of creative language use including similes inviting comparison; in this case, a perceived likeness in extract (9.2) between stained glass mobiles seen at a local craft fair and a colour wheel (lines 25–28), which is discussed below in greater detail. There is also a case for seeing some of the formality switches (for example, *pig out*, line 5) as constituting ironic-comic reversals of the kind not uncommonly connected with humorous creative effects. Sometimes the effect of these mainly pattern-reforming features is playfully to provide for humour and entertainment, but such patterns also generate innovative ways of seeing things and convey the speaker's own, more personalised representation of events.

We have dwelt in some detail on this example because it is prototypical. It challenges assumptions that creativity can be assessed on the basis of a single sentence or short text examples, or described with reference to the single, representational voice. Patterns form and reform dynamically and organically over stretches of discourse, and emerge through the *joint* conditions of production (in other words, we need to recognise how often creative language is *co-constructed*). We would challenge an underlying assumption in the analysis of much canonical literary discourse that creative language functions mainly for its own sake or for purposes of formal aesthetic presentation. Indeed, we would argue instead that creative language choices entail a variety of discoursal functions which compel recognition of the social contexts of their production: principally the construction of social identity and the maintenance of interpersonal relations. And at the same time we need a corpus of naturally occurring language to illustrate such features.

9.3   Corpora and creativity

But first we need to look at one other notion – that of creativity. This is yet another term used by Chomsky (1957, 1965) to demonstrate that the native speaker's competence includes a capacity, a creative capacity to form structures from their underlying competence that they could not possibly have heard before. Such a capacity, it is argued by omission, is not available to non-native speakers.

In our corpus studies, as we have seen, we do indeed find speakers who are constantly playing with words, creatively extending, deforming and re-forming them anew. And, as with all of our examples, an investigation of a spoken corpus will show that these are not isolated phenomena but are constantly ongoing and current. A couple of brief examples involve the words *like* and the morpheme *-ish*. Both these items, according to our searches, are especially active and mobile at the present time, creating new meanings, forms and functions before our very eyes.

Like is pervasive. The word is approximately five times as frequent in spoken English as in written English. It is a word that is in the top 30 words in spoken English in the spoken corpora we have examined (CANCODE, BNC, COBUILD) (see chapter 2). In addition to its familiar use as a verb, it is used to mark a quotation of direct speech (9.4), to make statements approximate (9.5), to add a note of deliberate vagueness to expressions (9.6), and to pose analogy-seeking questions (9.7).

(9.4)

> And my mum's **like**, non stop three or four times, come and tell your grandma about your holiday.
>
> (CANCODE)

(9.5)

> Just watching it all on TV was a shattering, frightening experience **like**.
>
> (CANCODE)

(9.6)

> When we were living there as students, we'd have lots of parties and stuff **like** that.
>
> (CANCODE)

(9.7)

> S1: What did you do today?
> S2: What did I do today? Erm. Oh. Had a good day actually. Got loads of stuff sorted out. Finished loads of odds and ends.
> S1: Did you? **Like** what?
> S2: **Like** my programme. Finished that off.
>
> (CANCODE)

-*Ish* is also very commonly used, mainly to hedge a statement (see chapter 8), to add a note of caution in descriptions, to express a little uncertainty and also to interact with other speakers so as not to sound too authoritative or certain of ourselves, not putting others down or making them feel we know everything. *Ish* is a 'democratic' morpheme and helps establish symmetrical and convergent speaking exchanges. And in (9.9) below it seems to have become a word in its own right.

(9.8)

> S1: What's he look like?
> S2: Well, for a start he's attractive . . . **attractiveish**.
>
> (BNC)

(9.9)

> S1: What time are they getting here?
> S2: Oh I don't know. Seven. **-Ish.**
>
> (BNC)

9.4 **Creative speakers**

Creativity is, however, not simply or exclusively the preserve of the native speaker, however subtly and adaptively such forms are being created and re-created here in the above examples. Extract (9.10) is taken from another corpus, a corpus of emails. Email is an interesting genre in that it falls somewhere between speech and writing. It is written through a keyboard but there is also something of the immediacy and interactivity of speaking, with minimal time for thought and revision as dictated by the online demands of the exchange. Email is a genre which is rich in creative possibilities. Here two non-native speakers are emailing each other as part of an ordinary, everyday exchange. The two writer-speakers, Viki and Sue, are both female undergraduate students at the University of Nottingham, UK. Viki is 21 years old; Sue is 22 years old. They are both from Hong Kong and are first language speakers of Cantonese.

(9.10)
[Cantonese translations: wei wei . . . lei dim ar – hi, how are you?; ng gan yiu la – it doesn't matter; ar, che, loh and la are discourse markers in Cantonese]

Viki:	it's snowing quite strong outside . . . be careful
Sue:	I will, thx
Viki:	wei wei . . . lei dim ar?
Sue:	ok, la, juz got bk from Amsterdam loh, how r u?
Viki:	ok la.. I have 9 tmrw
Sue:	haha, I have 2–4 . . . sooooooooooo happy
Viki:	che . . . anyway . . . have your rash gone?
Sue:	yes, but I have scar oh . . . ho ugly ar!
Viki:	icic . . . ng gan yiu la . . . still a pretty girl, haha!!

(University of Nottingham email corpus)

Note here in particular the creative mixing of email/texting shorthand (*thx* =thanks), (*tmrw* = tomorrow), (*9, 2–4* = classes at 9 a.m. and 2–4 p.m), (*icic* = I see, I see). There is also a creative play with voice and vocalisation (*sooooooooooo, ha ha*) as well as a constant creative insertion of interactive discourse markers transliterated from Cantonese.

Some may argue that such discourses underline the irreversible decline of standard English into a series of mutually unintelligible sub-languages, though the same might have been said over 100 years ago with the invention of the telegraph and the emergence of 'telegram' English, now widely accepted as an economically efficient and fully communicative 'shorthand'. Another way of seeing such exchanges is, however, to observe the richness and resourcefulness of which everyday users of English are capable and to praise the creative invention which results from the mixing. An even stronger interpretation would be to recognise the clear need the two students have to appropriate a language which is not simply English but their own English and to develop a repertoire of mixed codes which enables them to give expression to their feelings of friendship, intimacy and involvement with each other's feelings and attitudes – a discourse which would not be to the same degree available to them through the medium of standard written English.

The classroom may thus be a place where learners are encouraged to push back the boundaries by playing with email language, sharing with others in the class the different inventions, varying their creative words and phrases according to the person they are writing to and reflecting on the creativity inherent in the blending between speech and writing embodied in the medium. Typical tasks might include exploring ways of giving emphasis to key words, creating hybrid communication between languages known to both parties, rewriting formal into informal emails, serious into more playful and intimate emails and exploring what constraints there are to the topics that can be creatively engaged with.

9.5 Applications to pedagogy

Discussions of creativity in relation to language teaching and learning have tended to focus on issues of learners' own creativity in relation to language learning processes. For example, the teaching of literature in a variety of cultural contexts may be better informed by understandings of the pervasively creative character of everyday language and can support attempts by some practitioners (see Carter and McRae 1996; Cook 2000, part 3; Pope 2005) to establish continuities between literary and everyday language and establish stronger bridges between language and literature teaching. Appreciation of literary and broader cultural variation can also be supported by reference to what learners already understand and can do rather than by means of more deficit-related pedagogic paradigms. The idea that creativity exists in a remote and difficult-to-access world of literary genius can be de-motivating to the apprentice student of literature, especially in contexts where an L2 literature is taught, but where the primary goal is mastery of the foreign language.

But it is not only in the teaching of literature where the value of exposure to the more open-ended and creative aspects of language may be exploited. One criticism of notional-functional and task-based approaches to language teaching and learning is their tendency towards focusing on the transactional and the transfer of information, with the danger that language use comes to be seen only as utilitarian and mechanistic. While learners undoubtedly have survival needs, and while a language such as English has indeed become a utilitarian object for many of its worldwide users, learners in many contexts around the world relatively quickly pass from purely utilitarian motivations towards goals associated with expressing their social and cultural selves and seek that kind of liberation of expression which they enjoy in their first language. In such contexts, exposure to creativity can be enjoyed and understood in the most common of everyday settings. In these respects methodologies need to be developed which help learners better to internalise and appreciate relationships between creative patterns of language, purposes and contexts which can foster both literary appreciation and greater language understanding. Aston (1988) nicely refers to 'learning comity' (the book's title) as a desirable response to the transactional bias of contemporary language pedagogy, and much of his argumentation centres round bridging 'interactional' gaps, as opposed to the transactional information gaps so beloved of communicative pedagogy. Can our corpus-based insights into the relationship between language and creativity be further mobilised in this direction?

9.6   Corpus to pedagogy: creating relationships

Figure 1 shows sets of tasks for use with learners of English which draw on ideas about creativity discussed in relation to the above 'Sunday afternoon' (9.2) example. There is particular attention to some ways in which language is used to create more interactional affect and convergence. Both the data and the suggested tasks represent only a first step but the initial aim is to develop in learners an awareness of the properties and functions of patterns of language working creatively in everyday communication. The emphasis is on receptive skills but there is much research to support the view that greater language awareness, the development of noticing skills, the raising of consciousness about language functions can feed directly into more 'productive' creative language use.

The task sheet here is being further developed in the light of classroom use.

Further examples could develop 'interaction' gap activities and interaction gap-filling to build upon the more familiar information gap activities and transactional competence development which has been for so long a primary purpose within English language teaching. The overall aim is to increase learners' awareness of how they can creatively co-construct meanings and relationships. Such work may also encourage learners to *produce* more pattern-forming language. With increasing exposure to more examples, learners may also feel encouraged to play with words and to re-form patterns, becoming more creative in their language production and developing in the process a fuller interactional competence.

9.7   SUEs and creativity

This is not to suggest that there are not problems to be recognised when creative uses of language are encouraged and fostered in the language learning classroom. For example, Prodromou (2005) reports that many of the expert users (in his terms SUEs – Successful Users of English) he interviewed were cautious about being creative with their uses of language, especially when interacting with native speakers (see chapter 1 for more on SUEs). He gives a number of examples where successful advanced users of English played with the boundaries of the language only to be corrected by their interlocutors for misusing an idiom or for using a fixed phrase in what is felt to be an inappropriate way, commenting in the process that the same creative deviation or extension to a phrase would pass unnoticed or would be perceived as humorous or ironic in the discourse of native speakers. For example if a non-native SUE were to say *It's raining kittens and puppies*, he or she might well be corrected and have the idiom 'it's raining cats and dogs' reconfirmed for them, whereas the speaker here may simply be conveying a perception that it was drizzling or not raining hard

Figure 1: Task sheet

INTERACTIONAL LANGUAGE COMPETENCE: CREATING RELATIONSHIPS

Type A   **pattern-forming tasks**

1. Pre-task   Noticing exercise. What do you notice about the word *nice* in this exchange? Why do the speakers repeat each other's words? Do you do this in your own language? If so, why and when? If not, why not?

Task

A: Sunday's a really nice day, I think.
B: It certainly is.
A: It's a really nice and relaxing day.
B: Yes, it's really nice.

2. Pre-task   Noticing exercise. What is being talked about in the following conversation? What does it look like? What is the social setting for the exchange? How well do A, B and C know one another?

Task

A: What's that?
B: It's an earring.
A: Oh lovely.
B: It's fallen apart a bit.
C: I bet that's supposed to be straight.
B: I think it looks better like that.
A: There was another bit as well, another dangly bit.

Why task. Underline as many similar words and word patterns as you can. Which of these words have the same or similar sounds? Why do the speakers talk about the earrings using all these repetitions and echoes? One of the speakers then goes on to describe the earrings as *mobile* earrings? Why? How many meanings of the word 'mobile' can you find?

Type B   **pattern-reforming tasks**

Pre-task   Look up the words *blue* and *green* in the dictionary. How many words can you find which refer to these basic colours?

Task

A: What colour should we use?
B: Blue, I think.
A: Really, I'd go for green.
B: Well, bluey.
A: OK, what about blue-green. Or blue that's greenish.

Post-task   Why does each speaker change their word choice from blue to bluey and green to greenish? What kind of activity do you think A and B are doing? Would these patterns be created by speakers in, say, a job interview?

enough for the full adult form of the animals in the idiom to be invoked. Similarly, Prodromou reports an interview he held with a Polish SUE:

> When you try and play with idioms like those fixed ones . . . er . . . you know there was this . . . this party we had, you know, 'dine and wine' excessive, I would say, the . . . erm . . . next day I said that . . . something like . . . er . . . 'I was drinking' like a horse and . . . er . . . then I was told that you 'drink like a fish' but 'eat like a horse' and . . . er . . . my intention was that there was so much to drink and to eat that I wanted to . . . I wanted to blend the two idioms and come up with something new and original and I was sort of 'punished' for that (*laughs*).
>
> (Prodromou 2005: 311).

A similar situation is reported by a Greek SUE who uses a fixed phrase gambit, the expression 'you can say that again,' which is a common non-propositional conversational gambit, in a way that would be perceived as entirely normal for an L1 speaker.

> As a 'non-native speaker' I am not as free as native speakers to use the language creatively and idiomatically. For instance, yesterday I said something to a group of teachers and one of them commented 'you can say that again'. Humorously, I said 'OK, I'll say it again' and repeated myself more emphatically – embarrassingly, she said, 'no I actually meant that I agreed with you'. The assumption was, of course, that the meaning of the idiom was lost on me!
>
> (Prodromou 2005: 312)

The implication seems to be that, for L1 users, the language is mistake-proof but that the same rules do not seem to apply for the L2 user. Prodromou went further, and sent out 400 questionnaires to ELT practitioners (both native-speaking and non-native speaking), inviting them to judge the acceptability of an 'unusual' form (unusual in that it departs from the collocational norm that one can attest in large corpora). To one half of the informants he indicated that the form had been produced by a native speaker of English, to the other half that it had been produced by a non-native. Interestingly, where the informants thought a native speaker had produced the form, more tolerance was shown towards its acceptability than where the informants thought a non-native speaker had produced it. The form in question occurred in the sentence *I'm always very glad when for example I **bump into a new expression** . . .*. In the CIC, people bump into other people, bump into concrete objects in their path, but usually not non-concrete entities such as expressions. Figure 2 shows the distribution of responses.

The underlying assumption here seems to be, Prodromou suggests, that the L2 user is not normally seen to share the same schemata and cultural assumptions of exploiting words in novel ways, or using humour, banter, irony and purposeful play with language form that can obtain when speakers are, as it were, inexplicitly and subliminally, 'membershipped' by one another on account of sharing the same L1.

Figure 2: Acceptability (yes) or unacceptability (no) of *I'm always very glad when for example I bump into a new expression* (Prodromou 2005: 316ff)

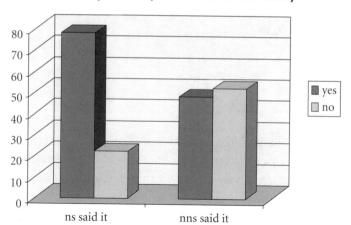

However expert their use of the language, somehow L2 users are seen to belong to a different club. As Prodromou says:

> When a proficient user of ELF attempts to play this game of humorous unpacking of idiomatic expressions, the result is often pragmatic failure – the subliminal becomes conscious, the implicit becomes explicit and the transgression is not seen as 'creative play' but as an error.

(Prodromou 1995: 312)

Cameron (2005) argues in the light of such evidence that courses for young learners and courses for beginners should therefore openly encourage and foster creative uses of language in order to allow L2 users to explore ways of finding their own meanings in the language. Being creative entails risks (people may not like or appreciate or may misunderstand what you are doing) and, in the light of Prodromou's examples, there is the real danger that L2 users may be unwilling to take the, as it were, extra risks.

Cameron argues as follows:

> Creativity is culturally evaluated, and children learn as they grow up what is valued as creative and what is not. Creativity involves taking risks and children learn which risks are appreciated in schools and which are not. If we want to encourage creativity in children's language, we have to give them space to experiment and encouragement to take risks.

She reports on research (Piquer Pirez forthcoming) in which data is assembled from young learners of English experimenting with the language, pushing back and playing with boundaries and rules and conventions in order to make meanings that are theirs. Learners of the language need to use the language in this way, she argues, as it is their language as much as anyone else's. Examples include the following in which children (young Spanish learners of English) interpret vocabulary for parts of the body that they have learnt (e.g.

hands, mouth, head, foot) when used metonymically in phrases such as *give me a hand, lend me your ear, the hands of a watch, the foot of the mountain*. Children were asked to explain how they would express in English the notion that someone needed help and were given the following options to discuss:

Give me a hand
Give me a head
Give me a foot
Give me a mouth

Discussion showed the children exploring the language, generating analogies with their own first language, making literal and metaphorical inferences and using visual and other juxtapositions to imaginatively create meanings. Collecting such examples further would be a challenge for corpus studies as we would have *learner corpora* that are illuminating not simply as a source of better understanding learner 'error' but rather as a source of learners showing how they use the resources of the language, underlining in the process that there need be no necessary disjunction between creativity and language learning skills, between exploiting creativity and developing accuracy, between expressing themselves and learning the patterns of a new language.

The emphasis in this type of creativity is on isolated pattern-reforming and the discussion of it both for purposes of developing language awareness and for developing the ability to talk about the language, seek analogies and respond to the contingencies and arbitrariness of much language. But alongside such overt and more obviously recognisable pattern-reforming, pattern-forming is also, as we have illustrated above, a significant component of creativity and is illustrated just as markedly in corpora of everyday spoken language. In the move from corpus to classroom creative patterns form a particular challenge for the researcher, the teacher and the learner. What cannot be ignored, however, is the corpus evidence of the truly remarkable extent of creative uses of language in everyday communication and not least for the expression of interpersonal involvement.

9.8 Quantitative and qualitative

It can be seen that our discussion here is in contrast with discussion in most other parts of this book. In preceding chapters, evidence of different forms and uses of language has mostly been drawn quantitatively from corpora. In this chapter we proceed rather more on the basis of observation and discourse analysis. Wang (2006) found this to be the only way of explaining apparent violations of the norms of sequencing in binomial expressions such as *upper and lower, black and blue, fame and fortune*; by applying qualitative text- and discourse-analytical techniques, Wang shows subtle relationships between unusual choices of word order and strategic planning and structuring of texts. It is difficult to identify creative uses of language a priori and then search a corpus for them, though Wang's work suggests that collocational anomalies (generated statistically) may be a good starting point for some types of creative manipulation. It is also difficult to recognise what may or may not be creative in the lists of words and chunks extracted from a multi-million-word corpus (although see Carter 2004: appendix 2 and pp. 222–226 for an initial foray into this area with the morpheme/word *-ish*). To make such assessments we have to read the corpus screen by screen and make judgements and evaluations of purposes and functions and then use these observations as a basis for qualitative assessment.

9.9 Conclusions

There is a long way to go in understanding creativity in the spoken language and in exploring the applications to the classroom of such understandings but the first steps have been taken in recognising that creativity is an everyday, demotic phenomenon, that it is endemic in spoken interaction and that it has been generally underplayed within the language teaching classroom. It is something that we need to work on to bring the best out of us as learners, teachers and collaborators in the language classroom. It is a fundamental aspect of a more humanistic approach to language teaching. And it is the kinds of evidence supplied by corpora of spoken language that enable these first steps to be taken.

10 Specialising: academic and business corpora

10.1 Introduction

As we saw in chapter 8, looking at small specialised corpora (such as shop encounters, radio interactions, family conversations, business meetings, and so on) can lead to insights that cannot as easily be gained by looking at large general corpora. In this chapter we build on this by taking two examples of more specialised areas of language and looking at how corpora can help us better understand how they work, and what distinguishes them from more general, everyday types of language. Specialised corpora have a number of advantages. Firstly, because they are carefully targeted, the data they consist of is likely to represent the target domain more faithfully than corpora which set out to capture everything about a language as a whole. Secondly, specialised lexis and structures are likely to occur with more regular patterning and distribution, even with relatively small amounts of data. Thirdly, the pedagogical goals in terms of how they are used and applied are likely to be easier to define and delimit. The two areas we examine in this chapter are academic English and business English. In the case of academic English we contrast spoken and written data, while in the business domain we look at a specially constructed spoken business English corpus and then compare it with the spoken academic corpus.

10.2 Written academic English

Academic English has been well studied, especially in terms of written forms and styles. One example of how a corpus of academic written texts was used to provide a very practical resource which has been applied pedagogically is the Academic Word List (AWL), developed by Averil Coxhead (Coxhead 2000). Coxhead used a 3.5 million word corpus consisting of written academic texts from journals, textbooks and coursebooks originating in different parts of the native English-speaking world, covering 28 subject areas subsumed under four major disciplinary areas (arts, science, commerce and law). She examined the distribution of words not included in the most frequent 2,000 English words from West's General Service List (West, 1953). Based on criteria of frequency (at least 100 occurrences in the corpus for members of each word family) and range (i.e. a minimum number of occurrences across the different disciplines and subject areas), Coxhead produced a list of 570 word families (base forms and their related inflected and derived forms) which accounted for around 10% of the total tokens in the corpus. The same word-families were found to cover less than 1.5% of the total words in an equally-sized written corpus consisting of fiction texts. The AWL therefore offers a 'fingerprint' of written academic vocabulary, the common core items which make it different from other types of writing. Most fruitfully, focusing on the AWL in vocabulary teaching and learning offers the possibility of increasing comprehension of academic text far more rapidly and efficiently than through just enlarging one's general vocabulary (see chapter 2). Coxhead (ibid.) proposes dividing the AWL into sub-lists of 60 items for practical learning purposes to provide a systematic framework for vocabulary teaching, and even though the AWL is simply a list, advocates teaching its members in context.

Written academic corpora have, not surprisingly, often been used to support the teaching of writing for students in academic settings. Here, questions arise as to whether the most suitable corpus is one drawn from the writings of fully-fledged academics (i.e. journal articles and academic books), or from the textbooks students are likely to read, or from the writing of those who aspire to be academics (e.g. thesis writers), or simply from a learner corpus of essays and other coursework, whether native-speaker or non-native speaker. All of these types of corpora exist. For example, Hyland's (1994, 1996a and b) much acclaimed work on academic writing conventions such as hedging is based on a corpus of research articles totalling in excess of one million words, drawn from many different academic disciplines (biology, engineering, mechanical engineering, linguistics, marketing, philosophy, sociology, physics). Other corpus-informed studies looking at this type of written academic data include Gledhill (2000a and b), Luzón Marco (2000), Oakey (2002), Silver (2003), Ruiying and Allison (2004), Harwood (2005), Hyland and Tse (2005), Biber and Jones (2005) and Kanoksilapatham (2005). On the other hand, Biber et al. (2002), using the T2K-SWAL[1] corpus (see appendix 1), range widely across written and spoken academic data and investigate written materials such as course packs, textbooks, and university catalogues and brochures. Biber and his associates have contributed several studies which distinguish the characteristics of academic discourse in general from three other basic types of language use: fiction, conversation and news. Biber and Conrad (2001) give a brief overview of this work and Biber et al. (1999) offer a more wide-ranging display of findings (see also Biber and Conrad 1999).

Studies comparing student textbooks and professional articles include Hyland (1999), who used a corpus of extracts from 21 university textbooks covering different disciplines and a similar corpus of research articles, and Conrad (2001), who compared textbooks and articles in biology and history. Academic textbooks also come under scrutiny by Reppen (2004), who contrasts their dense lexico-grammar with that of lectures. Meanwhile, Freddi (2005) looks at the introductions to linguistics textbooks in a 160,000-word corpus and notes the importance of individual stylistic variation.

Thesis and dissertation writing has been investigated by researchers using corpora, for example, the work of Paltridge (2002), who found that considerable variation existed in

---

[1] T2K-SWAL stands for TOEFL 2000 Spoken and Written Academic Language Corpus. It consists of 2.7 million words. For a full description see Biber et al. (2002). The corpus was designed to support the generation of test materials.

actual theses and dissertations compared with the published advice on dissertation writing. Charles, Maggie (2003) looked at the use of noun phrases to indicate stance through retrospective textual labelling in a half-million-word corpus of theses in the disciplines of politics / international relations and materials science. She concludes that the use of noun phrases to express stance is a valuable resource for thesis writers. Thompson and Tribble (2001) and Thompson (2005b and c) have also used corpora of theses both to examine how they are written in themselves and how the writing of novice student writers compares with them. Bunton (2005) examined a corpus of 45 theses, looking in detail at their concluding chapters.

Additionally, student academic writing has been examined, both on its own terms and in comparison with professional, published academic writing. Cortes (2004), for example, looked at a corpus of journal articles in history and biology, extracted the most frequent four-word lexical chunks from the corpus and classified them structurally and functionally. She then looked at students' use of the same chunks, and found that students rarely used those particular chunks in their writing. Student academic writing in its own right has been the basis of corpus studies, especially in the context of assessment and tests such as the IELTS test. Moore and Morton (2005), for example, compared an IELTS writing task with a corpus of 155 university writing assignments and found that there were important differences between the IELTS genre and the typical university essay. Binchy (2002) carried out a longitudinal study of a corpus of undergraduate essays, observing the use of personal pronouns by student writers and looking at possible correlations with grades given to the essays. Meanwhile, the multi-million-word corpus of student writing being developed at the University of Warwick, UK, described by Nesi et al. (2004), offers huge potential for the description and understanding of the characteristics of written student assignments at different levels and across different disciplines.

10.3 Written academic English: examples of frequency

In this chapter we intend to show how, departing from a quantitative standpoint, we can gain insights into the general characteristics or 'fingerprints' of specialist domains. This does not mean we think that 'academic English' is an undifferentiated, monolithic style; within different disciplines and genres we can expect a wide variation in conventions and individual uses, especially of lexis, but teachers are often tasked with teaching English for Academic Purposes (EAP) classes to mixed groups of students from different disciplines, and it does help to look at the somewhat broad brush picture of academic discourse which an initially quantitative study of a large corpus can provide.

If we generate a frequency list for an English written academic corpus and compare it with frequency lists for other types of written English, we find a degree of overlap, but also that certain words stand out as having noticeably different frequency in academic texts. Notably, the personal pronouns *I/me* and *you* are quite differently distributed. In the 19-million-word fiction sub-corpus of the British National Corpus, these personal pronouns are all found in the top 40 words. In a similarly sized corpus of British newspapers taken from the Cambridge International Corpus (CIC) the three pronouns just make it into the top 100. In the 12-million-word written academic segment of the CIC (consisting of academic books and articles), we have to trawl beyond the top 200 before *me* is found at rank 208. This obviously reflects the tendency to avoid too direct first- and second-person styles in academic writing and their greater prevalence in fiction. Other items also display marked differences: prepositions generally seem to be of slightly higher rank in the academic frequency list, reflecting the importance of logical relationships in academic writing (e.g. in prepositional phrases such as *in terms of, in relation to, from the viewpoint of, within the framework of, on the basis of,* etc; See also table 1), and the prevalence of noun-phrase postmodification using prepositional phrases (Carter and McCarthy 2006: 269–270). In particular, the prepositions *upon* and *within* occur with much greater frequency in the academic texts than in the newspaper or fiction texts, perhaps reflecting a preference for more formal choices.

Also notable in terms of providing a fingerprint for written academic texts are differences in the distribution of modal verbs between the three corpora (academic, newspapers and fiction). In a similar investigation to that of Biber et al. (1999: 489), we find that, in our three corpora, certain core modal verbs differ greatly in their distribution in the three kinds of texts (Biber et al. additionally compared their findings with a corpus of conversation). Figures 1 and 2 illustrate the differences. Here we deal only with the core modal verbs *can, could, will, would, shall, should, must, may* and *might*.

Figure 1: Modal verbs compared: academic texts and fiction texts

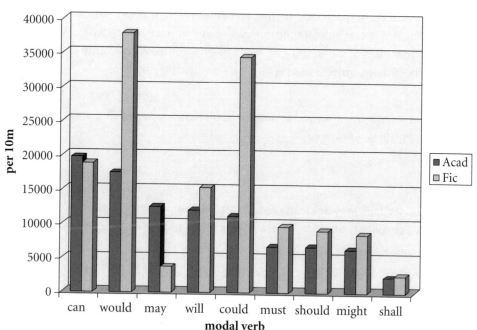

Figure 2: Modal verbs compared: academic texts and newspaper texts

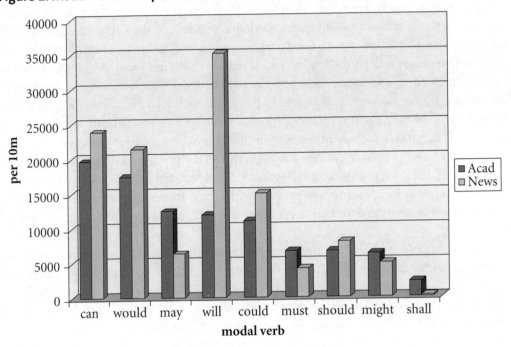

The graphs show that some modal verbs are fairly evenly distributed across the different text types (*can, should*), while others are markedly different. *Would* and *could* appear very high in fiction and *will* is high in newspaper texts. *May*, on the other hand, seems to be particularly preferred in the academic texts, and overall the academic texts seem to display a more even distribution of the verbs. *May* in academic writing, as well as having its meaning of possibility, is particularly common in examples such as (10.1) and (10.2), where its meaning is more factual, substitutable by *can*.

(10.1)

But the rearrangement **may** also have necessitated a move to find areas where the old skills could still be employed.

(CIC)

(10.2)

These connections **may** be clearly seen in a brief, comparatively less well-known poem, 'A Song,' which follows the three Teresa poems in the 1648 and 1652 collections.

(CIC)

These insights are to a great extent shared by Biber et al. (1999). Much can be gained simply by generating frequency lists for specialised corpora, but it is when they are compared with other specialised corpora or more general corpora that the really distinctive features emerge, providing a fingerprint for the type of language in the specialised corpus.

The prevalence of particular chunks also characterises specialised uses of language. In a smaller, mixed written corpus of one million words taken from academic books, theses and journals in a variety of disciplines, we find the following four-word integrated chunks occurring more than 30 times (table 1):

Table 1: Four-word chunks, more than 30 occurrences in a written academic corpus

	chunk	frequency		chunk	frequency
1	on the other hand	159	22	a large number of	40
2	in terms of the	128	23	the fact that the	40
3	in the context of	122	24	the way in which	40
4	at the same time	105	25	it is important to	39
5	in the case of	92	26	on the basis of	38
6	as well as the	84	27	the extent to which	37
7	at the end of	74	28	in relation to the	36
8	on the part of	74	29	the role of the	36
9	the nature of the	67	30	one of the most	35
10	as a result of	56	31	the analysis of the	35
11	in the course of	54	32	the relationship between the	35
12	the part of the	53	33	can be seen as	34
13	to do with the	52	34	as part of the	33
14	in the form of	49	35	in a number of	32
15	in the process of	47	36	to the fact that	32
16	a great deal of	46	37	has to do with	31
17	at the beginning of	43	38	in the same way	31
18	at the time of	43	39	it is possible to	31
19	on the one hand	43	40	that there is a	31
20	is one of the	42	41	the degree to which	31
21	a wide range of	41			

Quite clearly here we see the importance of phrases signalling abstract logical connections of various kinds, with a high incidence of prepositional constructions. If we compare this list with a list of four-word chunks from a general written corpus, we find the general corpus has more spatial and temporal prepositional phrases such as *in the middle of, for a long time, in front of the, on the other side,* etc.

10.4 Spoken academic corpora

Spoken academic corpora are a relatively recent phenomenon, spearheaded by the Michigan Corpus of Academic Spoken English (MICASE) (Simpson et al. 2002). This has been followed by the development of other spoken corpora in academic contexts such as the British Academic Spoken English (BASE) corpus and the Limerick Belfast Corpus of Academic Spoken English (LIBEL) (Murphy and O'Boyle 2005; see appendix 1). Additionally, the CANCODE spoken corpus contains a segment of seminars, tutorials and lectures recorded at British universities, amounting to some 344,000 words. Meanwhile, the ELFA spoken academic corpus of English as a lingua franca, under development at the University of Tampere in Finland (Mauranen 2003), promises to offer insights into how English is spoken within an academic community whose first languages are varied (in this case mostly European) (see appendix 1).

MICASE consists of 1.8 million words of data ranging widely across the spoken academic domain and extending beyond lectures, classes, tutorials, etc. to speech events such as service encounters on campus (e.g. libraries, computer centre) and campus tours. The corpus has already yielded some interesting and useful insights into spoken academic language (see references below). The BASE corpus includes 160 lectures and 40 seminars recorded on digital video across different university departments, while LIBEL CASE consists of one million words of spoken academic data, with equal amounts collected at each of two centres in northern and southern Ireland. These corpora are increasingly revealing the special characteristics of spoken academic discourse, both in its similarities to written academic language and in its reflections of more informal conversational genres. Here we examine the academic segment of the CANCODE corpus as an illustration of the kind of insights which can be gained from such a specialised corpus. We compare it in two ways: firstly in terms of its similarities to and differences from the CANCODE corpus as a whole, and secondly in comparison with the one-million word CANBEC spoken business English corpus.

10.5 Spoken academic English, conversation and spoken business English

Spoken academic English, as with written academic English, can cover quite a wide range of speech events, as we saw in the composition of the MICASE corpus. Students in typical English-medium third-level education experience not only lectures but a wide variety of seminars, classes of different sizes, small groups, one-to-one advisory sessions, pastoral consultations, encounters with departmental and faculty officials and administrators, conversations in libraries and other campus service centres. The academic segment of CANCODE is confined to lectures, seminars, classes, group tutorials and one-to-one advisory sessions, and consists of approximately 344,000 words, collected at two British universities across humanities and science departments.

Spoken business English (SBE) also covers a wide range of speech events, and the term 'business English' in general is an extremely wide-ranging term (St John 1996). SBE studies have focused on: business meetings, one major study being Bargiela-Chiappini and Harris (1997) (see also Dannerer 2001); buying and selling negotiations (e.g. Firth 1995; Charles, Mirjaliisa 1996), and office talk or workplace talk (e.g. Grimshaw 1989; Holmes 2000; Koester 2004, 2006). There has also been much discussion of the authenticity or lack of it in spoken business English as presented in teaching materials (Williams 1988), as well as of the language needs of students of business (Crosling and Ward 2002). There has, additionally, been considerable research into cross-cultural aspects of spoken business communication; for example, Yamada (1990); Garcez (1993); Halmari (1993); Ulijn and Li (1995); Ulijn and Murray (1995); Connor (1999); Gimenez (2001). Also notable are Pan et al. (2001) and Spencer Oatey (2000), both of which deal with Chinese English business communication.

Genre-based approaches have been strong in studies of the organisation of events such as meetings and phone calls, for example Yotsukura (2003), who uses a corpus of more than 500 phone calls recorded in commercial enterprises in the Tokyo and Osaka areas of Japan. Discourse analysis and conversation analysis have also played a significant role. Bargiela-Chiappini and Harris (1997) are typical of a blending of approaches in their examination of thematic (topical) development in business meetings, the use of pronouns and discourse markers, metaphors, and so on. Broader generic issues have also been investigated. For Charles, Mirjaliisa (1996: 21) business negotiation talk operates on distinct hierarchical levels, from the superstructural (the overarching situation in which the negotiation takes place), through the macrostructural (the event itself) to the microstructural (smaller cycles within the speech event). Other broad issues have come under scrutiny, such as questions of status and roles (Charles, Mirjaliisa, ibid.), as well as the nature of business cultures and the metaphors and other institutionalised constructs which underlie those cultures (Bargiela-Chiappini and Harris 1997). Firth (1990, 1995) investigates sales negotiations among business people using English as lingua franca, and uses a conversation analysis (CA) approach, though he notes interestingly that moments of difficulty in communication are often left unresolved, rather than repaired or successfully 'achieved' in the usual CA sense. In cross-cultural studies, differences arising from, for example, distinct perceptions of time and space among different cultures have been studied, as well as conversational management, including turn-taking (Yamada 1990; Ulijn and Li 1995).

In terms of the use of corpora in studying business English, some of the widely available large corpora include samples of spoken business data: the British National Corpus (BNC) includes 1.3 million words of 'events such as sales demonstrations, trades union meetings, consultations, interviews' (see Aston and Burnard 1998; see appendix 1). The International Corpus of English (ICE) project has the aim that each sub-corpus of English from the different countries and regions which supply the data should include around 20,000 words of spoken business data (appendix 1). Bargiela-Chiappini and Harris's (1997) important study is based on a corpus of approximately 18 hours of business meetings recorded in Great Britain and Italy. The Kielikanava (Turku, Finland) Business English Corpus (BEC) consists of one million words of spoken and written data, and includes spoken data from meetings, negotiations and telephone calls (Nelson 2000). Nelson compared the lexis of his business English corpus with the BNC as a benchmark corpus, and a corpus of published business English teaching materials. Nelson describes a business English lexicon, distinct from that of general English; the business lexicon embraces a limited set of semantic fields reflecting the institutionalized, activities, events and relationships of the world of business.

10.6 **The CANBEC business corpus**

Our investigation of Spoken Business English (SBE) is based on the CANBEC corpus. CANBEC stands for Cambridge and Nottingham Corpus of Business English[2] (see appendix 1). The corpus consists of one million words of spoken data recorded in a variety of different businesses, mostly in the UK but some recorded in other countries which included some non-native-speaker data. The data cover internal meetings (within the same company), external meetings (involving two or more different companies), office talk, sales presentations, telephone conversations and general office banter. Meetings form the largest part of the corpus; for full details of the corpus and data collection, see McCarthy and Handford (2004).

McCarthy and Handford (2004) was the first study to emerge from the CANBEC corpus. The question posed in that paper was: To what extent is SBE like or unlike everyday informal casual conversation? The question owed its provenance to the convention of identifying spoken language genres in terms of their similarities to and departures from everyday, casual conversation, using casual conversation as a benchmark. This method has been successfully used in the study of media talk such as interviews and talk shows (Greatbatch 1988; Scannell 1991; O'Keeffe 2006) as well as in the study of professional discourse (Drew and Heritage 1992: 25; Larrue and Trognon 1993; Boden 1994: 87).

McCarthy and Handford also pointed to the institutional dimension of business talk and argued that business talk evolves in and among business institutions, constructing and consolidating identities, roles and cultures which become institutionalised over long periods of time. It is therefore useful to study SBE as an institutional discourse, and, with that in mind, McCarthy and Handford compared CANBEC data with the academic segment of CANCODE, as we do in this chapter. McCarthy and Handford only had the benefit of a portion of CANBEC, which was incomplete at that time; here we explore the now completed one-million-word corpus. As a justification for the comparison of the two institutional varieties (academic and business), McCarthy and Handford hypothesised that one would expect to find similar degrees of discussion in non-conflictual environments, some presence of hierarchy or authority, a certain institutional formality, and a clear, purposeful task- and goal-orientation.

Here, in the way we have so often done in this book and elsewhere, we begin with comparisons of frequency lists for single words generated from CANBEC, the 340,000 word academic segment of CANCODE (referred to as ACAD in table 2) and a one-million word sub-corpus of the social and intimate conversation segments of CANCODE (referred to as CONV in table 2). Table 2 shows the top 50 words in each corpus, normalised to occurrences per million words.

The top 30 words in all three corpora are very similar, and few of the top 30 in CONV do not occur more or less within the same range in ACAD and CANBEC. Overall, spoken business English and spoken academic English clearly share a core, high-frequency set of

---

[2]   The corpus project was established in the School of English Studies at the University of Nottingham, UK, and is funded by Cambridge University Press. The corpus is copyright Cambridge University Press 2003.

Table 2: Top 50 words in conversation, business and academic English

	CONV	per m	CANBEC	per m	ACAD	per m
1	I	31,981	the	36,362	the	49,950
2	the	29,368	and	22,456	and	27,306
3	and	28,969	to	20,988	of	26,750
4	you	26,475	you	18,611	you	23,029
5	it	22,856	a	18,559	a	22,951
6	yeah	20,748	I	18,191	to	22,272
7	a	19,377	it	17,222	that	18,241
8	to	18,856	that	16,199	in	16,692
9	that	15,536	yeah	16,086	is	16,455
10	was	12,983	of	13,733	it	14,984
11	of	12,487	**we**	12,832	I	13,920
12	in	11,728	in	10,455	er	9,556
13	oh	10,333	is	10,085	so	9,338
14	it's	9,598	so	9,210	it's	8,280
15	know	9,227	it's	8,590	this	8,204
16	**no**	8,727	er	8,435	what	7,308
17	mm	8,566	but	7,729	yeah	7,288
18	**like**	8,516	on	7,638	erm	7,001
19	but	8,192	for	6,964	are	6,922
20	he	8,016	have	6,573	but	6,786
21	**well**	7,984	erm	6,493	on	6,313
22	they	7,771	they	6,175	have	6,009
23	is	7,501	know	6,143	be	5,684
24	we	7,352	be	6,140	we	5,516
25	er	7,229	if	5,972	right	5,504
26	have	7,018	do	5,692	know	5,478
27	so	6,995	**well**	5,393	as	5,229
28	on	6,944	just	5,356	they	5,159
29	what	6,554	that's	5,333	if	5,107
30	do	6,165	what	5,277	or	5,066
31	just	6,006	got	5,170	do	5,058
32	there	5,739	this	5,105	not	4,895
33	all	5,669	one	4,933	with	4,892
34	don't	5,635	with	4,831	all	4,858

Table 2: (continued)

	CONV	per m	CANBEC	per m	ACAD	per m
35	she	5,419	no	4,618	for	4,837
36	for	5,230	at	4,571	which	4,739
37	not	5,113	not	4,515	at	4,585
38	got	5,101	right	4,456	one	4,573
39	that's	5,095	all	4,438	there	4,544
40	be	4,967	was	4,298	can	4,510
41	erm	4,965	there	4,283	about	4,472
42	one	4,905	are	4,150	that's	4,391
43	this	4,836	can	4,129	like	4,188
44	right	4,812	think	4,113	was	4,063
45	then	4,762	as	3,857	mm	3,901
46	yes	4,688	then	3,725	just	3,773
47	think	4,380	or	3,653	very	3,666
48	with	4,123	get	3,635	he	3,570
49	at	4,106	don't	3,481	okay	3,564
50	get	3,967	them	3,382	because	3,422

word forms with everyday casual conversation. However, each of the special corpora does have distinctive features emerging from the frequency lists:

- Pronoun *we* is higher in CANBEC than in the other two corpora.
- Negative particle *no* falls outside of the top 50 in ACAD but is at 16 and 35 in CONV and CANBEC, respectively.
- *Well* falls outside of the top 50 in ACAD but is at 21 and 27 in CONV and CAN-BEC, respectively.
- *Like*, at 18 in CONV and at 43 in ACAD, falls outside the top 50 in CANBEC.
- None of these differences is terribly great, but the differences are suggestive. At this point it may prove more useful to look at keywords, which will provide a more statistically accurate fingerprint for the specialised corpora.

Keyword lists (see chapter 1) were created for the two specialised corpora, using CONV as the benchmark corpus. Nelson (2000) affirms in his study of business English that keyword analysis is a better way of defining the business lexicon, since crude frequency counts, especially when it comes to the very high frequency words such as those in our top 50 lists, show much overlap between business English and general English; it is apparent that this applies to spoken academic English too. Table 3 shows the top 50 keywords in CANBEC and ACAD. In the lists, industry- and product-specific words (e.g. *crane, rack, coal*), discipline-specific ones (e.g. *virus, stanza*) and numerals have been omitted so as to include as much as possible of a common core across the different companies and academic departments recorded.

Table 3: Keywords in CANBEC and ACAD

	CANBEC	ACAD			CANBEC	ACAD
1	**we**	the		26	**us**	therefore
2	**we've**	of		27	issue	effect
3	hmm	is		28	brand	analysis
4	customer	**which**		29	cent	particular
5	**we're**	are		30	two	associated
6	sales	in		31	if	examples
7	product	by		32	products	form
8	orders	this		33	website	cause
9	**need**	section		34	**so**	implied
10	customers	terms		35	client	a
11	meeting	okay		36	step	evidence
12	order	between		37	install	context
13	stock	example		38	batches	as
14	okay	these		39	gotta	means
15	company	process		40	list	society
16	marketing	**within**		41	markets	because
17	the	important		42	for	system
18	business	sense		43	batch	interpretation
19	mail	very		44	web	percent
20	gonna	will		45	**our**	surface
21	price	has		46	**problem**	structure
22	**we'll**	also		47	is	ways
23	per	contrast		48	target	more
24	month	an		49	market	question
25	will	common		50	which	fact

Here we are beginning to get a better picture of each of the two special uses of language. Of interest are the following:

- Ranks 1, 2, 5, 22, 26 and 45 in CANBEC are occupied by forms of the pronoun *we* (*we/us/our*), but neither *I* nor *you* appear in the top 50. None of the personal pronouns appear to be key in any way in ACAD.
- *Need* appears at rank 9 in CANBEC. *Need* is not a keyword in ACAD at all.
- CANBEC has many content items which are business-oriented: *customer(s) sales, product(s) order(s), market(s/ing), company, stock,* etc.
- CANBEC has *so* and *problem* in the top 50. ACAD has neither of these.

- ACAD has a very high rating of rank 4 for *which* (rank 50 in CANBEC).
- ACAD has many terms related to argumentation, such as *example, context, interpretation, question, implied, fact, important, particular*. CANBEC has none of these in the top 50.
- ACAD has content items expressing logical relations, such as *associated, section, means, ways, contrast, cause, because*. CANBEC does not have these in the top 50.
- ACAD has a high rank for *within* (16), which is not key at all in CANBEC.

The keywords are a kind of snapshot: they certainly tell us that predictable domains are frequently talked about in the two respective corpora (prices, customers, meetings, paperwork, examples, facts, interpretations, etc.), but they also reveal preferences for certain pronominal references in CANBEC (*we, us, our*) and a tendency to use particular modal expressions and expressions of stance. In the case of CANBEC, these key words and their contexts offer some insight into the interpersonal aspects of spoken business communication, and characterise it as (a) sharing properties with everyday informal casual conversation, (b) sharing properties with institutional discourses (in this case academic) and (c) different from conversation and academic discourse, a special or unique register or genre which can be described by observing the participants' activity in the construction of relationships and identities, both individual and corporate, and the creation of business cultures, that is to say a unique 'interaction order' (Roberts and Sarangi 1999). Similarly, spoken academic language creates its identities and cultures, and moulds the community of scholars into which young and new members are initiated through study, conventionalised styles of discussion and the transmission of knowledge through lectures and classes. We return to examples of both discourses below, after an examination of chunking in each corpus.

10.7 Chunks

In chapter 3 we looked at lexical chunks. A repeated claim in the literature on chunks is that such clustering of words recurs because the chunks become structuring devices which are register- (or genre-) specific. For example, Oakey (2002) looks at frequently recurring chunks such as *it has been* (*shown/observed/argued*, etc.) *that*, which are used to adduce external evidence in the three written genres he investigated (social science, medical and technical). Oakey notes that the chunks are distributed differently across the three domains. It is therefore reasonable to suppose that clusters in the CANBEC business data and the ACAD spoken academic data may show us something of the character of SBE and spoken academic language as distinct genres.

Space forbids inclusion of all of the chunks of different sizes (ranging from two words to six) in both corpora, but we reproduce here the top 20 three-word chunks for each corpus (table 4).

I don't know is high in both corpora, and in both cases it is frequently followed by reporting clauses beginning with *if* or a *wh*-word. *A lot of, a couple of* and *sort of*, all inherently vague expressions, are also evident in both (though not all shown in the table), as is the specifying expression *in terms of*. CANBEC has four chunks involving *think*, perhaps

Table 4: Three-word chunks in CANBEC and ACAD

	CANBEC	per m		ACAD	per m
1	I don't know	642	1	a lot of	477
2	a lot of	563	2	I don't know	469
3	at the moment	485	3	one of the	442
4	we need to	438	4	you can see	364
5	I don't think	378	5	this is a	358
6	the end of	376	6	you have to	343
7	in terms of	243	7	this is the	338
8	a bit of	241	8	in terms of	300
9	be able to	237	9	a sort of	297
10	at the end	235	10	there is a	276
11	end of the	230	11	and this is	271
12	and I think	229	12	look at the	268
13	I think it's	229	13	the end of	265
14	to do it	223	14	the sort of	265
15	we have to	208	15	at the end	253
16	have a look	196	16	you want to	253
17	I think we	194	17	you know the	250
18	you know the	192	18	do you think	247
19	a couple of	187	19	to do with	247
20	we've got a	184	20	and so on	239

reflecting the constant speculating and hedging in negotiative discourse; in ACAD there is only one in our list, perhaps reflecting a different range of expressions to indicate viewpoint or stance or speculation. Notably, *in terms of* occurs only 19 times in CONV, compared with 243 and 300 in CANBEC and ACAD, marking it out as a fingerprint of the two special corpora, where specifying is likely to be a frequent function of the discourse. Both corpora have chunks referring to looking at things (i.e. considering things), with ACAD also including *you can see*. CANBEC has a high occurrence of *at the moment*, perhaps suggesting the constant flux and change in business situations. The CANBEC list also brings together the high-frequency key words *we* and *need* (*we need to* at no. 4). This reflects the high incidence of statements of collective goals in SBE, even if this is only a projected or feigned collegiality (mirroring the corporate mantra *there's no 'I' in team*), for *need* is often used in SBE in face-protecting requests and directives. *We* in CANBEC carries a wide range of references, from very broad corporate references to smaller, group references and to the individual speaker, who may use it to shelter behind corporate authority or responsibility or to protect their interlocutors' face. Extracts (10.3) to (10.7), several of which are taken from

McCarthy and Handford (2004), all involving *we need to*, show different uses of *we* in operation:

(10.3)
(Broader, corporate *we*: includes people other than the speakers)
[The extract involves a British hydraulics company and an international coal company. They are discussing their advertising schedule.]

S1: Do you know what I mean? Erm and there again it it's a case of getting in front of people when the leads are produced.

S2: It is yeah. Yeah.

S1: That's what it's all about.

S2: We di= Yeah Obviously if **we** get leads erm if the if **we need to be wherever it is**. We need to be in+

S1: Mm.

S2: +China in Korea or wherever+

S1: Wherever.

S2: +**we need to be there**.

S1: That's right.

(CANBEC)

(10.4)
(Immediate group reference *we*)
[Group scheduling meeting with six participants]

S1: And we've got a contracts meeting, Dunc, on Monday afternoon with er Helen. Helen is+

S2: Yeah.

S1: +coming to the board meeting tomorrow in place of Peter to cover the property side. Okay. That's diary. Is there anything else **we need to be aware of**?

(CANBEC)

(10.5)
(Face-protecting request/directive using corporate authority *we*)
[Internal meeting among the sales and marketing managers of a British manufacturing company. The participants are reviewing and planning sales and marketing.]

S1: The spares side of things is another ball game altogether.

S2: Well.

S3: Right. Th= there's no need for us to concern ourselves with that is there really.

S4: No.

S1: No.

S3: I mean you're not, you're bothered.

S1: No.

S3: **We need to get our heads round and have a think about it as to the best way to go**.

(CANBEC)

We need to often frames corporate requests for information and for action issued by individuals with authority. As such it is an indirect form, protecting face and less direct than potentially face-threatening demands or directives:

(10.6)
[Meeting between a multinational car manufacturer and a British hydraulics company. They are discussing product development.]

> S1: I mean ultimat= ultimately it's your decision whether you want a+
> S2: True. But er o= o=
> S1: +a hard blow fuse if you like or a a resettable fuse.
> S2: You're right. But the thing is I mean **we need to know what your rationale is**. And if you say 'We prefer to have a resettable one because we we know this is a problem' then it will help Nigel to make that decision you see.
>
> (CANBEC)

(10.7)
[As for extract 10.6]

> We were just talking about the durability work. Erm we don't have any plans at the moment to do some tests on the assembly to the drop side body. And I think what we need to do is **we need to do some test work**. What I'd ask you to do then, it's good preparation for that test work, is, you've told me what you think your durability is from your calculating the er the durabi= the life of the crane.
>
> (CANBEC)

In ACAD, *we need to* only occurs 78 times per million, compared with the 438 occurrences in CANBEC. In ACAD, *we need to* mostly refers to gaps in knowledge, with *we* referring either to the academic community as a whole or to the students present, which will be filled or to which answers will be sought in the course of the lecture, seminar, etc., as seen in extract (10.8):

(10.8)
[Science lecture]

> DNA is essential for protein and also for cell specialisation in the expression of gene during cell specialisation occurring during development of an organism which is critical to er development. So **we need to understand** er growth. **We need to understand** cell development, cell specialisation. How those processes normally occur in the body. **We also need to understand** why these processes go wrong in the body. Why there are defects in growth. Or why growth becomes totally unregulated in the case of something like cancer. **We need to understand** what goes wrong.
>
> (ACAD)

Noticeable too is the incidence of chunks with *you* in ACAD, where clearly there is more direct instruction from teacher to students. We might compare, for instance, *you have to* in ACAD with the collective *we have to* in CANBEC.

Overall, the chunks illustrate the shared communicative resources and ways of approaching problems which characterise Communities of Practice (Wenger 1998), insomuch as the repeated patterns reflect institutionalised wordings that have become pragmatically specialised within SBE and academic discourse.

Need is by far the most frequent modal verb indicating obligation in CANBEC. Other possible exponents of obligation (e.g. *must, ought*) are very low in frequency. If we compare the occurrence per million words of obligation-uses of the expressions *need to, have (got) to / gotta, should, ought* and *must* in CANBEC, CONV and ACAD, we can immediately see that *need to* is high in CANBEC compared with the other two corpora. *Have (got) to, should* and *ought* are more evenly distributed across the three corpora. The high incidence of *need* and low incidence of *must* in CANBEC suggest that SBE prefers more indirect expressions of obligation, and how important the preservation of face is, even in a context where one might expect pressure and urgency to be part and parcel of everyday activity.

Even more notably, when individual transcripts are examined, variations in the patterns of use may be observed which indicate just how sensitive speakers are to face needs. In a CANBEC transcript of an in-company meeting between three managers there are 37 occurrences of *have (got) to / gotta*, where the managers discuss necessary actions and goals. There is no evidence of face-threat in the use of these rather direct forms among equals (see also Donohue and Diez 1985). However, when these goals and actions are communicated to others in subordinate positions, in two other in-company meetings at the same company, *have (got) to / gotta* drops dramatically in frequency (2 and 10 occurrences respectively), and in the latter of the two transcripts, where the manager is discussing changes which are needed with a subordinate, 40 instances of *should* occur. It seems that more face-protecting and indirect forms for issuing directives are preferred in order to maintain good relations and to promote the comity, motivation and corporate stability so essential in business institutions.

Hypothetical and speculative uses of *may* and *might* are very similar in CANBEC and ACAD, but lower in CONV. We might predict this in ACAD, where speculating and hypothesising are key recurring functions, but it also shows up a degree of speculation that characterise SBE, where, paradoxically, focus, goal-orientation and decision-making are also important. It would seem that speculation and hypothesising are an important part of the collaborative enterprise of consensus-forming, and is, once again, face-protecting both for those who speculate and those who respond.

10.8 *Problem* and its institutional construction in CANBEC

The words *problem(s)/problematic* are more than four times as frequent in CANBEC as in ACAD or CONV, and are thus worthy of special attention as 'fingerprints'. Their frequency can be accounted for by the fact that business meetings mostly take place to discuss and explore solutions to problems. Problems have to be evaluated and prioritized, and this is reflected in recurrent chunks such as *the main problem, the other problem, a big problem, the biggest problem, the only problem* which occur in CANBEC. Statements of perceived problems also reflect participants' agendas in meetings (Boden 1995). Boden (ibid.) notes the importance of how problems are framed by speakers and how this influences the course of their evaluation and solution. In CANBEC such framings can be seen often in the form of recurrent or extended metaphors and idioms. Wenger (1998) points to the importance of jokes, stories, lore, idioms and metaphors which become the routine ways of approaching problems in institutional contexts and which contribute to the construction of Communities of Practice. An example from McCarthy and Handford (2004) shows the use of metaphors and idiomatic expressions (the extract is edited for length, with time-hops indicated):

(10.9)

[Meeting between the sales staff of an IT company and a potential client. The latter is the managing director of an internet sales company. They are discussing computer server problems.]

S1: Erm as you know with application **problems** you just it it's+
S2: Yeah.
S1: +it's it's
S2: **It's a nightmare**.
S1: Yeah. [sighs]
S2: Sometimes the experts don't know.
[laughter]
S1: Yeah exactly. But **it can be a real**+
S2: Okay.
S1: +**er can of worms**. So. [inhales]
. . . [6 mins]
S2: +then if there is a **problem** and it's irretrievable they lose a day's transactions.
S3: Yeah.
S1: Yeah. Yeah. Which you can't=
S2: And **that's a nightmare**.
S1: Yeah.
. . . [20 mins]
S2: But we don't get the hosting+
S1: Mm.
S2: +on this particular customer because they we weren't offering a credible twenty four by seven+
S1: Yeah. Yeah.
S2: +erm support.
S1: Sure.
S2: And doing anything on their site **is a complete nightmare**+
S1: Mm.
. . . [20 secs]
S2: Because they're running something like sixty sites on one machine.
S1: Yeah.

S3: Wow.

S2: But but it **it just is a nightmare**.

(CANBEC)

Speaker 2, the client, frames the problem as a 'nightmare', while speaker 1 calls it a 'can of worms'. Such metaphorical and idiomatic frames contribute to the construction of the practices which build and maintain the cultures of businesses and their ways of communicating (see Mumby 1988).

10.9 Summary

We conclude that SBE and ACAD are institutional forms of talk. We also agree with Nelson (2000) that business English is not just general English with specialist terminology added, and believe that St John's (1996) misgivings, as to whether a lexico-grammar of something like business English can be easily defined, may be lessened by the use of corpora. However, as we have argued throughout this book, neither quantitative data alone nor the analysis of one-off conversational transcripts is sufficient; the former and the latter must be in a dialectical relationship with the analyst constantly moving from one to the other to gain maximum insight. This chapter has also attempted to show the value of comparative corpora: SBE is in some senses similar to spoken academic data and shares some of its institutional characteristics (*irrealis* domains of hypothesising and speculating, goal-driven discourse, chaired or teacher-led discussion, etc.). Both types of discourse derive from everyday conversation, sharing features with the banal talk of everyday life, displaying the primary human orientation towards comity, convergence, and good, non-threatening relationships. And all this occurs even in the face of hierarchically sanctioned institutional roles, what Boden (1995: 99) memorably sums up, in describing professional meetings, as 'the fine tinkering and manoeuvring of actors dancing around agendas and arrangements, accommodating each other locally for a variety of personal, political and institutional goals'.

10.10 Pedagogical implications

In light of our explorations of spoken academic and business corpus data, let us now reflect on pedagogical implications:

- A clear example of the applications of corpus study in academic English is Schmitt and Schmitt (2005). They base each unit of their book on a set of target words taken from Coxhead's Academic Word List (see 10.2 above), and present the target words explicitly at the beginning of each unit, inviting the user to conduct a self-test. Here is an example:

Figure 3: Extract from Schmitt and Schmitt (2005: 56)

<u>TARGET WORDS</u> — Assessing Your Vocabulary Knowledge

Look at each of the target words in the box. Use the scale to give yourself a score for each word. After you finish the chapter, score yourself again to check your improvement

1 I don't know this word.

2 I have seen this word before, but I am not sure of the meaning.

3 I understand the word when I see it or hear it in a sentence, but I don't know how to use it in my own speaking and writing.

4 I know this word and can use it in my own speaking and writing.

TARGET WORDS

___ accuracy	___ demonstrate	___ instance	___ perspective
___ achieve	___ deny	___ intensity	___ prior
___ alter	___ derive	___ mental	___ rejection
___ attribute	___ dimension	___ motivate	___ stability
___ challenge	___ emerge	___ participants	___ trigger
___ consistent	___ expose	___ perceive	___ vision

- We observed that academic English also possessed characteristic chunks. McCarthy and O'Dell (in press) include presentations and tasks based on frequent chunks from the academic segments of CIC (spoken and written), in contexts which are familiar to students. An example is shown in figure 4.
- A good many of the language forms which occur in SBE and academic spoken language overlap with casual conversation, in that interpersonal features of meaning are accorded at least equal status or with transactional (content) features, or indeed even more central status. A comprehensive SBE pedagogy would, for example, focus on areas such as personal deixis, modality, face-protection and indirectness.
- Nelson (2000) found that published business English materials focused more on concrete entities rather than abstract qualities and states, showed less variety and more politeness than the business people in his corpus. The CANBEC corpus seems to support that, and as regards politeness, CANBEC suggests that SBE is not amenable to over-simplifications of politeness and face-protection features. But the corpus evidence does suggest that training in lowering face-threats is

important, and that such training should stress core functions such as the appropriate use of particular modal expressions and the downplaying of others.

- Close observation of how speech acts such as requests and directives are realised while maintaining comity in SBE and academic contexts is a useful awareness-raising activity. Williams (1988), in examining the relationship between real data and published teaching materials, reminds us that the language of business meetings is far more complex than what a simple list of functions with suitable exponents can capture, and that on-the-spot linguistic strategies and awareness of interlocutors are crucial factors that must be taken into account.

- Many users of SBE and spoken academic language will be using English as a lingua franca in non-native contexts, but successful business relations and successful academic exchanges and relationships nonetheless rest, in the final analysis, on the building and maintenance of good interpersonal relations. Getting things done, either by oneself or getting them done by others, transmitting knowledge, discussing theory or hypothesising about solutions and processes are all facilitated by a raised awareness of what the linguistic resources have to offer in each conventional discourse type, even when outside of particular linguacultures and speech communities. It is for mature business people and students and academics themselves ultimately to decide whether and how to exploit those resources, but not to make them available to students of EAP and of business English is to offer an impoverished and narrow set of tools to the learner.

- As more and more spoken business and spoken academic corpora are constructed, data-driven learning using concordances and open access to corpus files becomes a real possibility, and corpus researchers and teachers may, we hope, no longer operate as gatekeepers but as facilitators, enabling business and academic users of English directly to access resources aligned to their own situations and linguistic goals. As with so much of learning to use a language appropriately, close observation and awareness-raising should be paramount; corpora and mediated corpus data enable such close observation in the reflective context of the classroom, self-study materials (including web-based materials) or the adequately equipped resource-centre. Tim Johns' *Kibbitzer*[3] web-pages are an outstanding example of how corpus concordance lines can be used in data-driven learning in EAP.

---

[3] See http://www.eisu.bham.ac.uk/johnstf/timeap3.htm

Figure 4: Extract from *Academic Vocabulary in Use* (McCarthy and O'Dell, in press)

---

16 Fixed expressions

If we look at a database of academic texts, we see that certain fixed expressions occur very frequently in spoken and written contexts. This unit looks at some of the most useful ones.

A Number, quantity, degree

Look at these comments written by a college teacher on assignments handed in by her students. Note the expressions in bold.

A good paper. It's clear you've spent **a great deal of** time researching the subject and you quote **a wide range of** sources. Grade: B	Some good points here but it's not clear **to what extent** you're aware of all the issues involved. Global trade affects nations **in a variety of ways**. Grade: C	I think you've misunderstood the topic **to some extent**. You've written **in excess of**[1] 3,000 words on areas that are not entirely relevant. Let's talk. Grade: F

[1] more than

B Generalising and specifying

In this class discussion, the students make fairly general statements, while the teacher tries to make the discussion more specific.

Marsha: Well, I think **on the whole** parents should take more responsibility for their kids.

Teacher: Yes, **with respect to**[1] home life, yes, but **in the case of** violence, surely the wider community is involved, isn't it? I mean, **for the purposes of** our discussions about social stability, everyone's involved, aren't they?

Marsha: Yes, but **in general** I don't think people want to get involved in violent incidents, **as a rule** at least. They get scared off.

Teacher: True. But **as far as** general discipline **is concerned**, don't you think it's a community-wide issue? I mean discipline **as regards**[2] everyday actions, **with the exception of** school discipline. What do you think, **in terms of** public life, Tariq?

Tariq: I think the community **as a whole** does care about crime and discipline and things, but **for the most part** they see violence as something that is outside of them, you know, not their direct responsibility.

Teacher: Okay. So, let's consider the topic **in more detail**[3], I mean **from the point of view of** violence and aggression specifically in schools. Let's look at some extracts from the American Medical Association's 2002 report on bullying. They're on the handout.

[1] or **in respect of**, or (more neutral) **with regard to**   [2] another neutral alternative to **with respect to**   [3] or (more formally) **in greater detail**

11 Exploring teacher corpora

11.1 Introduction

This chapter is very different from all of the other chapters in this book from a number of perspectives. Up to this point, we have focused on what corpora can teach us about language in use and what, in turn, this tells us about language teaching. Here we are not looking at what we can learn about language use from a corpus, rather we are looking at what corpora can tell us about our own teaching and ourselves as part of a professional cohort. For example, we draw on corpora of classroom interactions and compare them with other question-driven institutionalised contexts, such as media interviews, to show what makes classroom interactions different. We also look at the specifics of teacher talk, for example we survey studies of teacher questioning strategies and wait-time (after questions have been asked) based on corpus data collected in the language classroom. The overall aim of this chapter is to make a case for the development of corpora and corpus skills as a tool for reflective practice within pre-service teacher education and ongoing in-career development.

Another reason why this chapter differs so much from other chapters is because here we do not see a teacher corpus as something which is 'off-the-shelf'. A teacher corpus is something small and evolving over time. In this chapter we look at very small amounts of data very closely, usually turn by turn. A corpus of teacher interactions is seen as developmental in that, like a portfolio, it grows over a teacher's career and also in the sense that it becomes a tool for development itself. By building up classroom extracts, a teacher can reflect closely on classroom practice. We are also interested here in looking beyond classroom practice. Though the classroom is the primary site for teacher interaction, there are other aspects of a teacher's working life which merit attention and understanding. These areas are steadily acquiring attention; for example, interactions outside of the classroom with colleagues in meetings, one-to-one teacher education feedback sessions or within professional development sessions. We will also look at a project in Hong Kong where a corpus resource service has been set up for teachers.

Looking at the language of a corpus does not necessarily always mean looking at other people's language. As we have argued, corpora can also be used by teachers as tools for reflective practice and professional development. In a practical sense this means that small corpora are created by teachers and analysed so as to reflect on, better understand and enhance their own professional practice. In the case of classroom practice, transcripts from classroom interactions can facilitate close inspection and build up sensitivity to the language that we use so as to hone our judgements about what we say in the classroom. As Walsh (2006) notes, in a classroom context, where so much is happening at once, fine judgements can be difficult to make, and deciding to intervene or withdraw in the moment-by-moment construction of classroom interaction requires great sensitivity and awareness on the part of the teacher. Inevitably, teachers do not 'get it right' every time.

The overall aim of this chapter is to illustrate the growing application of corpora in teacher development and to provide frameworks within which teacher corpora can be used in different contexts. Looking at the language of the classroom is nothing new and many authors provide models for doing this (for example, Sinclair and Coulthard 1975; McCarthy 1991; Hatch 1992; McCarthy and Carter 1994; Johnson 1995; Riggenbach 1999; Celce-Murcia and Olshtain 2000; Hall and Verplaetse 2000; Hall and Walsh 2002; Mori 2002, 2004; Boxer and Cohen 2004; Kasper 2004; Markee 2004; Mondada and Pekarek Doehler 2004; Seedhouse 2004; Walsh 2006). Teacher educators will already be aware of commercially available video material which provides lessons for training and reflection in pedagogic practices. Here we are not arguing that these materials should be replaced by home-produced classroom corpora but we suggest that in-house teacher corpora can offer a valuable supplement to published training materials, especially in the area of methodological skills acquisition, because the practices of teaching must be interpreted within their contexts of realisation. In other words, socio-cultural and environmental factors which create and cast the lesson cannot easily be captured in their entirety by non-present third-party trainees in different educational and/or cultural surroundings. This is particularly true when the backgrounds, training conditions, and experience of trainees on teacher education programmes are socio-culturally at odds with that of the training materials available commercially. For instance, most teacher education videos are either British- or American-produced.

Another advantage of building and using a teacher corpus is that the transcript can then become a supplement to the video medium itself, or extracts from it can be examined as part of task-based activities on handouts. While a video clip could equally be used for this purpose, it is a far more ephemeral medium than the written transcript and does not allow for the same level of turn-by-turn analysis. For example, figure 1, overleaf, shows an example transcribed from a video clip, taken from O'Keeffe and Farr (2003) which, if played on video, involves less than 25 seconds of speech. However, when it is viewed as a transcript, it is frozen for turn-by-turn analysis.

With the advent of digital recording facilities, it is also possible to design such materials for teacher education whereby the audiovisual clip can be aligned with the transcript.

Figure 1: Sample material for awareness-raising in relation to teaching new vocabulary (O'Keeffe and Farr 2003: 401)

Student:	What's the difference between 'collaborate' and 'cooperate'?
Trainee:	Well 'collaborate' is generally used for something which is negative and 'cooperate' is more positive.
Student:	So can I say 'I am cooperating with Maria on this project'? Collaborate would be wrong here?
Trainee:	Well yes, no, mm I'm not too sure. What does the dictionary say? Let's check.

a)   Use a dictionary to find the differences in meaning between these two words.

b)   Use any large corpus from the electronic library to establish how these near-synonyms differ in terms of use and lexical patterns.

c)   Redesign the part of the lesson in the extract above to make it more effective.

11.2   Classroom discourse

Once a classroom corpus is created (see chapter 1 on building your own small corpus), the next step is to build up strategies and frameworks for its use. For the most part, classroom corpora will be used qualitatively; that is, extracts will be read and analysed manually. While applications such as concordances and word frequency list software will be used to search for certain words, phrases or discourse patterns, turn-by-turn analysis will be the main focus. Therefore, the corpus in this context is a large electronic resource that can be searched automatically to find extracts to suit one's pedagogical goal in a teacher education and professional development context, and it may be used very effectively as a supplement to existing video resources, as we noted above.

McCarthy and Walsh (2003) note that, for language teachers, understanding the discourse of the classroom itself is crucial. We teach *through* discourse with our learners; language teaching is unique in that language is both the medium and the content of teaching. In many parts of the world, the main exposure to discourse in the target language that learners will have is in the classroom itself, via the teacher. A number of studies have compared the discourse of the classroom with 'real' communication (e.g. Nunan 1987). But, as van Lier tells us (1988: 267), 'the classroom is part of the real world, just as much as the airport, the interviewing room, the chemical laboratory, the beach and so on'. A teacher corpus is therefore a resource of real-world interactions from the classroom and other sites of teacher interaction, and this database needs to be interpreted within a framework which will help us best understand the structure of the discourse that we find within it (see below).

11.3   Frameworks for the analysis of classroom language

We feel that there is no point in collecting classroom data without having an awareness of the main analytical models within which these data can be interpreted and understood.

We now survey three models, none of which is directly corpus-related but all of which offer powerful models for analysing classroom corpus data: Discourse Analysis (DA), particularly its concept of 'exchange structure', Conversation Analysis (CA) and Socio-cultural Theory (SCT). Data could be analysed using any one or even none of these models. However, we hope to show that by applying these models to actual data a triangulation of the three perspectives can offer a very rich insight for teachers. As we present each of these perspectives, we will also provide illustrations of the type of insights that they have brought to our understanding of language teaching and classroom discourse. Generally these are not corpus related, but they give a sense of how these models can be applied in a general sense.

Exchange structure

This approach to discourse analysis stems from a highly influential study by Sinclair and Coulthard (1975). Based on the analysis of recorded classroom interactions, Sinclair and Coulthard produced a model for understanding classroom discourse, which has subsequently been applied to the study of other contexts, for example doctor-patient interactions (Coulthard and Ashby 1975). In their analysis, Sinclair and Coulthard found that teachers divided their lessons into different phases of activity (called 'transactions'). Discourse markers (see chapter 8 for a detailed treatment) typically marked the beginnings and ends of transactions, along with intonational cues. These marking devices are termed 'frames' and are generally limited to items such as *okay, well, right, now, good,* uttered with strong stress, high falling intonation and followed by a short pause. It was noted that teachers frequently followed a frame (indicating the beginning of a transaction) with a 'focus', that is, a metastatement about the upcoming transaction. Here is an example from an EFL class where the teacher is setting up a task. The discourse markers *right, alright* and *okay* operate as frames and are followed by a focus, which functions as a signalling statement:

(11.1)

> Teacher: **Right** so what I'm going to do is I'm going to give you amm a thing. **Right?** I'm going to give you the thing an object **alright**? And I want you to decide what it is cos it may not be a hundred percent clear when you see the object what it is. **Alright?** You have to decide what it is. You decide what the selling points are and then we have to present it.

> (LIBEL)

Sinclair and Coulthard's (1975) model for the structure of a lesson involves a hierarchy consisting of levels, each composed of elements from the level below it (figure 2).

At the level of 'exchange', Sinclair and Coulthard observed the following as characterising classroom interactions:

(1) question-and-answer sequences
(2) pupils responding to teachers' directions
(3) pupils listening to the teacher giving information

Figure 2: Levels of Sinclair and Coulthard's (1975) hierarchical structure of a lesson

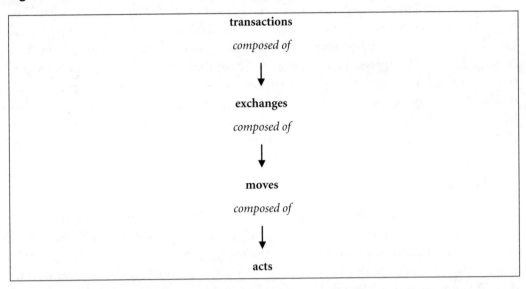

The question-and-answer sequence receives most attention. As a sequence, it consists of a minimum of three elements (often referred to as IRF):

(1) the question (or *Initiation*)
(2) the answer (or *Response*)
(3) the teacher's feedback (or *Follow-up*)

Here is an example from Sinclair and Coulthard (1975):

Teacher: . . . What else will cut the piece of wood?	*Initiation* (I)
Student: Saw.	*Response* (R)
Teacher: The saw yes.	*Follow-up* (F)

Note, in this example from Walsh (2001), the use of the discourse marker *so* whereby the teacher marks the new phase of activity. Here we see that the IRF sequence is repeated:

Teacher: So, can you read question two, Junya.	(I)
Junya: [Reading from book] Where was Sabina when this happened?	(R)
Teacher: Right, yes, where was Sabina?	(F)
In Unit 10, where was she?	(I)
Junya: Er, go out . . .	(R)
Teacher: She went out, yes.	(F)

Typically the teacher's follow-up evaluates the learner's answer (*right, yes*); such feedback is important to the learner. This is one of the distinguishing features of classroom discourse. Coulthard (1977) notes that the three-part exchange structure was suggested as the norm for classroom discourse for two reasons: firstly, answers directed at the teacher can be difficult for others to hear and so need repetition. Secondly, and more importantly, a distinguishing feature of classroom discourse is that the questions which a teacher asks are ones to which she already knows the answer (referred to as 'display questions', see below).

Often answers which are correct in terms of the question are not the ones the teacher is seeking and therefore it is essential for him/her to provide feedback indicating whether a particular answer is the one (s)he is looking for. For example:

Teacher: What does the food give you?	(I)
Student: Strength	(R)
Teacher: Not only strength we have another word for it.	(F)
Student: Energy	(R)
Teacher: Good girl, energy, yes.	(F)

(adapted from Coulthard 1977: 125)

IRF exchanges are also found in everyday conversation, but the follow-up element is not normally evaluative, for example:

(11.2)

S1:	What's the last day of the month?	(I)
S2:	Friday.	(R)
S1:	Friday.	(F)
	We'll invoice you on Friday.	(I)
S2:	That would be brilliant.	(R)
S1:	And fax it over to you.	(I)
S2:	Er, well I'll come and get it.	(R)
S1:	Okay.	(F)

(CANCODE. See also McCarthy and Walsh 2003: 176)

Very often in casual conversation, the response to an initiation involves tokens such as *great, brilliant, excellent, sure*. As we have discussed in chapter 7, these have a relational rather than an evaluative function, for example to show interest, surprise, shock and so on. For example, here they mark agreement between friends:

(11.3)

S1:	. . . it just goes to show you can't take people at face value.
S2:	No.
S1:	And you don't know what's going on either.
S2:	**Exactly**.

(LCIE)

The powerful nature of the three-part exchange as a classroom structure is illustrated by Coulthard (1977: 125) in this next example, where he notes that the absence of the feedback move signals to the student that the answer is wrong.

Teacher: Can you think why I changed 'mat' to 'rug'?	(I)
Student: Mat's got two vowels in it.	(R)
Teacher:	(F)
Teacher: Which are they? What are they?	(I)
Student: 'a' and 't'	(R)

Teacher:	(F)
Teacher: Is 't' a vowel?	(I)
Student: No.	(R)
Teacher: No.	(F)

(Coulthard 1977: 125)

However, the IRF routine in classroom interaction has been seen by many as unproductive as an interactional format, especially as a model for spoken interaction outside of the classroom. The argument put forward is that the IRF exchange is a poor model for learning pragmatics and discourse norms of the target language since it differs from everyday interaction (as the above examples show). IRF exchanges, it is argued, fail to give opportunities for tackling the complex demands of everyday conversation, especially since teachers usually exercise the follow-up role, while learners often remain in passive, respondent roles. Ohta (2001), for example, finds that the overwhelming majority of classroom follow-up moves are spoken by the teacher; learners get few opportunities to use typical listener follow-ups and only experience the teacher's moves as peripheral participants. Peer-to-peer interaction, Ohta argues, can provide the best opportunities for learners to produce appropriate listener responses (this ties in with the joint-production model of *confluence* that we discuss in chapter 7).

Walsh (2002), in his analysis of different modes of teacher talk, illustrates how these may hinder or optimise learner contributions. Kasper (2001), however, argues that the negative reputation of the IRF exchange may not be entirely warranted and that what really matters is the kind of interactional status assigned by the teacher to individual learners. Teachers can help their learners become actively involved in interaction, even within the typical IRF pattern, she argues. Exposure to the teacher's use of follow-up moves, along with explicit guidance on the use of responsive moves, can help students gradually move towards more productive use in peer-to-peer speaking activities.

Conversation analysis (CA)

CA gives us a framework for looking at 'local' aspects of interaction in detail, especially how participants in a conversation work hard to make it successful (see Pomerantz and Fehr 1997). CA focuses on how speakers decide when to speak during conversation, i.e. the rules governing 'turn-taking' (see Sacks, Schegloff and Jefferson 1974), and how they show they are listening (by using response tokens such as *umhm, yeah, right*, see chapter 7). It also deals with how speaker turns can be related to each other in sequence and might be said to go together as 'adjacency pairs', for example, complain + denial, greeting + greetings, or, as in Figure 3, yes/no question + yes/no answer:

Figure 3: Concordance line examples of adjacency pairs from CANCODE

```
1    Did you know that?      <$2> No I didn't.
2    Did you find them?      <$3> No I didn't.
3    Did you knock?          <$1> No I didn't.
4    Did you see that one? <$1> No I didn't.
```

Or in this example, from CANCODE:

(11.4)

[Speaker 2 has been relating how she was stung by a wasp while asleep]

S1: **Well perhaps it was nosing around minding its own business and you frightened it.**
S2: **Oh I see. It's my fault is it!**
S1: Well.
S2: He can never see my side.
S3: [laughs]
S1: Wasps don't sting unless threatened.

(CANCODE)

Not all second pairs have the same significance; therefore, there is said to be 'preference organisation', whereby some second-pair-parts are preferred and some are dispreferred (see Pomerantz 1984). When the two pair-parts do not fit, speakers have to work hard to repair potential problems, for example an invitation anticipates acceptance rather than rejection or hesitation. Compare the following:

S1: Would you like a cup of tea Ursula?   S2: Ooh I'd love one
                                                (preferred response)

                                        versus

                                            S2: (pause) You know I just don't know
                                                (invented dispreferred response).

(CANCODE)

Another important focus of CA is how turns are organised in their local *sequential* context at any given point in an interaction and the systematicity of these sequences of utterances (see Schegloff 1982). For example, one can talk about the sequentiality of greeting or leave-taking routines in different situations (as discussed in Chapter 8). CA also places great importance on how seemingly minor changes in *placement* within utterances and across turns are organised and meaningful, for example, the difference between whether a vocative is placed at the beginning, mid or end point of an utterance (see Jefferson 1973). Other concerns of CA include openings and closings of conversations (Schegloff and Sacks, 1973), and topic management (i.e. how speakers launch new topics, change the subject, decide what to talk about, etc.; see Gardner, 1987).

McCarthy and Walsh (2003) note that CA has brought a number of key insights for language teaching, including how teachers and learners have to deal with the special turn-taking circumstances of the classroom (only teachers normally select the next speaker, it is difficult to interrupt the teacher, teachers often do not wait long enough for students to answer, etc.). Pedagogically, CA insights suggest that some adjacency pairs will be easy to learn (e.g. the ritualised ones like greeting–greeting, offer–accept), but that dispreferred sequences will require skill and practice (see Dörnyei and Thurrell 1994). There has been growing support for CA as a means of understanding and improving speaking in pedagogical contexts in recent years (see Boxer and Cohen 2004). Mori (2002) uses CA to analyse a speaking activity in a class of non-native-speaking learners of Japanese, where students exchanged experiences and opinions with Japanese native speakers invited to the class. The resulting interaction resembled an interview, with a succession of questions by the students and answers from the native-speaker guests. Interestingly, more natural discussion came about when students made spontaneous utterances and when they seemed to be attending more to the moment-by-moment unfolding of the talk.

Wong (2000) notes that CA illuminates how local choices unfold in interaction and can focus on aspects of talk which are relevant for the participants themselves. A number of important studies into second language acquisition have been undertaken using CA (Hall and Verplaetse 2000; Markee 2000, 2004; Mori 2002, 2004; Hall and Walsh 2002; Lazaraton 2002; Seedhouse 2004; Kasper 2004; Mondada and Pekarek Doehler 2004, among others). Ducharme and Bernard (2001) look at learners of French, using micro-analyses of videotaped interactions and retrospective interviews to gain insights into the perspectives of participants. Mondada and Pekarek Doehler (2004) also look at the French second language classroom, providing an empirically based perspective on the contribution of CA and socio-cultural theory (see below) to our understanding of learners' second language practices. Mori (2004) focuses on a peer interactive task in a Japanese as a foreign language classroom. Through close observation of vocal and non-vocal conduct, Mori demonstrates how the students transform, moment by moment, their converging or diverging orientations towards varying types of learning and learning opportunities. Kasper (2004) examines a dyadic learning context in a German class between a native speaker and a beginning learner. Weiyun He (2004) appraises the 'uses and non-uses' of CA in the context of Chinese language learning. While she sees numerous applications of CA to teaching and research, such as in oral language assessment, she concedes that CA does not address introspective matters that may be important to language learning, and it is not designed to document learning longitudinally. Also pointing to the shortcomings of CA, Rampton et al. (2002) warn of the lack of a 'learning' dimension. Because CA is a very local kind of analysis, they argue, it lends itself less easily to providing evidence of actual development of language ability over time.

Sociocultural theory (SCT)

Sociocultural theories of learning focus on the social nature of the classroom interaction. Learners collectively construct their own knowledge and understanding by making connections, building mental schemata and concepts through collaborative meaning-making (Walsh 2006). Within this view, learners are seen as interacting with the 'expert' adult teacher 'in a context of social interactions leading to understanding' (Röhler and Cantlon 1996: 2). This notion has its origins in the work of Vygotsky (1962, 1978), a Russian psychologist who developed the sociocultural theory of mind. Lantolf and Appel (1994b), Lantolf (2000) and Lantolf and Thorne (2006) have been very influential in applying Vygotskian theory to language pedagogy. The concepts of 'scaffolding' and 'the zone of proximal development' (ZPD) are of central importance to this perspective. Scaffolding is the cognitive support provided by an adult or other guiding person to aid a learner, and is realised in dialogue so that the learner can come to make sense of difficult tasks. Scaffolded support is given up to the point where a learner can 'internalise external knowledge and convert it into a tool for conscious control' (Bruner 1990: 25). The ZPD is the distance between where the learner is developmentally and what (s)he can potentially achieve in interaction with adults or more capable peers (Vygotsky 1978: 86). According to Lantolf (2000: 17), the ZPD should be regarded as 'a metaphor for observing and understanding how mediated means are appropriated and internalized.' In the Vygotskian paradigm, instructors (or peers) and their pupils interactively co-construct the arena for development, it is not pre-determined and has no lock-step limits or ceiling. Meaning is created in dialogue (including dialogue with the self, often manifested in 'private speech') during goal-directed activities.

Walsh (2006) notes that central to the notion of scaffolding are the polar concepts of challenge and support. He points out that learners are led to an understanding of a task by, on the one hand, a teacher's provision of appropriate amounts of challenge to maintain interest and involvement, and, on the other, support to ensure understanding. Johnstone (1989) presents scaffolding as a strategy used by learners and teachers to overcome 'shortcomings' in the learner's interlanguage, while Anton (1999) advocates the use of careful and particular error correction as a means of assisting learners through the ZPD. Machado (2000) demonstrates how peer-to-peer scaffolding in the preparatory phases of spoken classroom tasks (mutual help with the interpretation of the tasks and the wording of meanings) is reflected in evidence of internalisation of such help in the performance phases of the same tasks. Machado suggests that peer-to-peer scaffolding may be just as important as expert-novice scaffolding (see also Kasper 2001; Ko et al. 2003).

11.4   Applying the frameworks to a corpus of classroom data

Bringing together the three frameworks that we have surveyed above, we will now consider some of their key insights and concerns in the context of actual corpus data. Figure 4 and example (11.5) are taken from an extract from an EFL class (from the LIBEL corpus, see appendix 1) where the teacher is trying to build a schema (or cognitive outline) for a newspaper text that the students are going to read as part of a reading lesson. She puts three vocabulary items on the blackboard. We begin the extract as she finishes writing the last two items:

Figure 4: Extract from an EFL class

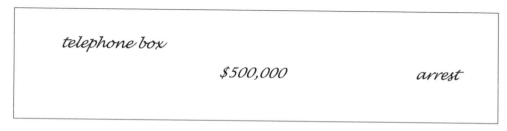

telephone box

$500,000   arrest

(11.5)
[the numbers on the left refer to turn numbers]

 1 Teacher: . . . ok ah so five hundred thousand dollars and arrest those are three
              things three items from a newspaper story. You can ask me yes no

questions that means I can only answer yes no or no okay? amm to find out a little bit more about the story. Now the dollar sign gives you a clue when asking the questions.

2 Student 1: Is it a fin=
3 Teacher: Is it a fine? No no it's not a fine.
4 Student 2: It's a robbery
5 Teacher: Yes yes a robbery umhm.
6 Student 3: Is it a re=
7 Teacher: A what? a reward? Sorry reward am no no that's not a reward no.
8 Student 3: Is it a phone=
9 Teacher: A coin box yeah
10 Student 3: [five syllables unintelligible] one phonebox.
11 Teacher: Not from one box. Not from one box from several boxes. Many boxes all right the five hundred thousand dollars came from many boxes yep ok. Anything else you can find out?

(LIBEL)

DA and CA: turn-taking in the classroom

The issue of the controlled or institutionalised nature of classroom discourse comes to the fore particularly in DA and CA models. Teachers have rights to initiation and evaluative feedback. Or in CA terms, there is a turn pre-allocation which assigns the questioning and evaluative role to the teacher, who is the holder of institutional power in a classroom context. Using DA and CA to examine extract (11.5) closely, we can make the following general observations about its turn structure:

discourse analysis	conversation analysis
• The teacher's move in turn 1 sets up the students as the initiators by getting them to ask the questions. • This seems to change the usual IRF structure by giving the students the right to initiate. • On closer examination, this is not so. Turn 1 is an initiation, turn 2, albeit a question from a student, is actually the response to the initiation in turn 1 by the teacher. • Turn 3 on the surface seems to be the teacher's response to turn 2, but it is in fact the teacher's evaluative feedback on turn 2.	• The teacher is normally in the role of questioner, but in turn 1 she sequentially allocates this role to the students. • However, while the teacher attempts to redress the teacher-centred turn pre-allocation of classroom discourse (i.e. where the teacher gets to ask all the questions), she merely replaces it with another turn pre-allocation (where students *have to* ask the questions). That is, students are normally pre-allocated the role of answerer; now they are pre-allocated the role of questioner.

discourse analysis	conversation analysis
• The exchange pattern, therefore, comprises the classic IRF structure, controlled by the teacher. • However, the teacher has decentralised the questioning role within the classic IRF structure so that the students are asking questions. She is not always answering the students' questions, in fact she sometimes responds with another question or gives feedback on theirs. • Students do not have the right to make evaluative comments on the teacher's questions.	• In reality, however, the teacher does not really change the turn pre-allocation or sequentiality of classroom discourse here: (1) she still usually selects the next speaker, (2) she manages and steers the topic by virtue of her responses, (3) she interrupts the students but they do not interrupt her, (4) she does not allow wait time between question and answer, (5) her responses to the students' questions are evaluative, and (6) on a number of occasions she does not adhere to the adjacency pairings of question + answer; instead she answers a question with another question.

Some of the pedagogical reflections from this close analysis of the extract are:

positive	negative
• Getting students to take on the role of questioner is a good idea because it is normally monopolised by the teacher. • By getting the students to ask the questions, the teacher decentralised the lesson. • As the students are asking the questions, the teacher has the opportunity to assess how much vocabulary they already know in relation to the text that they are going to read and to appraise the amount of new vocabulary which will have to be presented. • Students can learn from each other by listening to each other's questions and the teacher's responses to these. This sets up a peer–peer interaction as well as a student–teacher interaction.	• While the turn structure is devolved, the exchange is still highly controlled. • It would have been better to allow more wait time while the questions were being answered (see below). • The teacher interrupted the students in three out of five of their responses. • The teacher should have resisted reverting to the control position so soon. By turn 11, only after five contributions from the students, she intervenes. • In the teacher's initiation of the task, she says that the students must ask the questions and that she can only answer 'yes' or 'no'. However, she does not adhere to this arrangement and so never really hands control over to the students.

Socio-cultural theory: scaffolding and the ZPD

Extract (11.5) is an interesting one from the perspective of scaffolding. The teacher is preparing the students for a reading task. She needs to guide them through the ZPD by bridging the gap between what is known and unknown (figure 5). She does this by trying to build up the schema, or conceptual outline, of the story. The way in which she achieves this is interesting. Though it is teacher-led, it draws on peer-to-peer scaffolding. The teacher sets it up by giving three key words/concepts that she is confident the students will know.

Figure 5: Moving from the known to the unknown

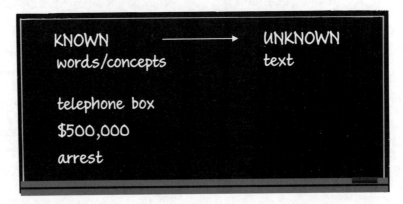

Peer-to-peer scaffolding is set up through her yes/no question routine. Students have to listen to each other's questions carefully so as to collaboratively increment the collective understanding of the schema of the text. Learning takes place interactively between teacher and student, as well as between students.

The issue of the amount of scaffolding provided by the teacher is interesting to consider here. She provides the following scaffolds:

Table 1: Teacher scaffolding, a turn-by-turn analysis

student	teacher scaffold	type of scaffold
Turn 2 student says *fin=*	Turn 3 teacher provides *fine*	lexical
Turn 6 student says *re=*	Turn 7 teacher provides *reward*	lexical
Turn 8 student says *phone=*	Turn 9 teacher provides *coin box*	lexical and schematic[1]
Turn 10 student suggests *one phone box* [as far as can be established]	Turn 11 teacher provides the information that *the five hundred thousand dollars came from many boxes*	schematic

---

[1]　On one level the teacher is giving an alternative lexical item to phone box, but at a schematic or conceptual level she is helping to add to the outline of the overall story by focusing on the phone box as a key factor in the story.

The following comments could be made about the teacher's approach, some positive and some more critical:

- She keeps the momentum of the guessing phase going by incrementing the new information at a steady pace, rather than letting it slow, so as to elicit the full or extended utterance from any one of the students. This sustains a high level of interest.
- She moves from lexical to schematic or conceptual scaffolds, building up key vocabulary before introducing schematic (or conceptual) information.
- She intervenes too soon in turns 3 and 7, for example, even before the students have had a chance to finish the words they are trying to construct.
- She provides too much scaffolding overall and should allow the students to engage in more guesswork for longer. This would promote more peer-to-peer scaffolding. Providing additional wait time would assist in this.
- By turn 11 when she provides the key information about there being many phone boxes, she has only had questions from two students at that stage.
- This could be counteracted by saying that the teacher knows the class and their level of need best and her goal is to build up a schema for the main task of the lesson, the newspaper story that they are going to read. She works at a pace that she knows will suit the class.

11.5 Looking at questioning in the classroom

Following on from this three-way analysis above, it is clear that questions have a central role in the classroom. Even when the teacher tried to hand over the questioning role to her students, she struggled with it, and that perhaps reflects the link between questioning and control. Classrooms, like a number of other institutional contexts such as political interviews, doctor-patient exchanges and courtroom interactions, are typified by a pervasion of questions. Raising an awareness of questions, how they are phrased, how many of them are asked, who they are asked to and how long the teacher waits for an answer are key issues to consider in teacher education and practice. Close scrutiny of classroom data can help considerably here. CA research tells us that the speaker who has high contextual status (e.g. lawyer in a courtroom, teacher in a classroom) normally controls the development of the discourse through questioning (see Coulthard and Ashby 1975; Sinclair and Coulthard 1975; Blum-Kulka 1983; Drew 1985; Fisher and Groce 1990; Heritage and Greatbatch 1991, among others). Hutchby and Wooffitt (1998) point out that institutional formats typically involve chains of question-answer sequences, in which the institutional figure asks the questions and the witness, pupil or interviewee is expected to provide the answers. This format is pre-established and normative rules operate, which means that participants can be constrained to stay within the boundaries of the question-answer framework.

In contrast, in casual conversation, roles are not restricted to those of questioner and answerer, and the type and order of turns in an interaction may vary freely. In this extract from a casual conversation, for example, we see how questions meander from speaker to speaker as the conversation evolves in real-time, without any pre-allocation of questioning turns or chains of question-answer sequences:

(11.6)

[Twix and Snickers are chocolate bar brand names]

S1:   I remember when I was in France ages ago when people were calling Twix Radars.

S2:   Radars?

S1:   Do you remember when Snickers were called Marathon?

S2:   Yeah.

S1:   And Twix were called Radars.

S3:   Were they called Radars? I never knew that.

S2:   Yeah the way they change the names of things like films.

S1:   They just translate them

S2:   No they don't 'Analyse This' right, they called it 'Mafia Blues'. It was an English word why change the name?

S1:   They probably didn't know what analyse meant or something.

S3:   Yeah do you know the 'Runaway Bride' is that what it is called?

S2:   Yeah.

S1:   Yeah.

S3:   Am in France it was called 'Just married'

S2:   'Just married' that was it

S1:   What?

S3:   It was in English like.

S2:   Yeah you used to see it on buses and it was like 'Just Married' and I was like that's 'Runaway Bride'. And I was like 'oh my god'.

S3:   I wouldn't mind if they translated it into a French word but it was in English as well.

(LCIE)

Though many institutional interactions are question-laden, the pattern of how they are used is not necessarily homogenous. It can be instructive to compare classroom transcripts with data from other settings. Here we consider how classroom interaction compares and contrasts with media interviews.

In media interviews, interviewers and interviewees generally confine themselves to a question–answer sequence, respectively. The power-role holder does not normally engage in a wider range of feedback responses (Greatbatch 1988). For example, (11.7) is an extract from the BBC TV programme *Breakfast with Frost* in which the host, David Frost, interviews the then Secretary of State for Education, Ruth Kelly:

(11.7)

[Speaker 1= David Frost, Speaker 2 = Ruth Kelly]

S1:   And would you like to see, I gather
      between the line you would, would
      you like to see more foundation

schools and more specialist schools as soon as can be managed?	*Initiation*
S2: I think the idea of a specialist school is an extremely important one. A school that has its own mission and ethos. A school that is strong and autonomous. And they have really a very important role to play in the future . . .	*Response*
S1: Will the 160 or so grammar schools survive under your system, under your aegis?	*Initiation*
S2: Well, as long as parents want them in the way they are, that's right. But I don't want to see more selection in the process. What I do want to see is really good state schools, strong and autonomous, who want to co-operate in the best interests of their students.	*Response*

(*Breakfast with Frost*, BBC TV, 23 January 2005)

Statements are often made by both interviewer and teacher as a follow up to a response. When an interviewer uses a statement, it normally refers forward as a preface to or as part of the next question (Greatbatch 1988), whereas when a teacher makes a statement it is typically referring back to the student's response in an evaluative way (as discussed above):

(11.8)

[In this extract from the BBC programme *Newsnight*, presenter Jeremy Paxman is interviewing Richard Caborn, then British Minister for Sports and Tourism, about the British government's intentions to liberalise licensing laws in relation to extending the hours within which alcohol can be legally sold. Speaker 1 = Richard Caborn Speaker 2 = Jeremy Paxman]

S1: . . . We have evidence to show where we have relaxed in England on Sundays, in Scotland when we allowed the opening hours to extend, there was a reduction in the problems related to nuisance through drink. Also you can cite many other countries that you don't get those problems on the Continent.	*Response*
S2: But we're not on the Continent. This is a north European and Anglo-Saxon problem.	*Statement as Initiation*
S1: France and Germany are north Europe. When they come over and go to a show at the Barbican and they can't get a drink after 11.00, they look at us bemused.	*Response*
S2: So we're doing it to placate French and German tourists.	*Statement as Initiation*

S1: Jeremy, when you're walking in Derbyshire and you
    can't get a drink at 4pm in the afternoon, because
    of the licensing laws, you get a little annoyed.   *Response*
S2: So we're doing it to placate French and German
    tourists and walkers in Derbyshire.   *Statement as Initiation*
S1: Plenty of other people who'd want of an evening to
    go and relax having a drink.   *Response*

(*Newsnight*, BBC TV Tuesday, 8 July, 2003, Full transcript
http://news.bbc.co.uk/1/hi/programmes/newsnight/3055548.stm)

The goal of the media interview is primarily to elicit information whereas the classroom goal is to facilitate learning, and so the teacher's questions and responses must increment knowledge rather than assume it. Many of the teacher's questions and responses serve to build up shared knowledge. Notice in extract (11.9) how the teacher stages her responses and questions so as to repeat what has been said for the benefit of others in the class. She gradually builds new information and extends vocabulary by repeating and recycling the students' responses.

(11.9)
[In this language classroom extract, the teacher is introducing a newspaper article on healthy eating for university students. They are discussing what constitutes a healthy lunch.]

Teacher: What do you think they might mean by a healthy lunch then?
Student: Having something else to ah eat.
Teacher: So what might they eat normally? Maybe.
Student: Chips, burger.
Teacher: Okay. Fries fries burger.
Student: Drinks.
Teacher: What kind of drinks? All right fizzy drinks?
[laughter]
Teacher: You know the expression fizzy drinks. Have you come across 'fizzy'?
Students: Yeah.
Teacher: What, Sebastian very kindly came in showing us there and what you just finished there. Is a fizzy drink am coke fanta fizzy drinks po= we also use the word pop am there tends to be a lot of chemicals in these drinks . . . .. So burgers pop what else might they eat normally?
Student: Eat sandwich.
Teacher: Yeah.
Student: Sweets.
Teacher: Yeah chocolate. Yeah cake. The food we like unfortunately. So what might be a healthy option?
Student: Vegetables.
Teacher: Vegetables okay what else?

[Three turns later]:

Student: Yogurt.

Teacher: Yeah yogurt am maybe water or if they don't like water and they don't like milk what else could they drink that's not fizzy?

Student: Juice.

Teacher: Orange juice apple juice . . . what system do we have in England and in Ireland for school lunches for kids in schools?

(LIBEL)

The classroom context differs greatly from the media interview in that there is a constant dialectic between student responses and pedagogic goals. In the media interview, as noted by Carter and McCarthy (2006), the interviewer typically does not follow up on responses in the same way that the teacher does; instead the listener or viewer is usually left to make his/her own evaluation of the interviewee's answer. The goal of the interviewer is to elicit information and to entertain rather than to teach the interviewee or the audience.

Something that the media interview and the classroom interaction have in common is the use of display questions. These are typically questions to which the questioner already knows the answer. As Carter and McCarthy (2006: 717) note, they are common in contexts such as classrooms, quiz shows and other tests of knowledge, and media interviews. The purpose of a display question is to put knowledge or information on public display. In the classroom, this is an important way of transmitting and testing knowledge for teachers and students. In these display question situations such as classrooms and quizzes, the questioner follows up the answer by stating whether it is the correct one or not. However, in media interviews, as we have noted, the follow up is very often left to the listener or viewer. We will now take a close look at other types of questions, including display questions, and the impact that they may have on the course of classroom interaction.

Questioning and question types

Questions are broadly defined as utterances which require a verbal response from the addressee and there are a number of types, based on a variety of structural patterns. Carter and McCarthy (2006: 715–727) distinguish between the following forms which function as questions:

1 Yes-no questions: these are one of the most common question types. The anticipated response is either *yes* or *no*.
   Do you know what a freebie is?

(LIBEL)

2 *Wh*-questions: questions with *what, when, where, which, who(m), whose, why, how* request specific information concerning persons and things, and the circumstances surrounding actions and events (e.g. time, manner, place, etc.). The anticipated response to such questions is not *yes* or *no*, but information which provides the missing content of the *wh*-word.

What adjective would you use to describe someone who says 'hi how are you I'm it's nice to meet you'?

(LIBEL)

3   Alternative questions: these questions give the answerer a choice between two or more items contained in the question which are linked by *or*. Alternative questions may be *yes-no* interrogatives or *wh*-interrogatives. An alternative question may offer the recipient the choice of one or all of the alternatives.
    Is this is this a word, a phrase or a clause?

(LIBEL)

4   Declarative questions: not all *yes-no* questions have interrogative form, and a declarative clause may function in context as a question. The intonation is typically rising (➚) (asking for confirmation) or falling (➘) (strongly assuming something).
    ➚ *You are sick today?*

(LIBEL)

   S1: ➘ *So you're going to be here about quarter past?*
   S2: *Yeah quarter past, twenty past, yeah.*
   S1: *That's fine.*

(CANCODE)

5   Tag questions: questions may include a tag after a declarative clause. Tag questions are highly interactive in that they may constrain the range of possible or desired responses from the addressee. Some patterns are more constraining than others.
    *You've worked hard **haven't you**?*

(CANCODE)

6   Echo and checking questions: echo questions repeat part of the previous speaker's utterance, usually because some part of it has not been fully understood. They often have declarative word order and a clause-final *wh-* word.
       S1: *He's called Oliver.*
       S2: *He's called **what**?*
       S1: *Oliver.*

       S1: *Steve was singing with the group.*
       S2: ***Who** was singing, sorry?* (stressed)
       S1: *Steve, Steve Jones.*
       S2: *Oh.*

(CANCODE)

A corpus of classroom interactions provides a very good starting point for reflecting on teacher questioning strategies and how these affect the classroom interaction, and ultimately the learning outcome. Farr (2002) looked at the questions in a corpus of classroom interactions of five pre-service teachers who were undertaking a language teacher education course. In these EFL classes, the teachers were working with advanced level students. Her research showed that declarative questions produced the longest answers:

Table 2: Question types and answer length (Farr 2002)

question type	average number of words per answer
yes-no	7.36
wh-	10.51
alternative	9.33
declarative	18.33

Research into classroom questions also uses a functional categorisation including display questions, as mentioned above, and referential questions (see Banbrook and Skehan 1989; Farr 2002):

1 **Referential questions:** genuine questions to which the teacher does not already know the answer

   Teacher: So how long have you studied English Jong?

   (LIBEL)

2 **Display questions:** questions to which the teacher already knows the answer

   Narrow display questions: display questions to which there is only one anticipated response in terms or either content or form

   Teacher: What do you call that what they're wearing?
   Student: Uniform.

   (LIBEL)

   Broad display questions: display questions to which there is a range of possible answers in terms of content or form from a range of possibilities already known to the teacher

   Teacher: Marie can you tell me what did you find in the third paragraph?

   (LIBEL)

Farr (2002) also looked at functional questioning strategies in her corpus of pre-service teachers and she found the following breakdown:

Table 3: Breakdown of functional questioning strategies (Farr 2002)

question type	total
referential	13
narrow display	38
broad display	74

Pica and Long (1986) examined the difference in linguistic performance between experienced and inexperienced teachers in Philadelphia. In terms of questioning, they found that, among inexperienced teachers:

- more display questions were employed in classroom talk than in informal conversation.
- almost four times as many display questions were asked as referential questions (see also Long and Sato 1983).

In another study, Brock (1986) examined the effect of using more referential questions in the language classroom. She found that by increasing the frequency of referential questions, students produced longer and more syntactically complex responses. While display questions produced an average answer length of 4.2 words, referential questions produced an average of ten-word answers. Farr (2002) found the following correlation between question type and length of answer in her corpus-based study:

Table 4: Question type and average length of student reply (Farr 2002)

question type	total occurrences	average number of words per reply in student answers
referential	13	17.92
narrow display	38	3.34
broad display	74	12.44

Another important factor in classroom questioning strategies that has arisen from research is the amount of time that the teacher pauses after asking the question; that is, the 'wait time' after asking a question before the teacher added a new or re-formulated question. White and Lightbown (1984) found that teachers rarely waited longer than two seconds for a reply from their students. Farr (2002) calculated that only 27% of all the questions that she looked at allowed any wait time. O'Keeffe and Farr (2003) suggest how a corpus of classroom interactions can be used to focus on questions and questioning strategies so as to promote teacher awareness and reflection.

11.6 Teacher corpora in professional development

Adolphs et al. (2004) look at communication in the professional context of health care in a corpus-informed study of staged telephone conversations between callers and advisers in the UK's NHS Direct health advisory service. They make a case for applied clinical linguistics, which involves the synergy of those involved in the health services, educators and corpus linguists. By looking at the communicative events within the profession empirically, they argue, a better understanding of the interaction can be reached and this can lead to better practice. This model lends itself even more readily to the broader professional context of language teaching since as a professional group we are more linguistically equipped to reflect on our own language use. Within this model, contexts beyond the class-room would be included so as to examine, for example, how we communicate with colleagues, trainees and administrators in non-classroom contexts such as meetings, staffrooms, offices, which are part of the wider situational matrix of teaching.

As noted by Sarangi (2002: 106), the primary focus of classroom-based teacher–pupil interaction is at the expense of looking at what happens outside the classroom. Corpora are beginning to have applications to teacher talk outside of the classroom, particularly in the broadening model of teacher observation. Two corpora have been independently developed to focus on this type of interaction and to learn from it (see Farr 2003, 2005; Vásquez and Reppen 2004; Vásquez 2004, 2005). Farr, working with the Post Observation Teacher Training Interactions (POTTI) corpus of over 80,000 words, looks at the interaction of trainers and trainees on an Irish postgraduate teacher education programme (see also chapter 6). Her work gives many insights into the post-observation interaction, including the role of relational strategies such as inclusive pronoun use when advising, so as to draw on professional solidarity, the use of first name vocatives, hedged directives, shared socio-cultural references as well as engaged listernership (responses, overlaps, interruptions) and small talk. Extract (11.10) is an example from Farr (2005: 214), where at the beginning of a post-observation session small talk is used as a relational strategy by the trainer to mitigate forthcoming criticism (the trainee had made a major organisational mistake in her teaching practice by preparing the wrong lesson). The small talk extends for 19 turns in all:

(11.10)

Trainer:	. . . are you feeling okay now cos you were you weren't feeling great earlier you said?
Trainee:	Em not any better I can tell you actually+
Trainer:	Really?
Trainee:	+I'm very tired and em I think I've an ear infection or something every time I talk I can it's like major feedback in my ear+
Trainer:	Oh
Trainee:	+yeah I I'll need to get to the doctor or something.
Trainer:	You need to be careful with that.

(Farr 2005: 214)

Vásquez and Reppen's work draws on a corpus of language teachers and their mentors in a longitudinal, action research study in an American university intensive English programme. Post-observation meetings between mentors and teachers were recorded and transcribed over a period of two years. The authors were involved as mentors in these interactions and their initial findings showed that they were responsible for the majority of the talk in the meetings and that teachers tended to be passive. Based on this, changes were made to their practice with the goal of eliciting more talk from teachers. Focusing primarily on interactional data from four teacher/mentor pairs collected over two semesters, Vásquez and Reppen (in press) describe how this study enabled mentors to become aware of the linguistic and interactional subtleties of their existing practices. They illustrate how mentors were able to successfully change the meeting dynamics from mentor-centered to more teacher-centered through changes in the distribution of talk among participants. Important changes came about, for example, as a result of the ways that teachers were positioned by mentors in the openings of meetings. As in Farr's work, Vásquez and Reppen have created their own corpus to look at their own professional practices in context.

Vaughan (in press) looks at a corpus of English language teacher meetings in which she participated. She applies Goffman's (1959) dramaturgical metaphor of *frontstage* and *backstage* to teacher discourse. She contrasts the teachers' highly regulated and formalised frontstage talk in the classroom with their less organised backstage identity. Somewhere between this highly regulated and formalised frontstage and less organised backstage lies the area of mediated interaction which has as its goal the facilitation of professional development (e.g. Edge 1992, 2002) and reflective practice (e.g. Walsh 2002, 2003). Vaughan argues that, while the frontstage interaction has been considered the most significant type of discourse that teachers engage in, interaction outside the classroom, the teacher's *backstage* (teacher to teacher) discourse, is equally significant and has not thus far received as much attention as it merits. Vaughan, working with a corpus of over 40,000 words of teacher staff meetings, looks at how characteristics of this Community of Practice (after Lave and Wenger 1991; Wenger 1998) may be realised in linguistic features, and how these features together comprise a 'badge of identity'. She finds, for example, that the type of vague language used by the teachers is specific to their practices and that humour is key to the establishment of a shared communicative space. She also highlights the creation of this space through the construction of in- and out-groups.

Corpora also have great potential as a linguistic resource for teachers who wish to either improve their own language awareness or want to find out more about a specific structure in a language that comes up for them in the classroom. A number of studies illustrate the role of using a corpus in developing teachers' linguistic awareness both in pre-service education and in-service development and support (see Hunston 1995; Allen 1999; Conrad 1999; O'Keeffe and Farr 2003; Tsui 2004, 2005).

Allan (1999) and Tsui (2004, 2005) provide details of an exciting Hong Kong-based corpus facility which supports English teachers' grammar queries online. The website, *TeleNex*, was set up in 1993 to provide professional support to English language teachers in Hong Kong schools (see Tsui 2004). It is supported by a team of language specialists at the Teachers of English Language Education Centre (TELEC) of the Faculty of Education, The University of Hong Kong (see Tsui 1996; Tsui and Ki 2002). The website is designed to include a conference area in which a number of discussion corners have been set up, including one on the English language. Within this 'corner', teachers send questions seeking help and advice on language issues. The questions are responded to by both school teachers and language specialists in TELEC, some of whom are full-time staff specifically recruited to support the website and some are academic staff in the Faculty of Education. The service has evolved so that teachers can now learn to use the corpus resources independently as well as avail themselves of the support team's responses, and obviously they can respond to each other's queries. In a period of eight years, more than one thousand questions were submitted (Tsui 2005).

When answering teachers' questions, corpus data is consulted for evidence of language structure and use. What is interesting is that this is done from both a local and an international context of use. Internationally, mostly British and American English corpora are used (the BNC and COBUILD Direct). Locally, the team has amassed data of considerable size to reflect how forms are used by successful users of English in Hong Kong. These include the Modern English Corpus (see Tsui 2005), a five-million-word native speaker collection consisting of one million words of spoken texts from radio phone-ins, panel discussions, casual conversations and lectures and two million words of literary and academic texts, and two million words from feature articles in the *South China Morning Post*, and the TeleCorpora, which includes a 20-million-word sub-corpus of articles from the *South China Morning Post* and a learner corpus of more than two million words. TeleCorpora is now available for on-line access by registered users of the TeleNex website (http://www.telenex. hku.hk). Reflecting on the project, Tsui (2005) believes that the process has led to many existing concepts about language being challenged (she provides a number of examples, including a query on whether *because* can be used to begin a sentence or turn). This offers an example of how a corpus can become an end in itself rather than just a means to an end. It can offer a tool for awareness-raising at all stages of professional development.

Meanwhile, at the Pennsylvania State University in the USA, a website is available to which teachers can upload their own data of any kind and gain assistance in coding and analysing it using the site's own online software, which, when fully developed, will include capabilities for measuring features such as lexical density and variation, as well as the more conventional tools of frequency lists and concordances, all linked to sophisticated databases. The site also encourages and enables data-sharing among practitioners, an invaluable step in the creation of a community of corpus-aware professionals. The website is under the aegis of the CALPER project (Centre for Advanced Language Proficiency Education and Research; see http://calper.la.psu.edu/).

11.7   Conclusions and considerations

A corpus as a complementary resource

As we have stressed here, we are not advocating a corpus of classroom interactions as a replacement for video resources, but rather we are saying that the one complements the other. A video offers the opportunity to look at the classroom interaction in close detail, its transcription allows us to look even closer (and commercially available videos often include transcripts, for example Bampfield et al. 1997). A teacher-made corpus of classroom interactions adds to this kind of resource because it comes from a local context, reflects local teaching conditions and can be viewed with local insights. It is something that can be built up gradually over time and not something that needs to be of a certain size before it can be of any use. Even one hour of recording can offer many reflective opportunities. As we have seen here, most is to be gained by looking at short extracts. In this way, a teacher corpus is one from which much can be gained qualitatively, where the corpus is an end in itself. In other chapters in this book, we sometimes used corpora as a means to an end, to help us identify lexical frequencies and language patterns, for example, which will inform *what* we teach. A corpus of teacher interactions, on the other hand, informs us about *how* we teach and interact in the classroom and with colleagues. Here, we have been concerned not so much with what can be gained *from* a corpus as what can be gained *by* it.

A teacher-made corpus provides a mirror for our own practice which we can hold up to ourselves and learn from what we see. In the future, the optimum situation will certainly be to have digital audio-visual corpora, thus merging image and transcript (the BASE corpus has already achieved this for the majority of its data; see appendix 1). The further down the line we go with audio-visual corpora, the more challenges we face. For example, how best should we code the visual aspects of non-verbal communications? How many cameras would be needed to capture a classroom interaction? Classroom interactions, like most social interactions, are *multi-modal* in nature, combining both verbal and non-verbal components and units (Saferstein 2005). If we are to properly transcribe the audio-visual interaction, should we transcribe and align teacher and student gestures and other non-verbal components such as position of teacher, direction of gaze, movement of hand and so on? Current research at the University of Nottingham, for example, is looking at ways of building an audio-visual corpus so that ultimately concordance lines can be generated with the visual as well as verbal (Carter et al. 2006; Adolphs and Carter (forthcoming)).[2] At a technical level this poses many challenges. A number of projects are underway to this end, for example see Pea (in press).

From turn to theory

Teaching and learning do not just happen. They are part of an interactional process built around teaching goals, learning styles, individual differences and classroom conditions, among other things. By extracting actual classroom interactions from a corpus and breaking them down turn by turn, we have been able to explore this interactional process very closely. However, to do so we have needed to draw on some existing frameworks. The importance of teacher awareness of frameworks for analysing discourse is something we see as fundamental since they help us interpret our practice. This also points to a wider issue in corpus linguistics: the question as to whether corpus linguistics is a theory or a method (see Tognini-Bonelli 2001). For us, a corpus is a database and the processes of corpus linguistics offer a powerful methodological tool. The interpretation of the results that we generate from either qualitative or quantitative analyses need to be interpreted within existing applied linguistic frameworks, as well as enabling us to refine those frameworks and generate novel ones, in the classic dialectical process. Here we have used three frameworks: DA (discourse analysis), CA (conversational analysis) and Sociocultural theory, but there are many others including CDA (critical discourse analysis) (Fairclough 1989, 1992, 1995),

---

2   See http://www.nottingham.ac.uk/english/research/cral/projects.html

Language Identity, Language Socialization and many Second Language Acquisition models that could have been applied (see McCarthy 1991; Hatch 1992; McCarthy and Carter 1994; Johnson 1995; Riggenbach 1999; Celce-Murcia and Olshtain 2000; Boxer and Cohen 2004; Seedhouse 2004; Walsh 2006).

Throughout this book we have drawn on frameworks to interpret what we find in language corpora and these frameworks often lead us to new insights which, in turn, suggest new ways of exploiting corpora. This process is unlikely ever to come to a finite end. Nor should it, for corpora are endlessly fascinating treasure-houses which always have something new to offer. There is no such thing as a used up, worn-out corpus.

Coda

This book set out to explore links between corpus linguistics and language teaching. We have argued that there are many connections to be made, but that forging the links has to be a two-way process. For corpus linguistics to adequately inform language teaching, teachers need to inform corpus linguists. In order for this to be realised, some form of corpus linguistics should ideally become a core part of teacher education and development. On one level, we have tried to show the application and importance of corpus-based findings for language teaching, but on another level, we have sought to raise teachers' interest in using language corpora themselves to pursue their own inquiries and enhance their professional development. Corpus linguists are interested in finding exciting insights about language, but these are not always relevant or exciting for language teachers. Here we have looked at a wide range of research findings in English corpus linguistics that have brought us forward in our understanding of pedagogy and materials design, but this is by no means an exhaustive treatment. While much has been achieved, it is only the start of the synergy between corpus linguistics and language teaching.

There are many more research questions to be explored which will lead us to insights and applications for language teaching in the future. These research questions need to be driven by teachers, and indeed a more critical response to the findings of corpus linguistics needs to come from teachers. Just because a corpus linguist tells us that a certain structure is the most frequent in a corpus does not necessarily justify giving it prominence in a beginners' level course. Similarly, when corpus linguists tell us that a certain lexical item is very low frequency compared with others in a lexical set, this is not a reason for not teaching this item as part of the lexical set (e.g. the low frequency of *Tuesday* and *Wednesday* which we find in British and American spoken corpora, compared to the other days of the week, as illustrated in chapter 2). Teachers know that learners will need to learn all seven days of the week, and they know this from practice, not from theory. Their tacit knowledge needs to be brought to bear more explicitly in relation to corpus findings and their practical applications. Language teachers must continually assert their role as mediators between corpus findings and practice. Their research questions about language that arise out of practice need to be pursued and incorporated into the research agenda. This will surely be realised as more language teachers are made aware of how to build and use corpora and critically interpret corpus findings for language teaching.

In looking to the future of corpus linguistics and its role in language teaching and vice versa, we see the next most important stage as that of evaluation or classroom-based enquiry and feedback. We need to focus on getting feedback on applications of corpus-based materials for teachers and learners. There is at present a dearth of work in this area. What has the impact been of existing corpus-based applications and materials in the classroom and how can this inform corpus-based research? The authors and publishers of the corpus-informed *Touchstone* adult course, which we have mentioned in several places in this book (McCarthy, McCarten and Sandiford 2005, 2006), are, at the time of writing, carrying out intensive feedback exercises with both teachers and learners, involving face-to-face meetings and written feedback from these users. On the positive side, the students and teachers who have used the course seem overwhelmingly to appreciate the naturalness of the spoken extracts and the items focused upon for practice, and feel they are experiencing 'real' language, with the consequent pay-off for learner motivation. On the negative side, some teachers worry that they will need special training as corpus analysts in order to use the course, and are relieved to be shown that the course in itself is just as easy to use as any other course, since the corpus information has been mediated by the authors and the students' and teachers' editions have a familiar look, with familiar tasks and exercises. But this natural fear and suspicion that many teachers feel is not to be lightly dismissed; the word 'corpus' suggests complex technology and yet another demanding level of expertise to be imposed on teachers' already busy lives. Once these fears are dispelled and teachers feel comfortable with the materials, they value the research and mediation that has already been done for them by the course authors. It is, after all, a mere two decades since teachers were first asked to accept and embrace corpus-based learners' dictionaries; in that short time the situation has transformed itself so that now few teachers would be impressed by a publisher which sought proudly to market a *non*-corpus-based learners' dictionary. In all probability, the way corpus-based dictionaries have embedded themselves in the stock-in-trade of our profession will be repeated as regards reference grammars, coursebooks and other resources. But this will take time, and applied corpus linguists must not assume that the profession at large will rush to share its enthusiasm for everything to do with corpora.

Other areas that we see as crucial to the development of the relationship between language teaching and corpus linguistics relate to actual corpora: 1) there is a need for a wider availability of corpora and corpus tools, especially online, and 2) there is a need for diversity in the type of corpora that are available. The increasing availability of online corpora at the time of writing along with 'teacher-friendly tools' helps greatly here (see appendix 1). However, as mentioned above, teachers need to be informed on how to search and use corpora within teacher education programmes or as part of their professional development programmes. On the second issue, that is, the type of corpora available, there is a need to broaden the range. We especially need more non-English corpora, not least of all, more corpora of spoken language, and corpora of non-native users (see below). The other deficit that we see is in terms of small, specialised corpus resources. For example, a small corpus of sales encounters, meetings, business presentations and office interactions is far more useful for someone who is developing materials for a business language course, as opposed to a multimillion-word corpus of general language. The CANBEC corpus is designed to fill such a gap, but many more such corpora are needed.

An increase in the number of small specialised spoken corpora from different languages would be invaluable in addressing an area that we see as under-exploited in terms of corpus-based research for language teaching, namely that of pragmatics, and particularly in a cross-cultural context (see McCarthy and Carter 2004). Corpora have so much to tell us about how speech-act patterns and phenomena such as politeness differ across varieties of a language and, even more significantly, how they differ between languages. Everyday routines of asking for information, apologising, thanking, and so on, manifest differently across languages and cultures. Corpora provide real instances that can be accessed and compared by language teachers. Teachers who are non-native users of English (or whatever target language) are best placed for this type of investigation and have much to offer in terms of developing materials that address cross-cultural pragmatic issues. Pragmatically specialised uses of language that we have illustrated in many of the chapters in this book only come to the fore when one works with a small, concentrated sample of language in a specific context. Large general corpora can subsequently provide a comparative baseline or benchmark.

Perhaps most pressing of all is the need to develop more types of corpora is in the area of expert users. Throughout the book we have reinforced the need to move away from the native versus non-native speaker dichotomy and to look instead at a continuum of successful or expert users of a language. The development of a corpus of expert users of a language would mean that the examples we draw on, as academics, teachers or materials designers are not exclusively the preserve of native speakers.

In terms of technological advances, we see multimedia corpora (involving non-verbal as well as verbal language) as offering major advantages over simple text-based written or spoken corpora (particularly in the case of pragmatic phenomena), while advances in automatic speech and image recognition will, one day, enable teachers to build their own spoken corpora quickly and inexpensively. At the time of writing, cost is still the most prohibitive factor and only large institutions can afford to build large corpora, a situation which often makes teachers feel excluded from the privileged world of their applied linguist peers who have access to funding bodies or are invited by publishers to participate in big corpus projects.

In this book we have tried to highlight the relevant research outcomes which, in our judgement, have informed or can inform pedagogy, or which challenge how and what we teach. However, as we pointed out in the preface, we stop at the classroom door. The ultimate judgement on our work, and the next steps, must come from the teachers within.

References

Aarts, B. (2001) 'Review of S. Greenbaum and G. Nelson, Elliptical clauses in spoken and written English' in Collins, P. and Lee, D. (eds.) *The Clause in English: in Honour of Rodney Huddleston. Journal of Linguistics* 37 (2) 423–428.

Aarts, J. (1991) 'Intuition-based and observation-based grammars' in Aijmer, K. and Altenberg, B. (eds.) *English Corpus Linguistics*. London: Longman, 44–62.

Adolphs, S. (2006) *Introducing Electronic Text Analysis*. London: Routledge.

Adophs, S. and Carter, R. A. (2002) 'Corpus stylistics: point of views and semantic prosodies in *To the Lighthouse, Poetica* 58: 7–20.

Adolphs, S. and Carter, R. A. (2003) 'Creativity and a corpus of spoken English' in Goodman, S, Lillis, T, Maybin, J. and Mercer, N. (eds.) *Language, Literacy and Education: A Reader*. Stoke-on Trent: Trentham Books, 247–262.

Adolphs, S. and Carter, R. A. (forthcoming) 'Beyond the word: new challenges in analysing corpora of spoken English', *European Journal of English Studies* 11 (2).

Adolphs, S. and Durow, V. (2004) 'Sociocultural integration and the development of formulaic sentences' in Schmitt, N. (ed.) *Formulaic Sequences*. Amsterdam: John Benjamins.

Adolphs, S. and O'Keeffe, A. (2002) 'Response in British and Irish English: go away!' Paper read at *The First IVACS International Conference*, University of Limerick, June 14th – 15th, 2002.

Adolphs, S., Brown, B., Carter, R. A., Crawford, P. and Sahota, O. S. (2004) 'Applying corpus linguistics in a healthcare context', *International Journal of Applied Linguistics* 1 (1): 9–28.

Ahmed, M. K. (1994) 'Speaking as cognitive regulation: a Vygotskyan perspective on dialogic communication' in Lantolf, J. P. (ed.) *Vygotskyan Approaches to Second Language Research*. Norwood, NJ: Ablex.

Aijmer, K. (1995) 'Do women apologise more than men?' in Melchers, G. and Warren, B. (eds.) *Studies in Anglistics*. Stockholm: Almqvist and Wiksell, 59–69.

Aijmer, K. (1996) *Conversational Routines in English. Convention and Creativity*. London/New York: Longman.

Aijmer, K. (1997) 'I think – an English modal particle' in Swan, T. and Westvik, O. (eds.) *Modality in Germanic Languages*. Berlin: de Gruyter, 1–47.

Alexander, R. J. (1984) 'Fixed expressions in English: reference books and the teacher', *ELT Journal* 38 (2): 127–134.

Alexander, R. J. (1985) 'Phraseological and pragmatic deficits in advanced learners of English: problems of vocabulary learning?' *Die Neueren Sprachen* 84 (6): 613–621.

Allan, Q. (1999) 'Enhancing the language awareness of Hong Kong teachers through corpus data: the Telenex experience', *Journal of Technology and Teacher Education* 7 (1): 57–74.

Altenberg, B. (1998) 'On the phraseology of spoken English: the evidence of recurrent word combinations' in Cowie, A. P. (ed.) *Phraseology: Theory Analysis and Applications*. Oxford: Oxford University Press, 101–122.

Altenberg, B. and Granger, S. (2001) 'Grammatical and lexical patterning of *make* in student writing', *Applied Linguistics* 22 (2): 173–194.

Altenberg, B. and Granger, S. (eds.) (2002) *Lexis in Contrast: Corpus Based Approaches*. Amsterdam: Rodopi.

Amador Moreno, C.P., McCarthy, M.J., and O'Keeffe, A. (2005) 'Language corpora in new learning environments: an examination of response tokens in spoken corpora of Spanish, French and British and Irish English'. Paper read at *The 10th International Colloquium on Foreign Language Teaching*, University of Limerick. June 10th–11th, 2005.

Andersen, G. (1997a) ' "They gave us these yeah, and they like wanna see like how we talk and all that." The use of *like* and other discourse markers in London teenage speech' in Kotsinas, U.–B., Stenström, A.-B. and Karlsson, A.-M. (eds.) *Ungdomsspråk i Norden*. Stockholm: MINS 43: 82–95.

Andersen, G. (1997b) ' "They like wanna see like how we talk and all that." The use of *like* as a discourse marker in London teenage speech' in Ljung, M. (ed.) *Corpus-based Studies in English*. Amsterdam: Rodopi, 37–48.

Andersen, G. (2000) 'The Role of the pragmatic marker *like* in utterance interpretation' in Andersen, G. and Fretheim, T. (eds.) *Pragmatic Markers and Propositional Attitude. Pragmatics and Beyond*, 79. Amsterdam: John Benjamins, 17–38.

Andersen, G. (2001) *Pragmatic Markers and Sociolinguistic Variation: A Relevance-theoretic Approach to the Language of Adolescents*. Amsterdam/Philadelphia: John Benjamins.

Antaki, C. (2002) ' "Lovely", turn-initial high-grade assessments in telephone closings', *Discourse Studies* 4: 5–24.

Antaki, C., Houtkoop-Steenstra, H. and Rapley, M. (2000) ' "Brilliant. Next question . . .", high-grade assessment sequences in the completion of interactional units', *Research on Language and Social Interaction* 33: 235–262.

Anton, M. (1999) 'The discourse of a learner-centred classroom: sociocultural perspectives on teacher-learner interaction in the second language classroom', *Modern Language Journal* 88: 303–318.

Arnaud, P. and Savignon, S. (1997) 'Rare words, complex lexical units and the advanced learner' in Coady, J. and Huckin, T. (eds.) *Second Language Vocabulary Acquisition*. Cambridge: Cambridge University Press, 157–200.

Aston, G. (1988) *Learning Comity*. Bologna: Editrice CLUEB.

Aston, G. (1995) 'Corpora in language pedagogy: matching theory and practice' in Cook, G. and Seidlhofer, B. (eds.) *Principle and Practice in Applied Linguistics: Studies in Honour of H. G. Widdowson*. Oxford: Oxford University Press, 257–270

Aston, G. (1997) 'Small and large corpora in language learning' in Lewandowska-Tomaszczyk, B. and Melia, P. J. (eds.) *PALC '97 Proceedings of the First Annual Conference*. Lodz: Lodz University Press, 51–62

Aston, G. (1999) 'Corpus use and learning to translate', *Textus* 12: 289. Available at http://sslmit.unibo.it/~guy/textus.htm.

Aston, G. (ed.) (2001) *Learning with Corpora*. Houston, TX: Athelstan.

Aston, G. and Burnard, L. (1998) *The BNC Handbook*. Edinburgh: Edinburgh University Press.

Bach, K. and R. M. Harnish (1979) *Linguistic Competence and Speech Acts*. Cambridge, Mass.: The MIT Press.

Bahns, J., Burmeister, H. and Vogel, T. (1986) 'The pragmatics of formulas in L2 learner speech', *Journal of Pragmatics* 10: 693–723.

Baker, M. (1995) 'Corpora in translation studies: an overview and some suggestions for future research', *Target* 7 (2): 223–243.

Baker, M. (1998) 'Réexplorer la langue de la traduction: une approche par corpus' (Investigating the language of translation: a corpus-based approach), *Meta* 43 (4): 480–485.

Bampfield, A., Lubelska, D. and Matthews, M. (1997) *Looking at Language Classrooms*. Cambridge: Cambridge University Press.

Banbrook, L. and Skehan, P. (1989) 'Classrooms and display questions' in Brumfit, C. and Mitchell, R. (eds.) *Research in the Language Classroom*. ELT Documents No. 133: Modern English Publications and the British Council, 141–152.

Bargiela-Chiappini, F. and Harris, S. (1997) *Managing Language: The Discourse of Corporate Meetings*. Amsterdam: John Benjamins.

Barlow, M. (1999) MonoConc Pro (Version 1.5) (Computer software). Houston, TX: Athelstan.

Barron, A. (2003) *Acquisition in Interlanguage Pragmatics*. Amsterdam: John Benjamins.

Barron, A. (2005) 'Offering in Ireland and England' in Barron, A. and Schneider, K. P. (eds.) *The Pragmatics of Irish English*. Berlin: Mouton de Gruyter, 141–176.

Barsalou, L. (1983) 'Ad hoc categories', *Memory and Cognition* 11: 211–277.

Barsalou, L. (1987) 'The instability of graded structure: implications for the nature of concepts' in Neisser, U. (ed.) *Concepts and Conceptual Development*. Cambridge: Cambridge University Press, 101–140.

Baynham, M. (1991) 'Speech reporting as discourse strategy: some issues of acquisition and use', *Australian Review of Applied Linguistics* 14: 87–114.

Baynham, M. (1996) 'Direct speech: what's it doing in non-narrative discourse?', *Journal of Pragmatics* 25: 61–81.

Benson, M. and Benson, E. (1993) *Russian-English Dictionary of Verbal Collocations (REDVC)*. Amsterdam: John Benjamins.

Bergstrom, K. (1979) 'Idioms exercises and speech activities to develop fluency', *Collected Reviews* Summer: 21–2.

Bernardi, S. (2000) *Competence, Capacity, Corpus*. Bologna: CLUEB.

Biber, D. (1993) 'Representativeness in corpus design', *Literary and Linguistic Computing* 8 (4): 243–257.

Biber, D. and Conrad, S. (1999) 'Lexical bundles in conversation and academic prose' in Hasselgard, H. and Oksefjell, S. (eds.) *Out of Corpora: Studies in Honor of Stig Johansson*. Amsterdam: Rodopi, 181–190.

Biber, D. and Conrad, S. (2001) 'Quantitative corpus-based research: much more than bean counting', *TESOL Quarterly* 35 (2): 331–336.

Biber, D., Conrad S., and Reppen, R. (1998) *Corpus Linguistics: Investigating Language Structure and Use*. Cambridge: Cambridge University Press.

Biber, D., Conrad, S. and Cortes, V. (2004) ' "If you look at . . .": Lexical bundles in university teaching and textbooks', *Applied Linguistics* 25 (3): 371–405.

Biber, D., Conrad, S., Reppen, R., Byrd, P. and Helt, M. (2002) 'Speaking and writing in the university: a multidimensional comparison'. *TESOL Quarterly* 36 (1): 9–48.

Biber, D. and Jones, J. K. (2005) 'Merging corpus linguistic and discourse analytic research goals:

Discourse units in biology research articles', *Corpus Linguistics and Linguistic Theory* 1 (2): 151–182.

Biber, D. Johansson, S., Leech, G., Conrad, S. and Finegan, E. (1999) *Longman Grammar of Spoken and Written English*. London: Longman.

Binchy, J. (2002) ' "Will I, Won't I?" Personal pronouns, grades, and changes over semesters in student academic writing', *Teanga* 21: 53–74.

Blum-Kulka, S. (1983) 'The dynamics of political interviews', *Text* 3 (2): 131–153.

Blum-Kulka, S. (1989) 'Playing it safe: the role of conventionality in indirectness' in Blum-Kulka, S., House, J. and Kasper, G. (eds.) *Cross-Cultural Pragmatics: Requests and Apologies*. Norwood: Ablex Publishing Corporation, 37–70.

Blum-Kulka, S. (1994) 'The dynamics of family dinner table: cultural contexts for children's passages to adult discourse', *Research on Language and Social Interaction* 27 (1): 1–50.

Blum-Kulka, S. (1997a) *Dinner Table Talk: Cultural Patterns of Sociability and Socialisation in Family Discourse*. Mahwah, NJ: Lawrence Erlbaum.

Blum-Kulka, S. (1997b) 'Discourse pragmatics' inVan Dijk, T. A. (ed.) *Discourse as Social Interaction*. London: Sage Publications, 38–63.

Blum-Kulka, S. and Olshtain, E. (1984) 'Requests and apologies: A cross-cultural study of speech-act realization patterns (CCSARP)', *Applied Linguistics* 5 (3): 196–213.

Blum-Kulka, S., House, J. and Kasper, G. (eds.) (1989) *Cross-cultural Pragmatics: Requests and Apologies*. Norwood, NJ: Ablex Publishing Corporation.

Boden, D. (1994) *The Business of Talk. Organisations in Action*. London: Polity Press.

Boden, D. (1995) 'Agendas and arrangements: everyday negotiations in meetings' in Firth, A. (ed.) *The Discourse of Negotiation: Studies of Language in the Workplace*. Oxford: Pergamon, 83–99.

Boers, F. (2000) 'Metaphor awareness and vocabulary retention', *Applied Linguistics* 21 (4): 553–571.

Boers, F. and Demecheleer, M. (2001) 'Measuring the impact of cross-cultural differences on learners' comprehension of imageable idioms', *ELT Journal* 55 (3): 255–262.

Bolinger, D. (1976) 'Meaning and memory', *Forum Linguisticum* 1: 1–14.

Bolinger, D. (1987) 'The remarkable double IS', *English Today* 9: 39–40.

Boucher, V. J. (2005) On the measurable linguistic correlates of deceit in recounting passed events. Paper read at *International Association of Forensic Linguists 7th Biennial Conference on Forensic Linguistics/Language and Law*, Cardiff University, UK, July 1st–4th 2005.

Boxer, D. (2004) 'Studying speaking to inform second language learning: a conceptual overview' in Boxer, D. and Cohen, A. D. (eds.) *Studying Speaking to Inform Second Language Learning*. Clevedon: Multilingual Matters, 3–24.

Boxer, D. and Cohen, A. D. (eds.) (2004) *Studying Speaking to Inform Second Language Learning*. Clevedon: Multilingual Matters.

Boxer, D. and Pickering, L. (1995) 'Problems in the presentation of speech acts in ELT materials: the case of complaints', *ELT Journal* 49: 99–158.

Braine, G. (ed.) (1999) *Non-Native Educators in English Language Teaching*. Marwah, NJ: Lawrence Erlbaum.

Braun, S. and Chambers, A. (2006) 'Elektronische Korpora als Ressource für den Fremdsprachenunterricht' in Jung, U. (ed.) *Praktische Handreichung für Fremdsprachenlehre*. 4th edition. Bern: Peter Lang, 330–337.

Breen, M. (1983) 'Authenticity in the language classroom', *Applied Linguistics* 6 (1): 60–70.

Brinton, L. (1996) *Pragmatic Markers in English: Grammaticalization and Discourse Functions*. The Hague: Mouton de Gruyter.

Brock, C. (1986) 'The effects of referential questions on ESL classroom discourse', *TESOL Quarterly* 20 (1): 47–59.

Brown, P. and Levinson, S. (1978) 'Universals in language usage: politeness phenomena' in Goody, E. N. (ed.) *Questions and Politeness: Strategies in Social Interaction*. Cambridge: Cambridge University Press, 56–310.

Brown, P. and S. Levinson (1987) *Politeness: Some Universals in Language Usage*. Cambridge: Cambridge University Press.

Bruner, J. (1990) 'Vygotsky: a historical and conceptual perspective' in Moll, L. C. (ed.) *Vygotsky and Education: Instructional Implications and Applications of Sociohistorical Psychology*. Cambridge: Cambridge University Press.

Bunton, D. (2005) 'The structure of PhD conclusion chapters', *Journal of English for Academic Purposes* 4 (3): 207–224.

Burns, A. (2001) 'Analysing spoken discourse: implications for TESOL' in Burns, A. and Coffin, C. (eds.) *Analysing English in a Global Context: A Reader*. London: Routledge, 123–148.

Burns, A., Joyce, H., and Gollin, S. (2001) *'I See What You Mean': Using Spoken Discourse in the Classroom*. Sydney: National Centre for English Language Teaching and Research.

Burrows, J. (2002). 'The Englishing of juvenal: computational stylistics and translated texts', *Style* 36 (4): 677–679.

Bygate, M., Skehan, P. and Swain, M. (eds.) (2001) *Researching Pedagogic Tasks: Second Language Learning, Teaching and Testing*. London: Longman.

Callahan, L. (2004) *Spanish/English Codeswitching in a Written Corpus*. Amsterdam: John Benjamins.

Cambridge Advanced Learner's Dictionary (2003) Cambridge: Cambridge University Press.

Cameron, L. (2005) 'Creativity and the language classroom'. Working paper, Faculty of Education: Open University.

Canale, M. and Swain, M. (1980) 'Theoretical bases of communicative approaches to second language teaching and testing', *Applied Linguistics* 1 (1): 1–47.

Candlin, C. (2000) General Editor's preface in Coupland, J. (ed.) *Small Talk*. London: Longman, 13–20.

Carroll, J. B., Davies, P. and Richman, B. (1971) *The American Heritage Word Frequency Book*. New York: Houghton Mifflin.

Carter, R. A. (1987) (2nd ed. 1998) *Vocabulary: Applied Linguistic Perspectives*. London: Routledge.

Carter, R. A. (1998) 'Orders of reality: CANCODE, communication and culture', *ELT Journal* 52: 43–56.

Carter, R. A. (1999a) 'Common language: corpus, creativity and cognition', *Language and Literature* 8 (3): 1–21.

Carter, R. A. (1999b) 'Standard grammars, spoken grammars: some educational implications', in Bex, A. R. and Watts, R. (eds.) S*tandard English: The Continuing Debate*. London: Routledge.

Carter, R. A. (2004) *Language and Creativity: the Art of Common Talk*. London: Routledge.

Carter, R. A. (2005) 'Spoken grammar' in Coffin, C., Hewings, A. and O'Halloran, K. (eds.) *Applying English Grammar: Functional Corpus Approaches*. London: Edward Arnold 35–49.

Carter, R. A. (2006) 'Common speech' uncommon discourse' in Martin, P. (ed.) *English: The Condition of the Subject*. Basingstoke: Palgrave, 34–54.

Carter, R. A. and Fung, L. (forthcoming) 'Discourse markers and spoken English: native and non-native use in pedagogical settings, *Applied Linguistics*.

Carter, R. A. and McCarthy, M. J. (1988) *Vocabulary and Language Teaching*. London: Longman.

Carter, R. A. and McCarthy, M. J. (1995) 'Grammar and the spoken language', *Applied Linguistics* 16 (2): 141–58.

Carter, R. A. and McCarthy, M. J. (1997) *Exploring Spoken English*. Cambridge: Cambridge University Press.

Carter, R. A. and McCarthy, M. J. (1999) 'The English get-passive in spoken discourse: description and implications for an interpersonal grammar', *English Language and Linguistics* 3 (1): 41–58.

Carter, R. A and McCarthy, M. J. (2001) 'Size isn't everything: spoken English, corpus and the classroom', *TESOL Quarterly* 35 (2): 337–340.

Carter, R. A. and McCarthy, M. J. (2004) 'Talking, creating: interactional language, creativity and context', *Applied Linguistics* 25 (1): 62–88.

Carter, R. A. and McCarthy, M. J. (2006) *Cambridge Grammar of English: A Comprehensive Guide to Spoken and Written English Grammar and Usage*. Cambridge: Cambridge University Press.

Carter, R. A. and McRae, J. (eds.) (1996) *Literature, Language and the Classroom: Creative Classroom Practice* Harlow: Pearson Longman.

Carter, R. A., Hughes, R. and McCarthy, M. J. (2000) *Exploring Grammar in Context*. Cambridge: Cambridge University Press.

Carter, R. A., Knight, D., Bayoumi, S., Mills, S., Crabtree, A., Adolphs, S. and Pridmore, T. (2006) 'Beyond the text: Construction and analysis of multi-modal linguistic corpora.' Paper read at *The 2nd Annual International e-Social Science Conference*, University of Manchester (http://www.ncess.ac.uk/research/sgp/headtalk).

Carver, R. (1994) 'Percentage of unknown vocabulary words in text as a function of the relative difficulty of the text: implications for instruction', *Journal of Reading Behavior* 26: 413–437.

Celce-Murcia, M. and Olshtain, E. (2000) *Discourse and Context in Language Teaching*. New York: Cambridge University Press.

Chafe, W. (1982) 'Integration and involvement in speaking, writing, and oral literature' in Tannen, D. (ed.) *Spoken and Written Language: Exploring Orality and Literacy*. Norwood, NJ: Ablex Publishing Corporation, 35–53.

Chafe, W. (1987) 'Cognitive constraints on information flow' in Tomlin, R. (ed.), *Coherence and Grounding in Discourse*. Amsterdam: John Benjamins, 21–51.

Chafe, W. (1994) *Discourse, Consciousness, and Time: The Flow and Displacement of Conscious Experience in Speaking and Writing*. Chicago: University of Chicago Press.

Chafe, W., DuBois, J. and Thompson, S. (1991) 'Towards a corpus of spoken American English' in Aijmer, K. and Altenberg, B. (eds.), *English Corpus Linguistics: Studies in honour of Jan Svartvik*. London: Longman, 64–82.

Chambers, A. (2005) 'Integrating corpus consultation in language studies', *Language Learning and Technology* 9 (2): 111–125.

Chambers, A. (in press) 'Popularising corpus consultation by language learners and teachers' in Hidalgo, E., Quereda, L. and Santana, J. (eds.) *Corpora in the Foreign Language Classroom*. Amsterdam: Rodopi.

Chambers, A. and Kelly, V. (2002) 'Semi-specialised corpora of written French as a resource in language teaching and learning', *Teanga* 21: 20–21.

Chambers, A. and Kelly, V. (2004) 'Corpora and concordancing: changing the paradigm in language learning and teaching?' in Chambers, A., Conacher, J. E. and Littlemore, J. M. (eds.) *ICT and Language Learning: Integrating Pedagogy and Practice*. Birmingham: University of Birmingham Press, 183–201.

Chambers, A. and O'Sullivan, Í. (2004) 'Corpus consultation and advanced learners' writing skills in French', *ReCALL*, 16 (1): 158–172.

Chambers, A. and Rostand, S. (eds.) (2005) *Le Corpus Chambers-Rostand de Français Journalistique*. (Oxford Text Archive) Oxford: University of Oxford.

Channell, J. (1990) 'Precise and vague quantities in writing on economics' in Nash, W. (ed.) *The Writing Scholar*. Newbury Park: Sage, 95–117.

Channell, J. (1994) *Vague Language*. Oxford: Oxford University Press.

Chappell, H. (1980) 'Is the *get-passive* adversative?', *Papers in Linguistics* 13 (3): 411–52.

Charles, Maggie. (2003) '"This mystery . . .": a corpus-based study of the use of nouns to construct stance in theses from two contrasting disciplines', *Journal of English for Academic Purposes* 2 (4): 313–326.

Charles, Mirjaliisa. (1996) 'Business negotiations: interdependence between discourse and the business relationship', *English for Specific Purposes* 15 (1): 19–36.

Charteris-Black, J. (2002) 'Second language figurative proficiency: a comparative study of Malay and English', *Applied Linguistics* 23 (1): 104–133.

Cheepen, C. (2000) 'Small talk in service dialogues: the conversational aspects of transactional telephone talk' in Coupland, J. (ed.) *Small Talk*. London: Longman, 288–311.

Cheng, W. and Warren, M. (1999) 'Facilitating a description of intercultural conversations: the Hong Kong Corpus of Conversational English', *ICAME Journal* 23: 5–20.

Cheng, W. and Warren, M. (2000) 'The Hong Kong Corpus of Spoken English: language learning through language description' in Burnard, L. and McEnery, T. (eds.) *Rethinking Language Pedagogy from a Corpus Perspective*. Frankfurt am Main: Peter Lang, 133–144.

Cheng, W. and Warren, M. (2002) '// \ ⁄ beef ball // → you like //: the intonation of declarative-mood questions in a corpus of Hong Kong English', *Teanga* 21: 151–165.

Chomsky, N. (1957) *Syntactic Structures*. The Hague: Mouton.

Chomsky, N. (1965) *Aspects of the Theory of Syntax*. Cambridge, Mass.: MIT Press.

Church, K. and Gale, W. (1991) 'Concordances for parallel text', *Using Corpora: Proceedings of the Seventh Annual Conference of the UW Centre for the New OED and Text Research*. Oxford: St. Catherine's College.

Clancy, B. (2002) 'The exchange in family discourse', *Teanga* 21: 134–150.

Clancy, B. (2005) '"You're fat. You'll eat them all". Politeness strategies in family discourse' in Barron, A. and Schneider, K. P. (eds.) *The Pragmatics of Irish English*. Berlin: Mouton de Gruyter, 177–197.

Claridge, C. (2000) 'Translating phrasal verbs' in Kettemann, B. and Marko, G. (eds.) *Teaching and Learning by Doing Corpus Analysis*. Amsterdam: Rodopi, 361–73.

Clark, H. H. and Lucy, P. (1975) 'Understanding what is meant from what is said: a study in conversationally conveyed requests', *Journal of Verbal Learning and Verbal Behavior* 14: 56–72.

Clemen, G. (1997) 'The concept of hedging: origin, approaches and definitions' in Markkanen, R. and Schröder, H. (eds.) *Hedging and Discourse: Approaches to the Analysis of a Pragmatic Phenomenon in Academic Texts*. Berlin: Walter de Gruyter, 235–248.

Coates, J. (1986) *Women, Men and Language: A Sociolinguistic Account of Sex Differences in Language*. London: Longman.

Cobb, T. (1997) 'Is there any measurable learning from hands-on concordancing?', *System* 25 (3): 301–315.

Coffin, C., Hewings, A. and O'Halloran, K. (eds.) (2004) *Applying English Grammar: Functional and Corpus Approaches*. London: Arnold.

Collins, P. (1987) 'Clefts and pseudo-cleft constructions in English spoken and written discourse', *ICAME Journal* 11: 5–17.

Collins, P. (1996) 'Get-passives in English', *World Englishes* 15 (1): 43–56.

Collins, P. (2004) 'Reversed *what*-clefts in English: information structure and discourse function', *Australian Review of Applied Linguistics* 27 (2): 63–74.

Collins, P. and Lee, D. (eds.) *The Clause in English: in Honour of Rodney Huddleston*. Amsterdam: John Benjamins.

Conley, J. M. and O'Barr, W. M. (1998) *Just Words*. Chicago: Chicago University Press.

Connor, U. (1999). '"How like you our fish?" Accommodation in international business communication' in Hewings, M. and Nickerson, C. (eds.) *Business English: Research into Practice*. Harlow: Longman, 115–128.

Conrad, S. (1999) 'The importance of corpus-based research for language teachers', *System* 27 (1): 1–18.

Conrad, S. (2001) 'Variation among disciplinary texts: a comparison of textbooks and journal articles in biology and history' in Conrad, S. and Biber, D. (eds.) *Variation in English: Multi-dimensional Studies*. Harlow: Longman, 94–107.

Cook, G. (1998) 'The uses of reality: a reply to Ronald Carter', *ELT Journal* 52: 57–63.

Cook, G. (2000) *Language Play, Language Learning*. Oxford: Oxford University Press.

Corbett, J. and Douglas, F. (2004) 'Scots in the public sphere' in Kirk, J. M. and Ó Baoill, D. P. (eds.) *Towards our Goals in Broadcasting, the Press, the Performing Arts and the Economy: Minority Languages in Northern Ireland, the Republic of Ireland and Scotland*. Belfast: Queen's University Belfast Studies in Language, Culture and Politics, 198–210.

Cornilescu, A. (1981) 'Non-restrictive relative clauses: an essay in semantic description', *Revue Roumaine de Linguistique* 26 (1): 41–67.

Cortes, V. (2002) 'Lexical bundles in freshman composition' in Reppen, R., Fitzmaurice, S. and Biber, D. (eds.) *Using Corpora to Explore Linguistic Variation*. Amsterdam: John Benjamins, 131–145.

Cortes, V. (2004) 'Lexical bundles in published and student writing in history and biology', *English for Specific Purposes* 23 (4): 397–423.

Cosme, C. (2004) 'Towards a corpus-based cross-linguistic study of clause combining. Methodological framework and preliminary results', *Belgian Journal of English Language and Literatures* 2: 199–224.

Cotterill, J. (ed.) (2002a) *Language in the Legal Process*. Basingstoke: Palgrave.

Cotterill, J. (2002b) *Language and Power in Court: A Linguistic Analysis of the O. J. Simpson Trial*. Basingstoke: Palgrave.

Cotterill, J. (2003) *Language and Power in Court*. Basingstoke: Palgrave.

Cotterill, J. (2004) 'Collocation, connotation, and courtroom semantics: lawyers' control of witness testimony through lexical negotiation', *Applied Linguistics* 25 (4): 513–537

Coulmas, F. (1979) 'On the sociolinguistic relevance of routine formulae', *Journal of Pragmatics* 3: 239–66.

Coulmas, F. (1981a) 'Idiomaticity as a problem of pragmatics' in Parret, H. , Sbisà, M. and Verschueren, J. (eds.) *Possibilities and Limitations of Pragmatics*. Amsterdam: John Benjamins, 139–51.

Coulmas, F. (ed.) (1981b) *Conversational Routine*. The Hague: Mouton.

Coulthard, M. (1977) *An Introduction to Discourse Analysis*. London: Longman

Coulthard, M. (2004) 'Author identification, idiolect, and linguistic uniqueness', *Applied Linguistics* 25 (4): 431–447.

Coulthard, M. and Ashby, M. (1975) 'Talking with the Doctor, 1', *Journal of Communication*, Summer: 140–147.

Coupland, J. (ed.) (2000) *Small Talk*. London: Longman.

Coupland, N. and Ylänne-McEwen, V. (2000) 'Talk about the weather: small talk, leisure. Talk and the travel industry' in Coupland, J. (ed.) (2000) *Small Talk*. London: Longman, 163–182.

Coupland. J., Coupland, N. and Robinson, J. (1992) '"How are you?": negotiating phatic communion', *Language in Society* 21 (2): 207–30.

Cowie, A. P. (1988) 'Stable and creative aspects of vocabulary use' in Carter, R. and McCarthy, M. J. (eds.) *Vocabulary and Language Teaching*. London: Longman, 126–39.

Coxhead, A. (2000) 'A new academic word list', *TESOL Quarterly* 34 (2): 213–238.

Crosling, G. and Ward, I. (2002) 'Oral communication: the workplace needs and uses of business graduate employees', *English for Specific Purposes* 21: 41–57.

Crowdy, S. (1993). 'Spoken corpus design', *Literary and Linguistic Computing* 8: 259–265.

Crystal, D. (1997) *English as a Global Language*. Cambridge: Cambridge University Press.

Cucchiarini, C., Strik, H. and Boves, L. (2000) 'Quantitative assessment of second language learners' fluency by means of automatic speech recognition technology', *Journal of the Acoustical Society of America* 107(2): 989–999.

Dagneaux E., Denness S., Granger S. and Meunier, F. (1996) *Error Tagging Manual Version 1.1*. Centre for English Corpus Linguistics. Université Catholique de Louvain, Louvain-la-Neuve.

Dagut, M. (1985) 'A "teaching grammar" of the passive voice in English', *International Review of Applied Linguistics* 23 (1): 1–12.

Dannerer, M. (2001) 'Negotiation in business meetings' in Weigand, E. and Dascal, M. (eds.) *Negotiation and Power in Dialogic Interaction*. Amsterdam: John Benjamins, 91–106.

Dash, P. (2004) 'Cross-cultural pragmatic failure: a definitional analysis with implications for classroom teaching', *Asian EFL Journal* (September). Available at: http://www.asian-efl-journal.com/Sept_04_pd.doc.

Davies, B. and Harré, R. (1990) 'Positioning: the discursive production of selves', *Journal of the Theory of Social Behaviour* 20: 43–63.

De Cock, S. (1998) 'A recurrent word combination approach to the study of formulae in the speech of native and non-native speakers of English', *International Journal of Corpus Linguistics* 3: 59–80.

De Cock, S. (2000) 'Repetitive phrasal chunkiness and advanced EFL speech and writing' in Mair, C. and Hundt, M. (eds.) *Corpus Linguistics and Linguistic Theory. Papers from ICAME 20 1999*. Amsterdam: Rodopi, 51–68.

De Cock, S. and Granger, S. (2004) 'High frequency words: the bête noire of lexicographers and learners alike. a close look at the verb 'make' in five monolingual learners dictionaries of English' in Williams, G. and Vesssier, S. (eds.) *Proceedings of the Eleventh EURALEX International Congress*. Université de Bretagne-Sud: Lorient, 233–243.

De Cock, S., Granger, S., Leech, G. and McEnery, T. (1998) 'An automated approach to the phrasicon of EFL learners' in Granger, S. (ed.) *Learner English on Computer*. London: Longman, 67–79.

Degand, L. and Bestgen, Y. (2003) 'Towards automatic retrieval of idioms in French newspaper corpora', *Literary and Linguistic Computing* 18 (3): 249–259.

Delin, J. L. (1990) 'A multi-level account of cleft constructions in discourse' in Karlgren, H. (ed.) *Proceedings of the 13th Conference on Computational Linguistics – Volume 2, Helsinki, Finland.* Morristown, NJ: Association for Computational Linguistics, 83–88.

Depraetere, I. (1995) 'Factors requiring, promoting and excluding the use of a (non-) restrictive relative clause' *Leuvense Bijdragen* 83 (4): 433–458.

Depraetere, I. (1996) 'Foregrounding in English relative clauses', *Linguistics* 34 (4): 699–731.

Dines, E. (1980) 'Variation in discourse – and stuff like that', *Language in Society* 1: 13–31.

Donohue, W. and Diez, M. (1985) 'Directive use in negotiation interaction', *Communications Monographs* 52: 305–318.

Dörnyei, Z. and Thurrell, S. (1994) 'Teaching conversational skills intensively: course content and rationale', *ELT Journal* 48 (1): 40–49.

Douglas, F. (2003) 'The Scottish Corpus of Texts and Speech: problems of corpus design', *Literary and Linguistic Computing* 18 (1): 23–37.

Drew, P. (1985) 'Analyzing the use of language in courtroom interaction' in Van Dijk, T. A. (ed.) *Handbook of Discourse Analysis, vol.3: Discourse and Dialogue.* London: Academic Press, 133–147.

Drew, P. and Heritage, J. (1992) *Talk at Work: Interaction in Institutional Settings.* Cambridge: Cambridge University Press.

Drew, P. and Holt, E. (1988) 'Complainable matters: the use of idiomatic expressions in making complaints', *Social Problems* 35 (4): 398–417.

Drew, P. and Holt, E. (1995) 'Idiomatic expressions and their role in the organisation of topic transition in conversation' in Everaert, M., van der Linden, E-J., Schenk A. and Schreuder, R. (eds.) *Idioms: Structural and Psychological Perspectives.* Hillsdale NJ: Lawrence Erlbaum Associates, 117–32.

Drew, P. and Holt, E. (1998) 'Figures of speech: figurative expressions and the management of topic transition in conversation', *Language in Society* 27: 495–522.

Drummond, K. and Hopper, R. (1993a) 'Some uses of *yeah*', *Research on Language and Social Interaction* 26: 203–312.

Drummond, K. and Hopper, R. (1993b) 'Backchannels revisited: acknowledgement tokens and speakership incipiency', *Research on Language and Social Interaction* 26: 157–177.

DuBois, S. (1993) 'Extension particles, etc.', *Language Variation and Change* 4: 179–203.

Du Bois, J. W., Schuetze-Coburn, S, Cumming, S. and Paolino, D. (1993) 'Outline of discourse transcription' in Edwards, J. and Lampert, M. (eds.) *Talking Data: Transcription and Coding Methods for Discourse Research.* Hillsdale, NJ: Lawrence Erlbaum Associates, 45–89.

Ducharme, D. and Bernard, R. (2001) 'Communication breakdowns: an exploration of contextualization in native and non-native speakers of French', *Journal of Pragmatics* 33 (6): 825–847.

Duncan, S. and Niederehe, G. (1974) 'On signalling that it's your turn to speak', *Journal of Experimental Social Psychology* 10 (3): 234–47.

Eastwood, J. (1994) *The Oxford Guide to English Grammar.* Oxford: Oxford University Press.

Edge, J. (1992) *Cooperative Development: Professional Self-Development Through Cooperation With Colleagues.* London: Longman.

Edge, J. (2002) *Continuing Cooperative Development: A Discourse Framework for Individuals as Colleagues.* Ann Arbor, MI: Michigan University Press.

Edmonson, W. and House, J. (1981) *Let's Talk and Talk About It.* München: Urban and Schwarzenberg.

Eggins, S. and Slade, D. (1997) *Analysing Casual Conversation.* London: Cassell.

Ellis, R. (1998) 'Teaching and research: options in grammar-teaching', *TESOL Quarterly* 32 (1): 39–60.

Erman, B. (1987) *Pragmatic Expressions in English: A Study of you know, you see, and I mean in Face-to-Face Conversation.* Stockholm: Almqvist and Wiksell.

Erman, B. (2001) 'Pragmatic markers revisited with a focus on *you know* in adult and adolescent talk', *Journal of Pragmatics* 33 (9): 1337–1359.

Evison, J., McCarthy, M. J. and O'Keeffe, A. (2007) '*Looking out for love and all the rest of it*: vague category markers as shared social space' in Cutting, J. (ed.) *Vague Language Explored.* Basingstoke: Palgrave, 138–157.

Fairclough, N. (1989) *Language and Power.* London: Longman.

Fairclough, N. (1992) *Discourse and Social Change.* Cambridge: Polity Press.

Fairclough, N. (1995) *Critical Discourse Analysis.* London: Longman.

Farr, F. (2002) 'Classroom interrogations – how productive?', *The Teacher Trainer* 16 (1): 19–23.

Farr, F. (2003) 'Engaged listenership in spoken academic discourse: the case of student-tutor meetings', *Journal of English for Academic Purposes* 2 (1): 67–85.

Farr, F. (2005) 'Relational strategies in the discourse of professional performance review in an Irish academic environment: the case of language teacher education' in Barron, A. and Schneider, K. P. (eds.) *The Pragmatics of Irish English.* Berlin: Mouton de Gruyter, 203–233.

Farr, F. and McCarthy M. J. (2002) 'Expressing hypothetical meaning in context: theory versus practice in spoken interaction.' Paper read at *The Teaching and Language Corpora (TALC) Annual Conference*, Bertinoro, Italy, July 27th–30th, 2002.

Farr, F., Murphy, B. and O'Keeffe, A. (2002) 'The Limerick Corpus of Irish English: design, description and application', *Teanga* 21: 5–29.

Fellegy, A.M. (1995) 'Patterns and functions of minimal response', *American Speech* 70: 186–199.

Fenk-Oczlon, G. (1989) Word order and word frequency in freezes. *Linguistics* 27: 517–56.

Fernando, C. (1996) *Idioms and Idiomaticity.* Oxford: Oxford University Press.

Fernando, C. and Flavell, R. (1981) *On Idiom: Critical Views and Perspectives.* Exeter: University of Exeter.

Fillmore, C. J. (1979) 'On fluency', in Fillmore, C. J., Kempler, D. and Wang, W. S. Y. (eds.) *Individual Differences in Language Ability and Language Behavior.* New York: Academic Press, 85–102.

Finell, A. (1989) '*Well now* and *then*', *Journal of Pragmatics* 13: 653–656.

Firth, A. (1990) 'Lingua franca negotiations: towards an interactional approach', *World Englishes* 9 (3): 269–280.

Firth, A. (ed.) (1995). *The Discourse of Negotiation: Studies of Language in the Workplace.* Oxford: Pergamon.

Firth, J. R. (1935) 'The technique of semantics', *Transactions of the Philological Society*: 36–72.

Firth, J. R. (1951/1957) *Papers in Linguistics.* Oxford: Oxford University Press, 190–215.

Fisher, S. and Groce, S. (1990) 'Accounting practices in medicine interviews', *Language in Society* 19: 225–250.

Fishman, P. M. (1978) 'Interaction: the work women do', *Social Problems* 25: 397–406.

Flowerdew J, (1993) 'Concordancing as a tool in course design', *System* 21 (2): 231–244.

Flowerdew, J. (1996) 'Concordancing in language learning' in Pennington, M. (ed.) *The Power of CALL.* Houston, TX: Athelstan, 97–113.

Flowerdew, J. (2003a) 'Register specificity of signalling nouns in discourse' in Meyer, C. and Leistyna, P. (eds.) *Corpus Analysis: Language Structure and Language Use.* Amsterdam: Rodopi, 35–46.

Flowerdew, J. (2003b) 'Signalling nouns in discourse', *English for Specific Purposes* 22 (4): 329–346.

Fonagy, I. (1982) *Situation et Signification*. Amsterdam: John Benjamins.

Fotos, S. and Ellis, R. (1991) 'Communicating about grammar: a task-based approach', *TESOL Quarterly* 25 (4): 605–628.

Fox, G. (1998) 'Using corpus data in the classroom' in Tomlinson, B. (ed.) *Materials Development in Language Teaching*. Cambridge: Cambridge University Press, 25–43.

Franken, N. (1997) 'Vagueness and approximation in relevance theory', *Journal of Pragmatics* 28: 135–151.

Francis, G. (1986) *Anaphoric Nouns*. [Discourse Analysis Monographs, 11.] Birmingham: English Language Research, University of Birmingham.

Fraser, B. (1975) 'Hedged performatives' in Cole, P. and Morgan, J. L. (eds.) *Syntax and Semantics (vol 3)*. New York: Academic Press, 187–210.

Fraser, B. (1980) 'Conversational mitigation', *Journal of Pragmatics* 4: 341–350.

Fraser, B. (1988) 'Types of English discourse markers', *Acta Linguistica Hungarica* 38 (1–4): 19–33.

Fraser, B. (1990) 'An approach to discourse markers', *Journal of Pragmatics* 14: 383–395.

Fraser, B. (1998) 'Contrastive discourse markers in English' in Jucker, A. H. and Ziv, Y. (eds.) *Discourse Markers: Descriptions and Theory*. Amsterdam: John Benjamins, 301–326.

Fraser, B. (1999) 'What are discourse markers?', *Journal of Pragmatics* 31: 931–952.

Fraser, B. and Nolen, W. (1981) 'The association of deference with linguistic form', *International Journal of Sociology of Language* 27: 93–109.

Freddi, M. (2005) 'Arguing linguistics: corpus investigation of one functional variety of academic discourse', *Journal of English for Academic Purposes* 4 (1): 5–26.

Fries, C.C. (1952) *The Structure of English*. New York: Harcourt, Brace.

Fukushima, S. and Iwata, Y. (1987) 'Politeness strategies in requesting and offering', *Japanese Association of College English Teachers Bulletin* 18: 31–48.

Garcez, P. (1993) 'Point-making styles in cross-cultural business negotiation: a microethnographic study', *English for Specific Purposes* 12: 103–120.

Gardner, R. (1987) 'The identification and role of topic in spoken interaction', *Semiotica* 65 (1/2): 129–41.

Gardner, R. (1997) 'The listener and minimal responses in conversational interaction', *Prospect* 12: 12–32.

Gardner, R. (1998) 'Between speaking and listening: the vocalization of understandings', *Applied Linguistics* 19: 204–224.

Gardner, R. (2002) *When Listeners Talk: Response Tokens and Listener Stance*. Amsterdam: John Benjamins.

Gavioli, L. (1996) 'Corpus di testi e concordanze: un nuovo strumento nella didattica delle lingue straniere [Text corpora and concordances: A new tool for foreign language teaching]', *Rassegna Italiana di Linguistica Applicata* 2: 121–146.

Gavioli, L. (2002) 'Some thoughts on the problem of representing ESP through small corpora' in Kettemann, B. and Marko, G. (eds.) *Teaching and Learning by Doing Corpus Analysis*. Amsterdam: Rodopi, 293–303.

Gellerstam, M. (1996) 'Translations as a source for cross-linguistic studies' in Aijmer, K., Altenberg, B. and Johansson, M. (eds.) *Languages in Contrast*, Lund: Lund University Press, 53–62.

Geluykens, R. (1988) 'Five types of clefting in English discourse', *Linguistics* 26: 823–841.

Gibbon, D. (1981) 'Idiomaticity and functional variation: a case study of international amateur radio talk', *Language in Society* 10 (1): 21–42.

Gibbons, J. (1994) *Language and the Law*. London: Longman.

Gibbons, J. (2003) *Forensic Linguistics*. Oxford: Blackwell.

Gibbs, R. W. (1986) 'Skating on thin ice: literal meaning and understanding idioms in conversation', *Discourse Processes* 9 (1): 17–30.

Gibbs, R. W. (1994) *The Poetics of Mind: Figurative Thought, Language, and Understanding*. New York: Cambridge University Press.

Gibbs, R. W. and O'Brien, J. E. (1990) 'Idioms and mental imagery: The metaphorical motivation for idiomatic meaning', *Cognition* 36: 35–68.

Gibbs, R.(1979) 'Contextual effects in understanding indirect requests', *Discourse Processes* 2: 1–10.

Gilmore, A. (2004) 'A comparison of textbook and authentic interactions', *ELT Journal* 58 (4): 363–374.

Gilquin, G. (2003) 'Causative "get" and "have". So close, so different', *Journal of English Linguistics* 31 (2): 125–148.

Gimenez, J. (2001) 'Ethnographic observations in cross-cultural business negotiations between non-native speakers of English: An exploratory study', *English for Specific Purposes* 20: 169–193.

Girard, M. and Sionis, C. (2004) 'The functions of formulaic speech in the L2 class', *Pragmatics* 14 (1): 31–53.

Gledhill, C. (2000a) 'The discourse function of collocation in research article introductions', *English for Specific Purposes* 19: 115–135.

Gledhill, C. (2000b) *Collocations in Science Writing*. Tübingen: Gunter Narr.

Gnutzmann, C. (1991) 'Linguistic and pedagogic aspects of English passive constructions', *Teanga* 11: 48–65.

Goffman, E. (1959) *The Presentation of Self in Everyday Life*. London: Penguin.

Goffman, E. (1971) 'Remedial interchanges' in Goffman, E. (ed.) *Relations in Public: Micro-Studies of the Public Order*. New York: Harper & Row, 95–187.

Graddol, D. (1998) *The Future of English?* London: The British Council

Granger, S. (1983) *The Be + Past Participle Construction in Spoken English*. Amsterdam: North Holland.

Granger, S. (1993) 'The International Corpus of Learner English' in Aarts, J. de Haan, P. and Oostdijk, N. (eds.) *English Language Corpora: Design, Analysis and Exploitation*. Amsterdam: Rodopi, 57–69.

Granger, S. (1994) 'The learner corpus: a revolution in applied linguistics', *English Today* 39: 25–29.

Granger, S. (1996) 'Learner English around the world' in Greenbaum, S. (ed.) *Comparing English World-wide*. Oxford: Clarendon Press, 13–24.

Granger, S. (1997) 'The computer learner corpus: a testbed for electronic EFL tools' in Nerbonne, J. (ed.) *Linguistic Databases*. Stanford: CSLI Publications, 175–188.

Granger, S. (1998a) 'The computerized learner corpus: a versatile new source of data for SLA research' in Granger, S. (ed.) *Learner English on Computer*. London: Longman, 3–18.

Granger, S. (ed.) (1998b) *Learner English on Computer*. London: Longman

Granger, S. (1998c) 'Prefabricated writing patterns in advanced EFL writing: collocations and formulae' in Cowie, A. P. (ed.) *Phraseology: Theory, Analysis and Applications*. Oxford: Clarendon Press, 145–160.

Granger, S. (1999) 'Use of tenses by advanced EFL learners: evidence from an error-tagged computer corpus' in Hasselgård, H. and Oksefjell, S. (eds.) *Out of Corpora – Studies in Honour of Stig Johansson*. Amsterdam: Rodopi, 191–202.

Granger, S. (2002) 'A bird's-eye view of computer learner corpus research' in Granger, S., Hung, J. and Petch-Tyson, S. (eds.) *Computer Learner Corpora, Second Language Acquisition and Foreign Language Teaching*. Amsterdam: John Benjamins, 3–33.

Granger S. (2003) 'The International Corpus of Learner English: a new resource for foreign language learning and teaching and second language acquisition research', *TESOL Quarterly* 37 (3): 538–546.

Granger S. (2004) 'Computer learner corpus research: current status and future prospects' in Connor, U. and Upton, T. (eds.) *Applied Corpus Linguistics: A Multidimensional Perspective*. Amsterdam: Rodopi, 123–145.

Granger, S., Hung, J., and Petch-Tyson, S. (eds.) (2002) *Computer Learner Corpora, Second Language Acquisition and Foreign Language Teaching*. Amsterdam: John Benjamins.

Granger S. and Petch-Tyson, S. (eds.) (2003) *Extending the Scope of Corpus-based Research: New Applications, New Challenges*. Amsterdam: Rodopi.

Greatbatch, D. (1988) 'A turn-taking system for British news interviews', *Language in Society* 17: 401–430.

Greenbaum, S. and Nelson, G. (1999) 'Elliptical clauses in spoken and written English' in Collins, P. and Lee, D. (eds.) *The Clause in English: in Honour of Rodney Huddleston*. Amsterdam: John Benjamins, 111–126.

Grice, H. P. (1975) 'Logic and conversation' in Cole, P., & Morgan, J. (eds.), *Syntax and semantics, volume 9: Pragmatics*. New York: Academic Press, 41–58.

Grimshaw, A. (1989) *Collegial Discourse: Professional Conversation among Peers*. Norwood NJ: Ablex.

Haastrup, K. and Henriksen, B. (2000). 'Vocabulary acquisition: Acquiring depth of knowledge through network building', *International Journal of Applied Linguistics* 10 (2): 221–240.

Hakuta, K. (1974) 'Prefabricated patterns and the emergence of structure in second language acquisition', *Language Learning* 24: 287–298.

Hall J. K. and Verplaetse, L.S. (eds) (2000) *Second and Foreign Language Learning Through Classroom Interaction*. Mahwah, NJ: Lawrence Erlbaum.

Hall, J. K. and Walsh, M. (2002) 'Teacher student interaction and language learning', *Annual Review of Applied Linguistics* 22: 186–203.

Halliday, M.A.K. (1961) 'Categories of the theory of grammar', *Word* 17: 241–92.

Halliday, M. A. K. (1966) 'Lexis as a linguistic level' in Bazell, C., Catford, J., Halliday, M. A. K. and Robins, R. (eds.) *In Memory of J. R. Firth*. London: Longman, 148–162.

Halliday, M.A.K. (1991) 'Corpus studies and probabilistic grammar' in Aijmer, K. and Altenberg, B. (eds.) *English Corpus Linguistics*. London: Longman, 30–43.

Halliday, M. A. K. and Hasan, R. (1976) *Cohesion in English*. London: Longman.

Halmari, H. (1993) 'Intercultural business telephone conversations: a case of Finns vs. Anglo-Americans', *Applied Linguistics* 44 (4): 408–430.

Harwood, N. (2005) 'We do not seem to have a theory … the theory I present here attempts to fill this gap: inclusive and exclusive pronouns in academic writing', *Applied Linguistics* 26 (3): 343–375.

Haslerud, V. and Stenström, A-B. (1995) 'The Bergen Corpus of London Teenager Language (COLT)' in Leech, G., Myers, G. and Thomas, J. (eds.) *Spoken English on Computer*. London: Longman, 235–242.

Hasund, K. (1998) 'From woman's place to women's places: class-determined variation in the verbal disputes of London teenage girls' in Despard, A. (ed.) *A Woman's Place: Women, Domesticity and Private Life*. Kristiansand: Norwegian Academic Press, 187–199.

Hasund, K. and Stenström, A-B. (1997) 'Conflict talk: a comparison of the verbal disputes of adolescent females in two corpora' in Ljung, M. (ed.) *Corpus-based Studies in English*. Amsterdam: Rodopi, 119–133.

Hatch, E. (1992) *Discourse and Language Education*. New York: Cambridge University Press.

Hatcher, A. G. (1949) 'To get/be invited', *Modern Language Notes* 64: 433–46.

Heffer, C. (2005) *The Language of Jury Trial : A Corpus-Aided Analysis of Legal-Lay Discourse*. Basingstoke: Palgrave

Henriksen, B. (1999) 'Three dimensions of vocabulary development', *Studies in Second Language Acquisition* 21: 303–317.

Heritage, J. and Greatbatch, D. (1991) 'On the character of institutional talk: the case of news interviews' in Boden, D. and Zimmerman, D. (eds.) *Talk and Social Structure*. Cambridge: Polity Press, 359–417.

Heritage, J. and Watson, D. (1979) 'Formulations as conversational objects' in Psathas, G. (ed.) *Everyday Language*. New York: Irvington Press, 123–62.

Hever, B. (1997) Tests for estimating vocabulary size. Göteborgs Univärsitet. Available at: http://www.wordsandtools.com/flat_structure.htm.

Hewings, A and Hewings, M. (eds.) (2005) *Grammar and Context: An Advanced Resource Book* London: Routledge.

Hoey, M. P. (1983) *On the Surface of Discourse*. London: Allen and Unwin.

Hoey, M. P. (1991) *Patterns of Lexis in Text*. Oxford: Oxford University Press.

Hoey, M. P. (2005) *Lexical Priming: A New Theory of Words and Language*. London: Routledge.

Holmes, J. (1988) 'Doubt and certainty in ESL textbooks', *Applied Linguistics* 9 (1): 21–44.

Holmes, J. (2000) 'Doing collegiality and keeping control at work: small talk in government departments' in Coupland, J. (ed.) *Small Talk*. London: Longman, 32–61.

Holmes, J. (2001) 'Ladies and gentlemen: corpus analysis and linguistic sexism' in: Mair, C. and Hundt, M. (eds.). *Corpus Linguistics and Linguistic Theory*. Amsterdam: Rodopi, 141–156.

Honeyfield, J. (1977) 'Word frequency and the importance of context in vocabulary learning', *RELC Journal* 8 (2): 35–42.

Hopper, P. (1987) 'Emergent grammar', *Berkeley Linguistics Society* 13: 139–157.

Hopper, P. (1998) 'Emergent grammar' in Tomasello, M. (ed.) *The New Psychology of Language*. Hillsdale NJ: Lawrence Erlbaum Associates, 155–175.

Hopper, R., Knapp, M. L. and Scott, L. (1981) 'Couples' personal idioms: exploring intimate talk', *Journal of Communication* 31 (1): 23–33.

Horn, G. M. (2003) 'Idioms, metaphors and syntactic mobility', *Journal of Linguistics* 39: 245–273.

House, J. (1999) 'Misunderstanding in intercultural communication. Interactions in English as lingua franca and the myth of mutual intelligibility' in Gnutzmann, C. (ed.) *Teaching and Learning English as a Global Language*. Tübingen: Stauffenburg, 72–88.

House, J. (2002) 'Communicating in English as a lingua franca', *EUROSLA Yearbook* 2: 243–261.

House, J. (2003) 'English as a lingua franca: a threat to multilingualism?', *Journal of Sociolinguistics* 7 (4): 556–578.

Howarth, P. (1998) 'Phraseology and second language proficiency', *Applied Linguistics* 19 (1): 24–44.

Hu, M. and Nation, P. (2000) 'Unknown vocabulary density and reading comprehension', *Reading in a Foreign Language* 13 (1): 403–430.

Hübler, A. (1983) *Understatement and Hedges in English.* Amsterdam: John Benjamins.

Hughes, R., and McCarthy, M. J. (1998) 'From sentence to discourse: discourse grammar and English language teaching', *TESOL Quarterly* 32: 263–287.

Hulstijn, J. and Marchena, E. (1989) 'Avoidance: grammatical or semantic causes?', *Studies in Second Language Acquisition* 11: 241–255.

Hunston, S. (1995) 'Grammar in teacher education: The role of a corpus', *Language Awareness* 4 (1): 15–31.

Hunston S. (2002) *Corpora in Applied Linguistics.* Cambridge: Cambridge University Press

Hunston, S. and Francis, G. (2000) *Pattern Grammar A Corpus-Driven Approach to the Lexical Grammar of English.* Amsterdam: John Benjamins.

Hunston, S., Francis, G. and Manning, E. (1997) 'Grammar and vocabulary: showing the connections', *ELT Journal* 51(3): 208–216.

Hutchby, I. and Wooffitt, R. (1998) *Conversation Analysis – Principles, Practices and Applications.* Cambridge: Polity Press

Hyland, K. (1994) 'Hedging in academic writing and EAP coursebooks', *English for Specific Purposes* 13 (3): 239–256.

Hyland, K. (1996a) 'Nurturing hedges in the ESP curriculum', *System* 24: 477–490.

Hyland, K. (1996b) 'Writing without conviction? Hedging in science research articles', *Applied Linguistics* 17 (4): 433–454.

Hyland, K. (1999) 'Talking to students: metadiscourse in introductory coursebooks', *English for Specific Purposes* 18 (1): 3–26.

Hyland, K. and Tse, P. (2005) 'Hooking the reader: a corpus study of evaluative *that* in abstracts', *English for Specific Purposes* 24 (2): 123–139.

Kanoksilapatham, B. (2005) 'Rhetorical structure of biochemistry research articles', *English for Specific Purposes* 24 (3): 269–292.

Iacobucci, C. (1990) 'Accounts, formulations and goal attainment strategies in service encounters' in Tracy, K. and Coupland, N. (eds.), *Multiple Goals in Discourse.* Clevedon: Multilingual Matters Ltd, 85–99.

Ihalainen, O. (1991a) 'A point of verb syntax in south-western British English: an analysis of a dialect continuum', in Aijmer, K. and Altenberg, B. (eds.) *English Corpus Linguistics.* London: Longman, 290–302.

Ihalainen, O. (1991b) 'The grammatical subject in educated and dialectal English: comparing the London-Lund Corpus and the Helsinki Corpus of modern English dialects' in Johansson, S. and Stenström, A.-B. (eds.) *English Computer Corpora: Selected Papers and Research Guide.* Berlin: Mouton de Gruyter, 201–214.

Irujo, S. (1986) 'A piece of cake: learning and teaching idioms', *ELT Journal* 40 (3): 236–242.

Itkonen, E. (1980) 'Qualitative vs quantitative analysis in linguistics' in Perry, T. (ed.) *Evidence and Argumentation in Linguistics.* Berlin: Mouton de Gruyter, 334–66.

James, A. (2000) 'English as a European lingua franca. Current realities and existing dichotomies' in Cenoz, J. and Jessner, U. (eds.) *English in Europe. The Acquisition of a Third Language.* Clevedon, UK: Multilingual Matters, 22–38.

Jefferson, G. (1973) 'A case of precision timing in ordinary conversation: Overlapping tag-positioned address terms in closing sequences', *Semiotica* 9: 47–96.

Jefferson, G. (1990) 'List construction as a task and resource' in Psathas, G. (ed.) *Interaction Competence.* Lanham, MD: University Press of America, 63–92.

Jenkins, J. (1996) 'Native speaker, non-native speaker and English as a Foreign Language: time for a change', *IATEFL Newsletter* 131: 10–11.

Jenkins, J. (2000) *The Phonology of English as an International Language.* Oxford: Oxford University Press.

Jenkins, J. (2004) 'Global intelligibility and local diversity: possibility or paradox?' in Rubdi, R. and Saraceni, M. (eds.) *English in the World: Global Rules, Global Roles.* Bangkok: IELE Press at Assumption University.

Jenkins, J. (2005) 'Teaching pronunciation for English as a Lingua Franca: a socio-political perspective' in Gnutzmann, C. and Intemann, F. (eds.) *The Globalisation of English and The English Language Classroom.* Tübingen: Gunter Narr, 145–158.

Jespersen, J. O. (1909) *A Modern English Grammar on Historical Principles.* Vol II. Heidelberg: C Winter.

Johansson, S. and Ebeling, J. (1996) 'Exploring the English-Norwegian parallel corpus' in Percy, C., Meyer, C.F. and Lancashire, I. (eds.) *Synchronic Corpus Linguistics,* Amsterdam: Rodopi, 3–15.

Johansson, S. and Hofland, K. (1994) 'Towards an English-Norwegian parallel corpus' in Fries, U., Tottie, G. and Schneider, P. (eds.) *Creating and Using English Language Corpora.* Amsterdam: Rodopi, 25–37.

Johansson, S., Ebeling, J., and Hofland, K. (1996) 'Coding and aligning the English-Norwegian parallel corpus' in Aijmer, K., Altenberg, B. and Johansson, M. (eds.) *Languages in Contrast Papers from a Symposium on Text-based Cross-Linguistic Studies,* Lund 4–5 March 1994. Lund: Lund University Press, 87–112.

Johns T. (1986) 'Micro-concord, a language learner's research tool', *System* 14 (2): 151–162.

Johns T. (1988) 'Whence and whither classroom concordancing?' in Bongaerts, T., De Haan, P., Lobbe, S. and Wekker, H. (eds.) *Computer Applications in Language Teaching.* Dordrecht: Foris, 9–27.

Johns T. (1991a) 'From print out to handout: Grammar and Vocabulary teaching in the context of data-driven learning', *CALL Austria* 10: 14–34.

Johns, T. (1991b) 'Should you be persuaded: Two samples of data-driven learning materials', *English Language Research Journal* 4: 1–16.

Johns, T. (2002) 'Data-driven learning: the perpetual challenge' in Kettemann, B. and Marko, G. (eds.) *Teaching and Learning by Doing Corpus Linguistics.* Amsterdam: Rodopi, 107–117.

Johns, T. and King, P. (eds.) (1991) 'Classroom concordancing', *English Language Research Journal* 4. University of Birmingham: Centre for English Language Studies.

Johnson, K. (1995) *Understanding Communication in Second Language Classrooms.* New York: Cambridge University Press.

Johnstone, R. (1989) *Communicative Interaction: a Guide for Teachers.* London: Centre for Information on Language Teaching.

Jones, L. B. and Jones, L. K. (1985) 'Discourse functions of five English sentence types', *Word* 36 (1): 1–21.

Jucker, A. H., Smith, S. W. and Lüdge, T. (2003) 'Interactive aspects of vagueness in conversation', *Journal of Pragmatics* 35: 1737–1769.

Jucker, A., (1993) 'The discourse marker *well*: a relevance-theoretical account', *Journal of Pragmatics* 19: 435–452.

Kagan, S. (1994) *Cooperative Learning.* San Juan Capistrano, CA: Kagan Cooperative Learning.

Kallen, J. L., and Kirk, J. M. (2001) 'Convergence and divergence in the verb phrase in Irish standard English: a corpus-based approach' in Kirk, J. M. and Ó Baoill, D. P. (eds.), *Language Links: The Languages of Scotland and Ireland*. Belfast: Cló Ollscoil na Banríona, 59–79.

Kanoksilapatham, B. (2005) 'Rhetorical structure of biochemistry research articles', *English for Specific Purposes* 24 (3): 269–292.

Kasper, G. (1992) 'Pragmatic transfer', *Second Language Research* 8 (3): 203–231.

Kasper, G. (2001) 'Four perspectives on L2 pragmatic development', *Applied Linguistics*, 22 (4): 502–530.

Kasper, G. (2004) 'Participant orientations in German conversation-for-learning', *Modern Language Journal*, 88 (4): 551–567.

Kellerman. E. (1986) 'An eye for an eye: crosslinguistic constraints on the development of the L2 lexicon' in Kellerman, E. and Sharwood Smith, M. (eds.) *Crosslinguistic Influence in Second Language Acquisition*. Oxford: Pergamon Press, 35–48.

Kendon, A. (1967) 'Some functions of gaze-direction in social interaction', *Acta Psychologica* 20: 22–63.

Kennedy, C. and Miceli, T. (2001) 'An evaluation of intermediate students' approaches to corpus investigation', *Language Learning and Technology* 5 (3): 77–90. Available (April 2003) at: http://llt.msu.edu/vol5num3/kennedy/default.html.

Kennedy, C. and Miceli, T. '(2002) The CWIC Project: developing and using a corpus for intermediate Italian Students' in Kettemann, B. and Marko, G. (eds.) *Teaching and Learning by Doing Corpus Linguistics*. Amsterdam: Rodopi, 183–202.

Kennedy, G. (1998) *An Introduction to Corpus Linguistics*. London: Longman

Kenny, D. (1997) 'Creatures of habit? What collocation can tell us about translation.' Paper presented at *ACH-ALLC '97* Queen's University, Kingston, Ontario, Canada, June 3–7, 1997. Available at http://www.ach.org/abstracts/1997/a006.html.

Kettemann, B. (1995) 'Concordancing in English language teaching', *TELL and CALL* 4: 4–15.

Kim, K. (1995) '*Wh*-clefts and left dislocation in English conversation: cases of topicalization' in Downing, P. and Noonan, M. (eds.) *Word Order in Discourse*. Amsterdam: John Benjamins, 247–296.

King, P. (1997) 'Parallel corpora for translator training' in Lewandowska-Tomaszczyk, B. and Melia, P. J. (eds.): *Practical Applications in Language and Computers (PALC '97)*. Łodz: Łodz University Press, 393–402.

Kirk, J. M. (1992) 'The Northern Ireland transcribed corpus of speech' in Leitner, G. (ed.) *New Directions in English Language Corpora*. Berlin: Mouton de Gruyter, 65–73.

Kirk, J. M. (1999) 'The dialect vocabulary of Ulster', *Cuadernos de Filología Inglesa* 8: 305–334.

Knowles, G. (1990) 'The use of spoken and written corpora in the teaching of language and linguistics', *Literary and Linguistic Computing* 5: 45–48.

Knowles, G. and Taylor, L. (1988) *Manual of information to accompany the Lancaster Spoken English Corpus*. Lancaster: Unit for Computer Research on the English Language, University of Lancaster.

Ko, J., Schallert, D. L. and Walters, K. (2003) 'Rethinking scaffolding: examining negotiation of meaning in an ESL storytelling task', *TESOL Quarterly* 37: 303–324.

Koester, A. (2004) *The Language of Work*. London: Routledge.

Koester, A. (2006) *Investigating Workplace Discourse*. London: Routledge.

Komter, M. (1991). *Conflict and Cooperation in Job Interviews: A Study of Talk, Tasks and Ideas*. Amsterdam: John Benjamins.

Kövecses, Z. and Szabo, P. (1996) 'Idioms: a view from cognitive semantics', *Applied Linguistics* 17 (3): 326–254.

Kramsch, C. and Sullivan, P. (1996) 'Appropriate pedagogy', *ELT Journal* 50 (3): 199–212.

Krashen, S. D. (1989) 'We acquire vocabulary and spelling by reading: additional evidence for the input hypothesis', *Modern Language Journal* 73: 440–464.

Krauss, R., Fussell, S. and Chen, Y. (1995) 'Coordination of perspective in dialogue: intrapersonal and interpersonal processes' in Marková, I., Grauman, C. and Foppa, K. (eds) *Mutualities in Dialogue*. Cambridge: Cambridge University Press, 124–145.

Kucera, H. and Francis, W.N. (1967) *Computational Analysis of Present-Day American English.* Providence R.I.: Brown University Press.

Kuiper, K. and Flindall, M. (2000) 'Social rituals, formulaic speech and small talk at the supermarket checkout' in Coupland, J. (ed.) *Small Talk*, London: Longman, 183–207.

Kunin, A. (1970) *Anglijskasa Frazeologija.* Moscow: Izdat'elstvo Vysšajaškola.

Labov, W. (1972a) *Language in the Inner City.* Oxford: Basil Blackwell.

Labov, W. (1972b) 'Some principles of linguistic methodology', *Language in Society* 1: 97–120.

Lakoff, G. (1972) 'Hedges: a study in meaning criteria and the logic of fuzzy concepts', *Papers from the Eight Regional Meeting Chicago Linguistic Society*, 183–228.

Lakoff, R. (1971) 'Passive resistance', *Papers from the Seventh Regional Meeting. Chicago Linguistic Society* 149–62.

Lantolf, J. P. (2000) *Sociocultural Theory and Second Language Learning*, Oxford: Oxford University Press.

Lantolf, J. P. and Appel, G. (1994a) 'Theoretical framework: an introduction to Vygotskyan perspectives on second language research' in Lantolf, J. P. and Appel, G. (eds.) *Vygotskyan Approaches to Second Language Research*, Norwood, NJ: Ablex.

Lantolf, J. P. and Appel, G. (eds.) (1994b) *Vygotskian Approaches to Second Language Research.* Norwood, NJ: Ablex.

Lantolf, J. and Thorne, S. (2006) *Sociocultural Theory and the Genesis of Second Language Development.* Oxford: Oxford University Press.

Lapidus, N. and Otheguy, R. (2005) 'Contact Induced Change? Overt Nonspecific *Ellos* in Spanish in New York' in Sayahi, L. and Westmoreland, M. (eds.) *Selected Proceedings of the Second Workshop on Spanish Sociolinguistics.* Somerville, MA: Cascadilla Proceedings Project, 67–75. Available at http://www.lingref.com/cpp/wss/2/paper1141.pdf.

Larrue, J. and Trognon, B. (1993) 'Organisation of turn-taking and mechanism for turn-taking repairs in a chaired meeting', *Journal of Pragmatics* 19 (2): 177–196.

Lattey, E. (1986) 'Pragmatic classification of idioms as an aid for the language learner', *International Review of Applied Linguistics*, XXIV (3): 217–33.

Lave, J. and Wenger, E. (1991) *Situated Learning. Legitimate Peripheral Participation.* Cambridge: University of Cambridge Press

Laver, J. (1975) 'Communicative functions of phatic communion', In Kendon, A., Harris, R. and Key, M. (eds.) *The Organization of Behaviour in Face-to-face Interaction.* The Hague: Mouton, 215–38.

Laviosa, S. (1998) 'Core patterns of lexical use in a comparable corpus of English narrative prose', *Meta*, 43 (4): 557–570.

Lazar, G. (1996) 'Using figurative language to expand students' vocabulary', *ELT Journal* 50 (1): 43–51.

Lazaraton, A. (2002) *A Qualitative Approach to the Validation of Oral Language Tests.* Cambridge: Cambridge University Press.

Lee, W. Y. (1995) 'Authenticity revisited: text authenticity and learner authenticity', *ELT Journal* 49 (4): 323–328.

Leech, G. (1974) *Semantics.* Harmondsworth: Penguin

Leech, G. (1991) 'The state of the art in corpus linguistics' in Aijmer, K. and Altenberg, B. (eds.) *English Corpus Linguistics*. London: Longman, 8–29.

Leech, G. (2000) 'Grammars of spoken English: new outcomes of corpus-oriented research', *Language Learning* 50 (4): 675–724.

Leech, G. N. and Short, M. H. (1981) *Style in Fiction: A Linguistic Introduction to English Fictional Prose*. London: Longman.

Lenk, U. (1998) *Marking Discourse Coherence: Functions of Discourse Markers*. Tübingen: Gunter Narr Verlag

Lenko-Szymanska, A. (2002) 'How to trace the growth in learners' active vocabulary: a corpus-based study' in Kettemann, B. and Marko, G. (eds.) *Teaching and Learning by Doing Corpus Analysis*. Amsterdam: Rodopi, 217–230.

Lennon, P. (1990) 'The bases for vocabulary teaching at the advanced level', *ITL. Review of Applied Linguistics* 87–88: 1–22.

Lewis, M. (1993) *The Lexical Approach: The State of ELT and a Way Forward*. Hove UK: LTP.

Lewis, M. (2000) *Teaching Collocation*. Hove, UK: LTP.

Liu, D. (1998) 'Ethnocentrism in TESOL: Teacher education and the neglected needs of international TESOL students', *ELT Journal* 52 (1): 3–10.

Long, M.H. and Sato, C. (1983) 'Classroom foreigner talk discourse: forms and functions of teachers' questions' in Seliger, H.W. and Long, M.H. (eds.) *Classroom Oriented Research in Second Language Acquisition*. Rowley MA: Newbury House, 268–286.

Louw, B. (1993) 'Irony in the text or insincerity in the writer? the diagnostic potential of semantic prosodies' in Baker, M. and Tognini-Bonelli, E. (eds.) *Text and Technology: in Honour of John Sinclair*. Amsterdam: John Benjamins, 157–176.

Luzón Marco, M. J. (2000) 'Collocational frameworks in medical research papers: A genre-based study', *English for Specific Purposes* 19: 63–68.

Macaulay, R. K. S. (1991) *Locating Dialect in Discourse: The Language of Honest Men and Bonnie Lasses in Ayr*. New York: Oxford University Press.

Macaulay, R. K. S. (2002) 'You know, it depends', *Journal of Pragmatics* 34: 749–767.

Machado, A. (2000) A Vygotskian approach to evaluation in foreign language learning contexts. *ELT Journal* 54: 335–345.

Maia, B. (1997) 'Do-it-yourself corpora . . .with a little help from your friends' in Lewandowska-Tomaszczyk, B. and Melia, P. J. (eds.) *Practical Applications in Language Corpora (PALC '97)*. Łodz: Łodz University Press, 403–410.

Makkai, A. (1978) 'Idiomaticity as a language universal' in Greenberg, J. (ed.) *Universals of Human Language, Volume 3: Word Structure*. Stanford California: Stanford University Press, 401–448.

Malinowski, B. (1923) 'The problem of meaning in primitive languages' in Ogden, C. K. and Richards, I. A. (eds.) *The Meaning of Meaning*. London: Routledge, 142–152

Malmkjaer, K. (1991) *The Linguistics Encyclopaedia*. London: Routledge.

Marinai, E., Peters, C. and Picchi, E. (1992) 'Bilingual reference corpora: creation, querying, applications', in Kiefer, F., Kiss, G. and Pajzs, J. (eds.) *Papers in Computational Lexicography Complex '92*. Budapest: Linguistics Institute, Hungarian Academy of Sciences, 221–229.

Markee, N. P. (2000) *Conversation Analysis*. Mahwah, NJ: Lawrence Erlbaum.

Markee, N. P. (2004) 'Zones of interactional transition in ESL classes', *Modern Language Journal* 88 (4): 583–596.

Markkanen, R. and Schröder, H. (1997) 'Hedging: a challenge for pragmatics and discourse analysis' in Markkanen, R. and Schröder, H. (eds.) *Hedging and Discourse: Approaches to the Analysis of a Pragmatic Phenomenon in Academic Texts*. Berlin: Walter de Gruyter, 3–18.

Márquez Reiter, R. (2000) *Linguistic Politeness in Britain and Uruguay*. Amsterdam: John Benjamins.

Martin, J. (1985) *Reclaiming a Conversation: the Ideal of the Educated Woman*. New Haven, CT: Yale University Press.

Massam, D. (1999) '*Thing is* constructions: the thing is, is what's the right analysis?', *English Language and Linguistics* 3 (2): 335–352.

Mauranen A. (2003) 'The corpus of English as lingua franca in academic settings', *TESOL Quarterly* 37 (3): 513–527.

Maynard, S. K. (1989) *Japanese Conversation: Self-Conextualization through Structure and Interactional Management. Advances in Discourse Processes*, vol. 35. Norwood, NJ: Ablex.

Maynard, S. K. (1990) 'Conversation management in contrast: listener response in Japanese and American English', *Journal of Pragmatics* 14: 397–412.

Maynard, S. K. (1997) 'Analysing interactional management in native/non-native English conversation: a case of listener response', *IRAL* 35: 37–60.

McCarthy, M. J. (1991) *Discourse Analysis for Language Teachers*. Cambridge: Cambridge University Press.

McCarthy, M. J. (1992) 'English idioms in use', *Revista Canaria de Estudios Ingleses* 25: 55–65.

McCarthy, M. J. (1998) *Spoken Language and Applied Linguistics*. Cambridge: Cambridge University Press.

McCarthy, M. J. (2000) 'Captive audiences: the discourse of close contact service encounters' in Coupland, J. (ed.) *Small Talk*. London: Longman, 84–109.

McCarthy, M. J. (2001) *Issues in Applied Linguistics*. Cambridge: Cambridge University Press.

McCarthy, M. J. (2002) 'Good listenership made plain: British and American non-minimal response tokens in everyday conversation' in Reppen, R., Fitzmaurice, S. and Biber, D. (eds.) *Using Corpora to Explore Linguistic Variation*. Amsterdam: John Benjamins, 49–71.

McCarthy, M. J. (2003) 'Talking back: "small" interactional response tokens in everyday conversation' in Coupland, J. (ed) Special issue of *Research on Language and Social Interaction* on 'Small Talk'. 36 (1): 33–63.

McCarthy, M. J., and Carter, R. A. (1994) *Language as Discourse: Perspectives for Language Teaching*. London: Longman.

McCarthy, M. J. and Carter, R. A. (1995) 'Spoken Grammar: what is it and how do we teach it?', *ELT Journal* 49 (3): 207–218.

McCarthy, M. J. and Carter, R. A. (1997) 'Grammar, tails and affect: constructing expressive choices in discourse', *Text* 17 (3): 405–429.

McCarthy, M. J. and Carter, R. A. (2000) 'Feeding back: non-minimal response tokens in everyday conversation' in Heffer, C. and Stauntson, H. (eds.) *Words in Context: A Tribute to John Sinclair on his Retirement*. Birmingham: University of Birmingham.

McCarthy, M. J. and Carter, R. A. (2002) '*This that and the other*: Multi-word clusters in spoken English as visible patterns of interaction', *Teanga* 21: 30–52.

McCarthy M. J. and Carter, R. A. (2004a) 'Introduction. Special issue on corpus linguistics', *Journal of Pragmatics* 36: 147–148.

McCarthy, M. J. and Carter, R. A. (2004b) '"There's millions of them": Hyperbole in everyday conversation', *Journal of Pragmatics* 36: 149–184.

McCarthy, M. J. and Handford, M. (2004) '"Invisible to us": A preliminary corpus-based study of spoken business English' in Connor, U. and Upton, T. (eds.) *Discourse in the Professions. Perspectives from Corpus Linguistics.* Amsterdam: John Benjamins, 167–201.

McCarthy, M. J. and O'Dell, F. (1997) *Vocabulary in Use: upper-intermediate.* Cambridge: Cambridge University Press.

McCarthy, M. J. and O'Dell, F. (1999) *English Vocabulary in Use. Elementary.* Cambridge: Cambridge University Press.

McCarthy, M. J. and O'Dell, F. (2001) *Basic Vocabulary in Use.* New York: Cambridge University Press.

McCarthy, M. J. and O'Dell, F. (2002) *English Idioms in Use.* Cambridge: Cambridge University Press.

McCarthy, M. J. and O'Dell, F. (2004) *English Phrasal Verbs in Use.* Intermediate Level. Cambridge: Cambridge University Press.

McCarthy, M. J. and O'Dell, F. (2005) *English Collocations in Use.* Cambridge: Cambridge University Press.

McCarthy, M. J. and O'Dell, F. (in press) *Academic English in Use.* Cambridge: Cambridge University Press.

McCarthy, M. J. and O'Keeffe, A. (2004) 'Research in the teaching of speaking', *Annual Review of Applied Linguistics* 24: 26–43.

McCarthy, M. J., McCarten, J. and Sandiford, H. (2005a) *Touchstone. Student's Book 1.* Cambridge: Cambridge University Press.

McCarthy, M. J., McCarten, J. and Sandiford, H. (2005b) *Touchstone. Student's Book 2.* Cambridge: Cambridge University Press.

McCarthy, M. J., McCarten, J. and Sandiford, H. (2006a) *Touchstone. Student's Book 3.* Cambridge: Cambridge University Press.

McCarthy, M. J., McCarten, J. and Sandiford, H. (2006b) *Touchstone. Student's Book 4.* Cambridge: Cambridge University Press.

McCarthy, M. J., McCarten, J. and Sandiford, H. (2006c) *Touchstone.* Level 4. Teacher's Edition. Cambridge: Cambridge University Press.

McCarthy, M. J., O'Keeffe, A. and Walsh, S. (2005) ' "… post-colonialism, multi-culturalism, structuralism, feminism, post-modernism and so on and so forth" – vague language in academic discourse, a comparative analysis of form, function and context.' Paper read at *the American Association for Applied Corpus Linguistics*, University of Michigan, Ann Arbor, May 12th–15th 2005.

McCarthy. M. J. and Walsh, S. (2003) 'Discourse', in Nunan, D. (ed.) *Practical English Language Teaching.* New York: McGraw-Hill, 173–195.

McConvell, P. (1988) '*To be* or double *be*? Current changes in the English copula', *Australian Journal of Linguistics* 8: 287–305.

McDavid, V. (1977) '*Which* in relative clauses', *American Speech* 52 (1–2): 76–83.

McEnery, T. and Wilson, A. (1996) *Corpus Linguistics.* Edinburgh: Edinburgh University Press

McEnery, T., Xiao, R. and Tono, Y. (2006) *Corpus-based Language Studies: An Advanced Resource Book.* London: Routledge.

McGlone, M. S., Cacciari, C. and Glucksberg, S. (1994) 'Semantic productivity and idiom comprehension', *Discourse Processes* 17: 167–190.

McLay, V. (1987) *Idioms at Work.* Hove: Language Teaching Publications.

Meara, P. (1996) 'The dimensions of lexical competence' in Brown, G., Malmkjaer, K. and Williams,

J. (eds.) *Performance and Competence in Second Language Acquisition.* Cambridge: Cambridge University Press, 35–53.

Meara, P. and Rodriguez Sánchez, I. (1993) 'Matrix models of vocabulary acquisition: an empirical assessment', *CREAL Symposium on Vocabulary Research.* Ottawa.

Medgyes, P. (1994) *The Non-Native Teacher.* London: Macmillan.

Meierkord, C. (2005) 'Interaction across Englishes and their lexicon' in Gnutzmann, C. and Intemann, F. (eds.) *The Globalisation of English and the English Language Classroom.* Tübingen: Gunter Narr Verlag, 89–104.

Meunier, F. (2002a) 'The pedagogical value of native and learner corpora in EFL grammar teaching' in Granger, S., Hung, J. and Petch-Tyson, S. (eds.) *Computer Learner Corpora, Second Language Acquisition and Foreign Language Teaching.* Amsterdam: John Benjamins, 119–142.

Meunier, F. (2002b) 'The role of learner and native corpora in grammar teaching' in Granger, S., Hung, J. and Petch-Tyson, S. (eds.) *Computer Learner Corpora, Second Language Acquisition and Foreign Language Teaching.* Amsterdam: John Benjamins, 119–142.

Meyer, C. F. (2002) *English Corpus Linguistics: An Introduction.* Cambridge: Cambridge University Press.

Mezynski, K. (1983) 'Issues concerning the acquisition of knowledge: Effects of vocabulary training on reading comprehension', *Review of Educational Research,* 53 (2): 253–279.

Miller, G. (1956) 'The magical number seven, plus or minus two: some limits on our capacity for processing information', *Psychological Review* 63: 81–97.

Miller, J. and Weinert, R. (1998) *Spontaneous Spoken Language: Syntax and Discourse.* Oxford: Oxford University Press.

Milton, J. and Meara, P. (1995) 'How periods abroad affect vocabulary growth in a foreign language', *ITL* 107–108: 17–34.

Mitchell, T. (1971) 'Linguistic "goings-on": collocations and other lexical matters arising on the linguistic record', *Archivum Linguisticum* 2: 35–69.

Mondada, L. and Pekarek Doehler, S. (2004) 'Second language acquisition as situated practice: task accomplishment in the French second language classroom', *Modern Language Journal* 88(4): 501–518.

Mondorf, B. (2002) 'Gender differences in English syntax', *Journal of English Linguistics.* 30 (2): 158–180.

Monoconc Pro Concordance Software, Version 2, (2002) Houston Tx: Athelstan. http://www.athel.com

Moon, R. (1992) 'Textual aspects of fixed expressions in learners' dictionaries' in Arnaud, P. J. and Béjoint, H. (eds.) *Vocabulary and Applied Linguistics.* Basingstoke: Macmillan, 13–27.

Moore, T. and Morton, J. (2005) 'Dimensions of difference: a comparison of university writing and IELTS writing', *Journal of English for Academic Purposes* 4 (1): 43–66.

Mori, J. (2002) 'Task design, plan, and development of talk-in-Interaction: an analysis of a small group activity in a Japanese language classroom', *Applied Linguistics* 23 (2): 323–347.

Mori, J. (2004) 'Negotiating sequential boundaries and learning opportunities: a case from a Japanese classroom', *Modern Language Journal* 88 (4): 536–550.

Mott, H. and Petrie, H. (1995) 'Workplace interactions: women's linguistic behaviour', *Journal of Social Psychology* 14: 324–336.

Mumby, D. (1988) *Communication and Power in Organisations: Discourse, Ideology and Domination.* Norwood, NJ: Ablex.

Murphy, B., and O'Boyle, A. (2005) LIBEL CASE: a Spoken Corpus of Academic Discourse. Paper read at *The American Association for Applied Corpus Linguistics* at the University of Michigan, Ann Arbor 12–16th May 2005.

Nash, W. and Stacey, D. (1997) *Creating Texts*. Harlow: Longman.

Nation, I.S.P. (1990) *Teaching and Learning Vocabulary*. New York: Newbury House.

Nation, I.S.P. (2001) *Learning Vocabulary in Another Language*. Cambridge: Cambridge University Press.

Nation P. and Waring, R. (1997) 'Vocabulary size, text coverage and word lists' in Schmitt , N. and McCarthy, M. J. (eds.) *Vocabulary: Description, Acquisition and Pedagogy*. Cambridge: Cambridge University Press, 6–19.

Nattinger, J. and DeCarrico, J. (1992) *Lexical Phrases and Language Teaching*. Oxford: Oxford University Press.

Nelson, M. (2000) 'A corpus-based study of business English and business English teaching materials'. Unpublished PhD Thesis. Manchester: University of Manchester, UK.

Nesbitt, C. and Plum, G. (1988) 'Probabilities in a systemic-functional grammar: the clause complex in English' in Fawcett, R. and Young, D. (eds.) *New Developments in Systemic Linguistics*. Volume II: theory and applications. London: Pinter, 6–38.

Nesi, H. (1995) 'A modern bestiary: a contrastive study of the figurative meanings of animal terms', *ELT Journal* 49(3): 272–278.

Nesi, H, Sharpling, G. and Ganobcsik-Williams, L. (2004) 'The design, development and purpose of a corpus of British student writing', *Computers and Composition* 21 (4): 439–450.

Nesselhauf, N. (2003) 'The use of collocations by advanced learners of English and some implications for teaching', *Applied Linguistics* 24 (2): 223–242.

Newbrook, M. (1998) 'Which way? That way? Variation and ongoing changes in the English relative clause', *World Englishes* 17(1): 43–59.

Norrick, N. (1986) 'Stock similes', *Journal of Literary Semantics* XV (1): 39–52.

Norrick, N. (1988) 'Binomial meaning in texts', *Journal of English Linguistics* 21 (1): 72–87.

Norrick, N. (2001) 'Discourse markers in oral narrative', *Journal of Pragmatics* 33: 849–878.

Nunan, D. (1987) 'Communicative language teaching: making it work', *English Language Teaching Journal* 41: 136–145.

O'Halloran, K and Coffin, C. (2004) 'Checking overinterpretation and underinterpretation: help from corpora in critical linguistics' in Coffin, C. Hewings, A. and O'Halloran, K. (eds.) *Applying English Grammar: Functional and Corpus Approaches*. London: Arnold. 275–297.

O'Keeffe, A. (2003) '"Like the wise virgins and all that jazz" – using a corpus to examine vague language and shared knowledge' in Connor, U. and Upton, T. A. (eds.) *Applied Corpus Linguistics: A Multidimensional Perspective*. Amsterdam: Rodopi, 1–20.

O'Keeffe, A. (2006) *Investigating Media Discourse*. London: Routledge.

O'Keeffe, A. and Adolphs, S. (in press) 'Using a corpus to look at variational pragmatics: response tokens in British and Irish discourse' in Schneider, K.P. and Barron, A. (eds.) *Variational Pragmatics*. Amsterdam: John Benjamins.

O'Keeffe, A. and Farr, F. (2003) 'Using language corpora in language teacher education: pedagogic, linguistic and cultural insights', *TESOL Quarterly* 37 (3): 389–418.

O'Sullivan, Í., and Chambers, A. (In press) 'Learners' writing skills in French: Corpus consultation and learner evaluation', *Journal of Second Language Writing*.

Oakey, D. (2002) 'Formulaic language in English academic writing' in Reppen, R. Fitzmaurice, S. and Biber, D. (eds.) *Using Corpora to Explore Linguistic Variation*. Amsterdam: John Benjamins, 111–129.

Oda, M. (1999) 'English only or English plus: the language(s) of ELT organizations' in Braine, G. (ed.) *Non-Native Educators in English Language Teaching*. Marwah, NJ: Lawrence Erlbaum, 105–122.

Oda, M. (2000) 'Linguicism in Action' in Phillipson, R. (ed.) *Rights to Language: Equity, Power and Education*. Marwah, NJ: Lawrence Eribaum, 117–121.

Odlin, T. (ed.) (1994) *Perspectives on Pedagogical Grammar*. Cambridge: Cambridge University Press.

Ohta, A. S. (2001) *Second Language Acquisition Processes in the Classroom: Learning Japanese*. Mahwah, NJ: Erlbaum.

Olshtain, E. (1989) 'Apologies across languages' in: Blum-Kulka, S., House, J. and Kasper, G. (eds.) *Cross-Cultural Pragmatics*. Norwood, NJ: Ablex, 155–173.

Oreström, B. (1983) *Turn-taking in English Conversation*. Lund: Gleerup.

Östman, J. O. (1981) *You Know: A Discourse-Functional Approach*. Amsterdam, John Benjamins.

Overstreet, M. and Yule, G. (1997a) 'On being explicit and stuff in contemporary American English', *Journal of English Linguistics* 25 (3): 250–258.

Overstreet, M. and Yule, G. (1997b) 'Locally contingent categorization in discourse', *Discourse Processes* 23: 83–97.

Owen, C. (1996). 'Do concordances need to be consulted?', *ELT Journal* 50 (3): 219–224.

Owen, M. (1981) 'Conversational units and the use of "well". . .' in: Werth, P. (ed.), *Conversation and Discourse*. London: Croom Helm, 99–116.

Paltridge, B. (2002) 'Thesis and dissertation writing: an examination of published advice and actual practice', *English for Specific Purposes* 21 (2): 125–143.

Roberts, C. and Sarangi, S. (1999) *Talk, Work and Institutional Order: Discourse in Medical, Mediation and Management Settings*. Berlin: Mouton de Gruyter.

Pan, Y., Scollon, S. and Scollon R. (2001) *Professional Communication in International Settings*. Oxford: Blackwell.

Pawley, A. and Syder, F. (1983) 'Two puzzles for linguistic theory: nativelike selection and nativelike fluency' in Richards, J. and Schmidt, R. (eds.) *Language and Communication*. New York: Longman, 191–226.

Pea, R.D. (In press) 'Video-as-data and digital video manipulation techniques for transforming learning sciences research, education and other cultural practices' in Weiss, J., Nolan, J. and Trifonas, P. (eds.) *International Handbook of Virtual Learning Environments*. Dordrecht: Kluwer Academic Publishing.

Peacock, M. (1997) 'The effect of authentic materials on the motivation of EFL learners', *ELT Journal* 51 (2): 144–156.

Pica, T., and Long, M. H. (1986) 'The linguistic and conversational performance of experienced and inexperienced teachers' in Day, R. R. (ed.) *'Talking to learn': Conversation in Second Language Acquisition*. Rowley, Mass.: Newbury House, 85–98.

Piquer Pirez, A. M. (forthcoming) 'Figurative capacity in young learners of English as a foreign language' in Zanotto, M. Cameron, L. and Cavalcanti, M. (eds.) *Confronting Metaphor in Applied Linguistics*. London: Continuum.

Pomerantz, A., (1984) 'Agreeing and disagreeing with assessments: some features of preferred/dispreferred turn shapes' in: Atkinson, J. and Heritage, J. (eds.) *Structures of*

Social Action: Studies in Conversation Analysis. Cambridge: Cambridge University Press, 57–101.

Pomerantz, A. and Fehr, B. J. (1997) 'Conversation analysis: An approach to the study of social action as sense making practices' in van Dijk, T. A. (ed.) *Discourse as Social Interaction.* London: Sage, 64–91.

Pope, R. (2005) *Creativity: Theory, History, Practice.* Routledge: London.

Powell, M. (1985) 'Purposive vagueness: an evaluative dimension of vague quantifying expressions', *Journal of Linguistics* 21: 31–50.

Powell, M. (1992) 'Semantic/pragmatic regularities in informal lexis: British speakers in spontaneous conversational settings', *Text* 12 (1): 19–58.

Prince, E. (1978) 'A comparison of WH-clefts and it-clefts in discourse', *Language* 54: 883–906.

Prodromou, L. (1996) 'Correspondence', *ELT Journal*, 50 (4): 371–373.

Prodromou, L. (1997a) 'Corpora: the real thing?', *English Teaching Professional* 5: 2–6.

Prodromou, L. (1997b) From corpus to octopus. *IATEFL Newsletter* 137: 18–21.

Prodromou, L. (2003a) 'In search of the successful user of English'. *Modern English Teacher* 12 (2): 5–14.

Prodromou, L. (2003b) 'Idiomaticity and the non-native speaker', *English Today* 19 (2): 42–48.

Prodromou, L. (2005) '"You see, it's sort of tricky for the L2-user": The puzzle of idiomaticity in English as a lingua franca'. Unpublished PhD dissertation, University of Nottingham, UK.

Qian, D. D. (2002) 'Investigating the relationship between vocabulary knowledge and academic reading performance: An assessment perspective', *Language Learning* 52 (3): 513–536.

Quirk, R., Greenbaum, S. Leech, G. and Svartvik, J. (1985) *A Comprehensive Grammar of the English Language.* London: Longman.

Rampton, B. (1990) 'Displacing the native speaker: expertise, affiliation and inheritance', *ELT Journal* 44 (2): 97–101.

Rampton, B., Roberts, C., Leung, C., and Harris, R. (2002) 'Methodology in the analysis of classroom discourse', *Applied Linguistics* 23 (3): 373–392.

Redeker, G. (1990) 'Ideational and pragmatic markers of discourse structure', *Journal of Pragmatics* 14: 367–381.

Redeker, G. (1991) 'Review article: Linguistic markers of discourse structure', *Linguistics* 29 (6): 1139–1172.

Reder S., Harris, K. and Setzler, K. (2003) 'The Multimedia Adult ESL Learner Corpus', *TESOL Quarterly* 37 (3): 546–558.

Reppen, R. (2004) 'Academic language: An exploration of university classroom and textbook language' in Connor, U. and Upton, T. A. (eds.) *Discourse in the Professions.* Amsterdam: John Benjamins, 65–86.

Reppen, R. and Simpson, R. (2002) 'Corpus linguistics' in Schmitt, N. (ed.) *An Introduction to Applied Linguistics.* London: Arnold, 92–111.

Ricento, T. (1987) 'Clausal ellipsis in multi-party conversations in English', *Journal of Pragmatics* 11: 751–775.

Richards, J.C. (1974) 'Word lists: problems and prospects', *RELC Journal* 5 (2): 69–84.

Riggenbach, H. (1999) *Discourse Analysis in the Language Classroom: Volume 1. The Spoken Language.* Ann Arbor, MI: University of Michigan Press.

Roberts, P. (2005) *Spoken English as a World Language in International and Intranational Settings.* Unpublished dissertation, University of Nottingham, UK.

Robinson, W. P. (1972) *Language and Social Behaviour.* Harmondsworth: Penguin.

Robinson, W. P. (1985) 'Social psychology and discourse' in van Dijk, T.A. (ed.) *Handbook of Discourse Analysis*, vol. 1, London: Academic Press, 107–144.

Roger, D., Bull, P. and Smyth, S. (1988) 'The development of a comprehensive system for classifying interruptions', *Journal of Language and Social Psychology* 7: 27–34.

Röhler, L. R. and Cantlon, D. J. (1996) *Scaffolding: A Powerful Tool in Social Constructivist Classrooms.* Available on the world-wide web at: http://edeb3.educ.msu.edu./Literacy/papers/paperlr2.html

Romaine, S. (1994) *Language in Society.* Oxford: Oxford University Press.

Rosch, E. (1978) 'Principles of categorization', in Rosch, E. and Llyod, B. (eds) *Cognition and Categorization.* New Jersey: Erlbaum Ass., 27–48

Rost, M. (2002) *Teaching and Researching Listening.* London: Longman.

Rounds, P. (1982) *Hedging in Academic Discourse: Precision and Flexibility.* Ann Arbor: The University of Michigan.

Ruiying, Y. and Allison, D. (2004) 'Research articles in applied linguistics: structures from a functional perspective', *English for Specific Purposes* 23 (3): 264–279.

Scannell, P. (ed.) (1991) *Broadcast Talk.* London: SAGE Publications.

Rutherford, W. and Sharwood Smith, M. (eds.) (1988) *Grammar and Second Language Teaching* New York: Newbury House/Harper Collins.

Sacks H., Schegloff, E. A., Jefferson, G. (1974) 'A simplest systematics for the organisation of turn-taking for conversation', *Language* 50 (4): 696–735.

Saferstein, B. (2005) 'Digital technology and methodological adaption: text on video as a resource for analytical reflexivity', *Journal of Applied Linguistics* 1 (2): 197–223.

Salkie, R. (1995) 'INTERSECT: a parallel corpus project at Brighton University', *Computers & Texts* 9: 4–5.

Salkie, R. (2002) 'Two types of translation equivalence' in Altenberg, B. and Granger, S. (eds.) *Lexis in Contrast. Corpus-based Approaches.* Amsterdam: John Benjamins, 51–71.

Salkie, R. and Oates, S.L. (1999) 'Contrast and concession in French and English', *Languages in Contrast* 2 (1): 27–56.

Santos, D. (1998) 'Perception verbs in English and Portuguese' in Johansson S. and Oksefjell, S. (eds.) *Corpora and Cross-Linguistic Research. Theory, Method and Case Studies.* Amsterdam: Rodopi, 319–342.

Santos, D. and S. Oksefjell (1999) 'Using a parallel corpus to validate independent claims', *Language in Contrast* 2 (1): 115–132.

Sarangi, S. (2002) 'Discourse practitioners as a community of interprofessional practice: some insights from health communication research' in: Candlin, C. N. (ed.) *Research and Practice in Professional Discourse.* Hong Kong: City University of Hong Kong Press, 95–136.

Schegloff, E. (1982) 'Discourse as interactional achievement: some uses of "uh huh" and other things that come between sentences' in Tannen, D. (ed.) *Analysing Discourse. Text and Talk.* Washington, D.C.: Georgetown University Press, 71–93.

Schegloff, E. A. and Sacks, H. (1973) 'Opening up closings', *Semiotica* 8(4): 289–327.

Schiffrin, D. (1987) *Discourse Markers.* Cambridge: Cambridge University Press.

Schiffrin, D. (2000) Discourse markers: language, meaning and context' in: Schiffrin, D. Hamilton, H. and Tannen, D. (eds.) *Handbook of Discourse and Analysis.* Malden, Mass: Blackwell, 54–75.

Schmitt, D. and Schmitt, N. (2005) *Focus on Vocabulary: Mastering the Academic Word list.* Longman: White Plains, NY.

Schmitt, N. (ed.) (2004) *Formulaic Sequences.* Amsterdam: John Benjamins.

Schmitt, N. (2006) 'Formulaic language: fixed and varied', *ELIA: Estudios de Linguística. Inglesa Aplicada,* 6.

Schmitt, N., and Carter, R. (2004) 'Formulaic sequences in action' in Schmitt, N. (ed.) *Formulaic Sequences.* Amsterdam: John Benjamins, 1–22.

Schneider, K. P. (1988) *Analysing Phatic Discourse.* Marburg: Hitzeroth.

Schneider, K. P. (1989) 'The art of talking about nothing' in Weigand, E.and Hundsnurscher, F. (eds.) *Dialoganalyse II: Referate der 2. Arbeitstagung Bochum, 1988, I and II.* Tübingen: Neimeyer, I: 437–449.

Schneider, K. P. (2000) 'Diminutives in discourse: sequential aspects of diminutive use in spoken interaction' in: Coulthard, M. Cotterill, J. and Rock, F. (eds.) *Discourse Analysis VII: Working with Dialogue. Selected Papers from the 7th International Association of Dialogue Analysis Conference, Birmingham 1999.* Tübingen: Niemeyer, 293–300.

Schneider, K. P. (2003) *Diminutives in English.* Tübingen: Niemeyer.

Schröder, H. and Zimmer, D. (1997) 'Hedging research in pragmatics: a bibliographical research guide to hedging' in Markkanen, R. and Schröder, H. (eds.) *Hedging and Discourse: Approaches to the Analysis of a Pragmatic Phenomenon in Academic Texts.* Berlin: Walter de Gruyter, 249–271.

Scott, M. (1999) *Wordsmith Tools.* Software. Oxford: Oxford University Press.

Searle, J. R. (1969). *Speech Acts: An Essay in the Philosophy of Language.* Cambridge: Cambridge University Press.

Searle, J. R. (1976) 'The classification of illocutionary acts', *Language in Society* 5: 1–24.

Seedhouse, P. (2004) *The Interactional Architecture of the Second Language Classroom: A Conversation Analysis Perspective.* Oxford: Blackwell.

Seidlhofer, B. (1999) 'Double standards: teacher education in the expanding circle', *World Englishes,* 18: 233–45.

Seidlhofer, B. (2001a) 'Closing a conceptual gap: the case for a description of English as a lingua franca', *International Journal of Applied Linguistics* 11: 133–158.

Seidlhofer, B. (2001b) 'Making the case for a corpus of English as a lingua franca' in Aston, G. and Burnard, L. (eds.) *Corpora in the Description and Teaching of English.* Bologna: CLUEB, 70–85.

Seidlhofer, B. (2004) 'Research perspectives on teaching English as a lingua franca', *Annual Review of Applied Linguistics* 24: 209–239.

Semino, E. and Short, M. H. (2004) *Corpus Stylistics.* London: Longman.

Semino, E., Short, M. and Culpeper, J. (1997) 'Using a corpus to test a model of speech and thought presentation', *Poetics* 25: 17–43

Serpollet, N. (2002) 'Mandative constructions in English and their equivalents in French – applying a bilingual approach to the theory and practice of translation' in Kettemann, B. and Marko, G. (eds.) *Teaching and Learning by Doing Corpus Analysis.* Amsterdam: Rodopi, 231–243.

Short, M. (1996) *Exploring the Language of Poems, Plays, and Prose.* London: Longman.

Short, M., Semino, E. and Culpeper, J. (1996) 'Using a corpus for stylistics research: speech and thought presentation' in Thomas, J. and Short, M. (eds.) *Using Corpora in Language Research,* London: Longman, 110–131.

Shuy, R (1998) *The Language of Confession, Interrogation and Deception.* London: Sage.

Silver, M. (2003) 'The stance of stance: a critical look at ways stance is expressed and modeled in academic discourse', *Journal of English for Academic Purposes* 2 (4): 359–374.

Simpson, R. and Mendis, D. (2003) 'A corpus-based study of idioms in academic speech', *TESOL Quarterly* 37 (3): 419–441.

Simpson, R., Briggs, S. L., Ovens, J. and Swales, J. M. (2002) The Michigan Corpus of Academic Spoken English. Ann Arbor, MI: The Regents of the University of Michigan. URL: http://www.hti.umich.edu/m/micase/ .

Sinclair, J. (1966) 'Beginning the study of lexis' in Bazell, C., Catford, J., Halliday, M. A. K. and Robins, R. (eds.). 1966. *In Memory of J. R. Firth*. London: Longman, 410–430.

Sinclair, J. (1987a) 'The nature of the evidence' in Sinclair, J. McH. (ed.) *Looking up*. Glasgow: Collins, 150–159.

Sinclair, J. (ed.) (1987b) *Collins COBUILD English Language Dictionary* (1st ed.). London: Collins.

Sinclair, J. (1987c) 'Collocation: a progress report' in Steele, R. and Threadgold, T. (eds.) *Language Topics: An International Collection of Papers by Colleagues, Students and Admirers of Professor Michael Halliday to Honour him on his Retirement*, Vol. II. Amsterdam: John Benjamins, 319–331.

Sinclair, J. (ed.) (1990) *Collins COBUILD English Grammar*. London: Harper Collins.

Sinclair, J. (1991a) *Corpus, Concordance and Collocation*. Oxford: Oxford University Press.

Sinclair, J. (1991b) 'Shared knowledge' in Alatis, J. (ed.) *Georgetown University Round Table on Languages and Linguistics*. Washington, D.C.: Georgetown University Press, 489–500.

Sinclair, J. (ed.) (1995) *Collins COBUILD English Language Dictionary* (2nd ed.) London: Collins.

Sinclair, J. (1996a) 'The search for units of meaning', *Textus* 9 (1): 75–106

Sinclair, J. (ed.) (1996b) *Collins COBUILD Grammar Patterns I: Verbs*. London: Collins.

Sinclair, J. (ed.) (1998) *Collins COBUILD Grammar Patterns 2: Nouns and Adjectives*. London: Collins.

Sinclair, J. (ed.) (2001) *Collins COBUILD English Language Dictionary* (3rd ed.) London: Collins.

Sinclair, J. (ed.) (2003a). *Reading Concordances*. London: Longman.

Sinclair, J. (ed.) (2003b) *Collins COBUILD English Language Dictionary* (4th ed.) London: Collins.

Sinclair, J. (2004). *Trust the Text: Language, Corpus and Discourse*. London: Routledge.

Sinclair, J. and Coulthard, M. (1975) *Towards an Analysis of Discourse. The English Used by Teachers and Pupils*. Oxford: Oxford University Press.

Sinclair, J. and Renouf, A. (1988) 'A lexical syllabus for language learning' in Carter, R. and McCarthy, M. (eds.) *Vocabulary and Language Teaching*. London: Longman, 140–158.

Sinclair J., Payne J. and Pérez Hernandez, C. (1996) 'Corpus to corpus: a study of translation equivalence', *International Journal of Lexicography* 9 (3): 179–276.

Skelton, J. (1988) 'The care and maintenance of hedges', *ELT Journal* 42(1): 37–43.

Solan, L. M. and Tiersma, P. M. (2004) 'Author Identification in American Courts', *Applied Linguistics* 25 (4): 448–465.

Spencer Oatey, H. (ed.) (2000) *Culturally Speaking*. London: Continuum.

Spöttl, C. and McCarthy, M. J. (2003) 'Formulaic utterances in the multi-lingual context' in Cenoz, J., Jessner, U. and Hufeisen, B. (eds.) *The Multilingual Lexicon*. Dordrecht: Kluwer, 133–151.

Spöttl, C. and McCarthy, M. J. (2004). 'Comparing the knowledge of formulaic sequences across L1, L2, L3 and L4' in Schmitt, N. (ed.) *Formulaic Sequences*. Amsterdam: John Benjamins, 191–225.

St John, E. (2001) 'A case for using a parallel corpus and concordancer for beginners of a foreign language', *Language Learning & Technology* 5 (3): 185–203.

St John, M-J. (1996) 'Business is booming: business English in the 1990s', *English for Specific Purposes* 15 (1): 3–18.

Stahl, S. A. and Fairbanks, M. M. (1986). 'The effects of vocabulary instruction: a model-based meta-analysis', *Review of Educational Research* 56 (1): 72–110.

Stenström, A.-B. (1995) 'Taboos in teenage talk' in Melchers, G. and Warren, B. (eds.) *Studies in Anglistics*. Stockholm: Almqvist and Wiksell International, 71–80.

Stenström, A.-B. (1997a) 'Tags in teenage talk' in Fries, U., Müller, V. and Schneider, P. (eds.) *From Ælfric to the New York Times. Studies in English Corpus Linguistics*. Amsterdam: Rodopi, 139–148.

Stenström, A.-B. (1997b) '"Can I have a chips please? – Just tell me what one you want" Nonstandard grammatical features in London teenage talk' in Aarts, J., de Mönninck, I. and Wekker, H. (eds.) *Studies in English Language and Teaching*. Amsterdam: Rodopi, 141–152.

Stenström, A.-B. (1998) 'From sentence to discourse: *cos(because)* in teenage talk' in Jucker, A. and Ziv, Y. (eds.) *Discourse Markers: Descriptions and Theory*. Amsterdam: John Benjamins, 127–146.

Stenström, A.-B., Andersen G. and Hasund, I. K. (2002) *Trends in Teenage Talk: Corpus Compilation, Analysis and Findings*. Amsterdam: John Benjamins.

Stevens, V. (1991) 'Classroom concordancing: Vocabulary materials derived from relevant, authentic text', *English for Special Purposes Journal* 10: 35–46.

Strässler, J. (1982) *Idioms in English: A Pragmatic Analysis*. Tübingen: Gunter Narr Verlag.

Stubbs, M. (1986) '"A matter of prolonged fieldwork": notes towards a modal grammar of English', *Applied Linguistics* 7 (1): 1–25.

Stubbs, M. (1995) 'Corpus evidence for norms of lexical collocation' in Cook, G. and Seidlhofer, B. (eds.) *Principle and Practice in Applied Linguistics: Studies in Honour of H.G. Widdowson*. Oxford: Oxford University Press, 245–56.

Stubbs, M. (2005) 'Conrad in the computer: examples of quantitative stylistic methods', *Language and Literature* 14 (1): 5–24

Sussex, R. (1982) 'A note on the get-passive construction', *Australian Journal of Linguistics* 2: 83–95

Svartvik, J. (1991) 'What can real spoken data teach teachers of English?' in Alatis, J. A. (ed.) *Linguistics and Language Pedagogy: The State of the Art*. Washington, DC: Georgetown University Press, 555–565.

Svartvik, J. (ed.) (1990) *The London Corpus of Spoken English: Description and Research*. Lund: Lund University Press.

Svartvik, J. and Quirk, R. (1980) *A Corpus of English Conversation*. Lund: CWK Gleerup.

Swan, M. (2005) *Practical English usage*. 3rd edition. Oxford: Oxford University Press.

Tabossi, P., and Zardon, F. (1993) 'The activation of idiomatic meaning in spoken language comprehension' in Cacciari, C. and Tabossi, P. (eds.) *Idioms: Processing, Structure and Interpretation*. Hillsdale, NJ: Erlbaum, 145–162.

Tajino A. and Tajino, Y. (2000) 'Native and non-native: what can they offer? Lessons from team-teaching in Japan', *ELT Journal* 54 (1): 3–11.

Tamony, P. (1982) 'Like Kelly's nuts' and related expressions. *Comments on Etymology* 11(9–10): 8–10.

Tannen, D. (1989) *Talking Voices: Repetition, Dialogue and Imagery in Conversational Discourse*. Cambridge: Cambridge University Press.

Tannen, D. and Wallat, C. (1993) 'Interactive frames and knowledge schemas in interaction:

examples from a medical examination/interview' in D. Tannen (ed.) *Framing in Discourse*. Oxford: Oxford University Press, 57–76.

Tao, H., and McCarthy, M. J. (2001). 'Understanding non-restrictive which-clauses in spoken English, which is not an easy thing', *Language Sciences* 2: 651–677.

Teubert, W. (1996) 'Comparable or parallel corpora?', *International Journal of Lexicography* 9: 238–264.

Teubert, W. (2002) 'The role of parallel corpora in translation and multilingual lexicography' in Altenberg, B. and Granger, S. (eds.) *Lexis in Contrast. Corpus-based Approaches*. Amsterdam: Benjamins, 189–214.

Thomas, A. (1987) 'The use and interpretation of verbally determinate verb group ellipsis in English', *International Review of Applied Linguistics* 25 (1): 1–14.

Thomas, J. (1983) 'Cross-Cultural Pragmatic Failure', *Applied Linguistics* 4 (2) 91–112.

Thomas, J., and Short, M. (eds.) (1996) *Using Corpora for Language Research*. New York: Longman.

Thompson, P. (2005a) 'Spoken language corpora' in Wynne, M. (ed.) *Developing Linguistic. Corpora: A Guide to Good Practice*. Oxford: Oxbow Books, 59–70.

Thompson, P. (2005b) 'Aspects of identification and position in intertextual reference in PhD theses' in Tognini-Bonelli, E. and Del Lungo Camiciotti, G. (eds.) *Strategies in Academic Discourse*. Amsterdam: John Benjamins, 31–50.

Thompson, P. (2005c) 'Points of focus and position: Intertextual reference in PhD theses', *Journal of English for Academic Purposes* 4 (4): 307–323.

Thompson, P. and Tribble, C. (2001) 'Looking at citations: using corpora in English for academic purposes', *Language Learning & Technology* 5 (3) 91–105.

Thornbury, S. (2004) *Natural Grammar*. Oxford: Oxford University Press.

Thornbury, S. and Slade, D. (2006) *Conversation: From Description to Pedagogy*. Cambridge: Cambridge University Press.

Thorne, J. (1988) 'Non-restrictive relative clauses' in Duncan-Rose, C. and Vennemann, T. (eds.), *On language: Rhetorica, Phonologica, Syntactica*. London: Routledge, 424–436.

Tiersma, P. (1999) *Legal Language*. Chicago: Chicago University Press.

Tiersma, P and Solan, L (2005) *Speaking of Crime*. Cambridge: Cambridge University Press.

Timmis, I. (2002) 'Native-speaker norms and International English: a classroom view', *ELT Journal* 56 (3): 240–249.

Tognini-Bonelli, E. (1996) 'Towards translation equivalence from a corpus linguistic perspective' in Sinclair, J., Payne, J. and Pérez Hernandez, C. (eds.) *Corpus to Corpus: A Study of Translation Equivalence. Special issue of International Journal of Lexicography* 9 (3): 197–217.

Tognini-Bonelli, E. (2001) *Corpus Linguistics at Work*. Amsterdam: John Benjamins.

Tottie, G. (1991) 'Conversational style in British and American English, the case of backchannels' in Aijmer, K. and Altenberg, B. (eds.) *English Corpus Linguistics*. London: Longman, 254–71.

Tracy, K. and Naughton, J. M. (2000) 'Institutional identity-work: a better lens' in Coupland, J. (ed.) *Small Talk*. London: Longman, 62–83.

Tribble, C. (1997) 'Improving corpora for ELT: quick and dirty ways of developing corpora for language teaching' in Lewandowska-Tomaszczyk, B. and Melia, P. J. (eds.) *Practical Applications in Language and Computers (PALC '97)*. Łodz: Łodz University Press, 106–117. Available at http://web.bham.ac.uk/johnstf/palc.htm.

Tribble, C. (2000) 'Practical uses of for language corpora in ELT' in Brett, P. and Motteram, G.

(eds.), *A Special Interest in Computers. Learning and Teaching with Information and Communications Technologies*. Kent: IATEFL, 31–41.

Tribble, C. (2003) 'The text, the whole text . . . or why large published corpora aren't much use to language learners and teachers' in Lewandowska-Tomaszczyk, B. (ed.) *Practical Applications in Language and Computers (PALC 2003)*. Frankfurt: Peter Lang, 303–318

Tribble, C. and Jones, G. (1990) *Concordances in the Classroom*. London: Longman.

Tribble, C. and Jones, G. (1997) *Concordances in the Classroom: Using Corpora in Language Education*. Houston TX: Athelstan.

Tsui, A. B. M. (1996). 'The participant structures of TeleNex – a computer network for ESL teachers', *International Journal of Educational Telecommunications* 2 (2/3): 171–197.

Tsui, A. B. M. (2004). 'What teachers have always wanted to know – and how corpora can help' in Sinclair, J. (ed.) *How to Use Corpora in Language Teaching*. Amsterdam: John Benjamins, 39–61.

Tsui, A. B. M. (2005) 'ESL Teachers' questions and corpus evidence', *International Journal of Corpus Linguistics* 10 (3): 335–356. (http://sitemaker.umich.edu/corpus_analysis_tools/files/tsui-corpustoolsforteachers.pdf)

Tsui, A. B. M. and Ki, W. W. (2002) 'Socio-psychological dimensions of teacher participation in computer conferencing', *Journal of Information Technology for Teacher Education* 11 (1): 23–44.

Turnbull, J. and Burston, J. (1998) 'Towards independent concordance work for students: Lessons from a case study', *ON-CALL* 12 (2): 10–21.

Turner, G. (1973) *Stylistics*. Harmondsworth: Penguin

Ulijn, J. and Li, X. (1995) 'Is interrupting impolite? Some temporal aspects of turn-taking in Chinese-Western and other intercultural business encounters', *Text* 15 (4): 589–627.

Ulijn, J. and Murray D (1995). Special issue on Intercultural Discourse in Business And Technology, *Text* 15 (4).

Van Lier, L. (1988) *The Classroom and the Language Learner*. London: Longman.

Van Lier, L. (1996) *Interaction in the Language Curriculum: Awareness, Autonomy and Authenticity*. London: Longman.

Van Peer, W. (1989) 'Quantitative studies of style: a critique and an outlook', *Computers and the Humanities* 23: 301–307.

Van Vaerenbergh L. (2002) *Linguistics and Translation Studies. Translation Studies and Linguistics*. Antwerpen: Linguistica Antverpiensia.

Vásquez, C. (2004) '"Very carefully managed": advice and suggestions in post-observation meetings', *Linguistics and Education* 15 (1–2): 32–58.

Vásquez, C. (2005) *Teacher Positioning in Post-Observation Meetings*. Unpublished doctoral dissertation, Northern Arizona University, Flagstaff, Arizona, USA.

Vásquez, C., and Reppen, R. (2004) What didn't you say? Increasing participation in teacher mentoring meetings. Paper read at *the 2nd Inter-Varietal Applied Corpus Studies (IVACS) Group International Conference*, June 25, Belfast, Northern Ireland.

Vásquez, C., and Reppen, R. (in press) 'Transforming Practice: Changing Patterns of Interaction in Post-Observation Meetings', *Language Awareness* 16 (3).

Vaughan, E. (in press) 'I think we should just accept . . . our horrible lowly status': analysing teacher-teacher talk within the context of Community of Practice. *Language Awareness* 16 (3).

Volk, M. (1998) 'The automatic translation of idioms. machine translation vs. translation memory systems' in: Weber, N. (ed.): *Machine Translation: Theory, Applications, and Evaluation. An Assessment of the State of the Art*. St. Augustin: Gardez-Verlag. Available at http:/www.ling.su.se/DaLi/volk/publications.html

Vygotsky, L. S. (1962) *Thought and Language*, Cambridge, MA: MIT Press.

Vygotsky, L. S. (1978) *Mind in Society: the Development of Higher Psychological Processes*, Cambridge: Harvard University Press.

Walsh, S. (2001) 'Characterising teacher talk in the second language classroom: a process approach of reflective practice'. Unpublished PhD thesis, Queen's University, Belfast.

Walsh, S. (2002) 'Construction or obstruction: teacher talk and learner involvement in the EFL classroom', *Language Teaching Research* 6 (1): 3–23.

Walsh, S. (2003) 'Developing interactional awareness in the second language classroom through teacher self-evaluation', *Language Awareness* 12 (2): 124–142.

Walsh, S. (2006) *Investigating Classroom Discourse*. London: Routledge.

Wang, S-P. (2005) 'Corpus-based approaches and discourse analysis in relation to reduplication and repetition', *Journal of Pragmatics* 37 (4): 505–540.

Wang, S-P. (2006) 'Corpus-based approaches and text analysis in relation to sound symbolism, reduplication and fixed expressions'. Unpublished PhD dissertation. Nottingham: University of Nottingham.

Ward, G. and B. Birner (1992) 'The semantics and pragmatics of "and everything"', *Journal of pragmatics* 19: 205–214.

Waring, R. (1997) 'A comparison of the receptive and productive vocabulary sizes of some second language learners', *Immaculata. The occasional papers at Notre Dame Seishin University*. Available online at: http://www1.harenet.ne.jp/~waring/papers/vocsize.html

Watts, R. J. (1989) 'Taking the pitcher to the "well": native speakers' perception of their use of discourse markers in conversation', *Journal of Pragmatics* 13: 203–37

Weinert, R. (1995) 'The role of formulaic language in second language acquisition: a review', *Applied Linguistics* 16 (2): 180–205.

Weinert, R. and Miller, J. (1996) 'Cleft constructions in spoken language', *Journal of Pragmatics* 25: 173–206.

WeiyunHe, A. (2004) 'CA for SLA: arguments from the Chinese language classroom', *Modern Language Journal* 88 (4): 568–582.

Wells, G. (1999) *Dialogic Inquiry: Towards a Sociocultural Practice and Theory of Education*. Cambridge: Cambridge University Press.

Wenger, E. (1998) *Communities of Practice: Learning, Meaning and Identity*. Cambridge: Cambridge University Press.

West, M. (1953) *A General Service List of English Words with Semantic Frequencies and a Supplementary Word-list for the Writing of Popular Science and Technology*. London: Longman, Green & Co.

White, J. and Lightbown, P. M. (1984) 'Asking and answering in ESL classes', *Canadian Modern Language Review* 40: 228–244.

Wichmann, A. (1995) 'Using concordances for the teaching of modern languages in higher education', *Language Learning Journal* 11: 61–63.

Wichmann, A., Fligelstone S., McEnery, T. and G. Knowles (eds.) (1997) *Teaching and Language Corpora*. London: Longman.

Widdowson, H. G. (1991) 'The description and prescription of language' in Alatis, J. (ed.) *Georgetown University Round Table on Languages and Linguistics* Washington, D.C.: Georgetown University Press, 11–24.

Widdowson, H. G. (1996) 'Comment: authenticity and autonomy', *ELT Journal* 50 (1): 67–68.

Widdowson, H. G. (1998) 'Context, community, and authentic materials', *TESOL Quarterly* 32 (4): 705–715.

Widdowson, H. G. (2000) 'On the limitations of applied linguistics', *Applied Linguistics* 21 (1): 2–25.

Widdowson, H. G. (2001) 'Coming to terms with reality: applied linguistics in perspective' in Graddol, D. (ed.) *Applied Linguistics for the 21st Century. AILA Review* 14: 2–17.

Wierzbicka, A. (1985) 'Different cultures, different languages, different speech acts: Polish vs. English', *Journal of Pragmatics* 9 (2–3): 145–178.

Wilks, C. and Meara, P. (2002) 'Untangling word webs: graph theory and the notion of density in second language word association networks', *Second Language Research* 18 (4): 303–324.

Williams, M. (1988) 'Language taught for meetings and language used in meetings: is there anything in common?', *Applied Linguistics* 9 (1): 45–58.

Willis, D. (1990). *The Lexical Syllabus: A New Approach to Language Teaching.* London: Collins COBUILD.

Willis, D (2003) *Rules, Patterns and Words: Grammar and Lexis in English Language Teaching.* Cambridge: Cambridge University Press.

Willis, D. and Willis, J. (1996) *Challenge and Change in Language Teaching.* Oxford: Macmillan.

Wilson, P. (2000) *Mind the Gap: Ellipsis and Stylistic Variation in Spoken and Written English.* London: Pearson Education.

Wilson, A., Rayson, P. and McEnery, T. (eds.) (2003) *A Rainbow of Corpora: Corpus Linguistics and the Language of the World.* München: Lincom Europa.

Wolfson, N. (1981) 'Invitations, compliments and the competence of the native speaker', *International Journal of Psycholinguistics* 24: 7–22.

Wolter, B. (2001) 'Comparing the L1 and L2 mental lexicon: a depth of individual word knowledge model', *Studies in Second Language Acquisition* 23 (1): 41–69.

Wolter, B. (2002) 'Assessing proficiency through word associations: is there still hope?', *System* 30 (3): 315–329.

Wong, J. (2000) 'Delayed next turn repair initiation in native/non-native speaker English conversation', *Applied Linguistics* 21 (2): 244–267.

Wray, A. (2000) 'Formulaic sequences in second language teaching: principle and practice', *Applied Linguistics,* 21 (4): 463–489.

Wray, A. (2002) *Formulaic Language and the Lexicon.* Cambridge: Cambridge University Press.

Wright, J. (1999) *Idioms Organiser.* Hove: Language Teaching Publications.

Wynne, M. (2005a) *A Guide to Good Practice in Collaborative Working Methods and New Media Tools Creation.* Oxford: Oxbow Books.

Wynne, M. (2005b) 'Stylistics: corpus approaches' in Brown, K. (ed.) *Encyclopaedia of Language and Linguistics.* Oxford: Elsevier. Available at: http://eprints.ouls.ox.ac.uk/archive/00001003/01/Corpora_and_stylistics.pdf

Yamada, H. (1990) 'Topic management and turn distribution in business meetings: American versus Japanese strategies', *Text* 10 (3): 271–295.

Yamashita, J. (1994) 'An analysis of relative clauses in the Lancaster/IBM spoken English corpus', *English Studies* 75 (1): 73–84.

Ylänne-McEwen, V. (1997) 'Relational processes within a transactional setting: an investigation of travel agency discourse'. Unpublished PhD dissertation. University of Wales, Cardiff.

Yngve, V. (1970) On getting a word in edgewise. *Papers from the 6th Regional Meeting, Chicago Linguistic Society*. Chicago: Chicago Linguistic Society.

Yorio, C. A. (1980) 'Conventionalized language forms and the development of communicative competence', *TESOL Quarterly* 14 (4): 433–442.

Yorio, C. A. (1989) 'Idiomaticity as an indicator of second language proficiency' in Hyltenstam, K. and Obler, L. (eds.) *Bilingualism Across the Lifespan*. Cambridge: Cambridge University Press. 55–69.

Yotsukura, L. A. (2003) *Negotiating Moves: Problem Presentation and Resolution in Japanese Business Discourse*. Amsterdam and Boston: Elsevier.

Zanettin, F. (1998) 'Bilingual comparable corpora and the training of translators'. *Meta*, 43 (4): 616–630.

Zanettin F. (2002) 'CEXI: Designing an English translational corpus' in Kettemann, B. and Marko, G. (eds.) *Teaching and Learning by Doing Corpus Analysis*. Amsterdam: Rodopi, 329–344.

Zimmerman, D.H. and West, C. (1975) 'Sex roles, interruptions and silences in conversation' in Thorne, B. and Henley, N. (eds.) *Language and Sex: Differences and Dominance*. Rowley, MA: Newbury, 105–129.

Appendix 1[1]:
Survey of corpora

Corpus	How to find out more
American National Corpus (ANC) • 22 million words of English • 83% written data including newspapers, books, magazines, letter, travel guides and internet postings. • Circa 17% spoken data including phone calls, narratives, lectures, seminars.	http://americannationalcorpus.org/
Bergen Corpus of London Teenage Language – (COLT) • 500,000 words of London teenager conversations • It was collected in 1993 and consists of the spoken language of 13 to 17-year-old teenagers from different boroughs of London. • It is a constituent of the BNC (see below)	http://torvald.aksis.uib.no/colt/ http://icame/newcd.htm
British Academic Spoken English (BASE) corpus • Being developed at the Universities of Warwick and Reading, it consists of 160 lectures and 40 seminars recorded in a variety of university departments. Holdings are distributed across four broad disciplinary groups, each represented by 40 lectures and 10 seminars.	http://www.rdg.ac.uk/AcaDepts/ll/base_corpus/

[1] In compiling this list, we have drawn heavily on the excellent, and far more extensive, information provided on the following websites complied at the University of Lancaster by:
    David Lee: http://devoted.to/corpora
    Richard Xiao: http://bowland-files.lancs.ac.uk/corplang/cbls/corpora.asp

Corpus	How to find out more
• Designed as a companion to MICASE (see below), however, unlike MICASE it does not include speech events other than lectures and seminars. • The majority of the recordings are on digital video rather than audio tape.	
British National Corpus (BNC) • 100 million words of English • Written (90%) includes, newspapers, periodicals and journals books letters and memoranda, essays, etc. • Spoken part (10%) includes conversation, recorded in a demographically balanced way, as well as a range of spoken language from business or government meetings, radio shows and phone-ins, etc.	http://www.natcorp.ox.ac.uk/what/index.html
Brown corpus • 1 million words of American English texts printed in 1961. • The Brown Corpus of Standard American English was the first of the modern, computer readable, general corpora. • Consists of texts sampled from 15 different text categories.	http://khnt.hit.uib.no/icame/manuals/brown/INDEX.HTM http://clwww.essex.ac.uk/w3c/corpus_ling/content/corpora/list/private/brown/brown.html
Collins Wordbanks Online English corpus • 56 million words, online corpus • American books, ephemera and radio (10m words) • British books, ephemera, radio, newspapers, magazines (36m words) • British transcribed speech (10m words)	http://www.collins.co.uk/Corpus/CorpusSearch.aspx
Cambridge and Nottingham Corpus of discourse in English (CANCODE) • 5 million words of spoken English discourse	http://www.cambridge.org/elt/corpus/cancode.htm

Corpus	How to find out more
• Represents spoken English in different contexts of use including casual conversation, workplace, and academic settings across different speaker relationships from intimate to professional.	
Cambridge International Corpus (CIC) • 1 billion words • British English: 450 million written, 17 million spoken including the CANCODE corpus, 20 million written academic, 30 million written business, 1 million spoken business (CANBEC see below) • American English: 200 million written, 22 million spoken the Cambridge-Cornell Corpus of Spoken North American English, 7 million written academic, 30 million written business • Learner English: 19 million learners' written English (the Cambridge Learner Corpus), 12 million error coded learner written English	http://www.cambridge.org/elt/
Corpus of English as a Lingua Franca in Academic Settings (ELFA) • Aims to collect 500,000 words of spoken English as a Lingua Franca in an academic context. • The data are being collected primarily in international degree programs and other programs conducted in English at the University of Tampere in Finland but also at the Tampere Technological University and at international conferences.	http://www.uta.fi/laitokset/kielet/engf/ research/elfa/project.htm
Corpus of Spoken Professional American English (CSPAE) • 2 million words of spoken American English • 1 million from White House question and answer sessions	http://www.athel.com/cspa.html

Corpus	How to find out more
• 1 million mainly from academic discussions such as faculty council meetings and committee meetings related to testing.	
Frown corpus (Freiburg version of Brown corpus) • 1 million word copy of the Brown corpus collected in 1991 by researchers at the University of Freiberg, Germany, making it a valuable resource for the study of language change in this period.	http://khnt.hit.uib.no/icame/manuals/frown/INDEX.HTM
Freiburg-LOB Corpus of British English (FLOB) • 1 million word copy of the LOB corpus collected in 1991, making it a valuable resource for the study of language change in a British context.	http://khnt.hit.uib.no/icame/manuals/flob/INDEX.HTM http://khnt.hit.uib.no/icame/manuals/lobman/INDEX.HTM (tagged version)
Hong Kong Corpus of Spoken English (HKCSE) • Two-millions words of audio-recordings comprising four sub-corpora, each consisting of half a million words of naturally occurring talk. • The four sub-corpora represent the main spoken genres found in the Hong Kong context: academic discourses, business discourses, conversations, and public discourses. • Each sub-corpus consists of a variety of discourse types and participants. • All the 200 hours of spoken discourse have been transcribed orthographically; 53% is also prosodically transcribed.	http://www.engl.polyu.edu.hk/department/academicstaff/chengwinnie.html
International Corpus of Learner English – ICLE • Over 2 million words of writing by learners of English from 14	http://www.fltr.ucl.ac.be/fltr/germ/etan/cecl/Cecl-Projects/Icle/icle.htm

Corpus	How to find out more
different mother tongue backgrounds (e.g. Brazilian Portuguese, Czech, Dutch, Finnish, French, German, Japanese, Polish, Spanish and Swedish)	
International Corpus of English – (ICE) • The International Corpus of English (ICE) began in 1990 with the primary aim of collecting material for comparative studies of English worldwide. • Each ICE corpus consists of one million words of spoken and written English produced after 1989. • To ensure compatibility among the component corpora, each team is following a common corpus design, as well as a common scheme for grammatical annotation.	http://www.ucl.ac.uk/english-usage/ice/ **ICE Great Britain** http://www.ucl.ac.uk/english-usage/ice/icegb.htm **ICE East Africa** http://www.ucl.ac.uk/english-usage/ice/iceea.htm **ICE India** http://www.ucl.ac.uk/english-usage/ice/iceind.htm **ICE New Zealand** http://www.ucl.ac.uk/english-usage/ice/icenz.htm **ICE Philippines** http://www.ucl.ac.uk/english-usage/ice/icephil.htm **ICE Singapore** http://www.ucl.ac.uk/english-usage/ice/icesin.htm **ICE Ireland** http://www.qub.ac.uk/ice-ireland
Lancaster/IBM Spoken English Corpus (SEC) • 53,000 words • Mainly taken from British radio broadcasts from the mid 1980s, and includes commentaries, lectures, news, etc.	http://nora.hd.uib.no/icame/lanspeks.html
Lancaster-Oslo/Bergen corpus (LOB) • 1 million words of British English texts printed in 1961 • Compiled by researchers in Lancaster, Oslo and Bergen. It consists of one million words of British English texts from 1961. The texts for the corpus were sampled from 15 different text categories.	http://khnt.hit.uib.no/icame/manuals/lob/INDEX.HTM

Corpus	How to find out more
Longman Written American Corpus • 100 million words • Consisting of running text from newspapers, journals, magazines, best-selling novels, technical and scientific writing, and coffee-table books.	http://www.longman.com/dictionaries/corpus/lcawritt.html
Longman American Spoken Corpus • 5 million words • Recordings undertaken by the University of California at Santa Barbara. • Represents the everyday conversations of more than 1000 Americans of various age groups, levels of education, and ethnicity, and includes speakers from over 30 US States.	http://www.longman.com/dictionaries/corpus/lcaspoke.html
The Longman Learners' Corpus • 10 million word computerized database made up entirely of language written by students of English	http://www.longman.com/dictionaries/corpus/lclearn.html
London-Lund corpus • 500,000 words • A combination of two projects: the Survey of English Usage (SEU) and the Survey of Spoken English (SSE). • Consists of spoken English in the form of dialogue and monologue collected recorded from 1953 to 1987.	http://khnt.hit.uib.no/icame/manuals/LONDLUND/INDEX.HTM
Limerick Corpus of Irish English (LCIE) • 1 million words of Irish English • Designed as a comparative corpus to CANCODE using the same design rationale based around speaker relationship and context of use.	http://www.ul.ie/~lcie/homepage.htm
Limerick-Belfast (LIBEL) Corpus of Academic Spoken English • 1 million words of spoken academic	www.mic.ul.ie/ivacs

Corpus	How to find out more
English recorded in two institutions on the island of Ireland. 50% from University of Limerick, 50% from Queen's University Belfast. • Consists of recordings from sites of teaching and learning, small and large lectures, tutorials, seminars, colloquia.	
Macquarie Corpus of Written Australian English (ACE) • 1 million words of written Australian English from 1986. • Designed to parallel the American Brown corpus.	http://www.ling.mq.edu.au/centres/sc/research.htm
The Macmillan World English corpus • Over 220 million words of spoken and written mostly British and American English. • The ratio is about 9:1 (written : spoken). • Sources include Academic discourse, print and broadcast journalism, fiction, recorded conversations (including telephone calls), recorded business meetings, general non-fiction, answerphone messages, emails, legal texts, academic seminars, cultural studies texts, radio documentaries, broadcast interviews, ELT course books, texts written by learners of English, including essays and examination scripts.	http://www.macmillandictionary.com/essential/about/corpus.htm
Michigan Corpus of Academic Spoken English (MICASE) • 1.8 million words available and searchable online • Consisting of 152 transcripts of spoken academic English recorded at the University of Michigan including lectures, labs, seminars, dissertation defences, interviews, meeting, tutorials and service encounters.	http://www.lsa.umich.edu/eli/micase/index.htm http://micase.umdl.umich.edu/m/micase/

Corpus	How to find out more
Santa Barbara Corpus of Spoken American English (CSAE) • Based on 100 of recordings of spontaneous speech from all over the United States, representing a wide variety of people of different regional origins, ages, occupations, and ethnic and social backgrounds. • It includes conversation, gossip, arguments, on-the-job talk, card games, city council meetings, sales pitches, classroom lectures, political speeches, bedtime stories, sermons, weddings, etc.	http://www.ldc.upenn.edu/ http://projects.ldc.upenn.edu/SBCSAE
SCOTS project • Project underway which aims to represent all the contemporary languages spoken in Scotland by building a corpus of spoken and written data. • Initially, its focus is on the collection of Scottish English and Scots texts, but it is also planned to include Gaelic and material from non-indigenous community languages such as Punjabi, Urdu and Chinese.	http://www.scottishcorpus.ac.uk/
TOEFL 2000 Spoken and Written Academic Language Corpus – T2K-SWAL Corpus • 2.8 million words; 490 of spoken and written texts • Representing spoken and written registers at four US universities including classroom teaching, study groups, textbooks, service encounters.	No webpage available, see Biber, D., S. Conrad, R. Reppen, P. Byrd, and M. Helt. 2002. 'Speaking and writing in the university: A multi-dimensional comparison'. *TESOL Quarterly*, 36 (1): 9–48
Webcorp • This interface site allows the user to run concordances using the internet as a corpus	http://www.webcorp.org.uk/

Corpus	How to find out more
Wellington Corpus of Spoken New Zealand English (WSC) • 1 million words of spoken New Zealand English collected in the years 1988 to 1994. • The corpus consists of 2,000-word extracts and comprises different proportions of formal, semi-formal and informal speech. Both monologue and dialogue categories are included and there is broadcast as well as private material collected in a range of settings. • 75% percent of the corpus is informal dialogue.	http://khnt.hit.uib.no/icame/manuals/wsc/INDEX.HTM http://www.vuw.ac.nz/lals/corpora/index.aspx
Wellington Corpus of Written New Zealand English (WWC) • 1 million words of written New Zealand English collected from writings published in the years 1986 to 1990. • The WWC has the same basic categories as the Brown Corpus of written American English and the Lancaster-Oslo-Bergen corpus (LOB) of written British English . The corpus also parallels the structure of the Macquarie Corpus of written Australian English. • Consists of 2,000 word excerpts on a variety of topics. Text categories include press material, religious texts, skills, trades and hobbies, popular lore, biography, scholarly writing and fiction.	http://khnt.hit.uib.no/icame/manuals/wellman/INDEX.HTM http://www.vuw.ac.nz/lals/corpora/index.aspx
Vienna-Oxford International Corpus of English (VOICE) • 1 million word target • Consists of naturally occurring, non-scripted and mostly face-to-face conversations in English as a lingua franca (ELF).	http://www.univie.ac.at/voice/

Corpus	How to find out more
• Speakers recorded in VOICE are described as 'fairly fluent ELF speakers from a wide range of first language backgrounds'. • So far, VOICE includes approximately 800 ELF speakers with 50 different first languages. • Interactions recorded in a variety of settings including (professional, educational, informal), functions (exchanging information, enacting social relationships), participants' roles and relationships (acquainted vs. unacquainted, symmetrical vs. asymmetrical).	

Business English Corpora

Corpus	How to find out more
Cambridge and Nottingham Business English Corpus (CANBEC) • 1 million words of spoken business English recorded in Britain and other countries. • Forms part of CIC (see above).	http://www.cambridge.org/elt/ http://www.nottingham.ac.uk/english/research/cral/projects.html
Wolverhampton Business English Corpus • 10,186,259 words of written business English • Collected from 23 different web sites around the world within a six period 1999–2000. • Includes a wide variety of categories including product descriptions, company press releases, annual financial reports, business journalism, academic research papers, political speeches and government reports.	http://www.elda.org/catalogue/en/text/W0028.html http://www.clg.wlv.ac.uk/projects/style/corpus/index.php

Some examples of non-English corpora (not comprehensive)

Banca dati dell'italiano parlato (BADIP) • 500,000 words of spoken Italian developed at the University of Graz (Austria) • Accessible online edition	http://languageserver.uni-graz.at/badip/
Basque Spoken Corpus • 42 narratives by native Basque/ Euskara speakers, who tell the story of a silent movie they have just watched to someone else. • Available with sound files in MP3 format as well as transcripts,	http://www.elda.org/catalogue/en/ speech/S0123.html
Chambers-Rostand Corpus of Journalistic French • Almost 1 million words of journalistic French. • Made up of 1723 articles published in 2002 and 2003, taken from three French daily newspapers: *Le Monde, L'Humanité, La Dépêche du Midi* • Articles are categorised into types: editorial, cultural, sports, national news, international news, finance.	http://www.ota.ahds.ac.uk/%20texts/ 2491.html
Chinese – English Translation Base • More than 100,000 English translation units together with their Chinese translation equivalents and vice versa.	http://www.corpus.bham.ac.uk/ccl/ chinese.htm
Corpus di Italiano Scritto (CORIS) • 100 million words of written Italian sampled from categories such as press, academic prose, legal and administrative and ephemera. • Accessible online	http://corpus.cilta.unibo.it:8080/ CORISCorpQuery.html
Corpas Náisiúnta na Gaeilge/ National Corpus of Irish • Consists of approximately 30 million words of text from a variety of	Corpas Na Gaeilge 1600–1882: The Irish language Corpus. 2004. Dublin: Royal Irish Academy.

contemporary books, newspapers, periodicals and dialogue. • approximately 8 million words are SGML tagged.	
Corpus Oral de Referencia del Español Contemporáneo. COREC • 1,100,000 of words of Spoken Spanish collected at Universidad Autónoma de Madrid. • Administrative, scientists, conversational and familiar, education, humanistic, instructions (megafonía), legal, playful, politicians, journalistic.	http://www.lllf.uam.es/corpus/ corpus_oral.html **Sample of corpus** http://www.lllf.uam.es/corpus/ corpus_lee.html#B4
The CREA corpus of Spanish • 133 million words • Sampled from a wide range of written (90%) and spoken (10%) text categories produced in all Spanish-speaking countries between 1975–1999 (divided into 5-year periods). The domains covered in the corpus include science and technology, social sciences, religion and thought, politics and economics, arts, leisure and ordinary life, health, and fiction. • The texts in the corpus are distributed evenly between Spain and America.	http://www.rae.es/ http://corpus.rae.es/creanet.html
Czech National Corpus (CNC) • Written component: 100 million words including fiction and non-fiction texts. • Spoken component: 800,000 words of transcription of spontaneous spoken language sampled according to four sociolinguistic criteria: speaker sex, age, educational level and discourse type.	http://ucnk.ff.cuni.cz/english/
Hungarian National Corpus (HNC) • 153.7 million words of texts produced from the mid-1990s onwards.	http://corpus.nytud.hu/ mnsz/index_eng.html

• Divided into five sub corpora, each representing a written text type: media (52.7%), literature (9.43%), scientific texts (13.34%), official documents (12.95%) and informal texts (e.g. electronic forum discussion, 11.58%).	
Le corpus BAF (English-French parallel corpus) • Circa 400,000 words per language. • Contains four sub-sets of texts: institutional, scientific articles, technical documentation, Jules Verne's novel *De la terre à la lune* in French and English.	http://rali.iro.umontreal.ca/
TRACTOR archive • Contains monolingual and multilingual language resources available on-line in the following languages: Bulgarian, Croatian, Czech, Dutch, English, Estonian, Finnish, French, German, Greek, Hungarian, Italian, Latvian, Lithuanian, Polish, Romanian, Russian, Serbian, Slovak, Slovene, Swedish, Turkish, Ukrainian and Uzbek.	http://www.corpus.bham.ac.uk/ccl/ services.htm#tractor

Appendix 2:
Classified list of 100 idioms extracted from randomly selected CANCODE files

	Evaluation of people's actions/states: clausal	occurrences
1	turn round and say	139
2	can't/couldn't help but/-ing	69
3	be/have a/some good laugh(s)	41
4	keep an/one's eye on	37
5	take the mickey (x3)	25
6	get on sb's nerves	24
7	be a (complete/right/bit of a/absolute/real) pain (in the neck/***)	21
8	pull to/take to/go to/be in pieces	15
9	be on the go	11
10	make sense of sth	10
11	have/go through a rough time	9
12	do/say sth behind sb's back	9
13	get it together	8
14	get the message	8
15	get a move on	6
16	chop and change	6
17	have a roof over one's head	6
18	pull sb's leg	5
19	have/give sb a hard time	5
20	be/get done for (crime)	5
21	drive (sb) round the bend	3
22	fall in with sb	3
23	put a stop to sth	3
24	have (got)/fix one's sights on	3
25	look down one's nose at sb	2
26	be in no mood to	2
27	be left to one's own devices	2

	Evaluation of people's actions/states: clausal	occurrences
28	suffer in silence	2
29	drag one's heels	2
30	tell/give sb the time of day	2
31	like the sound of one's own voice	1
32	ready, willing and able	1
33	drive like the clappers	1
34	jet off	1
35	wash one's hands of sb/sth	1
36	have/get the/an upper hand	1
37	dart round	1
38	can't/couldn't put it down (book)	1

	Evaluation of things/events: clausal	
39	make sense (x2)	157
40	be a (complete/right/bit of a/absolute/real) pain (in the neck/***)	52
41	be/go over sb's head	8
42	be/go (all) to pot	6
43	(let sth) wash over sb	5
44	bring sth to/come to the fore	4
45	can't go wrong	4
46	ring true	4
47	it's a small world	4
48	not be sb's thing	3
49	give sb/have this/that rosy glow	2

	Names for people	
50	whats-her-name/-face/whats-his-name/-face	16
51	man/woman of the world	3
52	male chauvinist pig	2
53	loose woman	2
54	no-hoper	1

	Names for things/events	
55	pub crawl	5
56	crazy paving	4
57	quantum leap	3
58	dead end	3
59	happy ending	2
60	slap-up (meal/party)	2
61	the arms race	1
62	magic mushrooms	1
63	the generation gap	1
64	stage fright	1

	Discourse routines and interjections (situation-bound)	
65	fair enough	240
66	there you go	209
67	good god	44
68	the only thing is/was	41
69	good grief	38
70	how's it going	21
71	let's face it	20
72	good heavens	16
73	for goodness sake	14
74	oops/whoops a daisy	8
75	or not as the case may be	3
76	by the by	3
77	now/look there's a thing	2
78	like mother like daughter	2
79	me and my big mouth	1
80	what's this, scotch mist?	1

	Miscellaneous adjectival/adverbial and prepositional phrases	
81	at the end of the day	221
82	all over the place [everywhere]	75
83	over the top	53
84	half the time	34
85	up to date	30
86	along those lines/the lines of	20
87	by and large	19
88	left right and centre	12
89	part and parcel	9
90	by the look(s) of it	8
91	out of the ordinary	6
92	true to life	3
93	over and above	3
94	tongue in cheek	2
95	safe and sound	2
96	give or take	2
97	by the sound of it	2
98	to and fro	1
99	back-breaking (work)	1
100	deaf as a post	1

Appendix 3:
Classified list of 100 idioms extracted from randomly selected CIC North American spoken files (5m words)

	Evaluation of people's actions/states: clausal	occurrences
1	figure sth out	348
2	screw up	151
3	freak out	56
4	get over sb/sth	54
5	piss sb off	53
6	put up with sth	44
7	be sick of sth	43
8	make fun of sb	40
9	stay away from sth	40
10	throw up	35
11	make out	25
12	hook up with sb	24
13	can't get over sth	24
14	get sth over with	24
15	put sth off	24
16	make up for sth	23
17	pick on sb	21
18	take it easy	21
19	have no clue	17
20	get one's hands on sth	17
21	hang on to	13
22	give sb a hard time	12
23	starve to death	11
24	keep sb company	9
25	hang around with sb	7
26	pump sth up	7
27	keep one's eye out	7
28	mess up on sb	7

	Evaluation of people's actions/states: clausal	occurrences
29	be in limbo	6
30	be hung over	6
31	give sb credit for sth	6
32	get a word in	4
33	be so out of it	4
34	fall into a/the trap (of)	2
35	not see hide nor hair of sb	2
36	compare notes	2
37	hit the jackpot	2
38	muck around	1
39	smack sth off	1
40	give sb the heat	1
41	look sb straight in the eye	1
42	be in for the kill	1
43	see stars	1
44	go back to one's old ways	1
45	be out like a baby	1
46	lose one's touch	1
47	rant and rave	1

	Evaluation of things/events: clausal	
48	(not) make (any) sense	276
49	how come X?	111
50	it all comes/came down to	40
51	it's a small world	12
52	come into play	8
53	(things/situation) go downhill	4
54	be/go over one's head	1
55	nothing ventured nothing gained	1
56	I say what the hell	1
57	you get your brains kicked out	1

	Names for people	
58	the bad guy(s)	12
59	what's-her-name	6
60	my loved one	2
61	best man	2
62	the ho patrol	2
63	a dead rag	1
64	big green giant	1
65	a piece of trash	1
66	sugar daddy	1

	Names for things/events	
67	(no) big deal	179
68	soap opera	24
69	rat race	12
70	odd balls	3
71	pony tail	3
72	small talk	2
73	shot in the dark	2
74	hot toddy	2
75	a roller coaster ride	2
76	cheat sheet	1

	Discourse routines and interjections (situation-bound)	
77	oh my gosh!	149
78	oh boy!	71
79	what's up with x?	30
80	I'll be darned!	30
81	take it easy!	27
82	bless you!	15
83	knock on wood	10
84	I swear to God	9
85	I/you wish!	8
86	you can't go wrong	7
87	here's the thing	6

	Discourse routines and interjections (situation-bound)	
88	God bless!	4
89	those were the days!	4
90	want to bet!	1

	Miscellaneous adjectival/adverbial and prepositional phrases	
91	once in a while	278
92	ahead of time	50
93	top notch	13
94	(no) strings attached	9
95	just for the hell/heck of it	9
96	bumper to bumper	5
97	hands on	3
98	smack dab in the middle	2
99	till you're blue in the face	1
100	right from the shoulder	1

Author index

Aarts, B., 114
Aarts, J., 105
Adolphs, S., 2, 4
Adophs, S. and Carter, R. A., 184, 244
Adolphs, S. and Durow, V., 76
Adolphs, S. and O'Keeffe, A., 154
Adolphs, S., Brown, B., Carter, R. A., Crawford, P. and
    Sahota, O. S., 240
Aijmer, K., 20, 164, 166, 171
Alexander, R. J., 54, 82, 164
Allan, Q., 242
Altenberg, B., 64
Altenberg, B. and Granger, S., 19, 23, 94
Amador Moreno, C.P., McCarthy, M., and O'Keeffe, A.,
    157
Andersen, G., 20, 171
Antaki, C., 148
Antaki, C., Houtkoop-Steenstra, H. and Rapley, M., 148
Anton, M., 229
Arnaud, P. and Savignon, S., 94
Aston, G., 4, 19, 23, 24 27, 191
Aston, G. and Burnard, L., 205

Bach, K. and Harnish, R. M., 166
Bahms, J., Burmeister, H. and Vogel, T., 94
Baker, M., 19
Bampfield, A., Lubelska, D. and Matthews, M., 243
Banbrook, L. and Skehan, P., 239
Bargiela-Chiappini, F. and Harris, S., 204, 205
Barron, A., 168
Barsalou, L., 179
Baynham, M., 23
Benson, M. and Benson, E., 62
Bergstrom, K., 98
Bernardi, S., 24
Biber, D., 1
Biber, D. and Conrad, S., 61, 199
Biber, D., Conrad S., and Reppen, R., 1, 2, 4
Biber, D., Conrad, S. and Cortes, V., 23, 62
Biber, D., Conrad, S., Reppen, R., Byrd, P. and Helt, M.,
    199
Biber, D. and Jones, J. K., 199
Biber, D. Johansson, S., Leech, G., Conrad, S. and
    Finegan, E., 4, 17, 61, 66, 100, 174, 201
Binchy, J., 200
Blum-Kulka, S., 168, 176, 233
Blum-Kulka, S. and Olshtain, E., 166
Blum-Kulka, S., House, J. and Kasper, G., 166

Boden, D., 206, 214–15, 216
Boers, F., 97
Boers, E and Demecheleer, M., 87
Bolinger, D., 59, 63, 134
Boucher, V. J., 20
Boxer, D. and Cohen, A. D., 221, 227
Boxer, D. and Pickering, L., 22
Braine, G., 28
Braun, S. and Chambers, A., 24
Breen, M., 26
Brinton, L., 171
Brock, C., 240
Brown, P. and Levinson, S., 73, 113, 166 174
Bruner, J., 229
Bunton, D., 200
Burns, A., 21
Burns, A., Joyce, H., and Gollin, S., 21
Burrows, J., 18
Bygate, M., Skehan, P. and Swain, M., 27

Callahan, L., 21
Cambridge Advanced Learner's Dictionary (CALD), 3
Cameron, L., 195
Canale, M. and Swain, M., 26
Candlin, C., 169
Carroll, J. B., Davies, P. and Richman, B., 48
Carter, R. A., 18, 21, 22, 27, 164, 184, 196
Carter, R. A. and Fung, L., 28, 172
Carter, R. A. and McCarthy, M. J., 3, 4, 12, 17–18, 27, 37,
    38, 68, 90, 114, 118, 120, 127, 128, 131, 134, 142, 166, 171,
    172, 184, 201, 237–8
Carter, R. A. and McRae, J., 191
Carter, R. A., Hughes, R. and McCarthy, M. J., 115–18, 130
Carter, R. A., Knight, D., Bayoumi, S., Mills, S.,
    Crabtree, A., Adolphs, S. and Pridmore, T., 142, 244
Celce-Murcia, M. and Olshtain, E., 221, 245
Chafe, W., 74, 120, 177
Chafe, W., DuBois, J. and Thompson, S., 120
Chambers, A., 24
Chambers, A. and Kelly, V., 24
Chambers, A. and O'Sullivan, I., 24
Chambers, A. and Rostand, S., 24
Channell, J., 74, 174, 177, 178
Chappell, H., 110
Charles, Maggie, 200
Charles, Mirjaliisa, 204, 205
Charteris-Black, J., 87
Cheepen, C., 159

Cheng, W. and Warren, M., 2
Chomsky, N., 60, 188
Church, K. and Gale, W., 19
Clancy, B., 176
Claridge, C., 19
Clark, H. H. and Lucy, P., 166
Clemen, G., 174
Coates, J., 142
Cobb, T., 24
Collins, P., 107, 108, 131, 133
Conley, J. M. and O'Barr, W. M., 20
Connor, U., 205
Conrad, S., 199, 242
Cook, G., 27, 31, 191
Corbett, J. and Douglas, F., 20
Cornilescu, A., 122
Cortes, V., 61, 66, 200
Cosme, C., 23
Cotterill, J., 20
Coulmas, R., 62, 63
Coulmas, E., 62, 96, 164
Coulthard, M., 20, 224
Coulthard, M. and Ashby, M., 223, 233
Coupland, J., 169
Coupland, N. and Ylanne-McEwen, V., 170–1
Coupland. J., Coupland, N. and Robinson, J., 169
Cowie, A. R., 63
Coxhead, A., 4, 50, 198–9
Crosling, G. and Ward, L., 205
Crowdy, S., 1
Crystal, D., 27
Cucchiarini, C., Strik, H. and Boves, L., 158

Dagneaux E., Denness S., Granger S. and Meunier, E., 23
Dagut, M., 118
Dannerer, M., 204
Dash, R., 183
Davies, B. and Harre, R., 164
De Cock, S., 23, 62, 63, 64–5, 94
De Cock, S. and Granger, S., 23
De Cock, S., Granger, S., Leech, G. and McEnery, T., 23
Degand, L. and Bestgen, Y., 82
Delin, J. L., 131
Depractere, I., 122
Dines, E., 178
Donohue, W. and Diez, M., 214
Dornyei, Z. and Thurrell, S., 227
Douglas, F., 20
Drew, P., 233
Drew, P. and Heritage, J., 206
Drew, P. and Holt, E., 63, 84
Drummond, K. and Hopper, R., 140
DuBois, S., 178
Du Bois, J. W, Schuetze-Coburn, S, Cumming, S. and Paolino, D., 120
Ducharme, D. and Bernard, R., 228
Duncan, S. and Niederehe, G., 142

Eastwood, J., 121
Edge, J., 242
Edmonson, W and House, J., 166
Eggins, S. and Slade, D., 169

Ellis, R., 118
Erman, B., 72, 171, 173
Evison, J., McCarthy, M. J. and O'Keeffe, A., 74, 178, 179

Fairclough, N., 244
Farr, F., 169, 176, 238–9, 240, 241
Farr, F and McCarthy M. J., 127
Farr, F, Murphy, B. and O'Keeffe, A., 175
Fellegy, A.M., 142, 148
Fenk-Oczlon, G. 82
Fernando, C., 90
Fernando, C. and Flavell, R., 62
Fillmore, C. J., 94, 158
Finell, A., 171
Firth, A., 204, 205
Firth, J. R., 33, 59
Fisher, S. and Groce, S., 233
Fishman, P. M., 1978
Flowerdew L , 24
Flowerdew, J., 24, 42
Fonagy, I., 164
Fotos, S. and Ellis, R., 118
Fox, G., 118
Franken, N., 177
Francis, G., 42
Fraser, B., 39, 171 174
Fraser, B. and Nolen, W., 168
Freddi, M., 199
Fries, C.C., 140
Frith, J.R., 18
Fukushima, S. and Iwata, Y., 168

Garcez, P., 205
Gardner, R., 140, 148, 227
Gavioli, L., 2, 24
Gellerstam, M., 19
Geluykens, R., 131
Gibbon, D., 93–4
Gibbons, J., 20
Gibbs, R. W., 79, 87
Gibbs, R. W. and O'Brien, J. E., 79, 87
Gilmore, A., 22
Gilquin, G., 23
Gimenez, J., 205
Girard, M. and Sionis, C., 77
Gledhill, C., 199
Gnutzmann, C., 109
Goffman, E., 166, 242
Graddol, D., 28
Granger, S., 23, 62, 107
Granger, S., Hung, J., and Petch-Tyson, S., 23
Greatbatch, D., 206, 234–5
Greenbaum, S. and Nelson, G., 114
Grice, H. P., 121
Grimshaw, A., 204

Haastrup, K. and Henriksen, B., 54
Hakuta, K., 63
Hall J. K. and Verplaetse, L.S., 221, 228
Hall, J. K. and Walsh, M., 221, 228
Halliday, M.A.K., 59, 105
Halliday, M. A. K. and Hasan, R., 42

Halmari, H., 205
Harwood, N., 199
Haslerud, V. and Stenstrom, AB., 20
Hasund, K., 20
Hasund, K. and Stenstrom, A-B., 20
Hatch, E., 245
Hatcher, A. G., 106
Heffer, C., 20
Henriksen, B., 54
Heritage, J. and Greatbatch, D., 233
Heritage, J. and Watson, D., 89
Hever, B., 84
Hewings, A and Hewings, M., 118
Hoey, M. R., 18, 42, 95
Holmes, J., 20, 21, 37, 169–70, 204
Honeyfield, J., 48
Hopper, P., 136
Hopper, P., 70, 136
Hopper, R., Knapp, M. L. and Scott, L., 94
Horn, G. M., 87
House, J., 28
Howarth, P., 63
Hubler, A., 174
Hughes, R., and McCarthy, M. J., 23
Hulstijn, J. and Marchena, E., 94
Hunston, S., 4, 242
Hunston, S. and Francis, G., 17
Hunston, S., Francis, G. and Manning, E., 17
Hutchby, I. and Wooffitt, R., 233
Hyland, K., 199
Hyland, K. and Tse, P., 199

Iacobucci, C., 159
Ihalainen, O., 20
Irujo, S., 94
Itkonen, E., 105

James, A., 28
Jefferson, G., 178, 227
Jenkins, J., 28, 29
Jespersen, J. O., 121
Johansson, S. and Ebeling, J., 19
Johansson, S. and Hofland, K., 19
Johansson, S., Ebeling, J., and Hofland, K., 19
Johns T., 24
Johnson, K., 221, 245
Johnstone, R., 229
Jones, L. B. and Jones, L. K., 131
Jucker, A. H., Smith, S. W. and Lildge, T., 178, 179
Jucker, A., 171, 178

Kallen, J. L., and Kirk, J. M., 20
Kanoksilapatham, B., 199
Kasper, G., 168, 221, 228, 229
Kellerman. E., 74
Kendon, A., 140
Kennedy, C. and Miceli, T., 24
Kennedy, G., 2
Kettemann, B., 23
Kim, K., 131
King, P., 19
Kirk, J. M., 20

Knowles, G., 2
Ko, J., Schallert, D. L. and Walters, K., 229
Koester, A., 204
Komter, M., 169
Kovecses, Z. and Szabo, R., 87
Kramsch, C. and Sullivan, P., 95
Krashen, S. D., 24
Kucera, H. and Francis, W.N., 122
Kuiper, K. and Flindall, M., 171, 185
Kunin, A., 62

Labov, W., 89
Lakoff, G., 174
Lakoff, R., 107
Lantolf, J. R., 228, 229
Lantolf, J. R and Appel, G., 55, 228
Lantolf, J. and Thorne, S., 228
Lapidus, N. and Otheguy, R., 21
Larrue, J. and Trognon, B., 206
Lattey, E., 96
Lave, J. and Wenger, E., 242
Laver, J., 169
Laviosa, S., 19
Lazar, G., 87
Lazaraton, A., 228
Lee, W. Y., 26
Leech, G., 2, 105, 169
Leech, G. N. and Short, M. H., 18
Lenk, U., 171
Lenko-Szymanska, A., 24
Lennon, R., 56
Lewis, M., 60, 63
Liu, D., 95
Long, M.H. and Sato, C., 240
Louw, B., 14, 18, 54, 104
Luzon Marco, M. J., 199

Macaulay, R. K. S., 171, 178
Machado, A., 229
Maia, B., 4
Makkai, A., 62
Malinowski, B., 169
Malmkjaer, K., 28
Marinai, E., Peters, C. and Picchi, E., 19
Markee, N. R., 221, 228
Markkanen, R. and Schroder, H., 174
Marquez-Reiter, R., 166
Massam, D., 134
Mauranen A., 28, 29, 204
Maynard, S. K., 140, 148
McCarthy, M. J., 2, 4, 11, 21, 23, 43, 62, 64, 80, 81–2, 87–90, 114, 147, 151, 152–3, 169, 170–1, 221, 245
McCarthy, M. J., and Carter, R. A., 23, 80, 89, 114, 118, 221, 245, 248
McCarthy, M. J. and Handford, M., 90, 206, 210, 215
McCarthy, M. J. and O'Dell, F., 10, 38, 43, 48, 60, 96–7, 217–18
McCarthy, M. J. and O'Keeffe, A., 21
McCarthy, M. J., McCarten, J. and Sandiford, H., 22, 77, 98, 101–2, 138, 139, 247
McCarthy, M. J., O'Keeffe, A. and Walsh, S., 180
McCarthy. M. J. and Walsh, S., 222, 227

McConvell, P., 134
McDavid, V., 122
McEnery, T. and Wilson, A., 1–2
McEnery, T, Xiao, R. and Tono, Y., 2, 4
McGlone, M. S., Cacciari, C. and Glucksberg, S., 87
McLay, V., 96–7
Meara, P., 54
Meara, P. and Rodriguez Sanchez, I., 54
Medgyes, P., 28
Meierkord, C., 94
Meunier, E., 23
Meyer, C. E., 3
Mezynski, K., 24
Miller, G., 66
Miller, J. and Weinert, R., 132
Milton, J. and Meara, R., 50
Mitchell, T., 61
Mondada, L. and Pekarek DoehIer, S., 221, 228
Mondorf, B., 20
Moon, R., 82
Moore, T. and Morton, J., 200
Mori, J., 221, 227, 228
Mott, H. and Petrie, H., 142
Mumby, D., 216
Murphy, B., and O'Boyle, A., 92, 96, 204

Nash, W. and Stacey, D., 184
Nation, I.S.P., 24, 50
Nattinger, J. and DeCarrico, J., 63
Nelson, M., 205, 208, 216, 217
Nesbitt, C. and Plum, G., 105
Nesi, H., 97
Nesi, H, Sharpling, G. and Ganobcsik-Williams, L., 200
Nesselhauf, N., 96
Newbrook, M., 136
Norrick, N., 82, 84, 171
Nunan, D., 222

O'Halloran, K and Coffin, C., 119
O'Keeffe, A., 74, 163, 178, 206
O'Keeffe, A. and Adolphs, S., 154
O'Keeffe, A. and Farr, F., 2, 4, 221, 222, 240, 242
O'Sullivan, I., and Chambers, A., 24
Oakey, D., 199, 210
Oda, M., 28
Odlin, T., 118
Ohta, A. S., 226
Olshtain, E., 168
Orestrom, B., 140
Ostman, J. O., 72, 171, 173
Overstreet, M. and Yule, G., 178
Owen, C., 24, 27
Owen, M., 1981

Paltridge, B., 199–200
Pan, Y., Scollon, S. and Scollon R., 205
Pawley, A. and Syder, E., 59, 63
Pea, R.D., 244
Peacock, M., 26
Pica, I., and Long, M. H., 240
Piquer Pirez, A. M., 195

Pomerantz, A., 277
Pomerantz, A. and Fehr, B. J., 226
Pope, R., 191
Powell, M., 62, 74, 84, 90, 177
Prince, E., 133
Prodromou, L., 24, 27, 29–30, 63, 76, 94–5, 145, 192–5

Qian, D. D., 54
Quirk, R., Greenbaum, S. Leech, G. and Svartvik, J., 17, 107

Rampton, B., 27
Rampton, B., Roberts, C., Leung, C., and Harris, R., 228
Redeker, G., 171
Redeker, G., 171
Reder S., Harris, K. and Setzler, K., 142, 156
Reppen, R., 199
Reppen, R. and Simpson, R., 7
Ricento, T., 114
Richards, J.C., 48
Riggenbach, H., 221, 245
Roberts, R., 27, 99
Roberts, C. and Sarangi, S., 210
Robinson, W. P., 170
Roger, D., Bull, R and Smyth, S., 142
Rohler, L. R. and Cantlon, D. J., 228
Romaine, S., 171
Rosch, E., 174
Rost, M., 26
Rounds, P., 174
Ruiying, Y. and Allison, D., 199
Rutherford, W. and Sharwood Smith, M., 118

Sacks H., Schegloff, E. A., Jefferson, G., 226
Saferstein, B., 244
Salkie, R., 19
Sallde, R. and Oates, S.L., 19
Santos, D., 19
Santos, D. and Oksefjell, S., 19
Sarangi, S., 241
Scannell, P., 206
Schegloff, E., 148, 227
Schegloff, E. A. and Sacks, H., 227
Schiffrin, D., 39, 171
Schiffrin, D., 171
Schmitt, N., 23, 63, 103–4
Schmitt, N. and Carter, R., 79
Schmitt, D. and Schmitt, N., 216–17
Schneider, K. P., 166, 169
Schroder, H. and Zimmer, D., 174
Scott, M., 5, 8, 12–13
Searle, J. R., 168
Searle, J. R., 166
Seedhouse, P., 221, 228, 245
Seidlhofer, B., 24, 27, 28–9
Semino, E. and Short, M. H., 18
Semino, E., Short, M. and Culpeper, J., 18
Serpollet, N., 19
Short, M., 18
Short, M., Semino, E. and Culpeper, J., 18

Shuy, R., 20
Silver, M., 199
Simpson, R. and Mendis, D., 83, 92, 96
Simpson, R., Briggs, S. L., Ovens, J. and Swales, J. M., 203
Sinclair, J., 4, 17, 18, 23, 27, 54, 59, 60, 75, 87, 100, 102, 103, 104
Sinclair, J. and Coulthard, M., 140, 221, 223, 233
Sinclair, J. and Renouf, A., 37
Sinclair J., Payne J. and P6rez Hernandez, C., 19
Solan, L. M. and Tiersma, R M., 20
Spencer Oatey, H., 205
Spottl, C. and McCarthy, M. J., 62, 77–8, 96
St John, E., 24
St John, M-J., 216
Stahl, S. A. and Fairbanks, M. M., 24
Stenstrom, A-B., 20
Stenstrom, A.-B., Andersen G. and Hasund, I. K., 20
Stevens, V., 24
Strassler, J., 62, 84
Stubbs, M., 14, 18, 37
Sussex, R., 110
Svartvik, J., 2, 23, 145
Svartvik, J. and Quirk, R., 2
Swan, M., 121

Tabossi, R, and Zardon, E., 87
Tajino, A. and Tajino, Y., 28
Tamony, R., 82
Tannen, D., 187
Tao, H., and McCarthy, M. J., 120, 121, 122–6
Teubert, W., 19
Thomas, A., 114
Thomas, J., 183
Thomas, J., and Short, M., 4
Thompson, R., 2, 4, 200
Thompson, R and Tribble, C., 200
Thornbury, S., 10
Thornbury, S. and Slade, D., 21, 23
Thorne, J., 122
Tiersma, P., 20
Tiersma, P and Solan, L, 20
Timmis, I., 27
Tognini-Bonelli, E., 19, 244
Tottie, G., 140
Tracy, K. and Naughton, J. M., 170
Tribble, C., 4, 24
Tribble, C. and Jones, G., 24
Tsui, A. B. M., 242–3
Tsui, A. B. M. and Ki, W. W., 242
Turnbull, J. and Burston, J., 24
Turner, G., 169

Ulijn, J. and Li, X., 205
Ulijn, J. and Murray D., 205

Van Lier, L., 26, 222
Van Peer, W., 18
Van Vaerenbergh L., 19
Vasquez, C., 241
Vasquez, C., and Reppen, R., 241
Vaughan, E., 242
Volk, M., 82
Vygotsky, L. S., 158, 180, 228

Walsh, S., 221, 224, 226, 228, 229, 242, 245
Wang, S-R., 82, 196
Ward, G. and Birner, B., 178
Waring, R., 84
Watts, R. J., 39
Weinert, R., 95
Weinert, R. and Miller, J., 131, 132
Weiyun He, A., 228
Wenger, E., 93, 214, 215, 242
West, M., 198
White, J. and Lightbown, P. M., 240
Wichmann, A., 24
Wichmann, A., Fligelstone S., McEnery, T. and Knowles, G., 24
Widdowson, H. G., 24, 26, 27
Wierzbicka, A., 168
Wilks, C. and Meara, P., 52
Williams, M., 205, 218
Willis, D., 17, 27, 37, 104
Willis, D. and Willis, J., 27
Wilson, P., 114
Wolfson, N., 169
Wolter, B., 52
Wolter, B., 52
Wong, J., 228
Wray, A., 63, 78, 163
Wright, J., 97
Wynne, M., 2, 4, 18

Yamada, H., 205
Yamashita, J., 122
Ylanne-McEwen, V., 169
Yngve, V., 140, 141
Yorio, C. A., 87, 94, 164
Yotsukura, L. A., 205

Zanettin, E., 19
Zanettin F., 19
Zimmerman, D.H. and West, C., 142

Subject index

a bit of, 68, 71
abroad, 15–17
age, 20–1
Academic Word List, 50, 198–9, 216
accent, 187
action research, 24
adjacency pairs, 226–7
adjectives, 37, 42, 43–5, 142, 181
   adjectival expressions, 84
adverbials, 45, 112–13, 84
adverbs, 37, 45, 142, 175, 177, 181
agency, degrees of, 107–9, 114
American English, 17, 21, 27, 68, 83–4, 85–6, 139
   as compared with British English, 3, 44–5, 67–9, 85–6,
     146–7, 221, 243
apologies, 20, 164
approximation, 177–80
articles, 12, 28, 104
aspect, 14, 46, 114, 136
attitudinal meaning, 14, 107–9, 111
Australian Corpus of English (ACE), 11–12
authentic teaching materials, 25–7
auxiliary verbs, 38

bargain, 3–4
British Academic Spoken English (BASE), 204, 244
be, 15, 101, 122, 133–6
binomials, 14–15, 56, 82, 196
body parts, 39–40, 51, 83, 97
border, 103–4
British English, 17, 20, 27, 29, 83–4, 85–6, 106, 179–80
British National Corpus (BNC), 20, 52–3, 205
Brown Corpus, 122

Cambridge and Nottingham Corpus of Business English
   (CANBEC), 90, 206–10
Cambridge and Nottingham Corpus of Discourse in
   English (CANCODE), 21, 22, 64, 204
Cambridge Advanced Learner's Dictionary (CALD), 3
Cambridge International Corpus (CIC), 11–12, 13–14,
   17–18
Cantonese, 190
cause, 14–15
chunks, 13–15, 34, 41, 46–8, 52–3, 56, 58, 60, 60–79, 80–1,
   136, 137, 163–5, 167, 210–14
   and deixis, 42
   and fluency, 76–7
   and intuition, 21, 61

   and native speakers, 76
   pragmatic integrity, 61, 63, 64, 69–70, 73
   processing, 77–9
   length of, 65–8
classroom interactions, 220, 226
cluster analysis, 13–14
code switching, 21, 190–1
cognitive metaphor, 83, 87
colligation, 61, 163
Collins Birmingham University International Language
   Database (COBUILD), 17
collocation, 4, 14–15, 18, 22, 37–8, 53, 56, 59–60, 63, 196
colour, 39, 44–5, 83
commissives, 166
communicative approach, 24
communities of practice, 214, 242
Computer Assisted Language Learning (CALL), 23, 24–5
conditional clauses, 127–30
concordance lines, 4, 8, 15, 24–5, 87, 155, 181
   in exercises for learners, 10, 24–5, 96
concordancing, 8–10,
conflict, 20, 206
conjunctions, 33
constructivist theories of learning, 24
contexts of use, 3, 10–11, 12, 18, 26, 63, 71, 83, 86–7, 95, 96,
   97, 105, 120, 137–8, 163
contractions, 68, 101
contrived examples, 21–2, 26–7, 136
conversation analysis, 63, 205, 223, 228–9, 230–1
conversational routines 62, 82, 84, 86, 163–8
copyright, 2, 5, 7, 8
corpora
   academic, 90–4, 198–205
   availability, 5, 59
   choosing suitable, 3–5
   comparable, 3, 19, 216
   cost of, 248
   business, 90–4, 206–16
   definitions, 1–2, 23
   internet as corpus, 27
   learner corpora, 17, 23, 196, 199
   limitations of, 33, 64, 82–3, 156, 196
   monitor, 17
   monolingual, 19
   multimodal, 2, 5, 142, 156, 183, 222, 244
   non-English, 157
   online, 24
   parallel corpora, 19

reference, 3, 12
spoken, 2, 4, 5–7, 11, 20–1, 23, 30, 44
teacher, 240–3
written, 2, 4, 5, 8, 11, 23
corpus data
collection, 2, 5–6, 8
database texts, 7, 8, 18
file formats, 8
obtaining consent from participants, 5–6 *see also*
copyright
corpus design, 1–2
building own corpus, 1–2, 5–8
criteria, 1, 4, 5, 8
ethics, 5
representativeness, 1, 3
size, 3, 4, 5, 55, 182
Corpus of London Teenage Language (COLT), 20–1
creativity, 18, 90, 184–97
critical linguistics, 119
culture, 26–7, 29, 40–1, 45, 53, 56, 74, 76, 80, 94–5, 98, 114,
155, 158, 179–80, 191, 210, 221
cross-cultural communication, 183, 205
business, 182, 210

days of the week, 39–40
data-driven learning, 24–5, 127, 219
decontextualised language, 26
deductive approach, 118
degree, 43
deixis, 42, 217
delexical words, 36, 37–8, 48, 71
demonstratives, 42
dialect, 20–1
dictionaries, 3, 15–7, 80, 87
directives, 73, 166, 176, 211
discourse analysis, 196, 222–3, 230–1
discourse markers, 20, 22, 33–4, 39, 43–4, 62, 71–3, 82, 84,
86, 122, 123–4, 160, 162–4, 171, 173, 181, 190–1, 205, 223
downtoners, 71, 174–5, 176–7
drilling, 77, 118

ellipsis, 22, 114–6
ELT Journal, 80
email, 190–1
emergent grammar, 70, 136
end weight principle, 122
English
as a first language, 27–8
as a global language, 27–8
as a lingua franca (ELF), 27, 28–9, 80, 98–9, 191, 204,
205, 219
as a second language, 27–8
English Language Teaching, 1, 26, 220–45
English for Specific Purposes, *see also* Language for
Specific Purposes
English for Academic Purposes, 50, 55, 200, 219
Business English, 219
error, 28–29, 95, 196, 229
coding in corpora, 17, 23
evaluation, 43–4, 82, 84, 87–9, 92, 96, 122–4, 126, 136, 185,
224–5, 230

exchange structure, 223–6
exclamatives, 187
eye, 10, 40, 83

face, 38, 71, 73–4, 113, 160, 166, 174, 211–2, 217
face, 83
feedback tokens, 44, *see also* response tokens
fluency, 61, 76–7, 144, 158
confluence, 142, 158, 226
figures of speech, 184
forensic linguistics, 13, 19–20
formality/informality, 90, 92, 96, 105, 106, 109, 113–4, 127,
137, 172, 177, 187
formulaic sequences, 63 *see also* chunks
French, 19, 24, 95, 157, 228
teaching of, 24
French learners of English, 23
frequency, 31–57, 65–6, 84–6, 96
and closed class noun sets, 40
and key words, 12
and native speaker vocabulary size, 31–3
and wordlists, 11
bands, 32, 48
comparisons across corpora, 11
cut-off points, 61, 65
in academic texts, 198, 200–3, 206–8
in business texts, 206–8, 214
of chunks, 13–14, 46–8, 52–3, 69–70
of idioms, 84–6, 96
of response tokens, 156
usefulness for teaching, 40–2, 55, 84
see also key words
functional words, 33, 37, 48

gender and language, 15, 20, 142
genre, 11–3, 17–8, 32, 61–2, 68, 74, 90, 138, 140–1, 145, 200,
206, 210
academic English, 11–2, 28, 50, 55, 68, 90, 92,
199–204
and idioms, 90–4
business English, 90–2, 182, 204–16
fiction, 18, 21
legal language, 20
service encounters, 11–2, 154, 160–2, 163–4, 168, 170–1,
175–6
General Service list, 198
German, 228
German learners of English, 23
get, 37, 48, 59–60, 163–4
get-passive, 18, 106–9
go, 15, 42, 59–60, 182
grammar, 17–18
deterministic, 104–5, 113
pattern grammar, 17
prescriptive grammar, 18, 23
probabilistic, 18, 43, 59–60, 104–5, 113, 116
traditionalist approaches to, 18, 121, 128, 181
Grice's Maxims, 121, 122

hedging, 22, 35, 71, 73–4, 128, 136, 162, 172, 174–6, 183, 187,
189, 199, 211, 241

hesitation, 20, 22
Hong Kong Corpus of Spoken English, 2
human agents/patients, 14–15, 43, 87, 106
humour, 188, 194

I mean, 13, 22, 34–5, 39, 71, 77–8, 124, 131–2, 160, 174, 177, 180
I think, 70, 74, 124, 174–5, 177
idiomatic items, 4, 10, 14–15, 81–99, 114
    and culture, 30, 80, 82, 94–5, 98
    and non-native speakers, 29–30, 94–9
    degrees of syntactic fixedness, 81, 87, 94
    degrees of transparency, 82, 84, 86–7
    frequencies in speech and writing, 52–3
    idiom and open choice principles, 60–1, 63, 75
IELTS, 200
inclusivity, 211–3
inductive approach, 10, 24, 118
intensifiers, 14–15, 38, 43, 112, 144
interpersonal communication, 38, 88, 95, 113, 114, 121, 136, 137, 151, 156–7, 184, 188, 210
International Corpus of Learner English (ICLE), 23, 205
interruptions, 39
intuition, 17, 21, 30, 47, 59, 61, 81, 86, 121, 142, 156, 230
Irish English, 20, 27, 86, 147, 167
Italian, 19

Japanese learners, 148, 227–8
Johnson, Samuel, 17
just, 35, 38, 176

key words, 12–13, 35, 208–9
    and genre, 13
Kielikanava Business English Corpus (BEC), 205

Lancaster/IBM Spoken English Corpus, 2
language contact, 20–1
Language for Specific Purposes, 13, 55, 90, 91, 182
latching, 22, 120
learner autonomy, 24, 47–9, 54–7, 117
    distinction from independence, 55
learner strategies, 56
learners
    advanced, 23, 31, 47–8, 49, 51–2, 54–7, 85
    low-level, 24, 31, 43, 46, 53, 58–9, 195
legal language, 19
lemmas, 32–3, 49, 198
    learner recognition of, 32–3
lexical bundles, 63
lexical density, 22
lexical syllabus, 17
lexical words, 33, 37, 46, 104 *see also* functional words
lexico-grammatical profiles, 14–7, 18
lexicography, 17, 19
like, 12, 20, 68, 188–9, 208
Limerick-Belfast, Corpus of Academic Spoken English (LIBEL CASE), 11–12, 92
Limerick Corpus of Irish English (LCIE), 6–7, 8–9, 11–12
listening skills, 77, 79, 137
literature, 18, 188, 191
London-Lund Corpus (LLC), 2, 145–6

Louvain International Database of Spoken English Interlanguage (LINSEI), 23

media interviews, 206, 234–7
metaphorical meaning, 10, 45, 51, 87
Michigan Corpus of Academic Spoken English (MICASE), 92, 203–4
modality, 21–2, 37, 122, 123–4, 175, 201–2, 214, 217
Monoconc Pro, 5, 8
motivation, 26, 50, 52, 55, 56, 95, 97, 191

narratives, 73, 89, 97–8
native speakers, 27–8, 49, 76, 190
    distinction from non-native, 28–30, 31, 76–9, 184, 192–6, 199, 219, 228
need, 209, 211–14
newspapers, 2
node word/phrase, 8–9
non-native speakers, 27, 95, 163, 188
Norwegian, 19
notional-functional approach, 191
nouns, 39–42, 104, 122
    noun phrases, 101, 178, 200, 201
    noun compounds, 82, 86

obligation, 214
overlaps, 22, 120

part and parcel, 81
passive voice, 61, 106–9, 119
past perfect, 23
past tense, 46
pausing, 22, 240
pay, 110–2
peace and quiet, 52–4
permission, 5
phatic communion, 169, 171
phonology, 28, 76–7, 185, 223
    intonation, 76–7, 120, 122, 154, 176
    pronunciation, 29, 158
    weak forms, 29, 76–7
phrasal verbs, 52, 81
phraseology, 62–4
plagiarism, 19–20
politeness, 71, 73–4
possessive phrases, 82
Post-Observation-Teacher-Training Interactions (POTTI), 127–30
power relationships in conversation, 39, 154, 176, 230, 233
PPP, 118
pragmatic categories, 71
pragmatic failure, 183 *see also* cross-cultural communication
pragmatics, 21
prepositions, 12, 15, 28, 33, 45, 177, 201
    prepositional expressions, 82, 84, 86
present tense, 28, 33, 105, 128
prim, 15
problem, 42, 134, 209, 214–6
problem-solution, 42, 91, 93, 94, 96, 214–6
productive skills, 76, 77–8, 98

pronouns, 68, 101, 200–1, 205, 208–10, 211
Punjabi, 20

qualitative analysis, 1, 2–3, 65, 181, 196–7, 222, 244
quantitative analysis, 1, 2–3, 55, 61, 196–7, 200, 244
questions, 237–40
    display questions, 224–5, 239–40
    echo, 238
    in classroom, 233–40
    tag, 237–8

reading skills, 24, 50, 54–5, 229–30
ready, 14
receptive skills, 76, 77–8, 96, 157, 181, 192
recording spoken data, 5–6
reduplication, 68
reformulation, 172
register, 17, 68, 90, 210
relative clauses, 12, 120–7
repetition, 20, 22, 43, 68, 185, 188
reported speech, 12, 23, 46, 114
representative, 1, 20
representativeness in corpora, 5
response tokens, 12, 22, 33–4, 43–4, 123, 136, 140–58, 187,
    226–7

saving/storing data, 6, 7, 8
say, 46
scaffolding, 158, 228–9, 232–3
schemata, 194, 228–9, 232
Scottish English, 20
Scots, 20
semantic prosody, 14–17, 18, 53–54, 71, 94, 101, 103–4, 106,
    109–11
semantics
    semantic associations, 51–2
    semantic restrictions, 14–15
shared knowledge, 34, 72, 74, 173–4, 177–80, 236, 241
similies, 82, 188
social class, 20–1
socio-cultural theory, 55, 228–9, 232
sociolinguistics, 20–1, 63
    variables, 1, 7
Soviet linguists, 62
space, 42, 75, 173, 203
Spanish, 21, 157
Spanish learners of English, 195–6
speech and writing, differences between, 11–12, 18, 33–5,
    38, 39, 41, 52, 56, 68, 106, 119, 139, 140–1, 177, 184,
    188–9
speech acts, 22, 71, 166, 183
    commissives, 166
    directives, 166
stance, 38, 45, 73, 109, 111, 136, 172, 175, 185, 200
stylistics, 13, 18
Successful Users of English (SUEs), 29–30, 63, 76, 80, 94,
    145, 193–6
Swedish learners of English, 23

syntax, 60–1, 62, 163
    syntactic restrictions, 14–15, 81, 94

taboo language, 20–21
tags, 20, 38, 178
    right dislocation, 114
task-based approaches, 191, 222
teacher training, 127–30, 176, 220–1, 241–3
TeleCorpora, 242–3
tense, 14, 46, 114, 136
TESOL Quarterly, 80
text signalling words, 42, 133
there, 10, 42
thing, 41–2, 74–5, 134
this, that and the other, 13, 75, 77, 81
time, 41
time and duration, 42, 71, 75, 89, 203
TOEFL, 199
topic
    boundaries, 34, 39, 72, 144, 173
    management, 227
    sentences, 131
Touchstone, 22, 77, 101–2, 138–9, 247
transcription (of spoken data), 2, 5, 6–7, 120, 156, 222
    conventions, 6
    level of detail, 2, 6
    time required, 2, 5–6
translation, 19
trinomials, 82, 86
turn taking, 22, 125–6, 141, 226–7, 230

Urdu, 20
Usage
    'bad', 39, 139, 190
    non-standard, 20–1, 114, 187
    see also scripted dialogues
utterance length, 20

vague language, 22, 38, 71, 74–5, 160, 162, 176–80, 187, 189,
    210, 242
Vienna-Oxford International Corpus of English
    (VOICE), 28
vocabulary
    core items, 4, 12, 35–6, 42, 46, 69, 156, 199
    receptive, 48–9
    size, 31, 47–8, 54–7

way, 8–9, 41
weather, 171
well, 33–4, 39
word class, 44, 46, 142, 181
word frequency lists, 11–2, 45, 155, 206–8
word play, 90, 186
Wordsmith Tools, 5, 8, 12, 13,

you know, 34–5, 39, 46, 69, 71–2, 76, 124, 131–2, 160, 173–7,
    180
yet, 100–2

Publisher's acknowledgements

Development of this publication has made use of the Cambridge International Corpus (CIC). The CIC is a computer database of contemporary spoken and written English, which currently stands at over one billion words. It includes British English, American English and other varieties of English. It also includes the Cambridge Learner Corpus, developed in collaboration with the University of Cambridge ESOL Examinations. Cambridge University Press has built up the CIC to provide evidence about language use that helps to produce better language teaching materials. This publication has also made use of the Cambridge and Nottingham Corpus of Discourse in English (CANCODE). CANCODE is a five-million word computerised corpus of spoken English, made up of recordings from a variety of settings in the countries of the United Kingdom and Ireland. The corpus is designed with a substantial organised database giving information on participants, settings and conversational goals. CANCODE was built by Cambridge University Press and the University of Nottingham and it forms part of the Cambridge International Corpus (CIC). It provides insights into language use, and offers a resource to supplement what is already known about English from other, non-corpus-based research, thereby providing valuable and accurate information for researchers and those preparing teaching materials. Sole copyright of the corpus resides with Cambridge University Press, from whom all permission to reproduce material must be obtained.

The authors and publishers are grateful to the following for permission to reproduce copyright material. While every effort has been made, it has not always been possible to identify the sources of all the material used, or to contact the copyright holders. If any omissions are brought to our notice, we will be happy to include the appropriate acknowledgements on reprinting.

Routledge for permission to draw on sections of Ronald Carter, *Language and Creativity* (Routledge, 2004) in the writing of Chapter 9; Cambridge University Press for permission of use in chapter 5 parts of an article Carter, R.A. and McCarthy, M.J. (1999) 'The English get-passive in spoken discourse: Description and implications for an interpersonal grammar', published in *English Language and Linguistics*, 3, 1: 41–58. Two chapters (2 and 3) also draw on: *What is an Advanced Vocabulary?* and *What is an Advanced Vocabulary?: The Case of Chunks and Clusters* delivered at the TESOL Symposium on *Vocabulary: Words Matter* held in Dubai in March, 2006 and published as Conference Proceedings by TESOL in 2006; Examples of usage taken from the British National Corpus (BNC) were obtained under the terms of the BNC End User License. Copyright in the individual texts cited resides with the original IPR holders. For information and licensing conditions relating to the BNC, please see the web site at http://www.natcorp.ox.ac.uk; Examples of usage taken from ICAME, were obtained from ICAME CD-ROM by licensed user. For further information please see the website at http://icame.uib.no/; Cambridge University Press for fig. 1, p. 3: 'Main entries for *bargain*' taken from *Cambridge Advanced Learner's Dictionary, (CD-ROM 2003)*, p. 10: Extract from *English Idioms in Use*, written by McCarthy and O'Dell, p. 22: 'Strategy plus' taken from *Touchstone Student's Book 1*, written by McCarthy, McCarten and Sandiford, p. 42: Cite 496634 *Living in Lincoln* written by Steve Brace, p. 78: 'Do you go straight home?' taken from *Touchstone Student's Book 1*, written by McCarthy, McCarten and Sandiford, p. 98: 'Reacting to what others say' taken from *English Idioms in Use*, written by McCarthy and O'Dell, p. 102: 'Yes-no questions and answers: negatives' taken from *Touchstone Student's Book 1*, written by McCarthy, McCarten and Sandiford, p. 115: 'Ellipsis in narratives' taken from *Exploring Grammar in Context*, written by Carter, Hughes and McCarthy, p. 116: 'Simple patterns of ellipsis in conversation' taken from *Exploring Grammar in Context*, written by Carter, Hughes and McCarthy, p. 117: 'Typical uses of get-type passives' and 'Choosing between different passives' taken from *Exploring Grammar in Context*, written by Carter, Hughes and McCarthy, p. 131: Cite 758623 *Cambridge History of American Foreign Relations Vol 4*, by Warren I. Cohen, p. 138: '*What* clauses and long noun phrases as subjects' taken from *Touchstone Student's Book 1*, written by McCarthy, McCarten and Sandiford, p. 139: 'Language notes, Unit 12' taken from *Touchstone Teacher's Edition, level 4*, written by McCarthy, McCarten and Sandiford, p. 218: Extract from *Academic English in Use*, written by McCarthy and O'Dell. All reprinted with the permission of Cambridge University Press; Oxford University Press for p. 10: fig. 7, 'Exercises' taken from *Natural Grammar*, written by Scott Thornbury. Reproduced with the permission of Oxford University Press. © Oxford University Press 2004; Professor Thomas Cobb for p. 25: 'Example of DDL task' taken from 1997 paper *System 25(3): 301–315*. Used with the permission of Professor Thomas Cobb; Thomson Learning for p. 97: 'Complaining or Commiserating' taken from *Idioms at Work*, written by McLay. 1st edition by RECGEN Canada. 1988. Reprinted with the permission of Heinle, a division of Thomson Learning: www.thomsonrights.com. Fax 800 730–2215; Associated Newspapers Ltd. for p. 131: Cite 1086421 'Your stars for today' taken from the *Daily Mail*, 29 July 2002. Used with permission. Pearson Education for p. 217: 'Target Words – Assessing your Vocabulary Knowledge' taken from *Focus on Vocabulary* by Diane Schmitt and Norbert Schmitt. Copyright © 2005 by Pearson Education, Inc. Reprinted with permission; TESOL for p. 221: 'Sample material for awareness-raising in relation to teaching new vocabulary' taken from *TESOL Quarterly*. © TESOL Teachers of English to Speakers of other languages, Inc. Reprinted with permission; Pearson Education Ltd for pp. 225–226: two extracts taken from *An Introduction to Discourse Analysis* written by M. Coulthard. © 1997. Used with the permission of Pearson Education Ltd; BBC for pp. 234–235: Transcript from Breakfast with Frost interview with Ruth Kelly, taken from the BBC website www.news.bbc.co.uk, pp. 235–236: Transcript from BBC Newsnight, Jeremy Paxman interview with Richard Caborn, taken from the BBC website www.news.bbc.co.uk. Used with the permission of the BBC.co.uk.